Neda

Maryam Rastegar

Library of Congress Cataloging-in-Publication
Data.
It was printed and published in
the United States of America.

ISBN 978-0-9760763-3-9: eBook Persian
ISBN 978-0-9760763-2-2: Paper. Persian
ISBN 978-0-9760763-3-9: eBook English
ISBN 978-0-9760763-4-6: Paper English

Dedicated

This book is dedicated to my children,
my friend T. and Iranian victims who
lost their loved ones due to the
Islamic regime crimes.
Thank you for giving my words a chance.
You may find something in these books
that resonates with you.

Neda
Table of contents

CHAPTER 1, NEDA

"Agha, pray for this girl; she was cursed."
"What is her name?"
"Neda."

I could see and hear their conversation by leaning on one of the pillars hidden from their view. Marzieh said that the Imam Jomaa (Friday Imam) is Sayed, a descendant of the Prophet Mohammed, and he can pray for you. People call them mullah-Qari. The older man with a goat's beard, wearing a dirty robe and green shawl, held a piece of clay in his hand and rubbed it like wax while grumbling under his breath. After Marzieh paid him, he placed a piece of clay in her hand and said, "Put this petition in the well. My hand is good; you will get what you wish. You must come to me seven times in a row for it to work well and will answer the prayer."

"Sir, we don't have the money to come seven times, so make sure that the first time is answered."

"Find a husband for her, a good husband. If you do not have one, I have one for you."

"No, sir, I don't have anyone. If you find one, God will reward you."

Qari put his hand on his white beard, when he checked Marzieh's head to toe, and asked:

"Do you have a husband?"

"Yes, sir, my husband is a printing shop worker."

"I am the prophet's descendant, and this green shawl symbolizes my lineage."

Sayed declared with pride and continued.
"My wife passed away, and my children are now married. I have a proposition for you. I will marry your daughter.

Talk to your husband and return with his positive answer
within three days, and I promise not to take the petition
money from you. Don't be late, your daughter was lucky
that I was here. The mosque would have been closed if you
had arrived a little later. Now, throw it into the well."

"God rewards you, wishes you well, and the prophet
Mohammed rewards you."

I was a mix of anxiety and curiosity, my heart aching
with the weight of Marzieh's unwavering determination to
find me a suitable husband. But this aged, goateed reciter
at the grave, who was as old as my great grandfather, how
dared was he to propose himself as my future spouse!

Marzieh hastened towards the well in the mosque's
center, clutching the clay petition. I thoughts to my father,
who toiled in a printing shop to support our family. It
pained me deeply to see Marzieh hand his hard-earned
money to the crafty mullah instead of using it for her
children. I was overwhelmed with regret for accompanying
Marzieh on this errand, torn between my loyalty to my dad
and my growing resentment towards the mullah.

I wouldn't want to be at home when my dad was not
there, but I couldn't bear to stay at Madam's house in those
days. They loved me, but I was consumed with a profound
longing because everyone was preparing for Ana's trip to
Tehran. The sadness that Ana was leaving and that I would
miss my friend was almost unbearable, so I returned home
earlier than usual and came to the cemetery with Marzieh,
Roya, and Sohrab.

Ana and I have been friends since elementary school,
but she would pursue further education after high school.

I was under influence of Marzieh's word to get married
as I was getting older, and I didn't even have a suitor yet.
This thinking was heavily influenced by Marzieh, who
believed that a good girl should be married by age eight
and was determined to find me a husband before it was too
late. During a bus ride to the cemetery, Marzieh repeated
the story about how her loyal mother visited his father's
grave weekly, which was boring to listen to her belief in
worshiping the dead.

Marzieh explained Friday Imam, Sayed Alireza was

previously a graveside reciter-Qari, was looked down upon. This made me wonder about transitioning from a grave reciter to a Friday Imam, recounted the story of my courtship of the important person and the birth certification by Sayed Alireza.

I inquired with Marzieh about the curriculum required for a grave Qari to study to become an Imam Jomaa, but she redirected me to Ana, suggesting that she was more knowledgeable due to her schooling. As we made our way to the cemetery and mosque, I contemplated the replacement of birth certificates, Sayed Ali Reza, and the general aversion towards mullahs. While at the cemetery, I observed the grave reciter and envisioned the possibility of him becoming the next Imam Jomaa. In contrast, Marzieh became irritated by the children playing around the graves, expressing her concern.

"Look, they are running, their socks might get ripped."

"How much money did you give the Qari? You could have bought socks for children with that money."

Marzieh ignored my question and led us to pray for her father and the Imam al-Zaman Well. Shiites believe Imam Zaman is the last of the twelve Imams who will come to carry out the Islamic mission and establish peace and justice in the world. Imam al-Zaman will kill and eliminate non-believers of Islam, which may lead some to claim that he has negative traits.

Imam al-Zaman was born in Samarra, Iraq, in 870 AD and disappeared as a child in a well in Samarra based on the story of Muslim believers. There are various wells named after Imam Al Zaman in different parts of Iran, which are used to collect money from people, such as the "Jamkaran Well in Tehran, where funds often go to the local religious leaders. It needed to clear whether Imam Zaman died about 1,400 years ago or if his life spanned about 1,400 years and involved traveling through underground wells.

These thoughts came to my mind while I watched Marzieh, holding a piece of clay and muttering something before throwing it into the mosque's well. She then remembered her children and called out for them. "Roya, Sohrab where are you?" She walked away from the well

In search of her children. I was standing there, and I saw
that the mullah was looking around carefully, he did not
see me. I wondered why he was looking around so
carefully. I tried to hide behind a column so he wouldn't
see me. He went to the well, leaned over, and a few
moments later, I saw a big basket as big as the well's
opening, in his hand while walking to his stool. I was
curious about what he was doing and surprised to see him
taking clay pieces from the basket and put them under the
chair. Those were the exact same clay pieces he had sold to
people in the pretense that throwing those clay pieces in
the well would answer their prays. There was a cloth on
the seat that covered its legs and hid the clay pieces from
sight. Then he returned with the basket to the well, and at
the same time, Marzieh was coming back with her children
and was looking for me. Mullah, who saw Marzieh,
angrily asked her:

"Where's the other girl?
"She was here." Marzieh answered.

I felt threatened and was holding my breath in my
chest so the cunning mullah would not know I was in the
mosque. My heart was pounding and coming out of my
chest. I looked back, there was a mosque entrance behind
me, quietly I emerged from behind the pillars when the
mullah asked me:

"Were you in the mosque?"
"No, I was waiting outside for them."
"Let me see your shoes". He ordered.
"Did not you take off your shoes?"

It was the rule that everyone should take off their shoes
in the mosque. I was lucky to be wearing a thin old shoe
that was silent while walking. He was relieved that no one
had seen him and did not know his secrets. He smiled and
spoke.

"Your daughter deserves new shoes." Traditionally,
buying new shoes for a girl meant he was a suitor. So, he
was implying that he was a suitor. He was standing there
when we left the mosque. At the exit door, I turned around
and saw him throwing the basket into the well.

On our way to return home, I reviewed the day that I

was listening to the radio, and Mr. President Rafsanjani said that women should propose to men too. My dad was outside I said that I also wanted to become the wife of an important person and go to suggest to him. Marzieh panicked and hit her head with both hands and said:

"What? This is dishonor. The people of our town talked behind our backs."

"Our town people do not know us; even the people of this alley do not know us." I responded.

"You need help understanding the meaning of these words. Okay, okay, that's enough. You must pray that someone will take you, and you will not stay with your father forever."

Those days I had to remain silent, Marzieh might have known better, but this thought was in my head and would not let go of my mind and I will share with you my courtship later.

I thought if this older man be my suitor, at least had one suitor, and according to Marzieh, if it had spell on me, this spell would be broken. I wanted to have a significant husband like a president; where did this dirty older man come from? How could I show off, if my future husband is the mullah of imam al zaman's Well? People would be laughing at me. What I wanted and this prospect of this old dirty men were two completely different things. My thoughts were distraught and remembering that Ana would leave this city, and sadness would overcome me and hurt my heart. I wanted to cry. I was thinking of my dad's advice, telling me not to go to the cemetery.

It is a pity that Roya and Sohrab were starved for food, yet Marzieh could not understand their basic needs and wasted my father's hard earning money on these cunning mullahs. My dad suggested that I read and understand the concept of "prayer" through the famous Iranian poet and philosopher Sohrab Sepehri's poem "Niaiesh" because he believed that the prayers of the mullahs were the most useless words.

My dad often expressed that no one could send a dead body to heaven. He was a good speaker, and I found a similarity between my crocheting work and his reading

which kept our minds busy. I used to be afraid of Marzieh.
Once, she punished me for losing a plastic ball. I was so
scared of her that I hid in the dark stairwells located
in the backyard, which led directly to the well and roof.
There was a deep water well with a large wheel attached to
a big bucket and a rope to pull water from the well. My
dad prohibited us from going there. It was dark, and I
feared falling into the well, trembled and waited for my
dad to return home in that dark area. After that, my dad
did not leave me alone with Marzieh; I stayed at Ana's
house and played with her until my dad came home. These
days, I have been upset and did not want to stay there
anymore. Our house was an old thatched-roof building,
exuding poverty, and despair, at the end of a dead-end
alley in a slum. Ana, Zubeida and Sara were my neighbor
and classmate in elementary school, and we would gather
in the cul-de-sac to play. Ana and Sara were thin and tall,
Zubeida was plump, and I was short and petite. Ana used
to compliment me on my clothes, saying they were the
most beautiful. Aunt Manijeh and Hossein Agha had
brought me nice clothes and shoes, mentioning that Zohreh
had sent them from America. They called my dad, Dr.
Soheil Khan. My dad told me that my Aunt Zohreh's sons,
played together when they were in Iran.

Marzieh quoted Hajieh Khanum as saying "every day,
my daughter Zubeida has a new suitor." It seemed that all
the boys in the city were Zubeida's suitors. I thought,
Zubeida had all these suitors, I did not even have one
suitor in my entire life. Those days, I did not realize that
Hajieh Khanum and Marzieh were the symbols of cunning
women, tricksters, and bluffs. The title of Hajieh and Haji
were unwarranted nicknames for the woman and man who
went to Mecca. According to Muslims, this title belongs to
the wealthy people who can afford one year of living costs
without working and can travel to Macca to fulfill their
Islamic obligation, Haj. This is just a commercial plan for
Saudi Arabia to earn money through Islamic tourism.

Zubeida's mother, who was in poor financial condition,
claimed this false title to attract a wealthy husband for her
daughter. She feared that her daughter would remain

single, and Marzieh hoped to have my daddy as a father for her children after me. I compared myself to Zubeida and was jealous of her, who was fat and short and had many suitors. I wished to be overweight and have a suitor, but it was never fulfilled. Marzieh said I was spelled cast; something like smoke or clouds surrounded me. I've always looked around to see where the smoke is. I've never seen it and told Marzieh I did not see smoke.

"You are stupid and do not understand these words."

I still need to understand those meanings. Zubeida soon married and left. The obsession with having a suitor lasted forever with me. Hajieh Khanum had talked about Zubeida's husband having a good job and doing well. He was the coal pollen seller at the end of the Arabs' pit. His title included many words, and I wish my husband would have a long title.

I analyzed our life situation, spending my time with my dad even in grocery shopping. My dad often bought me ice cream and allowed me to play with the girls next door without interruption. Every night, he would kindly wash and iron my clothes. Meanwhile, my dad also paid Marzieh to spend money on her children, but she would instead give it to the mullahs to pray for her father's soul to go to heaven, even though he had passed away years ago.

Ana was the daughter of Madam and Monsieur, Armenian. Her father had a salami shop on Namazi Street. In contrast, Namazi Street means the place of Muslim prayer, which they believe is forbidden to eat and sell pork meat, salami, and sausages. His customers were mullahs, and it was unlawful to have pork meat! At that time, I did not know that an illiterate mullah determined the concept of haram and halal, and the name of this statement was "Hadis" or "Fatwa". Marzieh afeared of Madam and spoke all the neighbors feared Madam, but Roya, Sohrab, and I feared Marzieh.

I was a good student, but I couldn't pass the oral exam in fifth grade. That was the same year the religious teacher was angry with me about why I did not pronounce the Arabic word "Oghuz" correctly. The teacher slapped my face firmly. My head was sore, and I was so ashamed of

why I couldn't pronounce Aqooz. My hand was full of
slimy liquid on my face, and I had a headache and was
embarrassed. Ana sat next to me on a bench and shouted:
  "Teacher, teacher, blood, blood comes out."
  "Varparideh, come forward." The teacher called:
  It was traditional that we called each other by the
surname. My surname, Varparideh, made my classmates
laugh. I wish Ana hadn't said anything.
  I walked two or three steps while I was dizzy, and my
knees bent. The teacher shouted out:
  "Good, good, don't pretend weakness like a dead rat."
  She came forward and pulled me toward the class
door, while he was furious and trembled:
  "Tell your mother that she should not send a child with
a bloody ear to the school."
  I heard Ana.
  "Teacher, her face was bloody after you slapped her."
  I trembled in fear. We had arrived outside the
classroom when she said:
  "Be a good kid. Tell your mother you have had her ear
discharge since you woke up. Don't come to school
tomorrow, rest at home."
  That day I understood the meaning of a good kid- a
liar. I was sick for several days. From that day on, I did not
answer the questions correctly. I was renewed that year
and did not want to go to school, and my dad told me not
to worry about the lesson. The summer when school was
closed, Ana asked me to go to her house and play ball
together. That's where I see the crochet handicrafts. Madam
was so fast hooked while looking at me. I wanted her to
teach me, and I learned to crochet.
  Madam was a kind and firm woman who had
crocheting classes and students. When she received an
order, pupils fulfilled that order. Her kind friend, Iran
Joon, live within her house and her left hand was
paralyzed, and she was the crochet expert. She placed the
other part of the crochet between her elbow and her knee
or table, not allowing her left-hand defect to prevent her
from doing her job.
  Madam loved her daughter Ana very much. Ana had

reported to her mother everything that happened at school, and Madam said that if the teacher had slapped my daughter, I would have torn her apart. When all the students were afraid of the teacher; Ana was not because she had the strong support quickly spoke for her. I have never seen Iran Joon be afeared of Madam. They talked and laughed and were very close friends, Iran Joon called her Gohar, and sometimes Iran Joon yelled at her. I asked my dad to continue the crocheting learning at Madam's house and play with Ana. My dad agreed that if I read a book and taught me lessons every night. I was so happy.

Madam and Iran Joon said, I'm the best crochet weaver. Whenever Ana was home, we played balls, ropes, and rock games in the backyard. I did not know that crochet was also a job, and I worked. After a few months, Madam paid me and said it was your salary, and I gave it to my dad. My dad used to give some money to Marzieh said this was Neda's money, and Marzieh was happy that I was an income source. Each Thursday, Madam paid the wedges while Iran sat next to her and kept the record of payments. One day, she asked me:

"I want to add your salary, tell me what you're doing with your money, you're a very good girl."

I looked at her, paused and I did not know what to say. She repeated.

"I gave it to my dad, who gave it to Marzieh to spend at home." Madam asked angrily:

"All of it?"

"Yes."

I trembled in fear. Iran's eyes were full of tears. Madam had never been angry with me except when she threw a beautiful cushion in my chair. She said in a firm tone that no one was allowed to sit in your chair, even Ana, Iran, and me. It was the first time; I had a unique chair. Madam was very kind, and Ana said her mother loved me.

I did not understand why she was angry with me that day. I regretted telling the truth, but I did not object, and my wedge did not change! When my dad wasn't home, I was happy to stay at her home, not with Marzieh. Ana insisted I return to school. I would tell her that my dad

worked in the printing shop, read all books, and taught me.
When Ana came home, Madam took the crochet away from
me and told me to go to play. We played or read Ana's
lessons together. Sometimes my dad was late; I stayed
there and had dinner until to hear my dad's motorcycle.
Sara, our neighbor, came to Ana's house. We played,
studied, and talked about our neighbors 'boys. Sara's father
had a fabric store, and her mother was a housewife. They
were Jewish. Little by little, Sara visited us less and less.
One day, she cried and said the kids at school told her she
was Jewish. Her mother said the stupid children mistook
and they were Guiim. It's better not to play with them. I
asked Sara.
    "What does Guiim mean?"
    "It means you are outside the religion."
    "Sara, where's the inside?"
    Ana laughed and said,
    "It looks like we're going to play hide-and-seek
together, I be inside, and you get me out. We play, and we
find each other."
    "Ana, you let me to see what Sara says. Where is the
inside and outside?"
    That day we laughed and kept playing. Not long after,
Sara and her family left our city. I still need to understand
the inside and outside of religion. It is not secret between
me and you that I need help understanding the meaning of
many phrases, such as Zubeida suitors, inside and outside
the religious, Hajieh Khanum flattering her son-in-law's
position!
    The coal pollen seller at the Arab's pit! I talked to
myself and wished I could get a husband with seven or
eight titles. I would be the wife of a significant person, such
as the president, the leader, the god, or the king. I wished
to find all these titles in one person.
    My mood rolled and thought about my dad, how
patient, calm, and kind he is, how much I love him, and
how he cared for me. He knew everything well, but our
home was different from Ana's situation. We only have one
room. We all lived and slept in the same room. We did not
have a full bathroom or a kitchen, but Ana had everything,

and each had a separate bedroom. If I went to school, I would have taken the entrance exam. I gave up on this thought. No, we don't have money to go to university. I was upset by annoying thoughts and impossible dreams; I fell asleep under the rubble of despair. My dad soon noticed my change and asked:

"What's wrong with you? Why are you upset?"

"No, nothing, I'm exhausted.

"I will take you to the doctor tomorrow."

"No, no, I do not want to see a doctor."

"Every problem has a solution. I love you very much, and I am with you. Nothing is important to me except you. If you want to talk, we will go outside and have ice cream. I was always happy with his offer to go out and have ice cream, but this time, it was different.

Also, Ana knew well that I was sad. And Iran Joon often asked:

"Neda, what's up? Why don't you talk?"

What could I say? I had nothing to say. I reluctantly worked, feeling too sad to engage in conversation. Both Madam and

Iran Joon expressed concern for my well-being repeatedly. Until one day Iran Joon asked:

"Are you upset because the mullah gave a negative answer?"

I was taken aback by her perception and the nature of her question. My gaze shifted to Iran Joon with a heavy heart. The weight of my emotions was palpable. Yet, she persisted,

"So why are you so depressed and upset?"

"Aren't you sad that Ana is leaving?"

"Yes, I miss her too. She studies and comes back. Don't be sad; we must go after our own lives.

That afternoon, Madam said:

"Iran told me why you were upset. Remember, Ana goes to study and comes back."

I did not say anything while I had tears in my eyes and couldn't bear them and I went to Imam Zaman's grave with Marzieh.

After we got home, we heard my dad's motorcycle

approaching. We laid out a tablecloth and prepared a simple dinner while I compared our situation with Madam's home, I enjoyed their dinners and preferred to dine with them. If I didn't want to eat at home, I would make up an excuse, like having a sore throat.

My dad quietly asked if Marzieh had taken me to the cemetery. "Sir, I took them to the mosque and prayed for Neda to feel better," She answered.

"Too bad. Neda, you shouldn't go to the grave."

Then I asked my dad about the green shawl the mullah wears around his waist.

My dad explained that this belief lacks credibility and contradicts the mullahs' words; according to them, if a child's father is Sayed, his son should also be entitled to Sayed. Muhammad only had a daughter and lived in Mecca and Medina, so it is illogical to assume he traveled to Iran and had sons. The cunning mullahs invented the term Sayed title to belittle Iranians. Someone with an inferiority complex tended to look down on others. The ignorant and uneducated mullahs act as pawns and adorn themselves with green shawls and black turbans.

The Iranians didn't speak Arabic and couldn't communicate against accusations of ignorance, which fueled the Arabs' contempt. Whenever one person says something in a different language, misunderstandings can arise, but the extent of the problem is concerning. A profound, knowledgeable poet like Ferdowsi dedicated his life to explaining that Iran's quietness was not due to ignorance or stupidity.

The Shahnameh, the longest epic poem composed by the Iranian poet Ferdowsi. Colonial powers supported individuals who capitalized on cultural exploitation to undermine the lives of Iranians."

"Astaghferallah"- God forbidden. Marzieh muttered her thoughts under her breath.

"Do you think she knows the meaning of this word? She is afraid of hellfire. I bought Hell, and Heaven is for the rest. My daughter remembers no radio, television, movies, dictionaries, or entertainment programs during Ferdowsi's era. Ferdowsi authored a unique book called Shahnameh, like a TV series. It covers history, especially before and after the Arab invasion, geography, industries such as shipping, agriculture, irrigation methods, job creation, healthy economy, spinning and weaving from animal hair, animal husbandry, and poultry farming.

The book also details the training of warriors, the making of war tools and clothing, the defense of the land, medical procedures such as cesarean section, people's lifestyles, including drinking wine in golden cups by soldiers, horse riding, and pure Iranian horse types. Nowadays, they are known as Arab horses, although everyone knows Arabs had camels and did not have horses. He also wrote about the right of girls to choose a husband, women's activity and social life, the method of selecting kings, and more. It showed that Iranians were a liberal people; even the famous prince had the right to have a child out of wedlock knowingly and freely, and there was no need to hide it." After a pause my dad continued.

"He adds romantic and exciting love stories to this collection, so it is not dull, but also it is a chart of people's lifestyle at that time when love was not a sin. He skillfully repeated all the Persian words and the usage of each term and vocabulary so that it is easily imprinted in people's minds by telling stories to each other and analyzing the heroes' lives, people used the words, in this way, saved not only the Persian language but also registered the Iranian identities in the world. He spent thirty years writing the Shahnameh to leave a reliable document, a complete dictionary, as a legacy for future generations. He said I had built a tall palace for you that will not be damaged by wind, rains, and storm. No one will fight over this inheritance. I wish people would read it, understand it. He clearly said: Wisdom is the eye of the soul; if you are blind, you are not happy in the world. He named the book Shahnameh (king of letters) and presented it to the Shah(king), who was surrounded by a beggar of flattery people.

He saved Shahnameh with a wisdom strategy, Shah respected the word Shahnameh and did not have Ferdowsi's knowledge to understand the book's essential message. Access to this precious treasure is one of the great fortunes of Iranians."

My dad sighed and continued.

"In a meeting in San Francisco, the Iranian poet Shamloo stated that the Shahnameh consisted of repeated words, inadvertently revealing his misunderstanding of Ferdowsi's main intention.

Shahnameh's repetition primarily aims to prevent forgetting Farsi and its pronunciation. Following strong protests from attendees at the same meeting, Shamloo corrected himself in a subsequent speech."

As my dad talked, visibly saddened, and lost in thought, I couldn't know what was causing his deep sorrow and amazement. He had gained profound knowledge. Reflecting on Ferdowsi's poetry, I realized that my dad's wisdom might transcend our understanding. He was eloquent, and I enjoyed listening to his pleasant and straightforward words. Despite his vast knowledge, our family's life wasn't ideal, and I worried about the possibility of Ana leaving. My heart felt heavy as I pondered my dad's words about reciting Sohrab's prayer rather than simply praying.

Feeling overwhelmed, I crawled under the quilt and tried calming my mind in my racing thoughts; I completely forgot about the impending marriage proposal and instead dwelled on the idea of Ana's departure and how swiftly time had passed. The school didn't even cross my mind. I remembered the problematic year when I despised everything related to studying.

The next day, I reluctantly went to work, I saw Madam and Iran talking and smiling unlike the previous days, Madam said:

"Neda, I have good news for you."

"Ana will stay here, won't go to Tehran... she won't go."

"She will go." Then she paused, looked at me, and laughed.

"I consulted with Ana, Arman, and Iran about you. Do you want to go to Tehran with Ana?"

"Me? I don't have money."

I was silent and thought, "I do not have money. What

would happen if I went, and who paid for the house?"

"Aren't you happy?

"I can't go because I don't have money."

"You have money, and you can."

"No, I have no money."

"Do you remember I asked you how you spend your money, and you told me to give it to my dad? From that day on, I regularly increased your salary and saved it to provide for your dowry when you married."

Dowry! What I should have thought about was dowry! I was happy I had money and remembered my siblings were always hungry.

"But the cost of the house?"

"We take care of it."

"What should I say to my dad?"

"I thought about it too. Do you want to go with Ana?"

"Yes, but one thing."

"What else?"

"I will do your work wherever I am, and you give the money to my dad."

Iran Joon was wiping her tears and said:

"Madam and I would care for your family, don't worry. Gohar was my classmate's friend, and when my husband abused me, Gohar helped me, and I became a member of her family. You are Ana's friend."

I was thinking about Iran's life; why is she living with them? But these issues were not important to me anymore.

"I will talk to your father." Madam said.

I was immersed in my sweet dreams. Going to Tehran and being with Ana was far beyond my dreams. I was happy, and sadness disappeared. Iran Joon was looking at me and overwhelmed by my happiness, and her generosity did it. At that moment, I did not want to know anything except to go to Tehran with Ana. Looking back today, I was so happy and forgot to thank them.

Their great dignity looked like a tree that created a shadow on a hot day for people and gave their branches to the crows without any expectation. Their goodness was so great all the time. No thanks could be worthy of their kindness. My childish joys spread the fragrance of happiness on their faces. Madam's voice took me out of the fantasy world.

"We will come tonight or tomorrow night to talk to your father."

When I returned to our home, I picked up Sohrab's book and read the prayer poem. Even Marzieh had noticed my mood change and said it was related to the petition! I read Sohrab's poetry after fulfilling the need, and I must attribute my change to Sohrab's poetry who emphasized on wisdom!

"We are impatient, and praying is contentless.
There are hidden vision seeds.
Send a cloud to rain and feed the seeds.
It might open the core, grow, and bloom out.
Improved vision. And we may reach the wisdom sun."

I suddenly remembered that Madam wanted to meet my dad. A strange anxiety gripped my heart. What should I do if my dad says no? I prepared myself for the meeting and how to tell my dad that she wanted to meet him.

My heart was pounding. Our dinner could have been more delicious. Marzieh put the leftover bread in boiling water to make a big food pot. The generosity of salt, a bit of flour, and two eggs will taste good and satisfy the hungry children. Sometimes, she added fried onions and potatoes. Oh, I just remembered that our yellowish face color was not due to malnutrition; it was related to turmeric powder. It was turmeric's fault! We had enough money to throw away, and Marzieh poured it into the cunning mullah's pockets. As usual, I sat beside my dad, and Marzieh, Roya, and Sohrab sat on the other side of the tablecloth on the floor for dinner. I ate a few bites and said fearfully.

"Daddy, Madam would come to see you tonight or tomorrow night."

My dad's gaze remained fixed on the bowl of food. The sound of the spoons hitting the bowls scratched the heavy silence. I regretted what I said, but it was too late. I looked at my dad. Marzieh's voice broke the silence.

"Madam has a son and come here for her son. They are Armenian."

In her mentality, the relationship between people goes

around in this closed circuit. It is evident that Marzieh
feared Madam and I would stay with my dad forever
because I did not have a suitor like Zubeida. Marzieh
continued. "I forgot to tell you that Sayed worked in the
mosque, prayed for you, and he would want to meet you
for Neda."

My dad, who had stopped eating after my words,
suddenly jumped up, looked at Marzieh angrily, and
roared.

"How dare you talk about my daughter, Neda."

His face flashed red, and he left the room. I had never
seen my dad so angry; I was so scared and blamed myself.
After a few moments, I quickly got up and took my scarf
to follow my dad. I blamed myself for that.

Marzieh spoke, "I know they were looking for you;
otherwise, why would they want to come here at this time
of night? Sayed is good. Say no to Armenian man is a sin."

I quickly put on my scarf and ran to the yard because
I thought my dad had gone to Madam's house. I heard my
dad calling me. My dad was at home. There was an
abandoned room in the corner of the old yard where an
old couple lived, and my dad paid them monthly rent. In
the other corner of the courtyard was an old bench that
could see in the moonlight. I ran towards him, scared and
trembling. I was constantly terrified of Marzieh and tried
to avoid contact with her. It was the first time I feared my
dad, and I wanted him to forgive me. I would tell them
not to come here if this matter upset him. I loved my dad
very much.

"Forgive me, Dad..."

My dad cut my sentence and spoke.

"My daughter, sit down."

He kept my hand in his hand. His kind voice trembled
and was noticeably sad. I sat beside him, and he put his
hand on my shoulder.

"Neda, I love you very much and will do whatever
you think for your happiness. You do not need to
apologize or be afraid of anything. What happened, and
why did they want to see me?"

I was afraid to tell him I wanted to go to Tehran with

Ana. The silence between us was annoying. My hands were shaking.

"Neda Joon, whatever it is, there is a solution. Do not worry; tell me. I love you."

I thought if I did not tell him, Madam would say to him.

"Ana will go to Tehran, and Madam will send me too if you allow me. I will not go if you disagree."

"That's it!"

I was surprised at how calmly he dealt with this issue and why he was so upset a few minutes ago.

"I work and give money for home."

My dad sighed. I thought he was crying, but I did not say anything.

"Don't worry about the household expenses; it is not your duty. You have enough money. I will arrange it myself. They seem like good people. What do you think?"

"Yes, they are particularly good people."

"I always watched you; I never heard you complain about them. You seemed upset recently. Has something happened?"

"No, nothing happened; Ana was supposed to go to Tehran, and it was tough for me to be away from Ana. Every night, I have a nightmare that it is a cold, rainy area; I grab your legs and wake up in fear."

My dad shook so hard that the bench also shook, and he held me tightly in his arms and spoke.

"You did not tell me. Why?"

At the same time, we heard someone knock on the door. We got up from the bench whose wood creaks played the moonlit night music for a worried father and daughter to walk to the door together.

My hand was in his hand, and I was squeezing his arm with my other hand. His bony arms were manifested in love and peace for me. I was happy that my dad agreed.

My dad spoke in his loving voice.

"Remember that I love you and will do anything for your happiness. Whatever it is, talk to me, and we will solve the problem. Never marry this mullah that Marzieh said, even if I am dead."

We arrived at the entrance, and a dim lamp illuminated it; my father opened the door and treated them kindly and respectfully. I saw Madam's surprised look, and I guessed she had not expected to see me with my dad behind the door. Ana and Iran Joon had also come with Monsieur and Madam. The tablecloth was folded when we entered our room, and our humble room was tidy. Iran Joon had brought a big box of sweets, which helped Marzieh's doubt to become a certainty that Madam had come to our house for Varouge. Marzieh made a brief inquiry, went to the kitchen, and prepared tea in a small part of our room separated by a curtain. The kitchen had a space for a samovar, a small stove, dishes, and pots. It was clear that Marzieh did not feel good about our guests.

My dad said to Monsieur, sitting next to him, in a calm and reserved tone, while he pointed outside the room with his hand.

"Neda said you wanted to talk to me."

Monsieur said something to Madam in Armenian. Madam shook her head and whispered in Iran Joon's ear while nodding to me. I went to the kitchen to bring tea to the only guests we had, but Marzieh did not let me serve them.

"Not you, I'll do it," she said.

In keeping with tradition, she gave a negative answer to my imaginary suitor. I reminded myself that Varouge had never paid attention to me, and Madam kindly treated me as her daughter. They deserved better treatment than this. I was grateful that I could rely on my dad's kindness and moral qualities; he treated them well.

I sat next to Ana. My dad and Monsieur had established a good relationship. I cherished my friendship with Ana over the years. Roya and Sohrab were sitting in the corner of the room, their eyes fixed on the present box.

Iran Joon, noticing their gaze, pushed the box toward Madam, who opened the package of cookies. Iran Joon placed the cup on the floor and handed the saucer to Madam. Madam filled a saucer with cookies and invited Roya and Sohrab to partake.

"Come on, they're delicious," she said.

Marzieh tried to speak, but Madam interrupted her and repeated.

"It is fresh, children, come forward."

She gestured for the children to come closer and asked Ana to turn the box around."

Monsieur took a cooky and spoke:

"I eat this cookie to your health and regret why I did not know you sooner. You are a knowledgeable person."

Listening to Monsieur's words, I wondered why I did not know my dad. Iran Joon gave the tea to the children. Monsieur spoke about himself and daily news as if my dad's comment were essential to him, and he replied,

"I have never assessed the depth of this issue."

Iran Joon was paying all her attention to me and asked my dad.

"Whom does Neda look like? It does not look like you."

"Neda looks like my sister and her grandmother exactly."

"Do you have any photos from her childhood?"

"Yes, it is in our stuff. I must find it."

I thought about which stuff. We do not have anything. A room with five thin mattresses on three sides covers the room's entire surface at night. In the corner of the room was my dad's mattress, on which he sat and slept, right above my head, and he used to hang his coat above his head. Next to his mattress was a wooden box full of books, a lamp, and my ironed clothes on the top of the box, and that was all we had. What stuff did my dad talk about? I was thinking, and they were talking, and sometimes I heard them. Noticeably, all were staring at my dad. I picked up the cups with a gesture from Marzieh to bring tea again when she followed me behind the curtain and said:

"Say no, they are Armenian."

"They did not come for me."

"Say no."

No one came for me, but I nodded my head in the affirmative. Then she poured tea on caps in a tray and handed it to me. My dad took the cup of tea said to Monsieur: "We will have this tea outside."

Monsieur got up and stood next to my dad, who took his coat and spoke to us.

"I am talking to our guest outside; you watch TV."

It was implied that only we would be out, and then they went to the same corner where the old bench was. I could hear moving metal tin. I told Ana.

"The dear guests sat on the couch, and my dad sat on the metal tin as the host. There was an old antique and aristocratic bench from France's noble "Varp" family in the corner of the yard. We reserved this antique sofa for our guests."

We laughed under our breath so that no one would notice. Our room, which no guest saw, had a different atmosphere. The important thing was the children had a good night, ate cookies as much as they wanted and slept comfortably. Little by little, I worried about why it had taken so long. My dad agreed, so why are they still talking to each other? Marzieh kept asking, "How long it took."

Ana was the only one who had quietly watched TV; she put her head on the mattress and fell asleep on the floor, as did Sohrab and Roya. Anxiety was crushing me; I got up and went quietly to the yard to find out what was happening. My dad noticed.

"Neda, go back to the room. We will come soon."

I was looking at my dad, dumbfounded and confused. I saw that they were crying when my dad had never moaned before. Iran Joon hurriedly said.

"It made them sad when I said my husband was beating me."

"Go, I'll come soon. My dad repeated."

Sadness squeezed my heart, and I returned to the room. Marzieh asked.

"What were they doing?

"They were sitting and talking and said they would come soon."

After a few minutes, they all returned to the room. Their voices were hoarse, and it was clear that they had been crying. I was staring at my dad, and Iran Joon noticed my curiosity. While looking at me, she said, "It is cold outside at night. We were cold."

Madam emphasized that was cold and spoke.

"Neda, come early in the morning. We have a lot to do."

Ana got up, when they left, my dad took a book from the wooden box and gave it to them. We returned to our room, and I noticed my dad's eyes were teary. He tried to avoid my gaze by pretending to be moving books.

"Sir, what did they want?" Marzieh asked."

"They talked about Ana and how she should study and work."

"Did they say anything about their son?"

"Their son is engaged to an Armenian girl and will have a wedding soon."

Marzieh was relieved, and my dad could tell what I was thinking.

"Madam and Iran Khanum complimented you and said you are good. They received one new order in another city and want to send you and Ana to that new job."

I calmed down for a while. I crawled under the quilt, and when Marzieh left for the bathroom, I took my head out of the quilt and quietly asked my dad,

"You cried; what happened?"

"Don't worry, you are going with Ana. Don't have any nightmares; I am always by your side and love you."

My father seemed sad. When I heard Marzieh approaching, I buried my head under the blanket and stayed quiet, feeling as still as a dead mouse. My mind was racing; I didn't know what I was searching for, and tears were streaming down my face. The pillow was a safe place to hide my secret tears. At night, when I couldn't sleep, I had this strange belief that if I exposed my head from underthe covers, the people around me could read my thoughts and understand what I was thinking. I was suffocating under the quilt, but I was too scared to stick my head out. Sometimes, like a thief, I would cautiously peek from under the quilt to see if Marzieh was asleep. When I saw that she was, I would cautiously lift my head, feeling relieved to be able to breathe easier. My mind was filled with sorrowful thoughts and hopeful dreams. When I thought Marzieh was asleep, I slowly lifted my head and called out for my father twice, but there was no response. I thought I had made a mistake. I couldn't recall how I fell asleep, but the important thing was that my father had agreed to send me to Tehran.

Years later, Madam recounted their conversation to me.

"One of the last nights of June had a beautiful full moon. The pale moonlight illuminated the house. Monsieur, Iran, and I were sitting as guests on a wooden bench, and the host was sorrowful man sitting on a metal tin and speaking."

"Neda is bright and has great faith in all of you. You've treated her well all these years, and she's never complained about you. She's right. I also shall leave her with a trustworthy person who will look after her after I'm gone. I will tell you everything related to her life and future and leave her in your hands.

If anything happens to me, please call my sister Zohreh in America or my friends, and they will cover all the expenses. Send Neda to them. Thank you for being kind to Neda and loving her. I know you had prepared a unique chair for her and sewed a beautiful cushion with beautiful stripes, even though your chair does not have a cushion. You told her that no one is allowed to sit on that chair. Your goal was for her to hear others well and not decrease her self-confidence. I saved all the money you gave her over the years. She can go to Tehran with your daughter. Neda was born in Tehran. I will tell you a little about her life tonight. I wrote these things in a notebook, and I will give it to you with her money. In that notebook, I wrote my sister's, acquaintances', relatives', and friends' phone numbers. I have been sick and worried about her future.

I did not want she would face adversity, especially tonight when Neda told me she had nightmares every night. I am sure the poison of bad memories has permeated her mind, and that's why she has such bad nightmares. Please do not tell anyone about what I am telling you, specially your daughter Ana; they are close friends and share everything. Ana may say something to Neda, and she will be annoyed. Iran Khanum asked me what Neda looked like and to whom. I said that she looked like my sister and her grandmother. My name is Soheil, and I graduated from Tehran University and became a professor at the same university at the age of twenty-four. I received the highest academic degree and became the first student to receive a medallion from the Shah of Iran."

Madam said. "I had seen you a year before you sent your daughter to school, and I told Iran that he is the only man caring for his daughter. He might have lost his wife and devoted his life to caring for his daughter. It shows that this girl is from a good family, and her clothes are clean and well-made, which is unusual for this neighborhood. When Ana said Neda was in her class, I asked the teacher to seat her next each other. They have been friends since childhood. Her behavior is different from others, and we love her."

Iran spoke, "I love Neda, and we found out that she is very depressed that Ana is going to Tehran. We ask you to allow Neda to be with Ana, and we will arrange everything."

Monsieur said, "I am happy that Ana is not alone. We love Neda, and they would be better together."

"When I got a birth certificate for Neda, I sent her to school. She was about four or five years old and started third grade. She is brilliant and learns quickly. Thank you for giving her your daughter's books. I am not worried about her education. She can pass the twelfth-grade exam easily at any time."

Madam surprised, "You didn't get a birth certificate for her until she was four or five years old. So, she is younger than Ana. I thought her mother was petite or did not have good nutrition." Soheil Khan briefly told us about your fate, how he got your birth certificate, talked about Hayedeh, Soroush, and Zohreh, and we cried. When Soheil Khan noticed the door opening, stopped talking and said,

"I think Neda is coming."

That night, Soheil Khan gave us a book, his diary, and an envelope of money. We returned home, Ana went to her room, and we were influenced by Soheil Khan's character, especially when we heard that he was sick, and his fate was in danger. We read his diary. Arman continuously drank,

and Iran cried, saying, "Now we understand Neda better."
Years passed until I read my dad's diary, listened to
Madam's words, and cried.

PROPOSAL

I heard Rafsanjani's words that ladies could propose to
men, and I was serious to find a top high rank husband
with titles. One day I heard that the government officials
would come to our city soon. I decided to propose to the
top one.

Madam would take Ana or me for shopping or send us
alone for shopping. I thought to find out when these crucial
people came in our town when I went for shopping. I find
out that a governor is essential, and they go to the
governor's home. I did not like the governor word because
it looked like a janitor to me, and I do not want this person.
I want an important person like the province's leader or the
president. When I was alone with Iran Joon, I asked her.

"Why do essential people go to the governor's home?"

"Because governments have nothing to do with people.

They are having fun with themselves. Our people's
misfortunes are ours when they have fun with their own
parties."

Madam entered the room and said:

"Listen, my daughter, a governor like the village's chief
to extort money from us, and the high rank government
came to collect the ransoms and put billions in their
 pockets. The government employees are thieves whose
hands are in people's pockets, except the decent Iran's
brother."

I did not know Iran's brother, Jamshid, worked in the
governor's office. I thought about what would happen if he
saw me in the governor's office. It is better to tell Ana and
Iran Joon. Ana was in the twelfth grade and preparing for
the final exams. All day, my mind was occupied with the
proposal and the governor's office. As if Madam and Iran
Joon read my mind and asked me several times:

"What's up today? Did something happen?"

I answered hurriedly.

"No, no, nothing."

Ana returned, and while playing, I asked her:

"Don't you want to marry someone such as Zubeida?"

"Leave me alone; I want to study. Who is Zubeida? Are you kidding?"

"I want to become the wife of a significant person like Mr. president. The government officials will come to our town, and I will propose to him as Rafsanjani's advice.

I did not finish talking when Ana laughed and pointed to her mother who was watching us behind the window. This was one of Madam's habits of looking at us as usual. Iran Joon was in the kitchen. I was scared; I hastily said:

"Don't say anything to your mother. She will throw me out."

Ana laughed. "Don't be afraid, my mom loves you."

At that time, Madam was in the yard. Ana said without any pause.

"Neda wants to propose an influential person."

I hid my face in my hands in horror and did not expect such an incident. My whole-body shook, and I cried. Madam was strolling, and the sound of her steps hit my head like a heavy hammer. I wish I had not told Ana what would have happened to me if Madam had told Marzieh. At this time, Madam's hand was on my shoulder, and Ana repeated that Neda had become an important person's wife and proposed to an important person. I did not hear the rest of Ana's words except Madam's laughter, and I thought she was making fun of me. But I immediately remembered that Madam never made fun of anyone, and she caressed my hair and said:

"Okay, who did you consider? I will help you."

I was puzzled that I am stupid. Ana said:

"An important person like the president."

"What did you say? President! He is old, and she should toss him into the garbage. You are a beautiful girl and should have a significant, handsome, and young husband."

I was surprised by what Madam told me and what Marzieh said. I spoke with fear:

"I want to be the president's wife."

"OK, when a woman decides that no one can change

her mind, it's okay. Well, my daughter, you know that he is an old, married man who is unsuitable for you."

I did not dare to say anything, kept silent and thought about how Zubeida's husband has seven titles and why my husband should not have a meaningful title. It would be wrong if I talked about what was in my mind, she would recognize that I was jealous. I thought what a difficult day I would have, but now that I looked back, I said that it was a good day because, for the first time, I could tell someone what was on my mind without any humiliation. It was night, and Monsieur returned home. He was kind, and I had dinner with them from time to time. But that night, I wanted to run away from there. Although no one was waiting for me at my home except my dad, I had not heard his motorcycle. Madam laughed at the time of leaving and said:

"We will talk about it tomorrow."

I came home and as always, in our home, our conversations were regular, and only my dad's words were fascinating. In Madam's home, we always talked about crochet and the beauties of handwork. We only had one room, a radio, and a television, which my dad said he bought with my salary. I sat in the corner of the room with a book and watched TV. Every year, Ana gave me her books from the previous year, and I would read Ana's books at night, and if I did not understand something, my dad would help me, and the next day I asked Ana about that lesson. Ana explained it patiently, she was in the twelfth grade and preparing for the final exams.

"It is perfect, you ask me these question that is course review for the entrance exam."

Sometimes I wished I went to school because I was happy to read books and understood the lessons well, but I remembered the renewal of the fifth grade, and Marzieh said I was a dumb child. That night, when my dad came, we spread the tablecloth on the floor. Roya and Sohrab were busy writing their homework, and Marzieh put the pot of broth on the tablecloth on the floor, and my dad started pounding and mixing the meat with beans and potato. When I did not want to have dinner, excused me, spread my mattress on the floor, and squeezed it under the quilt. My mind was busy, and I heard Sohrab:

"Give me more food."

He was always hungry, and he was right because our food was not delicious compared with the food at Ana's home. They had sausages for dinner, but Marzieh said that pork was haram- forbidden and did not buy it for us, but I had it at Ana's home. When I told my dad what Marzieh was saying and asked him about haram. My father sighed and bought us sausages that weekend. It was delicious. I preferred Madam's house to our house and school.

Although I liked school a lot before I did not understand the teacher's questions. That night, a thousand thoughts were raging in my mind. I could not sleep till early morning. I woke up in the morning to the sound of Roya and Sohrab getting ready to go to school, but I fell asleep again. I woke up of Marzieh's conversation with Madam. Madam said:

"I understand she's sick, it would be better to come with me."

I jumped up and called. "I will come now."

I was afraid that if I lost my job, it would be miserable, my siblings would be hungry, and worse; my dad would bear my living cost forever. I heard Madam.

"Okay, I'm waiting for you, there is a lot of work left."

Marzieh returned to the room and asked me to have a cap of tea. She thought I was sick and did not eat breakfast and gave my portion to Roya and Sohrab. Our breakfast was bread and sweet tea. We had to sweeten the tea with two or three sugar cubes or two spoons of sugar powder. Sometimes we had jam for breakfast. Marzieh shouted: "have a tea." I said no and left for Madam's home. The house door was open in the mornings because the students came one after the other. As soon as I arrived, sat on my chair and started crocheting. Fortunately, Madam and Iran Joon were not in the workroom. After a few minutes, Madam came, and I greeted her.

"You must buy yarn today." I was surprised.

"Ana bought it a few days ago, and we still have yarn."

"I know I got a new order; I want all threads to be from the same party." I told myself how well she had forgotten and focused on her work and did not remember yesterday.

Madam gave me the currency and a plate of fried egg and bread.

"Eat your breakfast first, and then go."

I ate breakfast, realized how hungry I was, and threw myself out. I heard Madam. "Neda, Neda"

I turned back, and she was behind me with a cup of tea. "Have a tea first."

I had tea, left the cup behind the door, and went to the same shop where I always bought yarn. The shop owner Nima Khan was a kind man who worked with his son. I have known them for years. Recently, he called his son when I was going to their shop.

"Aria, come here, someone from Madam's house."

I thought he would inform his son that a customer had arrived. Aria was beautiful, handsome, and polite. He came forward smiling, and I don't know why he was delaying me so much. It was as if he needed to be more focused on his work. I had to repeat the order several times. Once, he brought a different thread and once a distinct color.

When Aria went to the back of the shop, I said Nima Khan, it looks like your son is not paying attention; please give me the yarn. He said kindly.

"My daughter, be patient, everything will be fine, and you will be happy."

I needed clarification on what buying thread had to do with my happiness! Marzieh said I was dumb and did not understand the meaning of the words. After delaying Aria asked me again.

"How many yarns did you want?

I repeated it.

"We don't have it, and you can come back tomorrow."

Madam always called them to ensure they had the specific yarns before sending Ana or me.

"You did not tell Madam that you don't have it. otherwise, she wouldn't send me." I said surprise.

Aria's face flashed. Nima Khan kindly said:

"I will apologize to Madam. I misunderstood."

At the same time, Aria brought me a cup of tea. I rejected it, and returned home while thinking about Madam, who forgot about yesterday. I took the cup and went to the workshop. Madam was there and said:

"How soon did you come back?"

"Soon! they delayed me a lot."

"Ah, Nima Khan misunderstood, but they are good people. Was Aria there? Is Aria a good boy?"

"Is good for what, he is not more attended recently."

Madam laughed and spoke.

"There is a reason."

Iran Joon was also laughing and looking at me. I did not say anything and went to get on with my work. Madam and Iran Joon were in the kitchen when she called me as usual. I left work and went to the kitchen. The two were sitting friendly, like Ana and me. Madam motioned for me to sit down. My heart was pounding. I was scared and nervous; Madam started talking with a loving look.

"Neda, you are intelligent and beautiful girl, and when you went to school, you did well in your studies. You should marry a good person."

I was happy to hear from someone other than my father that I am intelligent and beautiful. My dad combed, dried my hair after bathing and said that my beautiful girl's skin was like moonlight and her hair was like silk, the most beautiful girl in the world, caressed my hair and kissed my head. My hair was black and straight; Ana also said she liked my hair and long eyelashes, while I liked Ana's brown hair. I remembered that Ana said that Madam likes me very much and her words just because she loved me. Marzieh had told me no one wanted me, and I am a fool. Madam doesn't know those words and doesn't even know that I did not have any suitor. If I marry a significant person, I will be an important woman. There was a heavy silence between us, and I was busy with my thoughts.

"Please tell me what you want to do, and I will help you."

Her sincerely was attractive and made me feel like I was talking to Ana.

"I want to be the wife of an important person, like a

leader."

"How is it possible?"

"I don't know, but I want to be significant, like the president." Again, Zubeida's important husband was prominent in my mind.

"Well, where can we get this critical person? These governmental people are all bastards."

"What does bastard mean? The baby's birth is the same. How did it become haram and another halal? Or are there two types of giving birth haram and halal?"

"I meant they are not good people; I do not know the rest. They would only reach the high positions without any merit, education, or skills if they related to the government party. Neda, you told Ana that you would propose to a significant person. How do you do this"

"When I saw him, I said marry me."

Iran Joon laughed and spoke:

"It is more complex than you think. What if he said no?"

"I will tell the next person."

"Well, you set your mind, I will help you."

I was relaxed, although initially afraid.

"Please don't say anything to Marzieh because she will kill me and say it is dishonor and people will talk badly about us."

Madam grunted: "These people bothered me with these ridiculous words of honor and dishonor. Which dishonor? No, I will not tell anyone. People do not even care about us. Our death and life do not change anything. Now she is clinging to the word of dishonor.

"Did you tell anyone?"

"No, I just told Ana."

"Your secret is safe with us so we can make a good plan; you must promise me that whomever you marry will not get pregnant. You are young and have many years ahead. Now sit down and eat lunch."

Then she left the kitchen. She always had her lunch with Iran Joon and left lunch for me. She trusted me; I must have been in the working room when they were not there. I thought about dishonor; what honor is Marzieh talking about? She never talked about children's hunger, but she constantly feared being humiliated for disgrace. Iran Joon stayed there and was watching me, I was never afraid of her, and she spoke.

"You know marriage is essential, do not gamble in your life. Our time was different from yours. My marriage was arranged, and the result was my paralyzed hand. Be careful, we love you and always care for you, but you must be wise."

There were tears in Iran Joon's eyes, and I was dumbfounded and wondered what a relationship could be between marriage and a paralyzed hand, but I did not dare to ask. There was a heavy silence between us, then she left the kitchen. Iran Joon took care of me. Once I got wet, and several times my clothes were dirty, she put me in Ana's dress, washed and dried my clothes, and wiped them so no one would notice. My dad was brilliant and understood everything I did and asked me who cleaned your clothes. I explained to him that I wet myself, and Iran Joon washed me and my clothes. I had lunch while I thought about proposing and returned to work's room.

Rudabeh, Rudy, was the students who worked very slowly because she was afraid of Madam. She trembled while working and feared making a mistake. I always finished her incomplete work, so Madam could not notice that she was working slowly. Little by little, her work was getting better. When I turned around, I saw that she was pale. I waited until Madam and Iran Joon left the room. I went next to her and asked what was wrong.

"Why Madam talked to you? I was afraid you might do something wrong. What will I do if they fire you? Please take me with you wherever you go."

Rudi was vulnerable and dependent was scary. She should be independent and self-sufficient. It was not right for me to finish her remaining work. I crocheted amazingly fast without looking at the knitting, talking with the students, and finishing their half-finished work. I should have used her needs toward her self-sufficiency.
I laughed and said: "Don't be afraid; I'm not going anywhere, and you will learn."

I took her knitting, as usual, finished her work, and was ashamed to repeat my mistake.

"Rudy, I'll give you a piece of yarn and a hook. At night, just crochet, then unravel and knit again. Keep the thread at home but bring the hook daily so that Madam and Iran Joon does not notice. Don't look at your hands while knitting, don't worry about any mistakes for one week, and your knitting will be fast."

I thought Madam needed someone to handle the job well and instruct the other students and Rudy should learn the job well because I would succeed in finding a good husband. Ana came, and we played together. Madam was watching us via the window. Ana did not ask me, and I did not say anything. In general, Ana never questioned me. I said goodbye and went home. All my thoughts were busy finding a high-position man's proposal. I said to myself; I will find an important person.

A few days later, Madam said that she heard from Varouge that the government officials would come to the town, and I needed a dress. Varouge, Ana's brother, had a bookstore near the city hall and always read magazines and newspapers. I asked:

"Dress? What dress is it?"

"You must wear a black robe, a mask, and a black veiling and chador, and keep it tight. How to stand and bend is also especially important."

I asked for clarification: "Where these customs and principles came from? We lived very simply. We had a robe and a headscarf. Neither the intention of showing off nor the thought of pretending, and how should I stand not important to me."

"You should hold the chador with your right hand firmly, then put the two edges of the chador together and keep it on your wrist with your left hand, like those women who stayed in the streets and bazaars, started mischief, and looked for an excuse to fight. In the old days, their name was jezebel, and now they are called faithful women! There is no problem with veiling as a head covering; on the contrary, people should be free to choose their clothes, but coercion, pretense, and false labels are problems. One wrapped 30 meters of fabric around his head and the other around his body. They named it the ritual faith. Look at the photo of the mullahs and the fat tent; you will see what I mean. All these tricks are not based on their faith and justice but on division and creating enmity. They separate people with different schemes so that they can rule."

I thought Madam's vision was perfect, so if there were a minor problem in our handwork, she would see it from a distance away when we could not see those problems up close. She must be right.

"I ordered some clothes from Hajieh Aghdas. She thought I wanted it for Ana."

"Ana is taller than me."

"Better, your dress collects the dust of the street; this is also a sign that this lady is so faithful that she does not want anyone to see the heels of her shoes."

"If my clothes are full of dust and dirt, it is show off that I am a believer, but if I am clean, it means that I am a terrible person.

"You just realized now. When Khomeini said that war is a blessing, or when the leader said that the oppressed means the leader of the religion, people misunderstood the oppressed meaning! Being dirty is a sign of faith! It would be best if you learned these lessons little by little."

I remembered the religious teacher telling me that I was a good girl if I lied and that I had bloody ear drainage when I woke up. Also, Hajieh Khanum's chador was always dirty, its face sides were like leather, and its bottom was full of street dirt. A dirty chador and lying are signs of a believer! Days passed, Ana was busy studying, and I was busy with proposals. Rudy's work was a little faster.

After two weeks, I asked her:

"Crochet whit closed eyes for one hour daily."

"Why? I am afraid to make a mistake."

"I meant it, close your eyes, nothing will happen, and at most, you will make a mistake."

She listened to me in disbelief, Rudi's work had improved significantly, and she did not need supervision, she could quickly knit without looking and finish her work on time. Madam and Iran Joon had realized, and one day

Madam said to me, I knew you would not let my business remain lame. I was happy that Madam was delighted. Later I found out that she was always following my work while I thought of hiding from her.

One day, when I was in the workroom Madam came in and said, "Ask Rudy to do all your work."

"I told her hastily that she supervised the students and could sit on my chair."

Madam growled. "No. I told you that no one is allowed to sit in your seat."

"Very well."

I wondered why Madam was so sensitive to my chair and my place. The workroom was a spacious room with a window on my left side, the table was along the window, and crocheting tools were on it. To my right side was the seat of the students. Madam and Iran were sitting at the other side of the table. I did not know why Madam had a strange sensitivity on my seat, but I know now. I am not telling you now, do not think badly, I did not have an accident at my place, and I promise to tell you later. Madam motioned to me to go with her. I followed her to Ana's room. It turned out that Madam received robes, veils, and chadors. Ana was at home study for the final exam. I never saw Madam tell her to study because she did her work on time. She gave me her book and spoke.

"I am happy to have a friend like you. Look at the book to ensure I answer everything correctly."

I was happy to learn lessons with her even though I did not go to school. Madam spoke:

"Put on your clothes, let me see your size."

I wore the robe, and I said."The sleeves were too long."

"Fine, wear a veil."

"I hate the veil, and why should I wear it?"

"If you regret it, there is no problem. You don't remember, but I remember well what Mr. President Beni Sadr used to say." At the same time, Iran Joon entered the room and said,

"Gohar, tell them that he was educated in France."

"Yes, he claimed he has a doctorate from France, and my relationship with Khomeini is the story of the lover and

beloved one (Mourid and Mourad). We did not understand
what he meant, and who was the lover! He was the elected
president of Khomeini and, in a speech at the National
University of Iran, said the women's hair creates radiation,
and they should cover their hair so as not to provoke men.
Yes, women's hair has radiation and irritates men, and you
must wear a veil."

I was confused and did not understand anything
Madam's words.

"No, no, I am not too fond of the veil. Ok, I will wear
it... yes, I will wear it... I will..."

I remember my friend Forough who lost her father,
and they became orphans without any income. Forough
was our classmate, and her father died of electric shock at
work. If the radiation can kill her father, surely the beams
of my hair can kill men. I could hear Madam's voice.

"Neda, Neda, where is your attention? You are in deep
thinking again. You want to get close to these devils, you
should dress like them and put your chin under the veil."

"Why chin? My chin has no hair. What sin has the chin
done?"

They all laughed, and Madam said:

"The same sin as the other parts of your body, pull a
veil to the top of your eyebrow and cover it with a chador."

I put the chador on it.

"Now cover your face, too." "It is not visible anywhere
on my body. Why should I cover it again?"

I thought my eyes, nose, and hands were parts of my
body and would be sinful if they were seen; what should I
do?

"What will happen to my hands and eyes? Will the sin
be attached to the rest of my body, or will it be counted
separately?"

Madam was laughing and said:

"For now, focus on wearing a chador. Look at the
picture of Zainab's sisters, they are all the same, and you
must repeat their movements. It is best to cover your face
with your right hand so that only your eyes are visible,
hold both sides of the chador with your left hand and put
your hand on your waist."

I was amazed to see myself, a stranger, in the mirror.

"Look what you did to me; it's a sin if your body parts are seen."

"My eyes and hands are also part of my body. If they are not covered, they become sinners."

Madam, under her breath, said, "Don't ask me; ask the mullah; he is omniscient and ignorant."

I need help understanding the meaning of ignorant, omniscient, and sin.

"What does sin mean?"

"In the dictionary, sin means crime and mistake, and a sinner is someone who has committed a crime or mistake."

"I did not commit any crime. This God who sent us naked is a sinner. How to punish him? Indeed, men whose bodies are naked are sinners. Does men's hair also have radiation or only women's hair?"

"Oh, oh, Neda, Neda." Madam shook her head and spoke.

"I put the veil on my nose so that only my eyes can be seen."

"No, you should do as Zainab's sisters do."

"Who are these Zainab's sisters?"

"Khomeini hired prostitutes and called them Zainab's Sister."

I noticed Madam's eyes were fixed on my feet, and she continued:

"I must buy you thick black socks and Galesh."

"Why?"

"In the old days, older women used to wear black, shapeless plastic shoes- Galesh, but now it is the Zainab's sisters' shoes, and it is one of the faith signs!"

"They are believers because of this dress, and if they take off their dress, do their faiths go away?

"Don't tell me. I know they used crazy words. Now practice and suppose that Ana is an important person. Talk, how do you say I will be your wife?"

The room was a comedy theater, and at the same time, Iran Joon, who had left the room for a few minutes, came back. They became the same age as Ana and me. All three were laughing. Ana was also happy with this play. I could not speak because Ana could not control her laugh.

"Talk, I want to be your wife. If the answer is negative, what do you do?"

"I will be sad."

"Oh, you will be upset; whoever likes you, you will become his wife."

I talked to myself; she did not know, nobody wanted me, only Marzieh knew.

"For example, if Aria loves you, will you be his wife?"

"No."

"Well, those people may not want you either."

It was hard to hear the truth because I had always imagined myself with them.

Madam said: "practice again."

"Will you marry me?"

The sound of laughter filled the air. Madam said:

"Practice and put your hand on your wrist and tightly cover your face with the chador."

I remember Rudy, who improved his work because of practice. So, I must practice. Ana's laughter was taking control of me. After repeating, I could say:

"I want to be your wife. Marry me."

"No, I will not marry you, and I do not want you."

"Why? I'm fine."

Madam was happy and said:

"Well done, you should tell him how good you are. Don't be upset; we all had dreams in our youth that were far from reality. You should follow your dreams. Just impossible is impossible. If you get your wish, what is better? If it does not happen, this ordinary life will remain here, and you will not lose anything. Just remember you promised me not to get pregnant. It's okay if you regret it; we will also regret our doing many times every day."

I was wondering how I said I was fine. It was strange for me too. After a long pause, Madam continued:

"Practice here every day. When you practice, you can speak well, and remember that you could not crochet so well; now, you can crochet better than anyone else."

Madam and Iran Joon left us alone. We were laughing and playing in the theater, which was set up to fulfill my wish. When Madam came back to the room, I asked:

"Why did they name the government?"

"The government should serve the people and be present in the scene. Conversely, our government stole wealth, happiness, and victory opportunity from the people. They brought nothing but fear and humiliation to the people. The government comes here to scare the people so they can steal and take away everything; they do not feel any responsibility for their duty to the people. They steal l billions from people and hide it in rat holes. They know what they have done to the people who hate them. They are clinging to this false hope that money will save them. They did not learn that if money and status can't save others, it won't save them either."

I did not understand anything from Madam's words, it was better to concentrate on my work and find the job of the person coming to our city and my future husband's position.

"Who is coming?"

"Vice President of Hojjat al-Islam Val-Muslim in, Mr. Mehdi..."

I could not hear the rest of the words because I had reached number seven in counting the titles. Do you remember the job of Zubeida's husband, coal 1, pollen 2, seller 3, Arabs 4, deep 5, pit 6. Now I have his long title, Vice 1 President 2 Hujjat 3al-Islam 4 Wal-Muslim in 5 Mr. 6. I thought it was good enough.

Madam had talked to me, and I had yet to hear.

"Hey Neda, where are you?"

I had woken up from a dream.

"Pay attention to me. I love you; you still want to be the wife of one of these bastards? I want you to be happy; it's not too late to think about it."

"I made up my mind."

A few days before the government's arrival, I was restless. I wanted the days to pass quickly, and I reach my beloved one. One more time I repeated my proposal to Ana when Madam was also present.

"Marry me. I want to be your wife."

"What is your name?"

"Neda Varpariedeh."

Madam jumped like a spring and spoke.

"What did you say? What is this? What kind of surname is this?"

I was used to these reactions for a long time. I told myself she was not the first to find my last name ridiculous and would not be the last. "What is Varpariedeh? We should change your surname—Varper Varpery."

My thought was totally on the stage of rehearsing my husband's proposal and an important person, and I must switch to my ridiculous surname "Varparideh" means disappeared or sudden death and is usually not a surname, and "Riedeh". Now that I am writing my memoirs, I know how strange names and characters lower children's self-esteem. Suddenly Ana shouted:

"Varp, Varp."

I was confused, and my eyes circled between Ana and Madam like a pink punk ball. "Yes, I like it. Varp is better. It is better to keep the "Varp" and discard the "Rideh". What do you think? Neda, do you like it?"

Between "Varp" and "Rideh"- shit, never I thought about this part.

Ana spoke "Neda Varp is better."

"What will happen if they see my birth certificate?"

"Don't worry, we will do something about it."

"What is your name?" Ana asked.

"Neda Varp. If they ask me, what does Varp mean? What do I say?"

"What is the meaning of Varparideh? So far, how many people have asked you what Varparideh means? If they ask, give the same answers as the stupid people. For example, say this is my grandfather's family name, who immigrated here from France. My honorable relatives are all from France."

"Is France the place that issued a doctoral title for Mr. president? Can I see France, my grandfather's country?"

"France is too far."

"Is it farther than Imam al-Zaman's grave?"

The only faraway place I had been was Imam Zaman's grave. Marzieh took us there, where Qari prayed at a

grave. Therefore, her father's dead corpus to go to heaven!
The tomb of Imam al-Zaman is outside of town; She said
that Imam Zaman was a small child who fell into the well
of Samaria and disappeared. Nobody took him out of the
well! Why? I do not know. But Marzieh said that there are
Imam Zaman's footsteps on the street. Did Imam Zaman
come out of the well and walk around there? I do not
know! My dad did not go to Imam Zaman's grave. I once
asked Iran Joon how Imam Zaman came from Samaria to
our city, and no one found this child on the way to hand
him over to his parents. Iran Joon said forget this bullshit. I
thought about where France is, far from the grave. I wish I
could see where my great ancestor came from. Madam
spoke.

"How do you know the grave of Imam Zaman?"

"Marzieh took us to the graveyard. Qari came, sat on
his knees, shook himself, said something, took the money,
and left. I did not understand what he said."

Suddenly, Madam sighed so profoundly that I thought
she was short of breath and said: "Enough, enough."

"Mom, what should we do with her birth certificate?"

"I am talking to Arman."

Madam called her husband by his name, Arman. But
Marzieh called my dad, Sir. In June, I became Nada Varp
and left "Rideh." Thursday was the day of the government's
arrival. I was restless lover who was feverishly waiting for
the meeting of my unknown beloved one and the proposal
ceremony. Sometimes, my heartbeat was faster, and my
face would bloom from seeing my lover. Indeed, loving
and being in love is a happy mood. In those days, I made
many tablecloths. Rudi was curious why I went to Ana's
room every day, and Iran Joon told her that Ana had an
exam, and they studied. On Wednesday, Madam watched
my show for the last time, which in my childish mind, was
the foundation of my future life.

"Neda, it is the last time I asked you, are you sure you
want to propose to one of these people? I know their evils."

"Yes, I want to be the wife of an important person."

"Very well, I talked to Arman. Don't worry; he will
arrange your birth certificate. This neighbor mullah, whom

you know, Sayed Alireza..."

"Imam Jumma, my father hates him."

"Yes, who would like this person? He was in the graveyard mullah and used to come to Monsieur's shop to buy alcoholic beverages and sausages. After the revolution, he became Hojjat al-Islam and Imam Jumma, and now he sent guards late at night to collect the ransom. He will do anything for money."

"Please don't expose me to Marzieh?"

"Don't worry. No one will consider Marzieh and me unless we were important, then maybe."

I did not sleep well, it was morning, and I hurried to the Madam's house. Madam was waiting for me in the clothes of Zainab's sisters, a black robe, a veil and chador, and a dirty chador in her hand. I was horrified to see Madam with that look!

"I will come with you. Don't worry; nothing terrible will happen."

"Why are you wearing this dress?"

" I told you; I will come with you."

Also, I changed my clothes. I saw that the bottom of the chador was full of dirt. Madam said, "I made it dirty on purpose."

Monsieur was still at home and said:

"Don't be afraid, my daughter. I will pray for you."

Then he said to Madam, "Wow, you are a stranger. If I saw you in the street, I wouldn't know you."

"Yes, they wear a chador and a veil so that no one will recognize them to do whatever they want. A person who does not do anything wrong does not need to hide herself."

Iran Joon was standing looking at me and shaking her head.

"Honey, don't worry, take care of yourself, call me if something happens. Monsieur said. Ana laughed and said:

"My father is right. Wow, you are some strangers. Do not be afraid; my mom loves you; we are always friends and will help you become important."

Madam and I walked away when she spoke.

"Stay on my left side. With these looks, no one knows us; even if we see anyone on the way, we pretend we did

not see them, and if something happens, we want to see
Varouge or Jamshid. You'll be successful. Hold your
chador firmly and keep your hand on your waist. Look
directly at their face while talking."

She was covering her face so tightly that I could not
even recognize her.

"These shops, photograph and deli, are spies. From this
moment on, be careful what we say. We will go to the
governor's office on a client's name. Varouge and Jamshid
don't know anything, either."

Although I had a calm appearance, I was restless at the
thought of seeing my beloved one and my future husband.
Vice President of Hojjat al-Islam Val-Muslim in, Mr.
Seyyed Mahdi. With these thoughts, we arrived at the
governor's office. We passed through the pretty
landscaping yard. Madam grumbled and whispered:

"This should be a place for poor children to play."

We entered the building and went to the lady's
inspection section which was separated from men. Three
women were there and told us to take off our shoes and
socks. A woman was in front of us and swore she did not
use lipstick. One of the three women had put her hand on
the back of the woman's head and neck and firmly rubbed
her lips with a tissue. The tearful eyes lady said, "You hurt
my lips when I showed you the handkerchief that I did not
use lipstick."

"It is okay, enough. Our ears were full of lies from
morning to night. What are you doing here now?"

"The Chief asked me to bring my husband's burial
certificate."

"Go to the room at the end of the corridor."

No matter how much I thought, my mind did not reach
the point of the relationship between God, religion, and
lipstick. It was time to check ours, and we had no
problems. They asked:

"What are you doing here?"

"We came for recruitment."

"It is clear from your accent that you are Armenian."

"Yes, I am Armenian, she is Muslim, and it was not in
the advertisement that I must be Muslim. I am Iranian."

"You must become a Muslim."

"Your job is inspection, and my religion is not your business."

The woman roared: "Look at the wall behind you. I am here to ask you about the Islamic orders. I must tell you to become a Muslim."

Madam and I could see on the wall. Order to good action and prevention of wrongdoing. It means violating the human rights, a hadith made up by the mullahs so that people can be forced to do something against their believe.

"Well, I am thinking about it." She asked me:

"Are you Muslim?"

"Yes."

"What do you know?" Madam answered:

"Her mother is sick and needs work."

"Very well, go to the third room on the right."

We left while we could hear: "An Armenian who does not pray, why did she come for employment?"

Madam talked loudly.

"I served people instead praying."

"How rude is she."

Madam didn't say anything; we went to the third room. Many customers were standing there. The weather was hot, and their stinging smell was suffocating. It wasn't easy to breathe. I remembered a small jar on the workshop table that Iran Joon said belonged to Varouge, who used it to cover his armpit smell. I wished I could tell Haji Agha that his room smelled and ask Varouge what he used. It was our turn.

There was a man behind the desk named Haji Agha. He had an unshaven beard, a dirty shirt collar, and dirty yellow irregular teeth. This man must be deeply religious because the dirtier his clothes, the more religious he is. Poor Haji Agha must not have a toothbrush. I remembered Sohrab and Roya brushing their teeth with my toothbrush. On the same day, my dad bought a toothbrush for each of us and threw away my old toothbrush. Madam turned to Haji Agha and said, "I came to get a job."

"You are from the minority."

"Yes, I am Armenian."

"There is no available position for you."

"I am Iranian, I was born in this land, and I have right to work. The job requirement was not Muslims only."

"We did not need to write. People know well that this is an Islamic country."

I recalled that everyone in the neighborhood was afraid of Madam, but Haji Agha was not scared of her. I thought this fear must be a local issue that only we experienced. Neither Haji Agha nor Madam was afraid. Madam growled.

"I'm going to the boss's room right now."

"Go, go wherever you want, I decide and rule here."

Madam left the room in the blink of an eye, and I followed her when she asked someone " Where is the governor's office?"

"It is upstairs." The governor's secretary was a young man with a thick beard.

"Sister, what are you doing here?"

"I want to see the governor."

"Haji Agha does not have time to visit the customer today."

"He told me to come here."

The door swung open, and a group entered the room, exuding an air of authority. The leading figure, a mullah with an impressively full beard and mustache, commanded the attention of the others. The rest put their hands over each other and stood before him like a criminal person. As I observed them, I found myself wondering about intimacy and marriage. How would I kiss my future husband? Would he have lips? I should find a solution. I pondered whether I should discreetly part his hair to glimpse his lips or playfully use hair clips.

I yearned to understand and embody the boldness of the actresses I had seen despite Marzieh's disapproval. I was determined to defy societal expectations. I also wanted to be like a shameless actress. I heard Madam.

"Sir, you are the vice president, and you tell people on TV that you are caring. I am Armenian and need a job, please ask them to hire me."

"Sister, talk to the head of recruitment."

"They told me that does not have a job for Arminian. I am an Iranian Arminian and have equal rights as Muslim."

"Yes, sister, we are brothers with minorities who have books."

He continued to walk to the next room when I rushed to him and said:

"I wanted to talk to you alone."

"Talk; they are all confidants."

I was calm and had no previous restlessness. There was no excitement in his meeting an unseen lover. And looked into his eyes and it's looked like I'm talking to Ana.

"I want to be your wife, marry me, and take me with you." As if he had an electric shock, he stopped moving, was restless and stared at me.

"What? What did you say?"

"I want to be your wife."

He looked at me dumbfounded, as if he had never heard this phrase and was experiencing his desirability for the first time. At that moment, I thought that my hair radiation, eyebrows, and eyelashes hair, must have done its job. I felt guilty and feared this poor man would die like Forough's father, and his children would become orphans. Also, it might be his joyful experience related to the fragrance of love that I could see the passion in his eyes. After a pause, he laughed and said:

"I have a wife; God takes you." He quickly moved away from me. He walked three steps and then turned back and stared at me. He might regret rejecting me. Who knows! All of them rushed the other room like grasshoppers. I was dumbfounded in the middle of the room when Madam pointed to me, and I understood that we should leave. Without showing that we were together, I followed her down the stairs while I was happy to leave their room and their disturbing smell. Two streets away, Madam took a taxi; we did not talk in the cab till we reached home.

I remembered how restless I was the night before, but I did not have any feelings for him when I saw him. Dreams created more passion. I thought all the way that he did not want me because he had a wife. Well, they all have three or four wives. Also, I thought if Varouge smelled the same. Puff, piffle. Humph. What about my dad and Monsieur? It is awful for a man to smell like this. If I marry him, I will endure the same smells every day. This matter occupied my mind, so the main issue was overshadowed. We arrived home. Madam asked:

"What did you say to him? No one heard you."

"I told him to marry me, and he said, I have a wife; God takes you."

"What? God takes him."

"No, he meant he did not deserve to have me, and someone higher than him should marry me."

They laughed. Madam shook her head and spoke.

"He said that God takes you, and then you will say that you are too good for him."

"Believe me, he did not think he was worthy, and in fact God is higher than him."

"Neda was a good start. You should know that you started a challenging task, and you should say to have me as a concubine, then you would have had a better chance. I wished it had come to my mind sooner."

"Ana hurriedly asked what does concubine mean?

"Concubine" means cohabitation for a certain period over a certain fee. In the dictionary, the meaning of prostitution is the same. A marriage contract is unclear whether it is temporary or permanent. People assumed it was a permanent contract. Mullah made this ceremony to exploit the people to the utmost. Interestingly, when reading the marriage verses, he says words that no one understands."

"What does he say?" I asked.

Madam took the book "Zan in Ebrahimi Religions" by Dr. Masoud Ansari and showed it to us. Mullah, whose name is a lawyer, says to the bride on behalf of the groom in Arabic ((Ankhtah wa Zavojth nafsi Eli Sadiq al-malum)) translated in English ((I will give you a certain amount of money for intercourse)) or you will let me tear and make holes, tearing and piercing in you. When the bride hears the above sentence from her lawyer, she says: Yes, I accept." The meaning of Ankhtah in the Dehkhoda

dictionary (Volume 9, page 721) ((marriage)) has two
intentions ((having intercourse)) and in English ((f...ing)).
Also, in the Arabic dictionary (Al-Tawqif Ali Mehmet al-
Ta'arif), marriage is explained in this way: ((Ilaaj Zikr Fi al-
Farj List Bzalik Kalshi Al-Wahid)) which means word for
word: (inserting the male penis into the female genital to
become a single object)) ;) "The wedding couple listened
and did not understand anything from the Arabic words
and said yes."

"Yes, to what? They do not know Arabic." Ana asked.

"This is the main point that 99% of people do not
understand what Mullah is saying. What answer do you
have to say when you don't understand something?

"Yes or no, both are wrong."

"Why don't they read in Farsi?"

"Ask them. There was no need for a grave reciter when
women and men married even Khadija, Muhammad's wife,
selected Muhammad and declared that he was her
husband. This matter is clearly stated in the book 63 years
of Prophet Muhammad's life. At that time, the Quran was
not created.

Quran had been written by Abu Bakr one year to 23
years after Muhammad's death, an adaptation of the Jews
book. In ancient Iran, when the Arians and Zoroastrians
got married, the text of the marriage was such that the man
said to the woman:

"I chose you as a wife from among all the good ones. I
am ready to live with you in the presence of these
witnesses. I tell you, and I will be loyal to you anytime and
anywhere. Do you accept my love?"

And the bride replied, "I will accept you now with all
my heart and soul, and I will be faithful to you at all times
and places."

Madam showed their marriage certificate in Iran:

Ministry of Justice,
Organization of Records and Property of the country,
Marriage certificate, price: 120 Rials.
"In the name of the creator."
Praise and thanks are due to the creator, who laid the

foundation of existence on the unity of the particles of reality and made the garden of life fertile by the union of souls, who strengthened the bond of marriage with the grace of marriage, and who purified the family with the smile of a child. And this sacred bond is the means of survival for humans."

Madame continued: "Note that there is not prophet's name because it was included all different Iranian religious."

Mullah has made fake verses for marriage, divorce, birth, and death to make money of people and attributes it to the Prophet. If you say its verses meaning in Persian, which is shameful, they will say that you have insulted us. The Muslims themselves who proudly have the worst attributes to their religion, and it is recorded in their books, such as murder (Jihad), theft (booty), lying (taqiyya), and violation of other rights (commanding the good and forbidding the bad). If you show Muslims their book, they will say it has a different meaning! It's as if we were their book authors, and religious promoters and ordered them not to read your religious books!

When Monsieur came home, didn't inquire about my proposal, and it seemed like he was aware of what had occurred. I overheard him conversing with Madame.

"Now, we have enough time to consider changing her surname. I asked Sayed Alireza's guard to bring me a birth certificate." Iran Joon said:

"Misfortune graveside reciter became versatile."

"Arman, we do not need a new birth certificate. It is better to tell the registry office to write a birth certificate for Neda."

"Okay, they should change their surnames together."

"Arman, no, I'm afraid they will hurt Neda."

"Honey, don't be afraid; no one will ever know that it was because of Neda unless you say something."

It was in my mind to find out if Monsieur smelled of sweat, but I didn't. I went home, and I wondered if my dad smelled sweat. Our dinner was baked potatoes with bread that night. As usual, my dad brought me a book, helped Roya and Sohrab with their lessons, and listened to the radio or watched TV. My dad calls Marzieh by her name and rarely talks to her. At the same time, Ana's father called Madam my dear, my love and honey.

My dad asked me about the book I had read. While answering, I asked him:

"Dad, why do men have stinging smells?"

He answered in surprise:

"Because they sweat and don't clean themselves on time. Does my body smell?"

"No, but today I went out with Madam; the men smelled terrible. Don't they know it is terrible to smell?"

"Perhaps they did not notice that it is better to clean themselves, and they can easily wash their armpits with soap every time used bathroom and they could take a bathe and changed the clothes every day. But remember that a worker who works on a sunny summer day cannot worry about the smell of sweat. Tell me where you went that you noticed the smell of men's bodies."

"In the shop."

I hated myself for lying! I remembered that my dad did laundry and iron my clothes and his own; on weekends, while I sat next to him, he would ask me about my weekly chores and lessons, and then we would go out together. I never washed my clothes. Marzieh washed Roya and Sohrab's clothes and herself.

It was the first time that my attention was drawn to my dad. I did not remember that my dad smelled like the people I had seen. He had a beautiful face, laughed a little, was calm, and clean, and shaved his face every day. He bought new clothes for me only, not for himself. He read books, and his books were in the corner of our room.

Our house did not have a shower room, but Madam's house had a full bathroom. There was a public bath near our home, with two separate sections for men and women, and each side had several private showers. My dad and I used to go there twice a week; he would send me to the women's section and ask a female worker to wash my body and hair, and he went to the men's section. His bath would finish early, and he would wait for me in the waiting area and pay the worker.

"What men rub under their armpits?

My dad said with a smile:

"Where did you see it?

"There was a small container on the table; Iran Joon said it belonged to Varouge who was rubbing it on his armpit."

"Antiperspirant is for women and men that should be used on the clean area, otherwise, it will cause a worse smell. Not long ago, I heard that people in America were not willing to be in the same elevator with some immigrants due to their breath of garlic smell, they made so many jokes about this issue on their televisions to help people to take care of this social matter and respect others. They all changed by joking and laughing, and the situation improved. A friend explained that this group tries to imitate the excellent behavior of others, which is a good thing. No one knows everything, but we should learn when we see something good. I wish the Iranian radio and television programs would bring up this issue with humor and suggest simple solutions for improving healthy environments."

"Daddy, you don't take a bath every day."

"When I go to the bathroom, I clean my body."

I wondered if my body smelled bad from sweat. That night, as usual, each of us crawled under our quilts, and the light was turned off, and we slept. Again, the idea of the proposal was with me finding someone higher position than the vice president and concubines are better than marriage. I fell asleep in thought. Day after when I woke up, my first thought was to smell myself in the bathroom so my body wouldn't smell. I should brush my teeth well, so my mouth does not smell, something I had never thought about until that day.

I looked at myself in the mirror. It was as if I saw myself for the first time and wanted to look at myself more. Usually, in the morning, Monsieur was not at home, but he was there with Madam and Iran Joon, so I greeted him and thought I should go near Monsieur and find out if he smelled. I told myself my body did not smell and felt good.

Monsieur: "Neda, can you bring me your birth

certificate?"

I was shocked, I had never seen a birth certificate, and I did not know what it looked like.

"Arman, I told you to arrange it yourself."

"Gohar, Monsieur must have the basic information." Iran Joon said.

"Well, Arman, after you buy the bus ticket, then we talk about it."

I went to the workroom where Rudy was as usual. I wanted to stand in front of the mirror again and look at myself. I was comparing myself with Rudi and Ana; Rudi is younger than me, and Ana is more beautiful. Rudy asked me which order we should finish things today.

"I asked you several times which order we should finish today," she said.

I didn't know, so I guessed, "The large tablecloth."

Rudy was right. When I focused on something, I tended to forget everything else. I started crocheting, which I could do easily without even concentrating. Crocheting kept me entertained and helped me analyze my thoughts. It was noon when I realized I had gone to the bathroom three times since morning. Usually, I would have gone after that time. I looked at myself in the mirror like a stranger, smelling my armpit and observing my face. I didn't feel beautiful; Ana is gorgeous. Rudi is lovely, but I'm not. I wasn't happy with my appearance and wished my hair was wavy. I became fixated on my appearance, comparing every part of my face with Ana and Rudy. I saw my face full of flaws and told myself that Ana was lucky because she had a shower at her house and could bathe every day. I believed I would be beautiful if I took a shower every day, just like her. Does Rudi have a shower room in their house? I felt like an inspector searching for everything. I spent the entire morning with these thoughts and internal conversations, thinking about things I had never considered.

The school was closed, and Ana was still sleeping. It was noon when Ana woke up, and we decided to have lunch together. I enjoyed talking to Ana about everything, including the smell of people's sweat, and we laughed together. Ana mentioned that she wants to go to Tehran and take entrance exams. Her father is supposed to buy the ticket for her. I had been in a good mood all morning, happy with my appearance, the mirror, and hair.

However, my good mood quickly turned to shock as I realized that Ana was leaving. I just realized how hard it is when I don't see her. At home, the subject of her trip to Tehran had put everything under the spotlight. There was a heavy sadness in my heart, everyone noticed my depression, and my efforts to hide it were useless. Those days, even Marzieh asked me why I was so sad. I was quietly crocheting and staring at a corner. I did not want to play with Ana, I did not think about the stingy smell crowd, and I did not care about proposal and marriage.

I went to bed earlier than usual. Under the duvet and in the bathroom were the only places where I, a helpless girl had privacy and could cry; I looked like a drowning person who was not even looking for a piece of board to save herself—wandering in the bottomless depression well and staring at the darkness helplessness.

CHAPTER 2, MADAM'S HOUSE

I wrote this part from my diary. In Madam's house, everyone treated me well, but their behavior was different after they met my dad. Ana was happy that we would be together. I was close to Iran Joon, at a suitable opportunity I followed her to the kitchen and asked her.

"Why did you cry last night?"

Iran Joon hugged me and said:

"I explained my life story to them."

I was in her arms and wished for endless moments because I felt like I had a kind mother like Ana. Madam always hugged and kissed Ana, but Marzieh had never hugged and kissed me. It was a pleasant feeling to be dear to someone. I knew my dad loved me very much, but he did not embrace me like this. I never felt that Marzieh might love me and cried involuntarily. I did not know if it was happiness or sadness. I tried to breathe slowly so that Iran Joon would not notice that I was crying and did not want to be separated from that warm embrace but hide my crying. I gently pulled myself out of Iran Joon's arms and went to the bathroom, where I could neutralize my warm tears with chilly water, cool my eyes, and stop crying. I consoled that it must not have been an essential issue except the Iran Joon's story. I went to the workshop, and Madam came in after me, took me in her arms, and asked.

"What are you doing here? You have the best father in the world, and we all love you very much. Why did you come here? Go to Ana's room; she is waiting for you."

This was the first time Madam hugged me like Ana, and I felt good, like a hungry person who had seen a piece of bread or a thirsty one who was drinking water. I was happy that I was beloved. Now, after years, I understand why Ana was kind and calm. She had tasted that being loved pleasant, reflected in her behavior. Her kindness touched my heart. Compared to Ana, I was the thirsty dessert and longing for rain.

I went to Ana's room. Ana was unaware of their crying, I did not say anything to her either, and wanted to believe that it was not an issue and that Iran Joon's words should be convincing. My mood quickly changed, and I was thinking about traveling. I imagined that in Tehran, I would no longer wait for government officials and propose marriage to the president or the leader; they live and work in Tehran. Does the leader have to work, or do the people work and give him money, and he is a consumer? These questions were paraded in my mind. The leader's responsibility should be more, and he should work hard, especially the leader of Iran, who is higher than God even he is the God lawyer.

I heard the leader is wealthy and must not work, unlike poor people. It is a phrase that said a camel dreamed of being a cotton grower, eating a lot, and being happy with his dream. I talked myself, wait, you will soon become his wife, and you will understand! I must buy new shoes and clothes; the leader must wear new clothes too, and he buys me new clothes like my dad, who regularly buys me something. He also gave Marzieh money to buy clothes for Roya and Sohrab, but she used my old clothes for Roya and gave the money to Mullah.

My dad's clothes were old and very loose, and he did not buy clothes for himself. My dad and madam said that I had money. But how can I find out how much money I have? I immediately censored myself that it was not good to ask.

My mood was changing again. Why self-censorship? I thought about self-censorship was chewing and swallowing my heart so no one would know about it. I never had any chat with Marzieh because she thought I was ignorant, and my dad did not have anything to say to her either when my dad is knowledgeable! If I say this to someone, they might think I'm stupid. It is better not to say anything and hide it. Also, I will keep secrets the becoming a concubine and imagined Marzieh's face; she understood that I had gone to Tehran and become a concubine. I was even afraid of my thoughts. Marzieh will indeed say that it is the result of filing a petition. It means the cunning mullah created the piece of dirty clay, and she threw it in the well, then he pulled it out and hid it under a stool for the next customer! Everyone knows that believing in the petition is far from wisdom.

Ana asked. "What are you thinking about? I yelled several times, but you did not answer, it was like you were in another world. Aren't you glad we are going together?

"I am so happy. I thought that Marzieh was paying Mullah that God take the dead body from the cemetery to heaven and prepare 72 angels in a river of wine for sex for his corpse. According to the Islamic code, in this world, prostitution is a sin, and alcohol is forbidden, but in heaven, it is permissible. It means that halal and haram changed their place. Does mullah pay the poor God? I am ignorant and do not understand that heaven is a place for halal or haram actions. And are these nymphs for men or women? We should refer to the dictionary book to see the name of God's job, which is to match ladies for men. Imagine that seven billion people worldwide order God fulfills their wishes, and Sayed Alireza's store makes easy money.

God takes the one-way trip from the grave to heaven and return to the cemetery empty? No one asks him to return his corpse from heaven to his grave. If people find out the corpse is not in the grave, they put a lawsuit against the cemetery administration."

Ana was staring at me, and we were laughing. Iran Joon came to our room. She was happy and spoke.

"These stories are not logical."

Ana asked me. "What else?"

"Another supplication is that God heals the patient as if God is a doctor and has a hospital. Some people die every day, which is God's fault. Those who have lost their loved one should sue God and ask for damages and blood money. I thought God had the treasure too, and I do not know on which occasion he distributed money. Marzieh said if you say, "God will", he will give you whatever you want! Ana, do you know the meaning of God's will?"

"I do not know."

"Because we do not know, it must be effective!"

We laughed.

Iran Joon: "Don't worry about these questions, it takes time for people to use their intellect and not have unreasonable expectations."

"Aunt Iran, we must prepare a list of what we want to take."

"Gohar and I made a list; you can play and have fun."

I was staring at Iran Joon.

"You too, my dear."

After the first meeting, a cordial relationship was established between my dad and Ana's family. They wanted my dad to come to their house. Monsieur treated my dad respectfully, like a great guest, and they talked for hours. Their home had a special guest room—mehmankhaneh, almost three times of our living area size.

My dad said that he could talk to Monsieur more easily here, but I suspected why they see each other frequently and my dad looked incredibly sad. When we were alone, I asked him. "What do you talk about?"

"I am talking to Arman about changing your birth certificate and arranging your high school exams. I am sure that you can easily pass the exams. It is essential you do not have the top student therefore you do not answer a few questions in each exam and do not tell anyone."

I asked in surprise:

"Why?"

"I will tell you later."

While we talked Monsieur entered the room. My father said. "Neda is worried about why we meet each other more often. I told her that we were talking about the birth certificate and her education, and she answered only some of the questions in the exam."

"Daddy, you told me not to tell anyone; you will tell Monsieur."

"Yes, except Monsieur, Gohar and Iran Khanum."

"My daughter, we love you very much and we are considering the best plan for you and my daughter Ana."

I was happy to hear his words, when my dad hugged

me. "Daddy, I wish you told me sooner because I was apprehensive."

Monsieur turned to my dad and spoke.

"I talked to Sayed Alireza's guard to get me a birth certificate, and I paid its fee."

When we were getting closer as we traveled, I had a strange anxiety, and I did not know if it was related to the excitement of traveling or other factors.

One day I noticed my shorts were stained, so I changed my clothes. At night, my father washed my clothes; he told me that I had my period and how to use a sanitary pad and to dispose the used one in a tied plastic bag and toss it in the trash can. I had heard that Ana had her period, but I did not, and the next day Iran Joon talked about it.

"Ana, I do not like to have my period, and my dad must have told Iran Joon and Madam. How did he know that I should use a pad?"

"I wouldn't like it too, but we must bear it. Your dad learns everything by reading books and newspapers."

In those days, my dad said that our place was tight, and he was repairing a small, dilapidated room in the corner of our yard. Monsieur had sent one, and they repaired and painted it. My dad left a mattress, a blanket, and his books there.

Monsieur, Madam, and Iran Joon were rarely my dad's guests in that small room, my father used to sleep in the same spot above my head if we were in our own house. After that night, Monsieur did not let us go home, and we stayed at their house more often. I slept with Ana in her bed. It was the first time I slept in bed, and we were happy to be together; my dad was sleeping in the guest room. Marzieh is satisfied that I leave soon! She might have thought she would have my dad and more food for Sohrab.

The unanswered questions disturbed my mind, why did they cry, what book my dad gave them and if they read it? I told Iran Joon that I know you talked about me that night, and you all changed, but I do not want to know what it was. On the same day, my dad told me about his chosen surname which I liked it.

Several years later, Madam told me that Soheil Khan

had said that the family name is essential, that Neda was born in Tehran, and her surname should combine sign of Pahlavi Street or Fereshteh Street. My dad also got a new birth certificate, so we don't have any problems travelling. Because the security guards stopped cars and asked people illegally for their identification cards. We met Monsieur's friend, the educational department employee, and I took the sixth to ninth-grade exams. Monsieur's friend said I should take the 10th, 11th, and 12th grades in one year in three different cities or regions of a big city like Tehran.

My dad was sure I would pass all the exams easily, and he reminded me to refrain from writing the answers to two or three questions, therefore I do not have the highest degree. If I shine well in the exams, everyone wants to know who the talented student is.

As usual, I had woven so many tablecloths that if Madam had ten orders, she could deliver them. My dad opened a joint bank account with Monsieur for me, deposited the money, and gave the bank book to Monsieur to send me monthly money. I wondered why my dad gave my money to Monsieur!

Madam also had a savings account for me and deposited my salary every month. Seeing the bank books, Monsieur said to my dad.

"Look, this is a significant amount, and we can buy a small house for the children to live comfortably."

However, my dad believed that the money should be spent on our education and studying without financial worries. The plan was Ana has taken the review course in Tehran before the university entrance exam, and I would take the exam for three high school classes in Tehran and participate in the university entrance exam year after and do not work. I told them that this knitting does not affect my studies because I knit it without looking at it.

Tehran Trip

At the TBT bus station, I cried in my dad's arms, Ana and Madam were there with me. When I said goodbye to my dad, he was crying too. The bus was crowded with two rows, each containing two seats. Ana was next to the window and Madam was behind us. As the bus left the city, I wiped my tears with my sleeve and spoke to Ana: "I never thought it would be so hard to be separated from my dad. I don't want anything except to be with him."

I knitted faster so that I can control my stress. Ana wanted me to teach her knitting. I gave her a hook and thread and taught her.

"A good craft. We can take it everywhere and put two tools and in your purse."

Madam noticed that Ana crocheted. She told me.

"You knit beautifully with your delicate and beautiful hands, encouraging everyone to learn. I wish I had brought a hook too."

I gave her a hook and a yarn.

"How many hooks did you have?"

"I had forgotten to take a hook and Iran Joon put a package in my purse and said a bundle is better do not pierce the purse."

"This way, we became three people crocheting, receiving passengers' attention. The first stop was a rest area, which was considered an exciting place for Ana and me! When we went to the bathroom, I quickly came back and complained.

"It is so dirty that I can't even use it."

"Neda Joon, there is no choice. It is the same along the road."

At the same time, Ana came back, and like me, she complained that the toilet was dirty. Finally, Madam convinced us there was no other way and we should use it if we needed. We went to the bathroom, and Ana said.

"From then on, I did not eat and drink anything."

"Me too."

We stopped eating lest we go to the bathroom. One of the passengers asked Madam by pointing at me.

"Your daughter is a knitting expert, and she taught you."

"Yes, she is the expert."

I raised my head and pointed to Madam.

"No, Madam is my teacher."

"I taught her who is so talented that she surpassed

everyone."

"What are you knitting?"

"Tablecloth."

"I wish I had bought some of these tablecloths as souvenirs."

"I would knit it for you if you bought it."

Madam looked at me with surprise. I continued.

"What size do you want? Tell me; I will knit it and teach you how to starch it and spread it on the table."

The passenger agreed, wanted a round tablecloth and gave me the size. She liked the same model I weaved it. I asked Ana to make the border strip and Madam to start from the opposite side. This way, group work began on a round tablecloth from three seats in two bus rows. It was interesting that we were knitting the same patterns at two different speeds. So that when Madam was less than a quarter of the way, I had completed half the circle, but no difference could be seen in the work. I changed the knitting order due to her work speed. Gradually, as the knitting circle increased, the tablecloth could rotate more smoothly. The tablecloth showed survey trees that rose from the center to the outside circle. Our collective work received the passenger's attention and was applauded.

At the last stop, the tablecloth was ready. The passenger paid Madam the fee and tipped each of us, which was surprising because we had never received a tip. The buyer was happy and said its price is higher in Tehran. I asked her.

"If you give me your address, we will make and deliver it to you in Tehran."

Her name was Niloufar to give her address to Madam, ordered a rectangular tablecloth, and wanted to pay in advance, which Madam refused. Madam and Ana laughed happily and said we made a portion of our ticket fee, and I was sad because I missed my dad. Afternoon, we arrived in Tehran, it was crowded, and people were running around in a hurry. We took a taxi, went to their relative's house, and stayed there for a night.

Rental Room

The next day, we went to the Tehran University area to search for a rental room. We got off the 24th of Esfand Square was named after Reza Shah's birthday, now called Revolution Square, and we went to the former Amirabad Street- Kargar Street. Ana and I were busy looking at the windows' shops, and Madam asked the shopkeepers if they had rooms for rent. Finally, one of them asked.

"Who do you want a room for?"

"For my daughters."

The shopkeeper perused Ana and me and said that you are coming from the city.

"Yes."

He spoke very kindly that I would take care of your daughters, handed Madam a house address.

"Go there and tell them that Ali sent me. It would be best if you did not stay here. Leave the girls to God's safety, and you return to your city. I take care of them, and whatever you want, come here, and I will do it for you."

We were happy. Madam thanked him and we went to the address near his shop. A woman was there. She accepted us and said that Ali was a good man, if he told you are reasonable, you must be good. This room is yours, and the rent is for you because of Ali, five thousand tomans. Madam agreed happily. The woman said that you should pay one month's rent in advance. Madam immediately paid her and received a key. We had lunch outside, got our luggage from their friend's house, and told them what had happened. They were surprised and said be careful not to trick you. Madam replied, what's the trick?

We rented a room. Their friend said to be careful and call me if you need help. In the taxi, Madam spoke, "we are strange in this city, so we should be careful. You study, and I'll stay here to ensure everything is safe."

We bought food, mattresses, and blankets and went home. Taxi also had an adventure in Tehran. Later we discovered that there are private taxis called a telephone taxi. Taxis in the city only went straight at total capacity; Madam found a taxi willing to take us home. The taxi had a row of seats in the front, and three of us sat in the front of the car, clinging to the driver, and went home.

On the first day, we provided the essential items, and I talked to my dad and said how much I loved him and regretted leaving him and cried. My dad told me not to worry and he would come soon. The telephone call was also a time-consuming problem. Although we did not lose time and crocheting, it was uncomfortable. We had to go to the telephone company, which had several kiosks with a phone in each. We had to give the number to the receptionist and sat in the crowded corridor till they called our name. Then we went to the kiosks and waited for the operator to take the number. The sound quality was not good, and we were satisfied to hear the voice of our loved one. I was always restless when talking to my dad. I did not know why! Let me tell you about our sudden move-out. One day Madam told us.

"Pack everything, and we will leave this place."

We wondered what had happened and why we had to leave here suddenly. Ana and I noticed that Madam silently sat behind the window and looked at the yard a day before. We knew her habit. Still, I looked in the yard and did not see anything, and I did not understand what Madam was looking at! Madam continued.

"Don't be afraid, I fight with the landlord, and we will leave here."

Ana and I asked why.

"This is not a suitable place, but for now, we will find an apartment and leave here."

"Won't you tell my dad?"

"No, Arman accepts my words."

"Humm, you always said I should ask your dad whenever I wanted something."

Madam laughed and said:

"Yes, everything is with his permission, but if I do something, your father will agree. We should find a place now."

When we came out of the house, a police officer was in the alley. Madam said:

"Look at this man; I will tell you later."

We passed him and reached the street, she spoke.

"This constable and the shopkeeper who introduced the house to us is the coworker of the property owner. Remember what I told you? None of them are reliable."

Madam asked people and shopkeepers for the address of the real estate agency. Finally, we arrived at the agency. Madam searched for a rental property.

"One-bedroom apartment is for rent for 7,500 tomans. Come in the afternoon and give 200 tomans to my assistant to show it to you."

"I will sit here and wait for him."

"I must go for lunch."

"I will give 250 tomans to show it now."

"Three hundred tomans."

Madam agreed, and at that time, he came and showed us a small apartment.

Madam said. "I rent it."

"Get your husband."

"My husband is out of town."

We were supposed to pay the rent and get the key in the afternoon. Madam said.

"My daughters are students, cloud you us discount."

"Come and see what I can do for you in the afternoon."

We returned in the afternoon, and the man was there; he rented the apartment to us for seven thousand five hundred tomans and said:

"Someone is looking for it if you do not want it."

Madam gave him the rent for one month. We thought it was expensive because we were not involved in the cost of living.

"Mom, we paid for that one, too; what will happen?"

"Don't worry; I'll take care of that."

Then we returned to the rented room. Madam made sure that all the items were ready to be moved out and said to us:

"Do not leave the room at all, these people who come here and the property owner are not good people, be careful; I will go to rent a taxi and come back. Be ready for me to move out."

"How and why do you say that? They were good people yesterday and they are not good today!"

Madam did not answer and went to get a taxi and returned. She said, "to hurry and put the things in the car."

We promptly put the only items we had in the car. We went to the new house, put the items in and returned to the rented room in the same taxi. Madam said: "Stay in this room, now I am going to fight and get my money back, do not be afraid. If the fight escalates, you will inform the police, not the police officer of the alley."

Madam went and knocked on the landlord's room; when the door opened, she roared: "Give me my money back; I want to go. This is the miscreants' house."
The owner, who was surprised by this move, began to curse loudly.

"The homeless villagers, hungry and beggars, they became human for us. You paid for a rented room. What do you want?

"Shut up, or I will call the police."

"Now, I will tell the police to come and arrest you."

At this time, Madam shouted:

"Listen, I am from a small city, but I am not a prostitute like you, and I do not have a brothel. You are calling the police officer in the neighborhood who is your partner.

My brother is the Brigadier General of the Tehran Police, and now I am telling my children to go and call him. I am telling you to give me my money because we will not be your customer. This is a brothel, the local police are your colleagues, and yesterday he brought you a customer. I watched you and saw what was going on here. You give me my money back, or I will call my brother. Children, call your uncle to come here and see what this house is for."

A man came out from another room. Said:

"Why are you making noise, disturbing neighbors, and not letting us sleep?"

Madam roared:

"You are also the accomplice of this woman."

"Watch your mouth. It is a pity that you are a woman. Otherwise, I would have shown you who I am."

"I am sorry that you are such a donkey, and I will not punch in the mouth of a donkey."

Then the madam turned towards the room and roared.

"Call your uncle."

Ana and I were looking at each other dumbfounded while I was shaking. I remembered Marzieh, who was afraid of Madam. I asked Ana:

"Do you know your uncle's number?"

"No, I do not know; I did not even know I had an uncle!"

She held me tightly in her arms.

"Don't be afraid, my mother said that we should not go anywhere from here, we should stay here."

At the same time, the man said: "What is the fight for? You want money, come, this is your money. How much did you give? Five tomans? Come on, get your money, and get out of here immediately."

The property owner said:

"So, what about these few days? There is no place for homeless beggars and hungry people to stay here for free, and you should deduct the fee for three days."

"This is our charity to these beggars."

"Close your mouth, or I will hit you with this shoe."

Madam was talking while she grabbed the money from the man's hand and quickly came to the room and said let's go. Excited, Ana and I followed Madam and ran out of the house. Then Madam told us there was a brothel, and the man at the store, the constable in the alley, and the people were in an invisible gang, and their goal was to fool innocent girls unfamiliar with these tricks. They assumed that we were from a small town and were easily fooled. I listened to our friend who said to be careful.

"Mom, where is our brigadier uncle?

Madam laughed and said:

"Uncle? There is no brigadier uncle. I wanted to show them we are not alone, have firm support, and are not afraid of the neighborhood police officer.

Ana asked in surprise.

"So, we do not have a brigadier general uncle."

"No, we do not have it, and we will become brigadier generals whenever necessary."

Living alone in a house was an excellent experience . The next day we walked to Ana's class .Ana went to class daily, and we studied all materials at night .We met Monsieur's friend in the educational department ,who promised to arrange my 10-12 grade exams .The day after , we delivered him the requirements document, and my registration was completed .September was the tenth-grade exam . He quoted Monsieur ,even though you know all the lessons but study all again because you might forget something due to the exam stress .I should take eleventh and twelfth-grade exams in another area and prepare for the university entrance exam. I made a rectangular tablecloth for two days. Madam called Niloufar Khanum , and we went to her house. She had a prospect palace . Madam gave her our address so that if she wanted to order again .She was kind and said she would tell all her friends and give us a hundred toman tip . We got it at her insistence because Madam did not accept it initially and later; she said that this lady was good and honest.

Public transportation

About the bus ride in Tehran: Tehran's buses were double decker, which we had never seen, and it was enjoyable. When Madam gave the driver the entrance ticket, Ana and I walked on the middle aisle to the empty seat at the back of the bus. Suddenly, with the driver's protest, we stopped because we assumed something had gone wrong and the passengers' laugh. We unawarded there were male and female sections on the bus, men sat in front, and women sat behind them or upstairs. Ladies should come from the front door, give the ticket to the driver, then get out of the bus and get on the bus from the back door.

"Ridiculous that you thought the bus was a bedroom, and people immediately cling to each other." Madam said.

The passengers laughed and cheered. We turned back and went through the back door to the upper floor, and Madam sat downstairs. On the bus, I thought my dad grew up in Tehran, he must know the streets; I wished he were there. I had missed him, and at night, I dreamed of him I was in a rainy place, and my dad was standing, and he was very tall. Madam called Monsieur and Iran Joon twice weekly, and I talked to my dad. I used to knit in a hurry for days, and Madam was knitting with me and saying thank you for making my hands work after so many years.

1996, Tehran University Entrance Exam

High school graduates can enter a university after they pass the entrance exam. My dad quoted aunt Zohreh, there is no entrance exam in USA. The entrance exam was approaching. Madam decided to stay with us until the entrance examinations in Tehran. We were overly excited on the entrance exam day.

I was sure Ana would pass the exam because we reviewed everything at night. I had become like my dad when he asked me a question, he made sure that I answered utterly, and I also ensured that Ana covered all details. I knew that Ana would pass if the questions were about those topics. Ana said.

"If I pass the exam, you will do it too. The teacher said it is essential to read all these materials carefully. Some students objected why the teacher reviewed so fast, and the teacher said that you should have learned these subjects in high school. Here is not the classroom; it is the review course. You study well, and if you know your lessons, the entrance exam is easy, otherwise, it is torture."

The night before the exam, Ana was a little anxious; Madam talked to her.

"You will pass; if you don't, you will take the exam next year with Neda."

Madam assured me that I would pass the exam when I did not believe I could get a diploma and go to college. It was my dream to study and be in Tehran with Ana, it happened. I missed my dad badly and cried during this challenging time.

On the day of the entrance examination, Madam and I walked with Ana to the university, which was busy. The police were standing at the entrance and only allowed the applicant to enter the university with the registration form. Madam and I returned home. I was worried and knitting faster than before, like someone is running away from something. Ana came back satisfied with the exam and spoke it was easy, and the result will be published in the newspaper. Madam said.

"Now we must have fun and visit interesting places."

In our idle moments, all three of us were knitting. Madam wanted to buy a TV, but we disagreed because we just wanted to study. One day we went to the Bazaar of Tehran which was surprisingly chaotic. I don't know why I remember Nima Khan and Aria's shop, and I missed them with the sincerity and simplicity of those good men. The yarn was cheaper, but the bazaar was crowded and noisy. Everyone is running. Tehran had large and beautiful parks and museums.

We visited Laleh Park Museum, learned a lot, and decided to visit the paintings later and to learn more about Iranian painters. Madam always said not to worry about money. Everyone assumed I was Madam's daughter. Madam asked the same real estate agent to find telephone line for us. The telephone service demands were more than supplies in Tehran, and it caused a chaotic situation (black market). Therefore, it was created a figurative job for someone to apply for a telephone line in advance and sell it in the free market. In the meantime, we called Niloufar Khanum, her friends had a shop and wanted to order some items.

We went to his shop, and he ordered a few tablecloths, and said it is easier to place an order by calling. We purchased all equipment for Starching the tablecloth when we went to the bazaar. From there, we went to Niloufar Khanum's home and took the tablecloth we sold to her to starch it. She wanted to pay again, and Madam refused, then she ordered two more. When we left her house on the bus, I asked Madam.

"Do you remember Niloufar bought the tablecloth as a souvenir, but she still did not give it!"

"She is a good lady who wanted to help us in this way without questioning the people's dignity. I saw nothing but simplicity in her house. I will tell her next time."

Finally, the real estate agent found a phone line for us. Madam agreed and paid two hundred thousand tomans instead of its actual price that was around eighteen thousand tomans! We had to buy a phone device separately. When we were in the store, Madam asked what color, and I said red without knowing that the red one was more expensive and imagined I would talk to my dad with this phone and my eyes were full of tears. Madam was staring into my eyes, and I was crying uncontrollably. Madam was hugging me, Ana was not beside us, and she did not hear us. She turned back, saw that I was crying, and asked what had happened.

Madam did not say anything and bought the red phone while Ana said it was more expensive. Ana laughed and said it must be for Neda. Three or four days later, our phone was connected. She called Monsieur and I talked to my dad who was there. As usual, my dad said to have fun, and he would come soon. I asked when and he repeated very soon.

Monsieur asked Madam to buy a house for us. Madam called Niloufar Khanum and gave her our phone number. Also, she told the agent to find a home for sale.

Buying a newspaper was tough on the day of the announcement of the entrance exam results and there was a long queue in front of the newsstand. The University of Tehran used to put the names of the results on the wall, which was very crowded with families. We bought a newspaper with great difficulty. Ana's name was on the front page. Ana was third from the top in the exams and we were all happy. Since we had a phone, we informed Monsieur as soon as we got home and then went to the cinema. The next day, the newspapers printed the photos of the top ten students on the front page, most of them were boys, and Ana was the most beautiful and the first among the girls. Ana was admitted to the medical school of Tehran University and said next year is your turn. Madam would wait until I took my exam because she missed her husband and Iran. Iran Joon had made many tablecloths that she would send us if we had a customer. Madam taught us to set a one-week deadline for order delivery. The shop owner said that sometimes a customer wanted within a short term, and if we prepare the work, he will pay twice as much if we deliver the work to the shop on time. Madam agreed.

The shopkeeper did not know that we regularly made more than demand. He advised us it is helpful to have an album so he can show it to customers and have more orders for us. Madam called Varouge and asked him to make an album and send it to us. In this way, we established our work, and I was happy to have income. Madam told me to keep the money and not spend it at home; I knew that she wanted to save it for me.

I passed the 10th-grade exam. During the exam, I had a doubt, why not write the answers when I knew all questions and I could become the first student. The temptation did not go away for a few minutes. Finally, I concluded that following my dad's instructions was better. As he asked, I wrote down the answers to some questions and passed the exam. Madam left us, and we expected my dad and Monsieur to come soon and buy a house. The following week, my dad came to Tehran. I was excited.

Years later, Iran Joon told me those day my dad was so ill and depressed. Monsieur took him to his house, made a doctor's appointment for him and tried to reduce his sadness by adding private students and increasing his teaching hours to keep Soheil Khan busy and did not leave him alone. Even though he had private students in the printing shop, regardless of the student's payment. Monsieur took the tutoring fee first and then set their time for teaching in a small room in his store. Monsieur did not accept Soheil Khan's proposal to divide the tutoring income. After visiting the doctor and repeating several tests from Soheil Khan, the doctor told him his weight loss was due to colitis ulcer not cancer. His condition improved with medication and diet, and he gained weight.

Iran Joon was talking about Soheil khan believed Marzieh should decide on their surname and Marzieh who claimed whatever sir said. But my dad did not interfere.

Marzieh told her story to Iran Joon that her husband Murad was her cousin, and his brother killed him in the name of honor. She did not want to choose Murad's name for her children because she was afraid of her brother

killing her and her children. She and Murad loved each
other and wanted to marry. Murad went on army duty,
and when he had a holiday break, she got pregnant by her
cousin and gave birth to Roya. Murad finished his army
duty and came back to marry Marzieh. His brother has
been very restless since childhood and used to fight all the
time. He was proud, had an honorable bias, and threatened
to kill Murad and Marzieh and he objected why Marzieh
loved and wanted to get married to Murad. One night
before Murad's murder, his brother fought with Murad,
saying irrelevant and obscene words to Murad. Marzieh's
mother also supported her son.

Murad replied patiently that he should grow up, it was
not nice he said such nonsense, and we are relatives. The
next day evening, his brother attacked Murad and killed
him with a knife. Marzieh, with her baby, stayed with her
neighbor for one week and then left her village, not
knowing she was pregnant again. One night, she reached
the road with her little child, and without having any
capital and knowing where she was going, she got on the
first truck that passed by the road and came to our city. The
truck driver told her that his name was Amir from Ahvaz.

Marzieh said they were two strong men and could rape
and kill me that night in the dark desert. And I was a
helpless woman who could not even support my weight on
my feet due to extreme hunger, so she was sitting on the
ground on the side of the road and terrified. When she sat
in their truck, they had gathered themselves in the front
seat so that their bodies would not accidentally touch her,
and they treated her well. At that time, she did not know
the name of the city.

Iran Joon said they were men, not her brother, who
killed his cousin in the name of honor and zeal. We should
salute the honor of truck drivers who are a refuge for the
homeless in the middle of the night and never sacrifice
their humanity and integrity for a few minutes of lust.
They are the best teachers of honesty on anonymous roads.
Marzieh had explained that she and her child slept in their
truck that night. They ensured her while she was with
them, they would not let anyone hurt her, and she could

relax and rest comfortably.

They dropped off Marzieh in this city and gave him some money without asking her why she ran away. Later, Marzieh found out about her second pregnancy and started begging to support her living expenses. Iran Joon and Madam suggested that she select a new last name, should work to support her children. Marzieh agrees to get a birth certificate with the actual name of her children's father. Monsieur arranged their new birth certification, paid its cost, and exchanged their old birth certifications.

Years later, when I read my father's diary, he wrote that these years were hard, but seeing Neda daily was a blessing. Neda was the love of my life. I survived because of her, endured my life, and hoped for a better life for her. I left far away from her with a galaxy of emptiness, loneliness, despair, and hopelessness. On this part of my dad's memories, I remembered that I missed him badly and did not miss Marzieh. Monsieur also contacted his friend, a university professor in Tehran, and told him about Soheil Khan, he liked to talk to Soheil Khan about teaching position in Armenian university. Two of their professors were Soheil Khan former students and knew him very well. Soheil Khan talked to the university dean and decided to meet him. Arman prepared tickets to Tehran, where he had bitter memories.

Monsieur talked about their chat about Zohreh with Soheil Khan along the way.

"I called her in America a few days ago, and she was good."

"I thought Zohreh was in Germany."

"She was in Germany and decided to go to US if the American visa is approved. Also, Manijeh and Hossein Agha decided to stay in Germany and continued her medical treatment, and care of Kaveh and Kamyar. Hossein Agha said Zohreh is young and should marry, and they took care of her children. Manijeh talked to Zohreh, and she replied that she was in love with Soroush, and the thought that he did not come is far from her mind, and she thought that he has gone on a journey and returned and was happy her children replica their father and did not want to know he is not coming. Manijeh stopped talking, but Hossein Agha believed that Shahriar was a good man to like Zohreh and call her regularly. Manijeh asked him not to say anything because Zohreh might be upset.

Zohreh told me to meet a kind Algerian foreigner in a cloudy day Manijeh left with Hossein Agha for a doctor's visit, and Zohreh was homesick and took her children to the playground next their building. Zohreh was alone in park when an older man came with his grandchild and sat next to Zohreh even all the benches were empty. Zohreh got up and sat on another bench. The man followed her. Zohreh wondered why he came next to her when there were many empty benches! The man spoke.

"Why are you sad. Why?"

He was an immigrant and talked with accent, and they talked with broken language when Zohreh denied her sadness.

"I saw you a few days ago. You were sad. I was looking out the window of my apartment and waiting you come, and I talk to you."

Zohreh looked at him with surprise. The man pointed to his grandchild.

"Do you see this child?"

"Yes, your grandchild."

"No, she is my daughter. I am Algerian, and one year France bombarded my hometown when I was there with my family for vacation. I lost my wife, three children, father, mother, sister, and house all together. I was very depressed for many years, and then I decided to marry a lady with three children who lost her husband. I worked in Germany for years and has have a good financial mean.

My wife can raise her children with my pension, and I asked her to go to school to learn some skills, and I will take care of the children. I want to help you. Talk to me."

"My husband was killed in Iran, and do not know who I am and what I want to do."

Algerian stated there is a program to support families with children who need their parents' supervision and provided an opportunity that the adults learn a skill for a better future and improve the German productions. People should refer to the labor office for job search. They have a list for recruitment and send the applicant to the appropriate places. I have experience that none of them hire you because you have small children at home and the language barrier. Then the government will support you and your children due to decreasing the Germany's population.

"I am not a German citizen."

"No matter. This law applies to you as a German resident. They must provide a salary and house for you, and you must file a lawsuit against your husband's killer."

"Lawsuit?"

"Refer to international organizations. Take immediate action against them and let the international organization access your husband's file. It would be best to complain that might save any innocent lives."

"I need to have money for the court."

"Some conscientious lawyers work free of charge on these issues, and I will find one for you."

"I do not know Germany, and an English-speaking country would be better for me.

"England is a poor developing country. Only go to the US if you do not want to stay in Germany. But remember, you have good support and do not worry about bread for your children here."

In this way, Zohreh received the government support when she was in Germany. Later, the Algerian man arranges for Zohreh to meet with a German lawyer-activist in human rights. Zohreh released all information about the Soroush murder via Nader and authorized him to contact Nader and filed a lawsuit against the Islamic regime.

Hossein Agha believed when Zohreh is involved in a lawsuit, she will suffer and hurt emotionally, and it is better to put her life in order. Manijeh said that if it is possible to take legal action, I will follow the case instead of Zohreh and go to the end of the line and avenge me brother's blood. This way, a complaint against the Islamic Republic for Soroush's murder was opened in the international court.

Nader and his friends went to Zohreh's house for

dinner. Zohreh shared the Algerian man's advice with them. Nader said that Iranians got support from the government and hid from each other, while it had nothing to do with them, and this is the government's decision based on its needs and interests.

Zohreh asked their choice between living in Germany and America. All except one said America because German people are racist. Zohreh decided to go to the US if the visa was approved and called Arash. On the other hand, Arash accidentally came across an ad the hiring a Persian language teacher with all benefits. Arash called Zohreh, and she applied for that position for Zohreh. At that time, American embassies were crowded of Iranian, and it was rumored that they would not give American visas under any circumstances. Zohreh applied and said someone other than me handled living with two hearts like this and got the visa.

Shahriar told Zohreh never to destroy the bridges behind, it might change your mind and want to return. Soheil described Shahriar had married a German girl at that time or having a girlfriend, and he separated after a brief period, when his father was there visited Zohreh. His father asked her if she considered to marry Shahryar and be his daughter in law? She gave him a negative answer. When Zohreh told Shahriar that she would leave Germany, he told Zohreh that he loved her and proposed her. Zohreh said that she did not intend to marry and should raise her children. When she left Germany, Shahriar came to the airport. Zohreh told him to promise that if something happened to her if no one could take care of her children, he would take care of them and hand them over to me. Shahryar said that she was depressed.

Zohreh replied that life had taught her not to be sure about anything. She and Soroush had a plan, and even Soroush told when we have children, our responsibility to take care of our health, check up regularly, and having a plan after the children leave us. But life had shown us differently, and when she wanted to use all the possibilities for the unknown day. Zohreh left Germany and all benefits others were counting on. The employee offer job and who

hired Zohreh should provide an apartment, and her
children would be in kindergarten while she was teaching.
Zohreh happily accepted their offer.

When Zohreh entered USA, the apartment was
unavailable, so she had to wait a few days. Arash took
them to his house to stay with them, his wife was upset
about having guests. Zohreh decided to go to the hotel,
which Arash opposed. Based on Arash's recommendation
Zohreh hired an immigration lawyer to follow her case.
After a few weeks, Zohreh recognized that living in that
area was incompatible with her spirit. Therefore, she found
a job in a store with working hours consistent with her
children's kindergarten. Arash told Zohreh to reconsider
her decision that everyone wished to find such a job, and it
is a big mistake that Zohreh committed and may hurt her
residency.

Zohreh said I decided we could live in a small room. I
rented a room and bought second-hand furniture. Arash
talked to Shahriar, who said she did not destroy the
bridges behind her and could return to Germany. Zohreh
said no, I did not want German
money either. I could work and raise my children.

Arash believed the employer might reject her if he
finds out about the legal residency. Zohreh said they did
not ask, and I did not say anything. I will start my job soon.
Arash helped Zohreh and her children stay in America and
signed a declaration of facts forms to pay the medical
expenses of Zohreh and her children if they needed it for
one year. Zohreh worked in the morning when her
children were at a childcare center, cared for some other
Iranian children, and taught them Persian in the afternoon.

Although the population of Iranians was small,
teaching and caring for the children made Zohreh's life
turn around until her residency was approved. After
obtaining the residence permit, she was hired as a teacher.
Her children are in high school and have a good life. As it
is known, Arash had a challenging situation with his wife,
and finally, they separated.

After their separation, Arash settled near Zohreh's
house and told Zohreh that he wanted to be with someone

like her, not like other people who were all strangers, even
when they spoke the same language. He said that when he
came to Iran, he had the same feeling, and if it was not
Soheil's help at the university, he would not have been able
to endure those first years as a professor at Tehran
University. You do not know how happy he was when
Soheil told me to come to his house so was not alone. He
wished my mother were alive, and he could repeatedly
smell the same food in our house. Later, Arash proposed to
Zohreh, but she refused, but they saw each other.

"Finally, they get married."

"I did not ask her about their relationship because I
trusted them. They are knowledgeable enough to make
their decisions. Zohreh said that Manijeh is traveling
between Germany and America, and she is in Germany
now. Nader has finished his studies, worked, married, and
has two daughters. His life is very independent of his
parents. Manijeh is upset with this kind of cold relationship
and said they are two neighbors who sometimes see each
other. Zohreh believed that living abroad means loneliness,
even in a group. I was the only one left in this corner,
unaware of everyone, and I no longer had any desire for
this community or that community. Now I must start all
over again."

"Every dark cloud has a positive aspect, and I am sure
you will have a good life.

They reach Tehran and take a taxi to Neda and Ana's
house. I remember how I was excited to see my dad when
reading my dad's diary. Here is part of my dad's note:
seeing Neda is essential to me, although the memories of
losing my loved ones tortured me, which is sad. Neda had
grown up instead of my little girl, a tall and lively beautiful
lady was sitting in front of me, and Ana was also more
beautiful than before. Neda told me that she passed the
exam well and did not write some answers, she learned to
cook and prepared dinner, but laundry is difficult for her.

Monsieur and I slept on a blanket in the hall of their
house. The next day, we went to the Armenian College,
and they hired me. My salary was several times higher
than that of Tehran University. However, living expenses

were on the rise. My former students, who have the professor's position, welcomed me well and were surprised at how old I had become. They happened to be close to Hayedeh, but they did not know anything about her fate when I told them, and they were highly impressed.
Before I came to Tehran, I had talked about renting a room in the faculty's house. They gave me its keys. Then we went to the bazaar to get the supplies I needed. We passed Hossein Agha and Shahpour Khan's shop.

Tehran was not where I was born and grew up, the names of the streets have changed, and it is very crowded and dirty, with disheveled and disturbed people. I only bought a few things; everything was costly. We went to the cemetery, which was still painful. Then we went to Masoud's house, at first, I thought we had come down to the wrong street. The street's name had changed, instead of Masoud's house, a multi-story apartment looked beautiful but did not match the city's texture. The neighbors had also changed, but it was one of the businesspeople there. We decided to go to Tajrish and Sultanate Abad Police Station.

In the taxi, Armaan suggested that we postpone going to the police station the next day and go home before Ana returned from university so there would be enough time to talk to Neda. I liked his idea because it was in my mind to speak to Neda as soon as possible. Monsieur, quoting Iran Khanum when she wanted to talk to Neda, she knew we talked about her that night, but she did not want to know anything. They returned home. Arman said I would pretend to take a bath so you can have enough privacy. Neda said:

"Daddy, I still need to make a meal, let me make you some tea. We had tea, and Arman went to the bathroom. I asked very casually.

"How is life in Tehran? Do you like it? The college hired me, and I will buy you a washing machine soon. The college has a faculty house and gives me a room for living."

Neda was happy and spoke.

"How great that you were hired as a teacher."

"I want to tell you something, don't be upset."

Neda suddenly changed, and tears covered her face.

In this part of reading my dad's diary, I remember not knowing what he wanted to say, but I felt it must not be good news. I thought about that night when my dad talked with Monsieur, Madam, and Iran, and they cried. I knew there was a problem that I did not know, and I did not want to know. That was enough for me to love him, and he loves me. I heard my dad's voice.

"I love you, I just wanted to say."

My heart was falling in my chest; I did not want to know anything. My dad also wrote down in his dairy that Neda interrupted me and told.

"Don't tell me anything. I don't want to know. If you wish, we will go back to our city. I will crochet and cover the cost of living."

I remember my dad's face; tears covered his cheeks.

"I love you."

And I did not let him speak. My dad wrote that Arman came out of the bathroom from the sound of Neda's crying and heard she refused to hear me.

My dad was moaning.

"Neda, I can't tolerate your crying; I just wanted to say that..."

Neda jumped up, cried, and spoke.

"I don't want to hear anything. Let me love you, that's all." She left the house without a scarf while crying.

Arman said: "don't say anything."

"My heart is broken. This child was suffering in silence, and I am unaware, so she was not ready to hear anything without knowing what I wanted to talk about.

It is the deep pain signs. Where did I fail?"

"Now, it is not the time for such words, it is better to go after Ana so that the atmosphere will change. Get up; this is not the time to cry."

I quickly put myself together and took her clothes and scarf, and we went towards the door. Neda was sitting on the stairs. Arman roared:

"Let's go after Ana, her class ends early today."

"You go; I will not come."

"Arman, I will stay at home too."

"Oh, I had left the house keys inside. Arman, do you

have the house keys? I left my key inside."

"I also left the keys in the bathroom."

This way, we all went to the university and reached a sandwich shop.

"I am so hungry; what day is today? Oh, no, I was wrong; Ana did not say today. So, let us eat a sandwich."

Unlike a few minutes ago, when Neda was aggressive, she had a calm appearance. In those moments, I thought that Neda had endured much pain, and I was analyzing Neda's recent changes in my mind, that all these changes did not happen suddenly. It grew gradually, slowly, and creepily. I see a particle of a volcano and a mountain of fire hidden under her calm appearance, which burns her inside and eventually kills me. I must be careful and see a psychiatrist Dr. Omid, or a psychologist, for help, and I should not trust her calm appearance. I remembered Arman's words when he said that now was not the time to cry; I pushed back my feelings and said:

"Arman, you are an expert in these restaurants and sandwich shops; tell me which one is good; these are pork!"

"Mr. Doctor, surely you want to say that it is impure."

We both laughed. There was no difference on Neda's face.

"No, Arman, when did I talk about impurity?"

"I was joking, Dr. Engineer, and University Professor. People say things that do not make sense."

When Monsieur said my titles, Neda looked at me with a half-smile. I showed that I did not notice her mood change.

Arman: "Tell me what you are eating."

"I am not hungry." Neda said.

"We all must eat something; I am hungry, if you do not eat, I must starve. If my love were here, she would order and would not ask me."

"Monsieur, I will have a sausage sandwich, and Neda too."

Without waiting for her answer ,I got up and brought three of the soft drinks that Neda liked.

"I like this drink. Ms. Gohar said that she had a

sandwich with you and Ana, which was unbelievably delicious. What was the sandwich that madam liked?"

Arman returned to the table.

"Are you talking about my love?"

"Madam liked that sandwich which was near Niloufar Khanam's house."

"Yes, my love told me; I wish we could go there."

"Now that we are here, may this sandwich also be good too."

I had no appetite at all. The atmosphere had changed, but a fire was burning inside me, and I thought there was a commotion inside all three of us. We should wait for Ana, and we decided to see a movie. This was the first time I went to the cinema with Neda. Fear of an unsafe environment prevented us from any social activity.

In this part of my father's memoirs, I was thinking about that day and my stress, and my intelligent dad knew me well. I was thinking about the pains and deprivations he had endured for me, that I had even robbed all his opportunity even to see a movie in the cinema. Let me go back to my father's diary, in which he wrote. In the cinema. Monsieur said with surprise and laugh.

"Look how distracted I am, the key is in my pocket."

We returned home. I stayed there that night, Arman called Ms. Gohar, and we talked with her. The rest of the night, we were passed in silence. Neda and Ana were studying together. We fell asleep. The next day Ana was at home and did not have class. Arman and I went out and decided to return in the afternoon.

We went to the Tajrish police station and talked about Neda until we reached the police station. We found out Payam had received a higher position and was transferred from there. Then we went to Saltanatabad police station to see Shahrukh, who was no longer there. The appearance of the polices had changed, the officers' uniforms were not neat, men with dirty clothes, and the dust of depression, rage, and anger was on their faces.

"Arman, do you think we find out what happened that night. What can we do with that data when Neda does not want to know, except to help her parents who have suffered for years. Sometimes we try to do something impossible. Neda is not ready to hear my words."

"Now, do not say anything; wait, she will grow up and understand more about life; you can talk to her then."

We decided not to tell Ana about this because Ana would tell Neda. They had prepared food for us, as I was not in a food trap, whatever was good. Monsieur said.

"Iran's hand-baked food is perfect."

"Father, you should bring them with yourself."

Neda was silent. For the first time, I also learned to express my feelings loudly before everyone.

"Whatever you cook is perfect for me. Ana, you know how much I love Neda. For me, Neda means my life. I love her, and Arman loves you; whatever you make is the best."

Neda looked at me and was silent.

"Neda, you tell me you agree, and I love you."

She did not say anything. It was important to me that she heard that I loved her.

Arman: "We should buy a sofa to sleep on the couch and not on the floor. What color sofa do you like?"

Neda and Ana wanted to go with Arman to choose the sofa, which I was happy to hear; we went together; I bought the furniture they liked and paid for it. I was looking Neda, who was knitting and studying with Ana, and the skill and creativity of my beautiful daughter were more than me. Arman was good in business and good living. I did not have a chance to live well. I had started my work the next day and wanted to go, but Neda asked me to stay and go tomorrow morning. I agreed; Arman and I slept on the sofa in the small hall of their apartment. I could not sleep even though it was not Monsieur's snoring, my eyes would not be dreamt of sleep. I thought that sometimes it is good to be forgetful and have Alzheimer, and I wish I had forgotten everything. I left home early in the morning and went to the university and came back in the afternoon, Neda asked me excitedly.

"How was university?"

"It was good."

I could see the excitement in her eyes. Although the university was an ordinary place for me, I explained it to her in detail. Arman had bought a car that day and spoke.

"You need a car. If I told you, you would prevent me from buying. We will count the money later."

He did not say how much he paid.

"Soheil Khan, I talked to the agency, there is a small house for sale two streets away from here, and I will see it even its price is high."

"Let the children study peacefully; I will think about it later.

"Don't worry. My business is good, the kids have money, and I pay the rest."

"Take the children so that they can express their opinion."

The next day ,I passed in front of the house where I lived with Hayedeh and stared at the home for a few minutes .Even though the face of the city had changed ,that house was still left in front of the tall buildings ,humbler than before. I was sad because I saw that with so much studying ,I did not have the financial ability to help the children .Neda insisted that I stay at their house ,but I saw that it was better for the two young girls to be alone ,they would be happy together ,and it was better for me to be near the college and see them twice a week .Arman had seen the home for sale and said that it was not good and asked the company to find a better one. The next day, I took Arman to the Mehrabad airport.

In this part of my dad's notebook, I remember how eager I was to see how he teaches at the university. My dad suggested washing my clothes, which I did not accept. I promised him that I would wash my clothes and not pour the water on the floor, and I told them the story of one winter night, when my dad did laundry inside the room, I was playing too much and accidentally spilled the water from the washing pan on the floor. My dad put me on top of the wooden box and tried to dry the floor because the same room was our bedroom. My dad bought me a washing machine and taught me how to use it. I cried because my dad used to wash my clothes at night after returning from work.

Those days, I understood that my dad was a doctor, and I remember my aunt Manijeh and Hossein Agha called my dad Dr. Soheil. I imagined myself in medical school and become a doctor. I did not believe I would take the 12th-grade exam. From the day we met Mrs. Niloufar on the bus, and she introduced me to that shopkeeper, I was earning a good income. Although I lived in a slum, money was a significant issue for me, my dad bought me everything and took care of me. In 1997 I got my diploma and was ready to take the university entrance exam.

CHAPTER 3, UNIVERSITY, CONCUBINE, and LOVE

Ana was at the medical school, and we talked about the school and her classmates, especially Abbas, the to student in the country's national exam. When Ana was in school, I did all the work and crocheted and read her textbooks, especially one lesson ahead that she would review. That year, I got the science high school diploma, and near the national exam, my dad asked me if I wanted to take a reinforcement class. I assured him that I reviewed all lessons with Ana last year and it was unnecessary. My dad and Ana were sure that I would pass the exam. Madam and Iran Jun came to Tehran to support me, and all accompanied me to the university on the exam day. According to my dad's advice, I left three questions blank and needed clarification on a few.

The results of the exams were announced, and I was among the first 20 candidates. It was due to my dad's endeavor that he made me used to reading books. Ana was thrilled and said that you are younger than me and passed the exam without going to school. My dad used to say he was proud of me. Iran Joon was pleased; she saw the manifestation of his failed maternal wishes in my fate and my successes.

A year after Ana, I entered medical school and was the youngest student in our class. Ana and I used to go to school together, but our classes were in two different buildings. In the university, we had to wear Islamic headcovers, and a veil, which I hated; we were not allowed to wear high heels.

We used to wear beautiful clothes at home that Aunt Zohreh sent for me. It was tough to wear a robe in the summer. We wore the same robe that Madam had bought for us. In university, everyone knew me as the knitting girl because I crochet. One Friday when we passed by the university that was very crowded, Ana said it was Friday pray, and the president was praying today, many flatters surrounded him, and others had come to show off. Again, the thought arose in my mind that I wanted to become the president's wife. I decided to find out the situation and to see the president. I had a strange obsession that would not let me go, and I hid the above matter from Ana.

That year, Madam convinced my dad to buy a house for us and pay the rest. They purchased a two-story house for us for three million tomans near Tehran University, each floor had two bedrooms, a hall, a living room, and a kitchen. Ana and I moved to the second floor. My dad refused to come and live with us, saying it was better to be near his university. We rented the first floor. Madam and Iran Joon used to come to Tehran more often.

My dad used to be with us on the weekend to have fun, I quickly grew and became taller than Ana, and no one believed I was under eighteen. My dad took us outside the city on Fridays and taught us how to drive. We loved driving; however, we could apply for a driving license after eighteen. The driving test was conducted in two stages, there was a practical exam after passing the written exam another turns. The motor vehicle department was in the police station, and the police officers were responsible for the driving test. Ana passed the written test on the first attempt. The police officer scheduled the practical exam three months later. In the practical test, she failed. We objected that Ana had done nothing wrong, which was not helpful. We had to wait a month to retake the exam, and she passed the second time. My dad offered Ana to have the car, but Ana said she would wait until I got my driving license. Two years later, I went through the same process, and it is evident that police officers did not approve the new young driver at the first attempt. I also got my driver's license.

When Ana and I were alone, our conversation was about Abbas. She had become obsessive towards Abbas.

"I mean that moody student, Abbas. I have a special feeling for him every time I see him. Recently, he talked to everyone except me. He knows all the lessons very well. He might be sad that I am also a good student. He went to a corner and sat quietly."

"Why do you think so?"

"I don't know, but he made me angry."

I was surprised because Ana never got angry, we grew up together, and I knew her well.

"This is the first time I hear you are angry with someone."

"I know, I don't understand why I became so sensitive to him. I like him to look at me and talk to me, and I'm angry about why he did not. He is very handsome; I don't know how to tell you."

"Ana, why don't you talk to him?"

"I don't know, I wait to see him every day. When he came, He ignored me."

"How is his behavior with others?"

"He doesn't talk to others; if someone asks a question, he answers in detail."

"Fine, ask him a question and see his reaction."

"He answered me briefly and did not look at me. I am nobody."

"He loves you."

"No, he did not want to look at me at all."

It was our regular and daily conversations about Abbas. I looked at Ana to see how passionately she talked about him, and she had never spoken about anyone like that.

"Do you wish he was here, and you were talking to him?"

"Oh, yes."

"You love him. I remember Madam telling me to look into his eyes and say I am good. Go ahead and tell him I'm fine."

Ana laughed and spoke. "You want me to go and tell him that I want to become a concubine."

"I was humiliated, and I was lost in my thoughts if she knew that I planned to see the president or Imam Jumma.

"Where are you, I asked you what else my mother said?"

"Your mother taught me to look into his eyes and say I

am fine."

"Wow, he did not look at me when I talked; it's like he hates me."

"Well, ask him one day, do you hate me?"

"Oh, Neda, what are you talking about? I thought the same; I couldn't talk to him at all. He sat in a corner and was
in his book, he was our country's first student on the test."

"Who was second?"

"He studies engineering."

"Does he know that you were the third one?"

"Yes, we used to talk daily, but now he tried to keep his distance.

"Look, as we read in books, it's like you fell in love."

Ana and I talked about Abbas for hours, but I did not tell her what was going on in my mind.

My dad often came to our house. Sometimes he was down. I felt sad to see his depressed face. I used to ask him; did you go to Your mother's grave, and he answered yes. I asked him.

"Did you like your mother?"

He nodded his head positively.

"I love you too, and my heart breaks when I see you sad. I'm afraid something will happen to you. You were a doctor and never told me I would become a doctor because of your efforts. I could crochet, and we could live in our old house. You used to teach me the letters of the newspaper, and I would tear the newspapers to pieces, stick them on the wall, and you would clean after me."

Then I hugged him, put my head on his shoulder, and cried.

"Don't worry, I take care of myself, and nothing will happen to me. My depression is related to losing my loved ones, and I could not forget them. I did not talk about my education and my title because I had been expelled from the university. You become a doctor because of your intelligence and talent. I told you not to answer the three questions because I did not want you to have my fate."

He was also crying with me. It was an exceptional opportunity when I talked to him about my feelings but was afraid to ask about his depression cause. I did not want to say that I did not like Marzieh, and I liked to have a strong mother like Madam.

Also, on Friday we had lunch outside, especially having sandwiches near Niloufar Khanam's house and went to the store to deliver his order. One of those days in the evening
when the weather was getting cold, on our way, he passed in front of his last house and spoke.

"This was my house."

"Uncle Soheil, why don't we go live there now?"

My dad was shaking his head: "I sold it years ago."

"Uncle Soheil, have you ever fallen in love?"

I was shocked by Ana's question because I never thought my dad might have fallen in love. He answered with a sad voice.

"Yes, Ana Joon, I fell in love too. I liked her very much."

I hesitated to hear about his love. Silence filled the air as if none of us dared to speak. After passing a few streets, my dad broke the silence.

"How much the city's appearance has changed, even the people's appearance has changed. There were never so many vendors in the streets; this is a sign of the people's poverty. Little children were not selling chewing gum and cigarettes. People did not come out unshaven with dirty clothes."

Ana interrupted him: "That means their clothes were clean."

"Yes, the men wore ties, their beards were all shaved or had a trimmed beard, and the people were neat. Now it looks like the Mongols have attacked here and intend to destroy everything. The traffic is awful, and the air pollution is intolerable."

Then, my dad changed the subject and asked about the university. Gradually the scope of the conversation was extended to speech freedom and girl-boy relationships.

Ana: "Girls and boys sat separately. Even some boys seem afraid to look at girls. They come highly late and leave early."

I was turning to Ana in the back seat, and we were smiling at each other.

"Uncle Soheil, why do boys behave like this? Are students sitting separately in your university, do boys ignore the girls in your classroom, and is their behavior are bad?"

"Ana Joon, our college is for Armenians and completely
private, and there are more boys than girls, only three girls are in my class. If a student ignores you, it means he likes you, and if you were indifferent to him, he wouldn't have to ignore you." Ana asked in a deep voice.

"Uncle Soheil, you mean that when a boy likes a girl, he ignores her, so what does he do when he doesn't?"

My dad smiled:

"People are different. Does someone ignore you?"

"No, I do not mean it."

"You grow up, you will gradually fall in love with a friend, giving yourself a chance to know him well sooner. Because he is a good student in your school is not enough to fall in love with him. There may be a thousand problems in his life that are not suitable for you."

"How do I know that he is good for me?"

"The standards of suitable marriage are different for people of different ages. It is important to consider mental, social, economic, and physical health. It may not be 100% perfect, but a minimum is necessary."

"Uncle Soheil, how do these factors affect the relationship between two people?"

"Everyone wishes to have a safe environment and live with someone who can proudly appear everywhere with him and not feel ashamed and embarrassed. You Will not be happy with a man not accepted by society.

It is tough to be with a man who does not care about morality and humanity, such as a not trustworthy drug dealer. He does not respect human rights and dignity and does not have a good character. Even though his appearance is attractive initially, he could not expect to have a healthy life with him."

My dad continued:

"Some people do not have an apparent mental illness but are unhealthy. For example, a suspicious person does not seem to have a mental illness to be admitted to a hospital, but it is healthy. These are symptoms that should be carefully checked. Sometimes there are special reasons for suspicion, but sometimes it is an illness. If one asks his partner why she looked at him, why did you go there, and why do you laugh are a sign of a lack of self-confidence; he does not accept himself and does not consider himself lovable. It is worse if he gestures as a sign of love. It is difficult to live under the same roof with a suspicious person. From a financial point of view, if a man cannot afford his expenses, how can he expect to provide the living expenses for his wife and children? Especially if the woman must stay home and take care of the children, it will greatly help you if you find out his financial qualifications.

Never think you could change people because it is impossible to change a person who does not want to change. Everything should be in balance. It is better to give yourself time to analyze in detail why you love him and what advantages he has over others.

You and Neda will become doctors soon, and it is better to find your future partner among medical students. If someone doesn't pay attention to you, he may love you."

I was listening to my dad's words when we reached the store. I delivered the tablecloth and received the money, then we went to the sandwich shop, and my dad ordered a sandwich. Ana always wanted to talk about Abbas and did not give me a chance to speak.

"Well, talk to him, look at his eyes, and tell him I'm fine and ready to be your wife."

"No, it can't be like that. He did not talk to me and left when the class was over. Let me tell you about Aria."

"Who is Aria?"

"Aria, do you remember Nima Khan's son used to sell yarn in the bazaar?"

"Han, what happened?"

"You do not know?"

"No, he was a good boy."

"He came to Tehran to study and live."

"Well, what does this have to do with us?"

"Iran Joon said that Aria would go to Tehran because of Neda."

"No, I don't think so. Iran Joon must have a fantasy." At the same time, my dad approached us, and we stopped talking.

"The sandwiches will be ready soon."

When we returned home, Ana asked my dad again.

"Why don't boys want to get close to girls?"

"There might be some problems and obstacles, and you attribute his behavior to yourself, and later you realize it was not related to you. He may be trying to solve a problem that
is important to him."

"Like what?"

"Sometimes even love is problematic. He might suffer social and economic issues that prevent expressing positive and negative feelings. There are many reasons that people have different approaches."

"What is the best response to this type of boy's behavior?"

"You may talk to him, or you may ignore him. You are a wise girl who could make the best decision. If there is anything I can help you with, please tell me."

Ana was silent and my dad did not say anything. In the following days ,as in the past ,we talked about Abbas as soon as we were alone .I have never experienced falling in love ,and I did not know this was a sign of falling in love.

One day Ana said. "I watched him all day to see if he did not see me or did not want to see me. Uncle Soheil is right. I will ignore him too. Abbas is always the last student to come to class before the teacher. He should stand in the corridor until the teacher arrives.

Tomorrow I will find out where he is so I can talk to him. I need to discover why he doesn't want to talk to me."

"I remembered your mom, tell her how good you are."

"Wait, tomorrow I will tell him who I am."

I was excited to find out what would happen between Ana and Abbas. Sometimes I saw Madam's character in

Ana. She spoke like her mother, I admired her, and I was afraid of her simultaneously. My dad had a steady and kind personality. I learned the fear from Marzieh. I even shuddered at the thought of two people fighting with each other. Although I had never seen Ana fight, I don't know why this image appeared before my eyes. I was restless and crocheted faster. I once asked my dad.

"Why do I knit faster when I'm restless?"

"With constant movements and repeated words, the human brain secretes hormones, creates calmness, and controls restlessness. Such as head banging, saying yahoo, repeated dance movements, or children hitting their heads on the bed rails in the orphanage, even repeated monotonous words or activities relax people that attributed to religion, ecstasy, mysticism, or God. Psychiatrists and neurologists can better describe the state of the brain and hormones. You can relax and sleep by listening to repeated musical rhythms."

"Is your friend a doctor in Tehran, and what is his name?"

My father lowered his head and said with tears in his eyes: "Yes, in Tehran, and his name is Soroush."

"Is he a psychologist?"

"No, Soroush's friend is a psychiatrist."

I did not want to know why my dad was sad when he talked about his friend Soroush. I was restless and did not know why. The topic of Ana and Abbas kept me busy. I was waiting for Ana
to come and tell what had happened. Ana came and was restless to tell what happened.

"When I arrived at school, I put my books on the desk and went to the toilet. It is interesting to tell you that a student girl who wears a chador and veil and pretends to be religious was having sex with a religious bearded boy in the bathroom. They stopped when they saw me and left quickly. I was laughing on the contrary. I amazed myself there for a while and returned to the classroom, but I did not see him in the corridor. I went out again at the same time as the class was starting. We met each other in the hall. When he saw me, he laughed and greeted me; I stood chest to chest with him and stared at him. His color turned red, and he lowered his head. Then I turned to see what he was doing, he was still standing there and looking at me and smile. The class was starting, so I had to return to the class. He came towards the classroom, and I tried to enter together. I did not even see him at lunchtime because he suddenly disappeared. I was so angry about his absence and I did not know what to do."

"So, contrary to your idea, he was not standing in the corridor on purpose."

"Yes, but when the class ended, I followed him to see where he was going in such a hurry."

"Well, where did he go?"

"He got on the bus."

"Does he work somewhere?"

"I do not know."

"How old is Abbas?"

"When he talked to me, he told worked for three years after graduation until he could attend the university. It might three years older than me."

"The first student in the country is three years late arrived university, which is odd."

"I was also surprised, but I did not ask anything."

"Is it possible that he is married and has someone?"

"I do not think so. I am sad that it is not like before. I know he is hiding something from me. He used to come and sit like a gentleman, and we would talk. Suddenly, without anything happening, his behavior changed. I have been restless all day to come and speak to you. I talked to myself about how good I have you and you came to Tehran with me. Otherwise, I would need to figure out whom to talk to and what to say in this loneliness."

The doorbell indicated that my dad had come; although he had our house keys, he always rang the doorbell, brought us fruit and we had dinner together.

At the table, Ana looked at him.

"Uncle Soheil, can I ask a question?"

"Ana Joon, ask whatever you want; I wish I knew how to give the correct answer."

I was scared, and various thoughts pressed into my

mind about what Ana wanted to ask about my dad falling in love. I don't know why I tried to stop her. I did not know why my dad did not say that he was a university professor. Was he in love with Marzieh and did not tell me. I did not see the intimacy between them, and I did not want to know anything about his love.

"My dad told me I should ask you if I have any problem because you are a university professor and understand better than other. My classmate used to talk to me all the time, but recently he doesn't speak to me. What do I do? You don't know how sad I am."

It was easy for Ana to talk to my dad like she was talking to me. Although I loved my dad very much, there was a distance between us. I did not feel the closeness that Ana had when talking about love with my dad. I was jealous of Ana for a moment and was relieved that the question was not about my dad's love. He answered calmly.

"Well, what were you talking about before?"

"We talked about everything like two friends, but now we do not."

"Did something extraordinary happen that he did not talk?

"No, nothing happened, he was noticeably trying to get away from me."

"What were you talking about the most?"

"About everything, books, lessons, and topics of the day."

"Where did you see each other?"

"In our class. He would come earlier and sit on a chair next to me, we would talk, and sometimes our classmates would join us. His behavior was friendly but suddenly changed."

"Did you ask him why?"

"I asked once, but he did not answer; he looked at me with a bitter smile."

"What is her name?"

"Abbas"

"From his name, it can be guessed that he is Muslim. May he be fanatical, especially since your name is Ana."

"No, Uncle Soheil, he once asked me and he knew that I am Armenian, and even asked me do not tell anyone that my name is Behrouz at home. He is not religious because it was prayer time. He told nobody does expect you to pray. Then he pointed to himself and said, look where we are stuck. Prayer is a personal issue in people's lives and has become a fundamental problem for students. We laughed together, and I said you should become a Christian. That day he also laughed and shook his head regretfully and said that the game of religion had become a disaster. I remember that his words were always charming and made me think."

My dad was silent for a few minutes, deep in thought, then he shook his head and asked.

"Has he ever talked to you about his private life?"

"No, we never talked about the details. But he said that he worked hard for three years to be able to come to university."

"Daddy, Abbass is the top student on the national entrance exam."

My dad asked in surprise.

"Someone with so much talent, three years out of school, something needs to be clarified."

"By the way, Neda told me too, but I never asked him anything."

"You did not understand and ask what he meant by working?"

"No, I did not think there would come a day when he would not talk to me."

"What is your suggestion z

"I don't know, and I get upset why he did not talk to me."

"Ana Joon, talk to him tomorrow, using a thousand excuses, for example, I did not bring a pen, give me your pen. I will come to your university one day to see him if you want. What kind of person do you think he looks like?"

Ana was talking with such an enthusiastic as if she were talking about a love person, while my dad was carefully looking at her. "He is perfect."

"Tell me which day is the best. Don't worry; let's see what the reason is. You are a beautiful and understanding girl, everyone should wish to love you."

I saw a similarity my dad's word with Madam words. I looked at beautiful Ana, everyone should wish to love her, and my dad was right. Ana was happy and spoke.

"Uncle Soheil, thank you, I must talk to him and see why he doesn't want to talk to me."

"Ana Joon, someone who doesn't talk to you might be okay. Remember that in a relationship between two people like you and your classmate, you are 40% of the whole story, 40% is him, and 20% are other factors. You should not worry about people's behavior and attribute it to yourself. He might have a crush on you, so he doesn't talk to you and other reasons."

"Uncle Soheil, you draw everything like a mathematical formula and show the solution to the problem."

It was sleeping time, my dad left us, it was Ana's time to talk about Abbas again and she liked my dad's proposal.

"Tomorrow, I will talk to him under any circumstances; I will take his notebook or pen."

"It's like you want to fight with him."

We laughed out loud.

"I want to fight with him, but I can't. I wish I could."

It was three am, I forced Ana to sleep. The next day Ana came back from school and spoke.

"I talked to him today, as Uncle Soheil said. I asked him to copy his note from his notebook, and I told him not to speak to me because I was Armenian. Behrouz stared at me, and after a long pause, he said:

"It may be the other way around."

I stared into his eyes. He smiled and said:

"I'm sorry if I upset you; I'll tell you one day."

"Ana, did you notice that you said Behrouz instead of Abbas?"

I did not notice, but I thought Behrouz was more beautiful than Abbas."

"Well, what happened next?"

"He was silent for a while and looked at me. I could

feel how heavy his gaze was, and his eyes were red. I don't know; I felt he wanted to tell me something, but he couldn't. He quickly said I must go to work. I gave him his notebook, but he did not go and stood there for a moment, looking around. I did not say anything, as if all the words had escaped from my mind. He said quietly, take care of yourself and go away."

I prepared dinner before Ana and my dad came. Ana explained to my dad that she had talked to Abbas and asked my dad to meet Abbas. They arranged for my dad to go to school the next day. That night, my dad stayed at our house and the second bedroom was for guests. We went to our bedroom, and again we talked about Behrouz. I could not sleep and thought Ana was stuck in a stormy sea. In the morning, we went to school, and my dad would come later. It was my dad's first meeting with Abbas.

Ana had returned and told me that she left the class when saw my dad from the window and gave him the Abbas's specifications. My dad entered the university between two sessions and asked Abbas where Ana was.

"She was here just a few minutes ago, please wait here. I will find her for you. Might she go to the bathroom?"

My father went with him to find Ana. My dad opened his conversation when they searched for Ana in the corridor.

"How is Ana at school."

"Ana is great student, and the world would be heaven, if all university students were like Ana."

"How your lessons are. Do you study, or do girls study more than boys?"

Abbas laughed. "I study well too, but Ana is better."

"There is only one student in your class whose knowledge is more than hers, his name is Abbas. What is your name?"

"My name is Abbas."

"So, you are the first student in the country."

He humbly says: "yes."

Daddy was looking at him said:

"I was also a first student and university professor. One day I must talk to you, which is especially important.

In short, study less!" Abbas is surprised:

"I heard correctly, should I study or not? Which one?"

My father was silent. Abbas said in a faint voice. "Ana did not tell me that her father is a university professor."

My dad looked at him: "I want to see you."

At the same time, Ana walked toward them from the end of the corridor; she approached them.

"Hi, what are you doing here, and do you know each other?" .

Abbass remained silent.

"No, we met now. This is Abbass, a first student at the university. I wanted him to come to our home and see me."

Ana turned to Abbass:

"Look, what a good uncle I have."

"I thought he is your father; you did not tell me that your uncle is a university professor."

Ana protested: "You last talked to me a while ago."

While my dad looked at Ana and said:

"Abbas, come to our house tonight; I want to talk to you."

Abbass' face and neck were red:

"I can work tonight and tomorrow night. I can come on night after."

"Okay, come on Thursday and ask Ana for the address."

Then he turned to Ana: "You left money on the desk this morning that I brought you money."

Ana took the money, and my dad left them. Ana asked my dad immediately "How was him, Uncle Soheil?"

My dad smiled and spoke: "He looks like a good boy."

"I am so glad that you invited him. How did you want him to come here?"

"Ana Joon, I understand that you like him, but before you let this feeling deepen and capture your heart, it is better to know him well. To know people better, you must hang out with them in a healthy environment with minimal stress. He looked like a good guy, but the question is he suitable for you? That's why I told him to come here."

"Uncle Soheil, you don't know how happy I am."

At the same time, Ana put her hand on my dad's neck and kissed him. Immediately my dad came to me and kissed me, and said: "Why do you quiet?"

I staggered: "I have waited since morning to see what happened, and I am not surprised that Ana is so happy."

My dad lowered his head while smiling.

Ana asked impatiently:

"How can I know Behrouz is good for me?"

"It is essential to know yourself first and who you are.

Collect information about yourself to make wise decisions based on facts and knowledge. Then what do you want and what is available? One should use the tried and tested scientific methods with general principles to check the obtained data, considering variable factors. When you are in a relationship, your level of vision is limited; it is like being inside a building; you only see a small part of it, but if you look at the building from the outside, you will see all the building dimensions.

The interface should be seen and examined in terms of time and place on a broad level to predict the result of today's decision in the next ten years. Accept your limitation to choosing skin color, place of birth, etc. We should learn from experiences and not allow bitter experiences to hinder
progress. Then you make the best decision based on the information you have. Although the best today may not be the best tomorrow and era. You may gain access to more knowledge in the future that you don't have it now and you should not blame yourself or someone else. Learning how to deal with adverse consequences is essential because men accept favorable effects. Then you can understand, based on your criteria, whether Abbass is the best for you or not."

"Uncle Soheil, you say everything systematically. We understand you. Do all people understand this?"

"Ana Joon, if the school students ask me, I will also tell them it depends on them to understand and use it or lose it. Here are your interests and future. I shall inform you and Neda before the events. These definitions will help you make a wise decision. You float like a fish in a pond. In real life, you should swim in the ocean. It would be best to learn how to direct the branches of wild trees without breaking them."

We had dinner and talking when Madam called. They were happy that my daddy was with us most of the time without knowing why. As if Monsieur had asked my dad about my aunt, my dad said that Zohreh is also good, but the exiles always have their glooms and wish to see us. My dad had a telephone in the professor's house, and sometimes Zohreh and his friend Arash called him. After my dad ended the phone call, Ana said to him:

"I'm glad to have you as my uncle. My father was right when he told me to ask uncle Soheil everything."

The day Abbass came, Ana and I were excited to see him. Aunt Zohreh sent me beautiful clothes that Ana and I wore. Ana finally wore a pink blouse after throwing all our clothes on the bed. We tried to cook well while we talked, laughed, and burned the food very well. Then we tried to get the burning smell out of the apartment, leaving the windows open for ventilations. My dad came and said:

"The food was burnt. I would buy dinner right now."

"We had prepared another dish."

Finally, the doorbell rang.

"Uncle Soheil, this is Abbas."

I looked through the window and did not see anyone.

"Ana, I did not see anyone."

My dad jumped up and looked at me worriedly.

"Do not come in front of the door. Let me see who is there."

My father's anxiety was strange to me. Ana spoke.

"How is no one?"

She quickly went to the window. My dad asked her to leave there. He immediately stood behind the window and looked outside like someone was afraid. There were difficult moments, and fear replaced the happy atmosphere that was filled with Ana's romantic feelings. Ana and I went to the room at daddy's order when the doorbell rang again, and my dad asked who it was. The sound of the door opening, we heard a man's voice greeting my father,

This is Behrouz." Ana said.

There was such an unspeakable joy and happiness in her voice, and her look that it made me happy. She touched her heart with my hand and spoke.

"My heartbeat."

"How happy are you?"

"Infinitive."

I watched her face.

"I am restless while you fall in love."

We quickly came to the front door. A handsome man in an ornate dress held a bouquet of red flowers and was busy greeting my dad. My dad's mood was noticeably different from a few minutes ago, and he looked happy. Behrouz shook hands with Ana and me and said while we were welcoming him.

"You must be Neda Khanum; Ana has told me a lot about you and how much she loves you."

There was no number in the entrance, and Behrouz suspected he had taken our house by mistake. He checked for the number of the neighbor, and we did not see him behind the door. I went to get tea, and Ana followed me into the kitchen, and while shaking with happiness, she said:

"I could not believe that he is here."

We had a good evening. Behrouz wanted to leave, but my dad asked him to have dinner with us. When Ana and I were setting the table in the kitchen, we noticed my dad and Behrouz whispering.

"Why do they whisper? What are they saying that they do not want us to understand?"

"Ana, do not worry; daddy will tell us."

Ana was always patient and calm, but now restless!

"No, I want to know right now."

We laughed while my dad asking:

"Do you need help?" At the same time, they arrived at the kitchen with Behrouz and helped us prepare the dinner table. The feeling of having guests was pleasant. At the table, Behrouz looked shy and spoke occasionally, and once he turned to Ana and said:

"You said my best and dearest friend is Neda; you did not say she is your cousin."

"You did not talk to me."

My dad extended the scope of speaking to universities. We were all busy talking during dinner.

"Behrouz told me something, and I wanted him to share it with you. I promised him that whatever he told us is always stay with us, and no one would hear it from us."

"I tried to distance myself from the students in the class because I am from a minority group."

"I do not understand, I am minorities, and there is no need to distance myself, so you are Armenian too."

Behrouz and my dad smiled, and he continued.

"No, I am not Armenian; I am a Baha'i."

We did not know what Bahai meant, but we did not ask. My dad guessed from our looks that we did not know.

"I told him that is no religious issue between us."

He looked happy. Ana talked about the beautiful flowers. I liked Ana's behavior who spoke straight. And I wished I could imitate her and tell my dad I wanted to become a concubine. Behrouz left after midnight and said no one knew my real name was not Abbas in the university. Ana and my dad assured him that the matter would remain the same. After Behrouz left, it was just the beginning of the night; Ana asked my dad's opinion.

"He looks like a good person, and you invite him when Arman comes."

"Uncle Soheil, my father always said that whatever you say is acceptable. Why did he change his name due to religion, and what is the relationship between religion and university?"

"After Khomeini came to power, he closed the universities and fired the professors. He knew that educated people could read their hands and learn about his tricks quickly, which are dangerous to their goals, and he tried to block and eliminate them. Non-Muslim students like Baha'i were not admitted to the university, and others were expelled from the university on various pretexts or false accusations that made them hate the study. After seeing this problem, Behrouz changed his name and entered the university as a Muslim to complete his studies.

His time was wasted for three years to change his name.He has passed through a difficult path and stayed away from you because he was afraid that after the university find out he is a Baha'i, they will reject expel him, and you will also be in trouble due to his situation. He thought that you have some problems due to your religion and that it is better not to add more problems, and he said that he loves you."

Ana was happy and asked excitedly.

"Uncle Soheil, he told you he loves me, and when he did not talk to me, I wanted to fight with him."

We laughed at Ana's words. My dad stayed at our house. We went to our room. I had fallen asleep while Ana kept talking about the roses and Behrouz. We woke up late. Daddy had prepared breakfast for us and spoke.

"At university, act like before and keep cautious, and if you want to see him, ask him to come here."

In fact, in the Islamic regime, love is forbidden, and marriage based on Islamic verses is shameful. Concubines are common due to creating the unlimited mullah income.

"Neda Joon, what do you think? How was Behrouz?"

"Abbass was good."

Ana had fallen in love and told Madam that she loved Behrouz. Madam called my dad and ensured everything was fine, and they decided to come soon and see Behrouz. I wanted to fall in love like Ana and be happy. After a few weeks, when Ana was studying, I went out under the pretext of shopping to see the Friday prayers and the president or Friday imam- Jumma imam. There were many women around who were employees. One woman asked me. "What are you doing here and looking for?"

"My mother is sick, and I want Imam to help me and heal her."

"God bless you, who and what they do to help you, no one."

When I persisted in seeing the imam, she said to write a letter, come here, and I will let you give it to the imam. I had a strange obsession and decided to write a letter and return there. Behrouz wrote letters to Ana at night when he was working. Ana and I used to read those letters, which were very romantic. Ana and Behrouz were very friendly and loved each other romantically, and I was looking for a love like theirs and assumed I could find it by becoming a concubine. I was ready to give my heart to a man in my dreams. At that time, I did not recognize that there was a deep valley between my imagination and real love.

Finally, one day I went to the Friday prayer to see the president; I just learned that imam Jumma changes every week, and sometimes the Imam Jumma is the president. It was crowded. I suddenly felt panic. I fear that if Ana finds out that I lied to her as well as the people around the imam, what will happen to me? I was shaking with fear or cold, afraid of the crowd and did not know what to do. I remembered Iran Joon, who said this is not an easy job. I told myself that I am stupid, and it was better to return. I slowly turned to go home. I had yet to go a few steps when suddenly someone tapped my shoulder. It saw a lady who said.

"Sister, that lady called you."

I saw the same lady who promised to help me to growl: "I called you several times, why don't you answer? Come with me."

I accompanied her with fear and shaking; my hand touched the letters in my pocket.

I was wearing a robe that the madam had sewn a big pocket inside the same shape and size as the outside pocket, and I put the letter that my mother is sick in the outer and the letter that I am willing to be your concubine in the inner pocket. She took me to the Masala which was a fossa place below the ground level for the imam Jumma to pray, and followers stood behind him when could not see him! Fortunately, there was only Friday and on weekdays wedid not pray. In fact, it was a brainwashing event by the cunning Imam Jumma on Friday. The cunning mullah deceived the foxes. The bodyguards were around to prevent killing him. I had reached a place of no return. The woman was part of their band, and there was no obstacle whenever we went. I regretted not telling Ana if something had happened to me. Poor Ana, who is waiting for me. One of the guards who called him brother.

"Give me the letter."

I showed him the letter.

"Fine, I will give it to Agha."

"No, I brought these sugars to be blessed, and my mother said that if Imam touches them, she will be healed."

"Very well, stay here."

That woman said to me: "Listen to the brother."

This man's talking manner differed from the others, as if he was a villain. I was afraid of him and the way he spoke. Everyone listened to him. Where I was waiting, I could see the prayer. My legs were shaking; I wanted to sit on the floor with a thousand scary thoughts. I suddenly remembered my dad came to our house. I was shivering and wanted to use the bathroom. My body was shaking, and my teeth were chattering, my spine was shooting, and my hair was standing on end. I did not know what to do. I said to myself, idiot, why did you write a letter? Do not give him the letter. Involuntarily, I remembered Madam's advice to look into his eyes and tell him that I am good and want to be his wife.

I met an awful imam and hoped this one would be better. In those moments, I thought about why I wanted to be the wife of these older adults, and Zubeida with her important husband's position as a coal pollan seller in the Arab's bottomless pit. Then we did not see her. Indeed, after I become the Imam's wife, I will become a public figure. I noticed that everyone was pointing and saying that Imam had come. I was nervous and thought about Iran Joon's words about rejection and I will find another one, my mother sickness is a good excuse, and he bless the sugar cubes. I did not know why I thought I'd come this far, and it's better to take it easy and tell him I want to be your concubine and see what happens. I wished that he would reject me. With these thoughts, my anxiety decreased a little. I did not see where the Imam was coming from, there might be an underground pathway to the Masala. The brother came forward and said:

"Did you just come to Tehran?"

"Yes."

Might my unkempt appearance show that I was not a city girl. I was lucky that he did not ask which villages I came from.

"After Agha comes, you give the letter, and when he blesses the sugar cubes, leave immediately."

"Yes. My mother is sick, and I must go soon."

"Come with me."

I Followed him who called a woman to inspect me, which was an examination. My only apprehension was to read the letter, which fortunately passed. No one paid any attention to me and the letter. They were all there, talking about property and buying and selling and the tyranny's properties that had been ravaged. I wondered why I wrote a letter. There were three steps below the street level as if the Imam wanted to hide there. The man took me with him to his place. There was an elderly man who looked like kind person. I thought why I was so scared. I stood in front of him when we were silent and I was looking on the floor, after a moment I raised my head and looked into his eyes and said in low voice.

"Imam, my mother is sick, and I came here to tell you that I want to be your concubine."

He had learned his lesson better than other one, stared at me and smiled and motioned to the man to stay away from us.

"How old are you?"

"Eighteen years old."

"Where do you live?"

"We have a room."

"If I tell you the address, you will memorize it."

"Yes"

"Do not tell anyone and come on Tuesday afternoon at five to this address??? X St # 0100. Do you remember it? Do you have a phone?

"No, we need more money to have a phone. I memorized the address.

"What is your name?"

"Neda Warp."

"What?"

"Neda Warp"

"Okay, there's a lady over there with a white blouse under her robe, and you wear a white blouse under your robe too."

"Yes."

He blessed the sugar, gave it to me, while he pointed to the guard and spoke.

"Your mother will recover."

"Thank you, sir."

"Go, go. The villain man said."

I left and ran from there to our home in a hurry. I thought about what I should tell Ana and how quickly I would find a husband better than Zubeida's husband. I saw from the alley that Ana and my dad were standing in front of our house. I recognized that the situation was awkward.

"Where were you? I died of fear."

"Neda, something happened."

"I went shopping, lost money, searched everywhere uselessly."

"I was terrified that you would kill me."

"Neda Joon, money is not important at all."

I did not know how this lie came to my mind, ashamed of their immense affection and sorry to take so much love for a childish game.

"Neda Joon, what did you want to buy? I will buy it for you or let us buy it together."

"The university is bustling."

"Uncle Soheil, we have everything at home, and the meal is ready."

We entered the house, and it was chaos inside me. My dad is reading a newspaper apparently and asked me.

"Neda Joon, there is something I can help you with."

"No.

I was looking at him, I wanted to put my head on his shoulder and cry, thought about him who worked in a printing shop, and we lived in poverty, although he was a university professor. I did not know what had happened in his life and did not let him tell me. My dad looked at me and continued.

"Neda, something is bothering you; whatever it is, you can tell me I love you. It does not matter what it is. What is on your mind?"

I was afraid that he might read my mind.

"No, Daddy, it is nothing. I was distraught when I lost my money."

I hated myself for lying while my dad looked at me.

"Do you want to go out?"

"No, I do not want."

Ana also wanted to be at home.

"Okay, I go and come back, then we will go out together."

I wanted to tell Ana where I was but as soon as my dad left, Ana started talking about Behrouz again and did not allow me to speak. I was wondering if I should tell her where I was, and I was thinking about my future husband when I heard Ana say we are going out. My dad returned and our usual Friday entertainment started with going to Niloufar Khanum's house and the store. In the car, I was listening to their conversation about the morals and character of good and trustworthy people, and I hated myself, a liar, and no one would trust me. I was figuring out why I was moving towards a vague, unclear, and incorrect goal. Why did I not tell the truth? This man is my dad and a scientist, but the important thing is that he loves me, and I imagined when he learned that I was the president's wife and became an important person. We reached the store, I handed over a tablecloth, and we went to a sandwich shop, and my dad was ordering a sandwich, so I told Ana.

"Let me tell you where I was. I lied, and I went to see Imam Jumma."

"What? Imam! So, you did not lose money?"

My dad returned to the table, and we were silent. When he left to get a sandwich, I told Ana everything. After eating the sandwich, Ana said.

"I must go home and study."

On the way back, at Ana's request, my dad stopped in front of a pharmacy and spoke.

"What do you want? I will buy it for you."

"Uncle Soheil, I must buy it myself."

My dad wanted to give her money, which she did not accept. We went to the pharmacy, a man with white hair was there, and Ana asked.

"Do you have birth control pills?" I did not know that
Ana wanted to buy pills for me. The man smiled and said:

"What kind?"

We both looked at each other; the man was smiling and
shaking his head.

"How many types are there?"

"Many."

"Whatever you think is good for your mother and
sister."

I looked at Ana and calmly said that this gentleman's
mother would not get pregnant anymore. We laughed
while we hid behind the pharmacy shelves. The man was
also laughing and said:

"Come on, this is good, 1000 tomans. Are you a
student?"

"Yes. Could you give discount, I only have eight
hundred tomans."

"Because you are a student, a thousand tomans."

Ana went to get money from my dad. I was laughing at
Ana's words that this gentleman's mother should take
birth control pills when we got into the car.

"I am glad that you're happy." My dad said.

My dad dropped us at our home. We talked that night
until two in the morning. We decided that if my dad came
and I was not at home, Ana should tell him that she had
gone to Niloufar Khanum's house to deliver an order. Ana
was afraid and wanted to call Madam, and I disagreed.
That night I took the first birth control pill.

I wore a white blouse under my robe on Tuesday, went
to university, and was worried all day long. I wondered
why I had done something wrong, but I still wanted to be a
concubine. In the afternoon, I went to the same address
Imam Jumma had given. A woman in a white blouse
examined me well instead of inspecting me. She did not
take off my shorts! I ignored it because I wanted to enter
this
dirty game. In her car, we went to a multi-story building in
Niavaran and took an elevator to an apartment. I should
wait for Agha and should leave immediately when Agha

ordered. Imam Jumma came, looked kind, sat on the sofa, and asked what did you say? My worries were gone. I looked into his eyes.

"I want to be your wife."

"Why?"

"You are the important person."

He laughed and asked about my family.

"We are poor; my mother is sick, and my siblings are hungry."

He spoke something in Arabic. "This is a concubine verse, and now you are my confidante and Muharram."

I listened but did not understand anything, and even the difference between Muharram and non-Muharram. All the time, I remembered that my right ear should be towards the Imam so I would not be disgraced. I was sitting with a robe and a veil, and the imam did not touch me. "What is your education?"

"I finished the fifth grade, and my mother said that you are stupid and couldn't learn more."

"Did you give the blessed sugar to your mother?"

"Yes, my mother said it would get better soon because Agha has blessed it."

"What is your job?"

"I make a tablecloth; I make it for you if you buy it."

"Fine, take this money and weave a tablecloth for me.

He gave me twenty thousand tomans.

"This is too much money, and how many do you want?

"Only small one for me, and the rest is yours." He paused and continued.

"It is for your grocery, and I will pay you the tablecloth money later."

Like Marzieh, Imam believed that I was dumb. I thought the Imam was kind, while people and the newspapers wrote severely about them. The imam considered me a stupid girl which was much better, and then I could ask him whatever I wanted.

"Did not say anything to anybody about here?"

"God kill me dumb if I say something."

"You will come here on Tuesday afternoon only and tell

me what's happening in the city."

I was scared that he would kill me if I told him that people cursed him. But I did not say anything.

"Go."

I was surprised, so I became his wife; I asked:

"Sir, I am your wife."

"My concubine, not my wife, I read the marriage verse."

I saw how easy it is to be a wife with one verse even though I do not understand it. It was a profitable easy job and has a good market. I will learn the marriage verse from the imam and become a verse reciter, it is easier than crocheting. I married with one verse, and did he marry me too? Having a husband one day a week is better than a permanent marriage because I had enough time the rest of the week to crochet, go to school, and study. If love and marriage are mutually inclusive, now that I got married and should experience love, but I still did not know what love is or even marriage.

Ana told me, you are younger than me, wait. Did the girls who become concubines know anything about love and marriage. Did they know anything about intimacy, or were they in the space of inanimate doll plays?

When I came out of Imam Jumma's house, the same woman was in front of the elevator. I walked to the street and then got on the bus. I thought someone might be following me. I reached Kargar Street; I saw a motorcycle rider next to the bus. I decided to get off two stops further. I went to the address of the rented room and worried that they might follow me. On my way, I saw a multi-story building with an open door. I went to that building, closed the door, and sat on the stairs. I was looking through the keyhole to see someone coming after me, but no one was coming. After a few minutes, a lady came out of one of the apartments and said: Whom are you working with?

"I'm tired, sit here to relieve my fatigue."

"Do you want water?"

"No, I'm leaving soon."

She returned to her apartment. Honestly, I was afraid to leave there. I decided to change my clothes. I switched

the blouse under my robe and put it on my bag, but I did
not have an extra scarf to change it. Then I slowly went in
the opposite direction, returned to the main street from the
side alley and walked to my house. On the way, I bought a
scarf and changed it so that if someone followed me, he
wouldn't recognize me. I got home; my dad was there. Ana
had told my dad that Neda had gone to deliver a tablecloth
to Nilofer Khanum.

My dad asked me. "Why did you not tell me?
"I forgot it."

I was nervous, had no appetite, and could not eat
dinner.

"Neda, why did you not have dinner? Did something
happen?"

"I ate a sandwich earlier."

At those moments, I wished I could tell my dad I had
become a concubine. The fear that my dad would hate me
if he found out occupied my mind, and I asked helplessly.

"Daddy, which magazine and newspaper are better?"

"Neda Joon, to understand people's lives, you must
read newspapers, but remember that you must quickly
learn to read the white line between the black lines and
remember that everything published passes under the
censor's blade."

"White lines between blackness? What is its meaning?

"When there is no freedom of speech, the writings are
the price of the author's life and his blood drips from his
pens. On the opposite side, there are self-selling authors
whose prices differ. Self-selling authors are liars. That's
why I say that every piece of content should be analyzed,
and facts extracted from the lies. Readers should learn the
writer's motivation and explore the content and the truth.
Don't rush; let's enjoy life."

We were silent for a while, then the conversation
between my dad and Ana continued, and the waves of
imagination took me and squeezed me. I assured my
daddy before he left to his home that I should not go
anywhere tomorrow, and he said he would come
tomorrow afternoon. We did not study that night. Our chat
was about my concubine. "I was thinking about you all day

as if I wasn't in class; you do not know how much I love
you, and you are the only one I have. You are my sister.
Tell my mother about the concubine; I'm afraid something
will happen to you."

"No, not now."

"How was the imam?"

"He was antique with white hair; he came and spoke
something in Arabic and said you had become my
concubine. He gave me money to weave a tablecloth, then
told me to buy food
with this money and he would pay for the tablecloth later.
Like Marzieh, he thought I am stupid."

We laughed.

"Neda, did he kiss you?"

"No."

"No! Slept with you."

"No, he did not even touch me and look at me as a
beggar girl."

"Well, what's the result?"

"I don't know, but I am curious and want a husband
like Zubeida to have a significant position."

"What do you think? Who is Zubeida?"

"Do you remember Haj Khanum showed off Zubeida's
suitors?"

"Are you stupid? Please leave me alone. You are
clinging to Zubeida and Haj Khanum."

I did not wonder even Ana knew that I was dumb,
asked in surprise.

"How is possible that you and Imam were in the same
house, he married you, and nothing happened? I mean the
events between the women and men. He could not do
anything!"

"Well, why did he read the marriage verse?"

"Do you know what the marriage verse is?"

"No."

"A fake and contentless mullah made words to make
money of people. It is their shop to get money."

"But he did not charge me."

"Yes, they don't lose the control of their fake jobs, and
it's their habit. He will marry you next time, and you will

go to bed, so take the pills and don't forget to take care of yourself."

"I have nausea because of the pill. I just started yesterday, and I feel bad. There is no other reason to be nauseous."

"Fine, that's enough; you wanted to get married; you must endure these things; this is just the beginning."

She was right, this was the beginning of the story.

"My mom told me Neda understands a lot and we should learn from her, now I know she was wrong, so what outcome do you expect? Why don't you tell my mother?"

"Look, a scary situation has happened; I am also scared sometimes, but I don't want to lose this opportunity, and I want to stay in this situation, but something bothers me."

"What?"

"I did not like to have his money."

"Do not make a mistake, if he gives money again, you must take it. You are not in a position not to reject his money, especially you told him that you are poor. You did a good job asking your dad about newspaper. We must know everything like Behrouz."

"I should try another birth control pills. I feel nauseous; even my dad noticed that I couldn't eat anything. You are the one who asked the pharmacy to give her mother's pill. She must have given us his old mother pills." We laughed.

"This time, I ask him what is good for his daughter."

"If he is a young man, and his daughter is three years old, he will throw us out of the pharmacy."

"We need to ask someone about the birth control pill."

Ana had fallen asleep, and thousands of questions were running through my mind. I thought about how I must fall in love with my Tuesday husband and assumed that love has its special time, and like Ana, I will enjoy the presence of love. I told myself I would ask my dad and immediately regretted not saying anything. I had terrible nausea and decided to go to the pharmacy near our house and find another type.

The next day, on the way to the pharmacy, I thought that the concubine meant prostitution, Imam was my concubine, or I was his concubine. Is Imam a prostitute or me, or both? Why do they say that a woman has become a concubine? We were both concubines. Muslims show off that the black Abyssinian and Sayed Qureshi have equal rights. But there is not equality right. Even men in conversation they used assaulting words for women.

What is equality? Concubine women shall serve and obey men, and men order. I used to say that the best scenario was that Imam looked at me as a poor, illiterate beggar girl. It was the best situation I wanted. What should I wear on Tuesday that my husband would like? Are we going to get married? Am I ready for him to kiss me? He seems kind, is he always kind, or I am wrong. I arrived at the pharmacy and asked the woman behind the counter.

"Do you have birth control pills?"

The woman looked at me and asked aggressively:

"Whom do you want for, how old are you?"

I noticed an awkward situation.

"My sister got married and takes pills that made her nausea; I want it for her." The woman took a deep breath.

"I was relieved; I thought how bad even this kid is talking about contraceptive pills, you need a prescription?"

"My sister told me to ask you what kind is good."

"It depends on the doctor; the more expensive, is better. Tell the doctor to write."

I came back with fruitless effort, and on the way, I thought the more expensive type was better! So, the pharmaceutical factory also makes shoes and bags; the Italian leather type is better! I reached home and prepared dinner before my dad came; I asked Ana:

"Tell me what to tell the imam on Tuesday. He wanted me to spy, and I will take people's words for him."

Ana growled. "No, are you Crazy? If you say anything, they will kill you."

"Don't be afraid, that's why I'm asking you; let's think together and tell him the daily issues as news and ask him for changing." Ana asked in horror.

"What are you saying, Neda? He could not make a change."

"On the contrary, he can."

"What?"

"My dad always brought me books. I remember I read a story that a king killed a girl every night, and one day, a wise woman told him a story and continued the story so much that she saved several innocent girls from death."

"I know which book you are talking about, the stories of Shahrazad and thousand and one night."

"Yes, it is."

"It was just a story."

"In the future, people will read our story and say it is a story. Stories are rooted in people's lives. We can do it."

Ana looked at me dumbfounded. "You have decided; I know you will not return from this way."

One evening, I was dared to ask my dad. "What is a marriage and a concubine, and how do people become halal haram or mahram with a single verse?"

"The real meaning of marriage is establishing an emotional relationship, belonging, being a partner in each other's joys and sorrows, and helping each other, which is the basis of a good relationship. The best relationship is a romantic feeling to have complementary differences that live and grow together and give life to each other. The effort to maintain that connection causes people to sign a contract and register it as marriage. Writing a marriage in the country's official is suitable for their children, and it brings living stability to children if the connection is stable; otherwise, most marriages are just attachments in the registry books.

Concubine is the same as prostitution, which leads to cohabitation and sexual intercourse by receiving money. Sex for money is prostitution. As I told you, the whiteness of the paper should be read before it turns black. The religion leader created a condition to take advantage of people; he recites verses in a language that others do not understand. I can recite a hundred verses, neither I know nor you, and I will tell whether it is about marriage or divorce.

Mulla made up the word halal, haram, and mahram with a Hadith or Fatwa and attributed them to God, Prophet, and Imam, which is entirely false and to exploit the gullible people. These far-fetched superstitions have contaminated the most critical events in human life. The Arabic verses of the marriage ceremony in Islam is shameful and not in the Quran. Moreover, the relationship between people, continuous or discrete, is not tied to an Arabic verse. Fortunately, countless people have awarded and no longer give the hard-earned money to the mullah to recite the contentless verses. They make a covenant and live together happily. They are equal, work together, and turn the wheels of life together. Remember, don't talk, or write about it in school because the regime is cruel and violent, and the weapon is in the hands of the ignorant and stupid killer."

It was past midnight, and my father was spending time with us. But I did not dare to say that I have become a concubine.

Nowruz (Iranian New year), Iran Joon, Madam, and Monsieur came to Tehran. One day, when we were all at home, Monsieur had gone to the bathroom and called Madam; we could hear their arguing in Armenian language. None of us knew what was going on.
We saw them come out of the toilet, and Monsieur went to buy something. Iran Joon said to Madam:

"Black peas."

Madam nodded her head in confirmation. I did not understand and asked Iran Joon. "What are black peas?"

"Madam sent him out to buy time and check the situation."

"What situation?"

"I don't know, wait, we will find soon."

Monsieur left the house grumbling. Madam made sure that he had gone and closed the door behind him. Then she called Ana and me and took us to the room because my dad was there. We went to the room to see what had happened.

"Ana, close the door." Madam spoke.

Suddenly I was afraid because Madam's face was angry, my heart was pounding, and my body was shaking with fear. Madam took out a pack of birth control pills from her pocket and asked Ana:

"What is this?"

We were staring at the birth control pills that nauseated me, and I left it in the bathroom cabinet drawer. I said quietly:

"It's mine."

"Don't take her side what is this?"

Ana remained silent, and I repeated.

"It is mine."

"You fell in love too."

"No."

"Do you have a boyfriend?"

"No."

"Monsieur saw these packages and was angry."

"I had nausea, and I did not take it anymore."

"Ana, tell me, what's going on?"

Ana, who was always ready to answer, remained silent.

"It's mine. Do you remember you asked me to take birth control pills?"

"Me!" Madam said with surprise.

"Yes, I became a concubine."

"What? What?"

"I became the concubine of Imam Jumma."

"I thought you were studying so well that you should forget this topic. Tell me how?" She immediately interrupted me and said:

"Arman will return soon, and I tell him the doctor's prescription for Ana to regulate her period. Don't forget."

"Why Ana, you tell Neda?"

"It doesn't matter that he is sensitive to both of you. Sometimes he is mad and screams. I will manage him. Neda, did you tell your father?"

"No"

I explained to her how I went to Friday prayers and became a concubine. Madam was laughing.

"It means he did not touch you; might he is not a man."

Ana laughed and said: "She is not allowed to examine him. We should know when she will become a doctor."

"He looked at me as a stupid miserable girl used for spying on people, and I liked my position."

Madam growled: "He is stupid that underestimated

you, son of a beach. I am proud that Ana was lucky enough to have a friend like you."

At the same time, we heard the doorbell ring. Iran Joon and my dad were in the kitchen. Iran Joon opened the door. Madam held me in her arms and said that "I would always love me."

We could see the different faces of people in exceptional situations. Monsieur had entered, and Madam took his hand and dragged him to our bedroom. Ana and I knew what was going on there. My dad looked at me and spoke.

"What did happen?"

"Nothing, Madam had a question for Ana and me."

I felt terrible and wanted to throw myself in his arms and say what a dangerous game I had started with my destiny. My dad understood something vague from me face, got up, hugged me, and spoke.

"Nothing is more important than you. You are love of my life." Hearing these loving words was water on the fire that burning me. Really, what was I burning from? Is it from my stupidity or from the motivation that drives me to the fire? I was incapable to analyze the situation, wanted to cry, and fragile. Monsieur entered the kitchen with a smile. My dad could very well read the difference in his face and asked him. "How are you?"

"Okay, I'm fine."

I understood the miracle of words that can turn someone 180 degrees quickly. Iran Joon and Madam were chatting in the other corner, and I knew it was about me. I sat at the table in the kitchen. I stirred the tea so that no unsolved sugar was left. It was my mystery, spinning around nothing to find myself. I thought about Ana and Behrouz's romance, a world of affection, solidarity, and unconditional love. The money, jewelry, and the difference in religious subjects were never raised. He said he had to work to support himself and his family financially. Ana did not care about his financial ability. Most of the time, Behrouz comes to our house, and Ana rarely goes to their house. Sometimes I went out with them. When Behrouz would buy groceries, Ana told him he did not need to do it.

There was no discussion about marriage, halal, or haram, they considered their love a precious phenomenon and counted the moments to be together. Behrouz wrote Ana a letter or a card on any special occasion and brought her flowers. Both were friendly and calm, as if they were made for each other. Behrouz sometimes looked sad due to religious and social issues.

He was surprised that I knew all their lessons and said with a laugh and a joke that I was jealous of you and Ana because I always thought I studied better than everyone else, but I see that you know the main concepts better than me. You must be the first student at the university. Ana said we have a religious problem like you, and we laughed. After that day, Behrouz did not ask me anything, and he uniquely looked at me. Behrouz had given Ana a notebook in which
part of his writings and the other part of poems by Iranian poets and writers about love. We were happy with those words. Behrouz had started to write this notebook when he kept his distance from Ana. Ana laughed and told him to be sad again and write more.

He came to our house daily when he was not working, especially during Norouz when the university was closed. Everyone loved him. We had an enjoyable time together; even his old scrap car made us laugh.

Ana had fallen in love, and I did not know what love was and emerged in imaginary romantic words and looked for love. In my imagination, I can weave love like a tablecloth! I did not feel any romantic feelings and the ridiculous concubine idea robbed wise thinking. In the same years, Behrouz asked Ana to marry him, and Ana wanted the ceremony to be simple and without religious traditions and asked my dad's opinion.

"It is important knowing what you want. Behrouz is a worthy man."

Unlike Anna and Behrouz, there was no compatible between my concubine and me. I thought it was too early to establish love between us. I was happy that Madam knew the subject of my concubine, but I did not want my dad to know it. Sometimes I tried to fit Behrouz's pleasant face into the wrinkled face of the Imam, which would not have been possible, no love, no passion, no relationship, and no marriage.

Even though my attempt to increase my heartbeat during his meeting was unsuccessful, I thought how about I have three concubines, may one of them would be good. I was like a gambler who couldn't resist the urge to gamble. I did the necessary research on this plan but did not say anything to Ana because I knew Ana would be afraid and try to stop me. I did not know what drew me to the castle of the witches.

Iran Joon told me this tribe was not worth even you talking to them. They are the same lice-contaminated grave reciters who read Vanyekad to get halva (votive) for survival. Now, the unoriginal and uneducated mullahs have become ghouls. Mullah's job was to work at the grave and pours water on the grave for money or the votive from the mourner. Vanyekad are a few verses from the Quran that Mulla recited at the tomb as if the dead person can hear it! Mullahs did not even know the meaning of those few verses. Iran Joon was right, at least I had tried one of them, although the mullahs changed their dress and washed their faces but still cleaned their noses with their sleeves, they were incompetent. Their illiteracy and stupidity are so ingrained in their existence that they never go. Even their talk is liked babble heads and big open mouths that spread humiliation and inferiority. Although I looked calm, I was confused. My dad sometimes stared at me and asked if something was bothering me. This was my dad's constant concern and his repeated question. We were staring at each other as usual and away from the conversation circuit. He wished to read my thoughts from my eyes and find an answer to his question. Even though I loved him the most and his assurances were enough for me, I was afraid he did not love me anymore, and hid behind the lying mask. He hugged me and said he loved me. My hands are knitting a tablecloth, and my mind is creating a lie. I hated myself and used to praise Ana, who never lied. My dad's fruitless questions continued in the following years.

Behrouz was curious about my statues, and Ana never told him anything about my concubine. Behrouz often said how I do not have a boyfriend. When I went to my concubine's husband's house and deliver woven tablecloths to the shopkeeper on the way. The same woman always waited for me and took me to Imam's apartment, and Imam was boring me with repeated questions. Ana was worried about me, and I was anxious and feeling threatened, but I did not regret it. The white shirt was a particular sign between them. It was interesting that Imam's apartment had tiny windows near the ceiling, like a bathroom window for ventilation. I could not see the inside of the adjacent apartment when standing on the sofa, might they consider their wife, which is their property, should not be seen by the adjoining apartment residents. I always sat on the same seat as the imam said, and he sat far away from me. I used to crochet because I could not sit idle, and when the imam came, I would put the crochet on the table.

Sometimes he came late; I was afraid to stay there alone. In my mind, I arranged to tell people's problems to him by adding a few irrelevant sentences to show off my stupid
personality. Some conversations and repeated questions between us were like this.

"Do you always crochet?"

"Yes"

"What is your education?"

"I finished fifth elementary school."

He always smiled and I was waiting for him to ask what was going on in the city so that I could talk about the people
in the town were cursing all the Mullahs.

"Did you buy food for your family?"

"Yes, I did, the prices are incredibly high. Shopkeepers and people curse mullahs. I'm afraid to say that they curse you; my mother told me to bless these candies for her."

He frowned and asked:

"You told your mother where you are going?"

"No, she said that if Sayed touches this sugar cube, she will be cured."

"How many times I tell you that I'm not Sayed."

"No, my mother said that Mullah is Sayed, he is the son of Mohammad. The daughter of Muhammad is not Sayed, only his son is Sayed. You are the son of the Prophet Mohammad."

"You are foolish. What are you saying? The Prophet was 1400 years ago; what is he doing now?"

"Forgive me; if I say these words to my mother, she will say that Imam is stupid and does not understand. May I ask you a question?"

"Ask."

"Am I your wife?"

"I read a concubine verse, and you became my concubine."

"I saw in the movies that the woman sat on the man's lap."

"Shut up, rude and shameless girl."

"Does your wife sit on your lap?"

"If you talk about Haj Khanum again, I will slap your face."

"I did not talk about Haj Khanum, Zubeida's mother. I said your wife."

"Who is Zubeida?"

"She was our neighbor. All men of our town propose to her. Did you propose to her too?"

"Was Zubeida beautiful?"

"No"

"Was he rich?"

"No, I did not see any money and she did not give me money."

"You are a fool. Whom is wealthy should not give you money."

"Look, you give me money, that means you are rich. I buy food."

"Enough, I am stupid that I brought the donkey here."

"Where is the donkey? I did not see him."

"Well, enough, tell me what's going on in the city?"

"People told me that the mullahs are thieves, and they swear at you and don't know that I am your wife."

"Shut up."

Then, I would shut up according to Imam's order; he was dozing on the sofa where he was sitting. I also crocheted until he would say.

"How are you going home?"

"By bus."

"Take this money and go by taxi and let me know what people say."

He gave me a lot of money, which I had never seen before.

"Imam, all this money is mine, so how about you?"

"Take the money and get out of here."

I should leave immediately. The same woman was in front of the elevator; I was careful that no one followed me, and I did not lose caution. I got into the taxi that went straight and changed several taxis even though I did not see anyone chasing me. No one cares about unfortunate people. Ana always waited for me with concern. During those years, when I visited my contactless concubine, I reviewed new things with Ana and told her. I am an unintellectual beggar who is only suitable for spying. It is better in the minds of short-sighted people to be too small than to abandon their weapons. I asked imam once:

"Do you go for grocery shopping and know how expensive food is?"

"Silly girl, it is not suit with my prestige."

"So, the Netherlands queen went shopping daily on her bicycle, which is low level for her position."

In this way, the conversations between the imam and me revolved around daily issues. Once, I asked him.

"Why do you twist these fabrics around your head? Is your turban made of cotton?"

"Stupid girl? It is a holy turban."

"Isn't it made of chelvar (kind of the cheap fabric?"

"No, it is made of Malmal (the expensive fabric)."

"What is Malmal?"

"Your mother is right that you are stupid."

"Yes, you are right, but I don't understand why you tie your fabric around your head."

"Shut up; when you come here, sit in the corner, and talk about what's happening in the city. I pay you."

He spoke to me full of insults and contempt as if he
had a burden of a thousand years of hatred in his chest. I
knew his humiliation root.

"Sir, do you talk to your wife the same way at home?"
He was aggressive when I used his wife's name.

"You mentioned Haj Khanum's name again."

"Your wife's name is Haj Khanum in her birth
certification. You said that I am your wife."

"Okay, okay, shut up, stupid."

I was looking for love and how exciting it would be to
speed up the heartbeat like Ana and create a romantic
feeling. Ana's world was full of love, and the world of the
concubine was devoid of romantic feelings. This bitter,
childish illusion that was dressed in adorable clothes and
rooted in the inferiority complex of my childhood. Years
later, I recognized that my dirty mind had robbed my
thinking ability. On Nowruz, Imam asked me not to go
there for a few weeks and gave me money to buy new
clothes for myself and my family. I was happy because
money was my favorite toy, and Behrouz's love was Ana's
favorite. I used to knit the tablecloths and to glue the
irrelevant words together for lying, hoping that light
turned on the Imam dark's brain. Yes, in my wild
imagination, his brain death cells could revival. This
situation continued, and I thought about becoming the
concubine of another imam.

Ana and Behrouz got married without any religious
ceremony. My dad performed their marriage ceremony in
our apartment, told them to take care of each other, and
called them husband and wife. Later, they registered the
marriage in the city office. Behrouz liked writing, and his
writing was excellent. Ana and I were voyeurs, to know
what he was writing, and we would look at his notebook.
He wrote that his family was not happy with changing his
name, but he was in a situation to choose between continue
and stop his education. Elsewhere he wrote that in the
Baha'i community, freedom of religion was not accepted,
even if I had to choose this path because of my love for
studying, and did not abandon my faith, but it was a
problem for my family to accept me and it is 'sit is a waste

time. Ana, Neda, and I can learn all these materials in a short time except the practical lessons. If I knew the content of university courses was this, I would learn by self-study. The educational system should be changed because it is suitable for lazy students and a time killer for talented students. My only happiness and luck were to meet and find my love, Ana. When Ana and I read this section, we noticed we had ignored this critical issue.

When I read the anatomy of the ear, it refreshed my memory of the teacher slapping my face, and this situation tormented me for years and reduced my self-confidence. Madam arranged a special seat for me to hear others well. I cried that day and thought that teachers' physical attacks must have crippled countless children with different intensities. The effect of the negative and positive behavior of the teacher on the child's life is undeniable. My fault was mispronunciation Arabic word and a religious phonetic teacher pretending to do so or throwing her anger at the weaker student. Some people may never know that their dislike of lessons and school is rooted in the teacher's behavior not school. I liked classes and school before that day. I also remembered when Ana was in the 11th grade, she told the young teacher was rubbing himself on one of the students. That girl got up and slapped his face, and the fighting started. She was called to the school office. No one asked her why she beat the teacher. The student was banned from studying throughout the country's schools for 3 years.

So many have never told their pains or have not been heard, and their destinies have changed due to the teacher's mistake, and many caring teachers have changed the students' behaviors with their sacrifice. Another example is the leader barber, a reciter of the Quran sexually assaulted 19 male teenagers. When their parents put a lawsuit against him, he claimed he would name 100 senior government officials if he were condemned. The Islamic regime banned the reporter from pursuing the problem! The Islamic regime claimed they are the justice regime! It is clear there should be a system to prevent child abuse.

That day my dad looked into my eyes as usual and

asked what had happened. I cried and said that I read the anatomy of the ear and remembered my fifth-grade teacher. My dad hugged and kissed me and explained that after that incident, he complained and sent many letters to all departments, and finally, that teacher was fired from the school. When I refused to go to school, he knew why. I was lucky that Ana was our neighbor. He was sorry for his limitation, and the Shah banned student physical punishment. Unfortunately, when a teacher of the Islamic regime sexually abuses a student; they say it is the child's fault! I thought how lucky I was to have such a good father; otherwise, what could I do with a low education? Another exciting event was the second concubine. I consciously and willingly chose my second concubine.

I met Imam with a prior appointment on Tuesday when he saw me dumber than the day before. He was a patient man, and I was a toy for him to the extent of talking. He was calm, while everyone knew that killing innocents were his and his accomplices' orders. He was better than other brainless mullahs, while the rest were the dinosaurs' fossils and at the level of the Taliban that the woman should be in the bag. Although Mullah=Taliban=ISIS=Al-Qaeda= Hezbollah etc. They are all under the same blanket, and their policy is to kill people.

These sponger mullahs beg door to door before, and they are rich financially now due to stealing Iranian wealth and becoming God's attorney on earth! They knew very well that all their words were lies. Here is a real story about mullahs' financial situation. One imam on life radio interview said that our food was Eshkeneh. For your information, he was born and grew up in a city where the poor people's food was Eshkeneh, who could not afford to buy meat. He also wrote in his diary book, published in Iran, that one day he and two mullahs wanted to visit a city in the north of Iran, but they did not have two thousand tomans to buy a second-hand car! The teacher's salary was around three thousand tomans per month at that time. As a grave reciter, Mullah used to have votive food in a piece of newspaper and tie it in the corner of his robe to take it home. Now the amount of their stealing money from the bread of helpless people is skyrocketing. Each mullah took shares of one of the people's most basic food items, monopoly, and abused the people. They are friends when they are accomplices in a robbery and kill each other when they want to divide it. Suddenly, seventy-two mullahs were killed in one place in one assembly. People were pleased and celebrated their death and said that less mullah = better life, or good mullah = dead mullah.

One day I begged the imam to see the leader imam.

"You are miserable child to select that stupid man."

This was neither the first time nor the last time I was ignorant and exposed to these assaultive words, and it did not matter to me. The stupid man's words surprised me because he praised the leader in the crowd. Finally, one day I went to see the imam who claimed to be a god representative in the earth. My concubine's husband arranged this meeting and expected me to spy on him. He wore long white clothes like Arabs. There was no excitement at his meeting, just a few moments of fear of what I did with my destiny and nothing else. Like him, I did not have any feelings.

One imam's speech was primitive. His speech started with "but it should not be like this!" He spoke with a unique accent and a monotonous voice. I imagined Madam was by my side, saying to look into his eyes and talk. There were
several people in the room.

"I want to be alone with you."

Everyone went out of the room on his order."

"I want to be your wife; marry me."

Contrary to the people who thought about mullahs' power, these words are in people's minds and become monsters. Cowards were scared and carried weapons; they knew their weakness.

During the Friday praying, Imam prayed with a gun in his hand. They were afraid of people and knew the people hated them and did not trust them. Their fear signs were observable. People created a monster of them and advertised them with their speeches. People should

remember that their words about them are their
advertisement. I used this trick device and speech, toward
my own goal. It was interesting that he did not ask me if I
loved him. They never saw themselves as loveable and
worthy. It is easier to reach and talk to the superior due to
his immense loneliness surrounding him instead of going
their guard. He laughed and spoke.

"I do not need you. I have nymphs that you never
could compare with their prettiness."

"Just let me see you and marriage is the most halal way
to see you. I have no intention of sleeping with you."

"Sleeping is okay too, but I am busy."

"I only want to see you for a few hours."

"Where is your home?"

"We have a rented room, and my mother is sick. You
bless these sugar cubes for my mother to believe that if you
touch them, she will heal."

I do not know how a few sugar cubes became my
excuse to try these idiots, but it was working. He rubbed
his hand on the sugar cubes that made me sick. I thought
that if this peanut head knew I made fun of him, he would
surely kill me. After blessing the sugar cubes, he took my
hand unexpectedly, which was disgusting. He was a vulgar
man, and I was used to the behavior of the first concubine
and did not expect this stupid older man's action.

"My daughter, I will have mercy on you and make you
a concubine for two or three hours, but no one should
know. You will come wherever I say and do whatever I
want."

"Agha, having your name over my head is enough for
me. I will not say to anybody."

"Do you know English?"

I wondered why he concerned about the English.

"No, but I can go to class. We have a neighbor who
goes to class."

"You are literate."

"Yes, I finished fifth grade."

"Samaya's sister will tell you where and what day you
should come. Have you ever smoked opium?"

I was stunned.

"No sir, how about you? Do you smoke opium?

"Samaya will teach you." Then he clicked the button. I noticed that he had a device like a TV remote control in his hand, which had different letters, and he carefully selected the button. Each bottom was for a specific order or person. A woman entered the room. Imam said something in her ear. My right ear was towards them.

"See, it is easy to find one. I found it." The woman asked him.

"Are you sure?"

"I spent my life among people; I am an anthropologist."

The woman did not say anything. I told myself, yes, he is knowledgeable! Samaya talked about the plan.

"Do you have a phone?"

"No."

"What day?"

"One or two day per month."

"Agha, thank you for accepting me. God bless you. I became your wife."

"Concubine"

"Thank you Thank you. God wants good for you."

"Very well, nobody should know anything except Samaya and me."

"Did not you read the marriage verse?"

"I read."

I did not say anything, and he might have recited the verse! Or it was occult verses. Since I was stupid and dumb, it was better not to pry and speak. The second concubine became what I wanted. What seems impossible and complex from the outside becomes easy when it is solved. The high public figure seemed so gross, but they were empty. It might have met them at a suitable time when they had looked for someone! The second concubine was older than the first,with poor physical condition. He wanted to hold my hand while he could not clean his nose. He was very stingy to pay money when I asked several times. I was sick of the second one, and although I did not like the first one, but he was more tolerable.

Surprisingly, he had a butterfly collection, and the

good childish feelings could not repel the ferocious headsman character. He used to smoke opium, and I heard he played the instrument and was in love with his son's wife and had a party where the poets read their new poems to him. People assumed the leader role was more important than the present, Imam Jumma, when the true story was different. Their believers closed their minds to reality. Dr. Roshangar's book, Allah Akbar, said "an ignorant person needs religion so much that he even turns to worship cows".

In that situation, Imam Jumma used him and his weakness and forced the leader to obey his orders and to accept an unwanted situation who claimed he had drunk a cup of poison! There was a time when Imam Jumma, had drowned in the pool with the presence of his bodyguards, and the wise people know the secret.

The second concubine's apartment smelled of opium and it was a smoke party place. He chose me for the nights when he was alone. I was again afraid that something might happen, so I started taking a contraceptive pill. This time Ana and I had learned which one was better, but not the pill that was good for the pharmacist's mother! Because Madam had asked Ana to go to the doctor, the doctor prescribed the pill that caused mild and tolerable nausea. I used the same pills as Ana. Contrary to the expectation, I would not become a bride. Fortunately, the old hyenas were impotent.

I was not attractive enough to motivate them, a simple country girl without makeup. While everyone around them had heavy makeup, covered in thick foundations. I wasn't an exciting creature to motivate the Turban men who hung themselves with a sex rope. The evidence showed that these men's lives were summed up in the sex lines, and now the tools were useless. I once asked the Imam.

"You would not sleep with me."

"Trashy girl, you are nothing to me to sleep with you. I have many nymphs, and you are nothing compared to them, do makeup."

I looked at him like a foolish child and said:

"My mother is sick."

While I evaluated his stupidity in my mind and how he hid his inability in contempt for other or saw a woman as a doll and used it for show off! One of those days, he told me to smoke opium; I knew well that smoking opium was the beginning of addiction, and I studied about side effects of using opium which were nausea and itching. He gave me the pipe (Wafoor) and showed how to put it in my mouth and breath. I hesitated to touch the device that he had mouthed, I immediately pretended to burp, which means that I am vomiting, and I poured my saliva onto the pipe and quickly ran to the bathroom and stayed there for a few minutes and repeated the sound of vomiting and then came out and started to scratch my body. Imam started cursing.

"Dirty girl. Idiot, you ruined my pipe."

"Agha, I have itches. I vomited. My body itches."

"Poor foolish, you are dirty, take a bath if you itch."

"Itching started when you gave me the pipe, I bathed once a month."

"Learn from me; I bathed once a week Friday morning after Thursday's night. Early Friday morning, good memory with Haj Khanum."

"Agha, what happened? Haj Khanam died."

"Idiot, I remember, Haj Khanum came to my room on a good Thursday night, good memory. Haj Khanum came then; my goodness, I was a young man."

I knew the comment referred to the Muslim tradition should have sex on Thursday night, then take a bath Friday morning for the praying.

"She does not come, so you go to her room."

"You are dumb, stupid; I mean, Thursday night."

"My mother said that I am stupid. Why do you take a bath on Friday morning?"

"Foolish girl, for pray."

"Do you pray only on Friday?"

"You are dumb."

"We bathe once a month. My mother says we have no money. Good for you to bathe once a week."

"That is why you are dirty and have itching."

"Sir, give me money for bathe."

As usual, I said several times until he paid. The first concubine used to travel sometimes, and I was sincerely happy. The second concubine did not go anywhere because he knew everyone was waiting for his absence.

Someya was very nosy and curious about what I did daily. My dear knitting has always been my helper when I showed it and explained about my source of income for our living expenses. She also ordered me to knit some tablecloths for free. Interestingly, she asked me each time about how much I got and took some of it before I left. Some money accumulated gradually. Madame was my secret keeper and suggested to buy a house for me. I did not agree and asked her to open a class and teach more students to have a job for their lives. Madame took the money, bought a house next door to her home, establish classes for girls and boys and hired a teacher to teach them textiles and sewing. I was pleased, and my love of my concubine had increased due to money! I kept complaining about the cost of living and food expenses to make more money of them. At the same time, I was asking them about the cause of inflation.

My concubines had skills in sophistication, which was cleared to have been fed from one source. They used a bad language, stated that you are not literate, you do not understand, women are all ignorant, and words like this have always been the prelude to their conversation with me. Then They shook their head like a goat and said they knew what they were doing, both aware of people's misfortunes and the killings of innocent people. Because the victims' photos with the stature of an angel and a smile on their lips in the execute rope (like Majid) were published in the journal, and they received all journals.

They did not care about the people's misfortune; the soldiers killed at war, the writer's bus downing in the canyon, the plane crash, and the killing did not matter. The protestors were arrested and executed by Khalkhali, Lajevardi (Khomeini agents), and their coworkers without trial and court under the name of fighting with God or accusations of sedition against the regime.

Without any documents or court order, they killed bus

after bus full of passengers with one order and the Nojeh
Air Force national officers. Then both liars spoke about
healthy life for Iranians in the Friday prayers. It was when
the cost of living especially food items had increased
significantly, and the dollar price had reached 700 seven
hundred tomans from 7 tomans. And this was just when
the government encouraged people to put their money in
the bank and not work and get twenty percent interest. In
other words, they planned people to be idle without any
production and earn money! The government, the
graveside reciters, was taking steps towards crippling of
the economy and people's lives. They knew very well what
valley people would fall at the end of the pathway because
Khomeini had said that the economy belonged to a donkey.

On the other hand, as a young girl, I felt how chaffy my
life was compared to Ana and Behrouz's passion, love, and
lifeful. There was a big gap and difference between Ana's
romantic relationship with my contentless concubines.
They were living, and I was pretending to live like a clown.
This was the concubine life. I thought, do concubine girls
understand the concepts of love and marriage? Did they
share their experiences with other girls?
It might the poor living in a small town deprive me of
understanding these phenomena.

The definition of the concubine is a woman sleeps with
a man after receiving money. They must satisfy the man's
appetite for sexual pleasure. So that man can get the sexual
pleasure he wants, which is precisely equal to the
definition of prostitution in the dictionary. In Islam, they
believe that men's sexuality is God-given and don't need to
control it; on the contrary, women's bodies have evil
properties that cause sexual desire in men. Therefore,
Muslim women should be limited to the Islamic hijab
because it provokes men. Men can have concubines outside
their marriage and have sex for pleasure without immoral
labels, but women cannot.

If women have sex outside of their marriage, they are
called deviant and should be stoned, but not the men.
Women belong to their husbands. Also, concubines are
considered a matter of reproduction. Young concubines

often live in married men's houses, a form of polygamy. Men are a superpower in the concubine interface. Muslims have double standards for similar behaviors, and these issues are rooted in the Muslim mentality. Concubinage is a type of female slavery. Illusions and social superstitions, such as roaring slaps, drag uninformed and inexperienced women to the witches' castle.

It is necessary to clearly define the concubine and illuminate these dark alleys for immature young girls to prevent them from being captured by witches. Concubine is a toy of social misconceptions that has no truth and has been spread by the mullahs of the godless false religion.

In the Islamic Republic regime, love and affection are considered invalid and a crime; it is forbidden to establish a relationship between a man and a woman outside the rules of Islam. The Islamic Republic regime has medieval laws to create fear and terror, revealing their terrifying nature by arresting, publicly flogging, imprisoning, and stoning women. May this help the world learn Mullah's nature and religion?

The Islamic regime has reduced girls' marriage age to 13 as "Islamic justice," The new law has been approved by the parliament, which allows a man of a family to marry his 13-year-old adopted daughter (shameful)! Khomeini's religious treatise states that men can touch a baby's thighs for sexual satisfaction (what is it called in modern society? Newborn molestation). In the same treatise comes if men have sex with an animal, they must kill the animal! This is the content of Khomeini's religious message.

In the Islamic regime, the malignant concubine cancer spread, so the grave reciter, Imam Alamalhoda, established the concubine income source in Mashhad. The real meaning of the concubine house is a brothel. Also, young girls from low-income families are attracted to men's glamorous castles with the illusion that they will achieve happiness by gaining money and power. They suffer from an inferiority complex that pulls them toward the empty fortresses. Also, it is a game for devilish adventurer girls to take advantage of wealthy elderly because older men have the illusion that if they sleep with young girls, they will become young again. Adventurists were aware of men's fantasies that they took advantage of and made money in this way.

Sometimes the concubines attribute the man's impotence and his projection. Men claimed my wife was not attractive and selected to concubine to show off that he still had the sexual ability and hide his disability, while wise people knew. In the world of concubines, money is like the winning ace in the gambler's hand in the male sexual casino corruption. Men tried to cover their sexual or brain impotence or lack of human emotions in the shade of gold. And on the other side of the gambling table is that women bear the humiliation. A concubine is a toy for men who throws money at women to cover up his inferiority complex. Concubine women accept cash because they might need it or not know the meaning of self-respect and consider the burden of humiliation as a regular thing because she is humiliated enough and cannot see the manifestations of self-respect.

MEDICAL SCHOOL OFFICE 2002

I was a diligent student at university. A new professor who had just joined the university faculty used to question me often, and I would answer his queries without hesitation. One day, I was called to the faculty office. When I arrived, I found several professors and the dean waiting for me. They pointed out that my exam papers, there were three unanswered questions.

I was stunned, and although I felt scared, I remained composed and remembered my dad's advice. I guessed that the new professor, who frequently questioned me, might be involved in this situation. Despite being disconcerted by his intense gaze, I managed to stay calm and composed. It was surprising how casual I sounded when I reiterated my earlier explanation, considering the seriousness of the situation. It became evident to me that the professors were more focused on my unanswered questions than on the students who were not studying. After repeated questioning, the dean expressed disappointment that I was not being truthful. Despite my repeated responses, they requested that I visit the dean's office the following day with my father. I informed them that my father was traveling and that I would discuss the matter with him upon his return. Despite their insistence, I left the office feeling like the matter was far from being settled. That night, I discussed it with Ana, but we couldn't come to a decision. Ana seemed to think that everything would be fine once my dad was informed, but I felt compelled to solve the problem on my own. We decided not to involve Behrouz, and instead, Ana was excited to share the news that Iran Joon was getting married. I loved Iran Joon very much; he was kind and caring .

Ana said that when Aria came to Tehran, Nima Khan was alone and talking to Iran Joon .Finally ,they decided to marry. Nima Khan was the expelled university professor , opened a yarn shop ,and lived with his only son. I was thrilled to hear this news as well. They would be visiting Tehran soon before heading to northern Iran for a few days. At the same time, our upstairs tenant moved out, and Aria, a handsome engineering student, moved in. Although we didn't see much of him due to his work schedule, he did have a question for Ana whenever we met. Ana also mentioned that Aria's mother was beautiful and tragically stoned to death by mullah. Ana and I had taken an English course together, primarily because most of our science books were in English. Behrouz was more proficient in English than us. I had pretended to take the English course at the suggestion of my concubine, who wanted me to go abroad for money laundering. I feigned ignorance to hide behind a façade. Despite all this, Ana and I found it amusing to teach English to the mullah.

I asked the mullah to learn English and remarked that 'two teas' sounded like 'parrot', 'bill'- 'invoice,' 'feel'- 'elephant,' 'sea'- 'thirty,' and 'sad'-'hundred' in Persian. It seemed like he was commending himself each time he repeated a word, and I played along. This seemed to amuse both Ana and me to find some words like this, and it was my job to get more money from him and help the talented man learns English with a silly girl! He was happy learning English, and I had to repeat the exact words in the next session because he forgot it. It was a funny game.

Bijan first meeting

Ana was in the first year of surgical residency and had to prepare an article, but she was sick and resting at home, asked me to prepare the case summary and make a copy for the file. I asked the CCU secretary for Ana's patient file and explained that Ana was sick. She knew Ana and respected her well. She believed that Ana's diligent work saved her daughter's life and allowed me to have the patient's file. She pointed to the next room where Dr. Bijan had the file. I went to the adjoining room, and a handsome man was busy flipping through the files. I could see his profile's beauty, standing helplessly and looking at him for a while. He was reading the file and did not notice my arrival, and I don't know why I did not dare tell him that I wanted the file. I had enough time until the next class and would wait for him to finish his work. There was a medical journal on the other table. I sat down to look at the magazine, But he was the center of my attention and noticed he was looking at me. I thought to myself that I must be wrong. I slowly raised my head to see if I was right and saw that he was still looking at me.

"What year are you?" He smiled and asked.

I was confused and said:

"I wanted the file."

"Do you have a presentation?"

He got up, came to the table where I sat, and stood before me. I was looking at the magazine. He laughed, and I raised my head to see what he was laughing at. When I had a strange feeling. He brought out his hand, turned the magazine, and said:

"Now, you can read from this side."

I noticed that I held the magazine upside down, embarrassed, and tried to hide my face behind the magazine, and he tried to control his laughter. There was silence for a few seconds.

"We can read the file together. When should the article be submitted?"

"I do not know."

He was looking at me with surprise. I pulled myself together.

"It was for my friend."

He laughed and spoke.

"Cheating!"

"No, my friend is a good student; she is sick. I wanted to copy some pages for her."

"It is a fascinating case. I read the whole file. More tests and a thyroid radioisotope are necessary. How old are you?"

He sat, put his hand on the file, ignored my request, and stared at me. I was embarrassed. My hands shook, my heart came out of my chest, I couldn't bear to look at him.

"I took some notes and will give them to you for your friend; it may be helpful. My name is Bijan. What is your name?"

I was speechless and did not dare to look at him and answer.

"What is your friend's name?"

"Ana"

"I asked your name."

At the same time, Behrouz entered the room. They knew each other. Behrouz greeted him and said to me:

"Why did she bother you? It was my fault that I told Ana that my work was taking too long. I wish I had said I would try copying the file for her."

"So, your fiancé is sick. You must have made her sick."

Behrouz laughed and said:

"It's always my fault. We were gone, Abali, and it was cold. I should have gone back to the room immediately. I was delayed, and Ana was in freezing weather for a long time. I did not realize the cool weather, and she had caught a cold."

I lowered my head, afraid to look at him, and couldn't breathe. I got up and said to Behrouz:

"You take a copy of the file, and I go."

When I came out, I could hear. "It is an interesting case, and you must read it. Talk to your fiancé; I can come to your home tonight and write an article together if she wants."

I did not hear the rest of the conversation or understand my feelings. How charming and handsome he was. I wondered why I thought about him. A typical encounter, why I made it big. I told myself that this was just momentary feeling. I went to my class and had enough time to read something, but no matter how hard I tried, I couldn't concentrate on understanding even one word and knitted faster.

I wished I had not created so many problems for myself; I was free now and could quickly deal with my feelings. But it was too late. I thought he wouldn't even look at me when he knew I was a concubine. It is better to control my emotions. Then, I analyzed my behavior and judged myself. I reviewed my childhood memories of severe poverty. Marzieh humiliated me, and her words spread the seed of inferiority. I thought no one would ever want me, and I would stay with my dad forever. Haji Khanum complimented her daughter's suitors and her husband. I never saw myself as good enough even to have one suiter. Worse, I hid all these words, and countless complications were born, and did not pay attention to the class at all.

I looked at the professor dumbfounded. The teacher noticed my change and asked where you were today. I did not care and tried to get him out of my head. His visit was explosive in my emotions. I left the class, decided to go home, thought about him all the way, and repeated that I did not want him. It was an instant feeling; I could get him out of my mind. Why was I worried about nothing? I got home. Ana was still in bed. I told her a doctor had the patient's file and Behrouz would bring a copy. I tidied up her room.

"Something is bothering you." Ana asked.

"I don't know how to tell you that I don't understand why I was shaking when I saw Dr. Bijan. All the time, I tried not to think about him, and I wanted to cry. I thought about my destiny and analyzed my life in detail.

"I don't know why I feel sad."

"Might you fall in love at one glance?"

"No, I don't want to be in love. I heard he wanted to

review the patient's case with you tonight."

"He might like you and use this as an excuse."

"No, he studied this file before, took some notes, and offered to give it to me before Behrouz entered the room.

"What were his name and his shape?"

"Behrouz comes and tells you I did not look at him properly because I couldn't bear to look at him, but I remember his name was Bijan."

"Do you remember when I was in love with Behrouz? I was in the same state. Well, tonight, I will find out what is going on. You are sure that he will come tonight."

"I don't know, I heard him say to Behrouz, I did not hear the rest of his words. I am going out tonight. I do not want to see him at all, which doesn't matter."

I organized some of her report papers with Ana for two or three hours. We talked, although it was the first time I did not want to speak to Ana. In the afternoon, I went to the house of my concubine's husband. There was chaos in my heart. I felt that this was the beginning of a storm, and I had a strange feeling and felt helpless, like a poor child who shivered from the cold on a windy and rainy barren desert and looked for a shelter. I cried, took my dad's excuse like that day Marzieh punished me, and I hid on the stairs. I wish my dad would come and hold me in his arms. When I was at the concubine's house, that was like always, but I was not. I was walking around the room and remembered the poem of Forough Farokhzad:

"Staring at the eyes of my life.

Those two fearful anxious eyes ran away from my gaze.

They sought a shelter in the solitude of the eyelids like a liar, and I don't fit into my lonely cocoon."

I was running away from myself." What a life I made for myself. I wish I listened to Madam and Iran Joon. I was so restless that nothing could calm me down. I sat on the sofa and realized the concubine was not coming. This was not the first time he did come; it did not matter to me whether he came or not. There were some days that I had exams and wished for free time, but for the first time, I wished he would come and distract my attention for a few minutes. And I want to hang around to pass the time. Unwanted things are rare when we need it. Reading books and television could not occupy my mind. Moments later, I said it was better that mullah hadn't come, and I wondered how I could talk to him when I was restless and upset about the current situation. I was talking to myself that I had ignored Bijan, but he was with me. I was enduring inner conflict and did not know that this storm would take me away like a straw. I used to take the excuse of my dad, who was close to me and far away from me. I was crying. When I got home, I was anxious again behind the door. Did he come, and is he still here or gone?

I entered the house with the tip of my steps. It was clear from the house's silence that no guest was there. Ana and Behrouz were sleeping. I went to my room and slept.

I woke up several times with the same childhood nightmares. I don't know if I cried in sleep or when I woke up. I dreamed of holding my dad's leg tightly in my arms in a cold and dark place, and I was afraid he would leave me alone. As usual, I woke up in the morning and had to go to university. When I came out of the room, Ana sat at the table and a bouquet of red roses on the table.

"Dr. Bijan came here, he is very literate. As I guessed, he liked you and asked Behrouz what your name is and whether you are engaged or love someone, and he knew that we live together and brought these flowers on purpose. When he was leaving, he asked Behrouz why you were not at home."

"What did Behrouz say to him?"

"Behrouz said that Neda worked. Also, he told Bijan is excellent and must like Neda very much because he asked about her many times. I don't know anyone better than this man."

We ate breakfast in the kitchen when Behrouz came and said excitedly.

"Neda, I have good news for you. You saw Bijan; he asked me about you. He is the best man I have ever met in my life."

I looked at him dumbfounded and he stared at me and spoke.

"Aren't you happy? What does bother you?"

I did not say anything because I had nothing to say.

"Are you okay today? Are you sick?"

At the same time, the phone rang. Ana picked up the phone; I guessed it was Madam or Iran Joon called to find out how Ana was doing, but the call was for me. My dad was on the phone when he asked.

"Are you worried?"

"No, there are many lessons."

"Take two days off and go around. I dreamed last night that you were upset."

"No, I'm fine."

"Take care."

"Okay, Daddy."

Ana was resting at home, and I got in Behrouz's car to go to school. Behrouz turned several times, looked at me, and asked.

"Neda, how are you? You must have fallen in love too."

"No, I don't want any love in my life."

I talked to myself; Ana knew what my pain was. It's better that you don't know it. We reached the hospital, and he went to his ward. The restlessness killed me all day. Like a person standing on the edge of a precipice behind a high roof, there is a fear of falling on one side, and on the other side, a predatory tiger is lurking. How could I want him or forget him and pass from the impasse? I had filled out the paper in class with I do not like him phrase. I thought Rudi learned how to weave fast with practice, and I could do it too. I will practice. My childish experiences were the base of my emotional issues. I ignored that a different measurement unit is needed to measure length and weight. One primitive experience is not a tool to weigh the feeling, the pressure on the springs of the feeling increases its force. I was trying to push back the emotional feeling firmly and keep them under control. I thought it was not necessary; I would succeed. It is momentary feeling, and it passes. I can. I can. Unaware that the emotional volcano cannot be controlled with weak hands, and I lost the gamble.

My inside war was raging that I did not want him, this feeling was inner fight and flight, and I kept telling myself that I did not want him...I don't want him. I was a lost person that had a dream to pass off this impasse. I excused my illness, went home, and blamed myself for the silly concubine games. At home, Ana was sleeping, and I had tea slept, and woke up from the door sound, it was Ana.

"What's wrong with you? Do you think you have a cold?"

"No, I was tired and fell asleep."

She sat on the edge of my bed and spoke. "Why are you
upset, afraid that he will find out about the concubine?"

"Well, he won't like me when he finds out. It's better that I don't like him and end the story here."

"Nothing has yet to happen to terminate."

"You are right, Ana; why am I so sad?"

"You worry about the concubine. If your relationship becomes serious, we will think about it."

"He is wealthy, and our financial situation is incompatible. He does not want me when he knows we are not on the same level."

Ana said in surprise: "What are you saying? Everyone should wish to have someone like you. This is a lack of self-confidence. You are a lovely person."

"You and I grew up together since childhood. You think so, but I don't believe these words. He is a charming, intelligent, and wealthy man who will not want me when he knows."

"Oh, so you are afraid. This is normal; you remember when Behrouz did not talk to me, I interpreted that I was Armenian, and he was Muslim and did not like me. In contrast, he was in love and afraid of rejection. Our thought was childish.

I am glad I told Uncle Soheil. Let me talk to him."

"No, not at all. I love my dad very much, don't want to tell him anything, and our situation were different."

I was sure Ana did not tell Behrouz anything, but I said. "You did not say anything to Behrouz."

"No, I did not, but he asked me why Neda was not

happy. Might she be in love with someone and hide it from us? We had agreed that when the university was over, you would terminate all the concubines; you could do it now. In the meantime, you will know Bijan to see what you want to do. You did nothing, and I am proud of you for taking such a significant risk. Do you remember my mother saying that we should learn selflessness from you. If there were none of these problems, you would have been upset that you met him or that he likes you."

"Well, of course not. But Ana, we have a different class; he came from a prosperous family, and I am from a family where we were always hungry when I was a child."

Ana was distraught and spoke.

"You never told me that you were hungry."

"Ana, I did not say it, but it did not mean I wasn't hungry.

"Well, now think that there is none of those issues and get to know him; after a while, it might you do not like him, or he does not like you."

Behrouz returned home and said:

"What's wrong? Ana gave you a cold; I will make you some soup."

"No, I am not sick and hungry."

"Well, get up and make soup for us. Ana gave me a cold, and the penalty for coming home early was to prepare dinner. We can also have guests, of course, if you want."

"No, I am working tonight."

I do not know why I lied. Later my dad came and said that he was worried about me. I was resting in bed. My dad sat on the edge of the bed, and I put my head on his knee and cried. My dad was worried and kept asking me to tell him what happened; everything had a solution, except death. Did something happen in the school?

"No, only the teacher understood that I answered only some of the questions purposely."

"You cry because of this; you should not be afraid of anything. I am always by your side. Do you want me to talk to the university president?"

"No, I told them that my dad was traveling. The next

day, I went to the dean's office and repeated the exact words."

"The maximum is that I will send you from Iran to Zohreh."

"I will go if you come with me. Otherwise, it is impossible; I will stay wherever you are."

"It's better to finish the school this year but remember, I lost my loved ones; I don't want you to take any risk to get a degree, so only you are important."

"Daddy, you always look sad because you lost your dearest ones. Did I understand correctly?"

"Yes"

"I don't want to know who that dear was; it's sad to tell." My dad remained silent and did not say anything.

"Uncle Soheil, Neda has worked so hard; it's a pity to leave the university."

"Ana Joon, you're right but at what circumstances and at what price? It is okay if she can wait, but if she can't or doesn't want, the lesson is not essential; she's important. I am sure that Neda has understood very well, and it is better to travel for a few days and then decide what she wants. Experience showed that these successes are insignificant compared to the whole of life, and one should not look for success when the essence of life is under question."

We looked at him in amazement. I could manage my life with knitting, and why should I be afraid? One day from the school dean, one day because I fell in love with someone higher than me and may leave me, one day because I am afraid of being scandalized by the concubine issue. It is better to leave him now before anything happens between us. I heard my sobbing and saw how my innocent dad must constantly be worried for me; I could control myself and told him, please forgive me if I hurt you. My dad looked sad and spoke.

"Cry, if it calms you down, take it easy. Ana Joon, you know why Neda is sad, tell me."

"Uncle Soheil, I never tell anyone what we say to each other. She can tell you if she wants. Do not worry; she is okay and cry for nothing."

Dinner was ready; I did not have an appetite and pretended to have a headache and rest .The thought of leaving here opened a window of hope .

I thought about Ana's words that I should give myself a chance to know Bijan ,and she was surprised by my behavior. Then I concluded that Ana loved me when Bijan knew she wouldn't like me .This is wrong from the beginning and does not have a good ending. This feeling was so strong, and my classmates and teachers noticed my change from my unbalanced behavior. I had become introverted and sought isolation. I was running away from everyone. In agony in this effort, days passed with inner challenges and running away from logic and from him.

My condition was getting worse day by day. It was an internship period, sometimes I saw him in the hospital and changed my way as if I did not see him .I did not go wherever I knew he was. One day when I had to report the patient's condition to the surgical professors .Bijan arrived and stood next to the professor ,face to face with me .I was restless and moved to the bottom of the patient's bed because I could not bear his gaze .It caused everyone to smile. The professor asked ,is the weather better there? And they all laughed .The hot flash was pouring from my face.

I was so shocked that I did not know what to do .I put the patient's file on her bed and ran out of the room .I heard his footsteps behind me as he came a few steps .I reached home and immediately called my dad ,but no one was there. I collected some of my clothes and decided to leave the city. I wish I could go to Aunt Zohreh, but I can't. I would go to Madam and Iran Joon. In the afternoon, I called my dad again and said I wanted to go to Drood. My dad said I would come soon. He came and spoke.

"Nada, wait, we will go together tomorrow."

"I want to go now. I can't breathe here."

I was surprised that Ana came home at the same time. Later, I heard Bijan told Ana that I left the ward. Ana insisted me on waiting; she will come too.

"I want to go tonight."

My dad called a travel agency and reserved tickets and tried to discover my impulsive behavior.

"Ana what was wrong with Neda? Is there a political issue, or is someone chasing her?"

We were surprised and my dad continued.

"In the university age, several problems may upset a student, love, different beliefs, conflict with vigilante groups, SAVANA and Harasat, political issues, or studies."

"No, Uncle Soheil, not at all."

"Girls either fall in love with someone or someone falls in love with her and causes trouble. Is it about love?"

"No, it is not love." I answered harry.

"Another common issue among the people is the issue of the virginity, and I hope that at least you, as doctors, will clear these superstitions from the minds of society. Virginity is not about torn and bleeding. The untruthful doctor repaired and made money from naive people, a kind of robbery that fueled myths and superstitions. People falsely created stories about the virginity, which were rooted in
ignorance.

"Uncle Soheil, how do you know so well? Do they talk about such superstitions in engineering universities?"

"At all academic and non-academic levels, these illusions and nonsense are attached to people who are satisfied with the listening principle, not studying the facts. They carry these superstitions with them and, in turn, poison the atmosphere and
cripple people. Superstitions penetrated some minds; the charlatans take advantage of the donkey wherever the donkey are stuck.

"I would like to know, Uncle Soheil, what you know about the virginity."

There was no surprise because Ana always expressed her words quickly.

"Wisdom people who are interested going to a library and do not need to have access to medical books. Even in ordinary dictionaries that are not censored, you can read that the hymen is an annular membrane attached to the inside of the vagina.

And there is no reason for a woman to bleed during intercourse. The dishonest doctors repaired and knew very well that there is nothing to repair. They use people's ignorance as a money-piggy box, like mullahs. Poor and ignorant people who never get rid of ignorance to pay the penalty to these two groups."

I thought it might my dad assumed I had some relationship and worried him.

"Daddy, I have never had a relationship with any boy."

"My daughter, there is nothing wrong with you having a relationship with someone, it is a natural need, and this relationship should not be seen as abnormal. Do not have a relationship is unusual and abnormal, but I'm not worried about that."

That night, we went to Drood, and I did not consider it would be painful for my dad to repeat his bitter memories.

Madam and Monsieur met us at the bus station and took us to their house. My cushion was on my chair with a doll, and a doll was sleeping on Ana's bed. Madam set Ana's room for me. "Tell me, I love you as much as Ana and can't see you being upset."

Madam spoke decisively, and I felt safe with her. I told the story of Bijan. Madam laughed and said:

"You suffered so much because you love someone. It's a pity that you are a medical student. What did you learn from university books? Bijan should be happy to love you. Did he tell you that he doesn't love you?"

"No."

"Well, why did not you tell him that you love him?"

"No, I don't want to love him."

"Well, you don't like him. Whenever he says he loves you, tell him to go away, you don't love him."

"No, it is not like that."

"I don't understand you ,let me call Ana."

She picked up the phone and spoke to her .At the same time ,Iran Joon came ,kind and loving as always ,and she ended her phone call with Ana.

"Iran, sit down and see how our daughter is."

She turned to me.

"What is this behavior? Everyone agrees that he is the

best university doctor and likes you. How did you make this mess? The issue of the concubine is nothing. What are you talking about? You told Ana that he might not like you. You did not beg him to love you. What are these rejections?"

"We have a different class."

Madam growled: "What nonsense are you talking about? Did you buy or sell goods? Its condition is better so. It is enough if you love each other. Unless there is another problem that you should have told me about."

"I don't know why my heart tells me he doesn't like me when he knows my situation."

"Well, you are not in a bad situation where no one wants you. In opposite, he wishes to have someone like you. If the day comes that he doesn't want you, then we will give it a thought. Are you afraid of concubines? They are with me to finish it."

"No, they are harmless monsters. Two illiterate and unintelligent coward mullahs see me as a parasite. I am not even a human being to them."

Madam spoke: "Mullahs go to heal, who are dumb because they could not know you, stupid mullah. I will fix that issue. How much you bothered me, I was afraid. What happened that you skipped class once, and Ana did not say anything. You love him and are scared."

"I am afraid he will reject me when he finds it out."

"He made a mistake if rejecting you. He wishes to have you. I will come to Tehran and talk to him."

"No, no, I don't want to. I want to stay here."

She looked at me. "We will talk about it later."

I used tiredness as an excuse, and she left me alone in Ana's room, and I fell asleep. I felt that I needed solitude more than ever. I had a thousand thoughts. Ana called me and said that Bijan had come to our house, asked Ana if Neda love someone then he get out of her way. Ana told him that if he is in love, he must wait, and Behrouz assured him that no one is in Neda's life. Iran Joon lived with her husband. The next day, she came to Madam's house and spoke.

"Aria came to see us when he heard Neda is here."

I heard Madam telling Iran Joon it was useless, and Iran Joon also said that my heart was broken for him. I needed clarification on what they were talking about. My dad was talking to Monsieur. He was calmer than before. I think Madam told him. Because my dad told me, Neda Joon, if you love someone, you can be with him to see if your morals are compatible. I was bored and did not even want to crochet .Rudy was still working there .

Marzieh was at Madam's house .Roya and Sohrab became tall and beautiful ,and Sohrab worked in the shop and went to school .Monsieur had promised to buy him a bicycle if the shop was always clean and tidy and if he studies. Varouge still had the bookstore. It was a good city.

Madam told me I deserve more than all of them and appreciate myself more than anyone else. Go ahead, don't let anything stop you. Madam's words, "You can be above all," shook me. It was the third day that I told my dad I wanted to return. Madam said wait; I will come too. I said no, I could solve this problem myself. I said to myself, I can stand in front of Bijan like others, look into his eyes, and speak. For me, Madam always had the authority of a coach or psychologist who changed my view of the world and increased my abilities. I did not know why I did not see Bijan as an ideal man. My shortcomings had crippled me, and I saw myself as weak against his abilities. I needed to see Madam till to believe myself; although I still doubted, he had a noticeable class difference from me. It was better to refrain from saying any more to Madam, which is useless because she judges Bijan without seeing him. I thought about why I had come and returned, but my dad never said why.

We returned to Tehran. Along the way, my dad talked about me and my love which is the best experience, and when he can see Bijan. He wondered why I was bothering myself. My dad dropped me at home and left. The next day, I did not want to go to the hospital and stay home. I slept all day. It was night, Ana and Behrouz had come, and I used the excuse of being tired and sleeping in my bed when I heard my room door opening, but no one came. I turned to find out who was coming.

Bijan stood at the door with a smile that covered his face in happiness, just like when I held the magazine upside down. He was leaning on the door and said can I visit the patient. But he did not come and was still standing at the door's threshold and smiling. My face was towards the door, and I could not escape his gaze. It was Behrouz's voice that answered, please.

The air in the room was heavy, I could hear my heart, and I did not know how to tolerate his presence at that moment. I closed my eyes to avoid looking into his eyes. I could hear the door locking. He slowly came forward, sat on my bed edge, and took my hand. I resisted but he did not let me release my hand from his hand. I tried hard to remain immobile. He kissed my hand. I had goose bumps, and we stayed silent for a while. After a long pause, Bijan spoke.

"Neda Joon, I love you very much, and when you denied me, I talked to Ana, and she said that I shall wait if I love you. I have reached to a point where my patience is exhausted, and I can no longer see you denying me and my love. If you want, I will wait longer, but tell me why. I know there is something that prevents you from approaching me. I thought about everything and why you were running away from me. I don't care about anything, and regardless of what happened in your life that prevents you from getting close to me, I care about you; only you are important. I love you. Let us be together. I promise not to bother you if you see something wrong with me that you don't like. I tried extremely hard not to get close to you in these few months, especially when I saw that you changed your ways every time you saw me, it was excruciating for me, but I said to myself, if seeing me bothers her, it doesn't matter how much it bothers me. I was talking to Ana. Ana told me that you don't love anyone else. This gave me hope that you might love me one day and helped me to be patient. Tell me why. Why don't you want to see me? Do I look terrible?" Meanwhile, he kissed my forehead and placed his forehead on my face. I was motionless like a statue. I had nothing to say. I loved those moments and his warm breaths and wanted to stay at that position forever.

He would whisper that I love you and say that you love me too. I don't know how the moments passed. We heard Behrouz's voice saying that dinner was ready, and he laughed.

"You couldn't speak; let me answer that we are ready."

The sound of a knocking door caused Bijan to take his head off my face. Ana opened the door and quietly told.

"Dinner is ready for the princess."

Bijan laughed and Ana continued.

"My Uncle Soheil is here."

"Hope Uncle Soheil likes me, then may Neda Joon look at me."

They laughed. Bijan pulled my hand to get up. I said I would come and pulled my hand out of his hand. The memory of those moments is always with me. Behrouz came and left the room with Bijan. I stayed with Ana, who was laughing.

"Neda, Bijan loves you very much. Getting up is dinner time. My uncle may talk to Bijan. And we will do whatever Uncle Soheil says."

I had a strange feeling.

"Ana, what should I do if he knows about the concubine?"

"Well, that's enough; we will solve that issue and tell him. Do you want to get help from Uncle Soheil?"

"No, we will not say anything to my dad."

"My parents told me to ask Uncle Soheil about any matter, whether complex or private, even women's issues. I believe they want the best for us; I don't know why you don't see that Uncle Soheil knows better than anyone and can quickly help you and me. However, I will only say something if you want me to."

At their insistence, I went for dinner and sat next to my dad to talk very casually, and Bijan used to answer Behrouz's questions, which made him talk. My gaze was fixed on my plate, and there was unspeakable chaos inside me, and in this way, our love entered a new phase. A few days later, Madam and Iran Joon came to Tehran to see Bijan. Iran Joon looked upset and said Aria had fallen in love and decided to vacate the lower floor. I liked Iran Joon very much and asked her to talk to Aria that he should express his love to her. Iran Joon shook her head and said that the problem is that she was in love with someone else I was sorry for Aria. In this way ,Aria left our neighborhood ,and I got involved in the crisis of falling in love.

CHAPTER 4, NEDA & BIJAN

I returned to the hospital, and most of the time, Bijan was with me, Behrouz, and Ana. I loved him so much and wished to spend all my moments with Bijan. Sometimes I stared at a corner. Bijan said I know something is bothering you. Please tell me whatever it is; it doesn't matter to me, don't bother yourself. It was a pleasure to hear those loving words, but I knew that my past mistakes could not be justified. I thought he would hate me when he knew about my concubines. The roaring flood of his love brings me to the peak of happiness, and the storm of regret from past actions dragged me into the sadness trap. I felt like a mentally ill person who sometimes lapses into mania and depression.

I regretted my past adventures. My mind was pounded between the rock of regret and happiness poles. Bijan's love led me to a world of affection; I learned the meaning of freedom from the trap of lying and deception. I was no longer that girl who weaves thousands of lies as an excuse; although I did not dare enough to say what I had done ,I hated lying. Even in front of my concubines ,my lies were significantly reduced ,and I was no longer the rude and careless girl, and my anxiety was different; knitting did not relieve me ,so I knit less. The first concubine imam a calm man ,noticed my change earlier than the second addicted imam ,and I replied that my mother's illness had become worst, and I was worried about her .

Madam kept reminding me that my mother's sickness was a good excuse ,and my mother vowed to go to Mashhad to be healed of such superstitions; I believed that to get rid of them ,I would continue to play the role of the dumb girl. On the first visit, Bijan told my dad that he lost his parent at early age, grew up in his aunt's house, his aunt and uncle were his parents and loved them. Bijan spent most of his time in our house near the hospital.

I went to Bijan's home several times, where there was prosperity, high class, and high financial situation. Bijan's cousins lived in the USA, and his parents went there for treatment. He was very close to his family and told them he had fallen in love and wanted to marry me. Little by little, the marriage matter had become profoundly serious. When I saw his wealthy house and car, I told him his financial situation differed from mine. Bijan noted that these are not important; we love each other. I told my dad that Bijan is very wealthy, and his situation differs from ours. He replied that you did not go after him because of his money, so it doesn't matter if he is rich.

Bijan insisted on knowing where I work, and I told him that his curiosity made me feel that I had lost my freedom, and he did not ask about it anymore. I started birth control pills again. Now I am a doctor, and I should not ask the pharmacy what pill I take. I decided to use an IUD because I lost my appetite and weight.

One night, when we were at our house, and my dad was present, Bijan told my dad that he had talked to his parents about when they would come because he wanted to arrange the marriage ceremony sooner. His mother said he should not wait for anyone, and it would be best if he had a wedding yesterday. Also, he asked for my dad's permission to buy rings and get married if my dad and I agreed.

"Neda, what do you think?"

I had no idea what to say.

"Give me some time."

I stared at a point again. My dad, who was aware of our close relationship, looked at me with surprise and said:

"I will talk to Neda."

Bijan was looking at me with concern and surprise when Ana came to help and said:

"We, as girls, are different from boys. We should talk to each other."

After that night, Ana and I decided to finish the concubine, tell Bijan about it and see his reaction. One day I tried to talk to Bijan, but I could not because he was

different from other men. In his presence, I became a
clumsy girl who did not even have the strength to speak.
We decided that Ana would tell Bijan about the concubine
and evaluate his reaction. During this time, Bijan always
wrote romantic expressions in my notebook and books,
such as my dear, Shakespeare did not know to be or not to
be is not the issue. He should write that being with you or
without you is the issue. I remembered that sentence
because it was the same day that Ana told Bijan about the
concubine. Ana had told Bijan that she wanted to have
lunch together and talked to him alone. She said to him
that we loved Neda very much, and I want to tell you why
she looked depressed.

"Yes, whenever I wanted to ask Neda, I faced her
resistance, and I did not say anything because no matter
what was, it would not effect on my love for her."

"I wanted to tell you that Neda has become a
concubine." Bijan said surprisingly.

"It was not possible! I know her, and you must be
joking.

"No, I'm not kidding; I'm serious. Bijan paused for a
moment and said:

"Well, no matter what, I love her, and I don't care what
happened before." Ana did not say anymore when Bijan
paused. When Ana told me, I was happy initially, then I
was sad and spoke.

"He has the right to know everything and love or hate
me and I should accept whatever happens. Each of us must
make a conscious decision, if he decides to leave me, it's his
right, I can't do anything, and it's better to know as soon as
possible, especially now when we talk about marriage."

That night, Bijan came to our house, and he started
before I could say anything.

"Ana told me about the past. I told you whatever is it
did not matter to me. Why did not you think I loved you so
much that nothing mattered to me?"

"I wanted to talk to you."

The feeling of losing him was killing me.

"What else, why don't you say now, and bothering
yourself?"

"Behrouz is coming now, and I want to have a good moment so that if something goes wrong, I will keep the memory of these moments with me."

He looked into my eyes.

"Did I get it quickly and to lose it fast? What will ruin it? Everything will remain the same or better. I promise to make you happy; this was my promise to your father."

Behrouz came, and we had dinner together, and I was silent at the dinner table. I remembered Madam's words that I should look into his eyes and talk. The first night she came to my room and sat on my bed, I could not even look into his eyes. I was still the same weak person, and this man was different from all the men in the world. He was my dearest man; I was not afraid of him but losing him was the most incredible sadness. He was also silent and was different from before, and might he wait for an unknown event or a storm. Ana was the only person who knew my worries. Behrouz was on call and returned to the hospital. We went to our room, and I called Ana. I wanted her to be present when I tell him everything and I spoke.

"I am still a concubine."

"No, you are joking."

"I am serious, and I am still a concubine."

He laughed and spoke.

"It is not possible."

Bijan finally asked in amazement.

"Well, do you love me?"

"More than you believe."

"Very well, finish the concubine."

"I am a concubine in two people."

He laughed and spoke.

"I am sure you are kidding; how is that possible?"

Then Ana slowly told him what had happened. When he found out that I was the imam's concubine, he stared at me for a long time out of fear and asked.

"Why? Are you not a pity?"

It took minutes for him to mastered himself and asked.

"What do you want to do now?"

"Neda had planned to finish the concubines by the end of this year, and now she will do it sooner."

Bijan squeezed me tightly in his arms and spoke worriedly.

"What dangerous thing did you do? They are dangerous."

I was shaking and crying due to the fear of losing him.

"So, it was the reason you only wrote the answers to some of the questions."

I wondered how he knew.

"No, they do not know that I am a student. They consider me a stupid beggar girl."

He said with horror.

"What should we do now?"

My hands were on my face and crying while Ana whispered.

"Bijan, Neda is a great person. My mother said I am lucky to have a friend like her. None of us have his heart and soul."

"If you play with fire, you will burn, it is extremely dangerous."

Bijan was terrified. It was painful to think it might be the last time I would have the pleasure of being in his arms and smell his aroma. He was quiet, and I could hear Ana's voice.

"The vital thing is that you love each other."

My heartbeat was in my temples, and his silence was killing me. I said quietly.

"Bijan, I will accept your decision and never lose a bit of my love for you, don't worry about me."

Ana roared.

"Nothing has happened."

I do not know if my words or Ana's loud voice caused Bijan to break his silent.

"Nothing has happened. Nothing has happened."

Unexpectedly, I heard those words as if he were talking in his sleep. Again, a long pause, and then Bijan spoke.

"I love you, and we will solve the problem together."

I just burst out and cried loudly.

"Don't worry, we will do something, but you did a dangerous thing, as you heard about the Lajvardi's

murder. Lajvardi was the head of Evin prison ,and he
arrested and killed people without any court order and
trial; he was known as Tehran's executioner . When his
murder was announced, people were happy ,and the
Islamic regime pretended to mourn .But people knew that
there was a dispute between them .No one knew what the
fight was about ,but it was clear that the battle was so fierce
that people had found out about the secrets .There was a
roamer that Lajvardi killed at the order of his master .This
tyrannical government was the mafia group in the God
Father movie ,who killed his brother .The dictators were
friends during the murder and theft and were enemies at
the time of disbursing .The power-seekers used to talk to
each other with the guns and people wished to target each
other successfully.

Bijan's voice freed me from my thoughts.

"I was worried about you, and we should do
something as soon as possible."

"Bijan, Neda decided to get rid of them soon."

Bijan asked in horror. "It means she kills them."

"No, I meant to end up being a concubine."

Bijan kissed me.

"Don't cry; we will give it a thought."

I was relieved to tell Bijan about such a complex
matter. I whispered. "There is one more thing I want to
say."

Bijan shook violently.

"What else? Is there a third concubine?"

Ana also said with surprise. "What do you want to
say?"

"No, there is not third concubine; I have a disability."

"What?"

"I have a hearing problem in one ear."

"So! It does not matter."

Bijan asked about my mother, and I said I do not know;
my dad raised me, and I love him very much, and he did
not continue. He probably had recognized my family's
unusual situation.

Later, Ana told me that she was scared when heard

there is another issue because I hide the second concubine. I had a strange peace like a peace after a storm and it was time to rebuild the ruins. Since that day, Bijan has been in deep thought most of the time, and whenever I asked, he denied it and said that there was nothing, and when I insisted, he said that I was worried about me. I told Bijan about my plan, to tell them that my mother was sick, and I wanted to take her to Mashhad for healing.

"Do you not believe in these superstitions? Am I right?"

"No, I do not believe these foolish words, but in my position, I must have the same tactics."

"You are wrong if you thought they believe these superstitions when they knew these stupid and ridiculous words."

"You are right, and I should act the same role."

Sometimes I felt that although Bijan was sitting next to me, he was not present and was somewhere else. Unlike in the past, he hugged me, leaned his head on my head, his breaths were deep and avoided looking into my eyes. He was in deep thinking; his face was sad and did not look directly into my eyes. Contrary, I wanted to look at his eyes so that I could read what was going in his mind. There was a gap between us.

I told myself it might be the last days of our relationship, and I would be happy to see him because it was my fault. I was relaxed in his arms and did not know that his hugs were a sign of fear, the end of the relationship, or a sign of disappointment from a woman who called her an angel. There was no choice I should tolerate it. Ana knew my sadness symptoms only, and I replied to her question that Bijan's behavior is different; I am satisfied with it instead of nothing, and you do not say anything.

Security Office (Harassment)

In 1980, the security office was established in universities and hospitals to spy and control students and doctors. One day, the guard took Bijan and me to the security office for being alone in the patient's room. We were not next to each other and stood on one side of an alert patient. They were looking for an excuse to harass us, and time was going hard for us. The illiterate mullah said you are unmarried and were alone in the same room.

Bijan was upset and said that I had a question for her about the patient, let her go, and ask me any question you have. I was also scared to see Bijan's frightened face. Fortunately, our friends saw us and informed our professor Kiani who came to the security office. They released us because of Professor Kiani, who was treating mullah's son.

When we got out of there, Bijan told me that we should get married as soon as possible and he talk to his father immediately. Hearing Bijan's words made me happy. Bijan called his parents that night, and his father said that he had enough money in his account, and Bijan could buy anything he needed and have a wedding and not wait for them. And they will arrange an elaborate wedding party for us when returning to Iran. I called Madam that night and asked for her help. She understood what I meant, and her presence boosted my confidence. Madam's powerful performance significantly affected my life, and Bijan's fear weakened me. Might I be a weak person that external factors changed me? Whatever it was, the existence of all these kind and loving people by my side could not provide me with the self-confidence Madam always gave me. Marzieh planted Madam's powerful image because she was afraid of her. Although everyone approved of my dad, I saw Madam as a victorious warrior.

At the same time, my dad bought a small house near our house with a bank loan. He moved to his house with one of the university professors, a genuinely kind lady named Sahar. My dad seemed happier than before, and I was pleased about his happiness. He did not explain about his friend, and we did not ask either. It was enough that he was happy. I was thinking about how far my dad was from Marzieh, and there was not any intimacy between them.

Sahar was very understanding and had a pleasant constructive conversation. She told me that her husband was a university professor and had a doctorate from Stanford University in America. As soon as he arrived in

Iran, he was arrested at Mehrabad airport and killed by
Khalkhali without trial. After the Bam earthquake in Iran,
the Islamic regime sought an earthquake expert. Stanford
University introduced him, and they noticed that their
executioners had killed the innocent man. Sahar was very
compatible with my dad, and they seemed like a perfect
couple. I told my dad about the security office and Bijan
discussing marriage as soon as possible. My dad said
Bijan's words are essential, but what you want is the most
important. Do you want to marry him and see yourself
with him for a lifetime?

"Yes, I was happy with his proposal."

"Bijan is a worthy man; I am glad you like him, too; it
will be a good marriage."

When I saw my concubines, I did not plead like before,
and my silence caused them to question me. My answer
was my mother's severe illness; she wished to go to
Mashhad, and I was afraid that something would happen
to her before I fulfilled her expectations. I thought I was
pitiful and ignorant with so many lies for nothing, and I
must leave that era behind. It was a long time since the
workshop was self-sufficient, and according to Madam, all
her expenses were covered by its product selling. Although
I did not need money, I was interested in getting more
from the concubines. It became my habit. The first
concubine was more generous, paid well, and always had a
smile on his face. The second concubine was as arrogant
and haughty as the monopoly of necessity items. He was
stingy too, and I had to tell him many times that I wanted
money so that he would pay. His words were repetitive
and primitive.

I learned to look at him, occasionally say hah, and
entertain myself by knitting. Knitting helped them consider
me miserable person with a low-level job for living
expenses, and I was grateful to be underestimated. After
telling the truth to Bijan, I acquired a chronic fear. I hid my
anxiety with knitting because I had enough customers from
the same shop. I put the money aside and gave it to
Madam.

I had several friends in the university and hospital ,but

no one was Ana .I met Dariush ,a surgical resident ,via Ana and Behrouz. He was a handsome man with a good figure and liked to sew tapestry ,which was not within the standards of male society. The reaction of the uneducated was terrible ,and even worse was the reaction of educated people and doctors ,which was very annoying .They accused him of having feminine feelings ,but this was not based on my observation. His girlfriend ,Nasrin ,was a lovely girl. Since the beginning of my studies at the university ,I used to knit without paying attention to the students' attitudes and was known as a knitted girl.

My indifference had caused them to lower the weapons .I was bullied in elementary school for my surname and in university for knitting ,even though I did not write a few answers! I am surprised that not answering was also a topic of fun for me .I was sure that an inexperienced professor had spread this issue .I did not care about those behaviors; I was so traumatized that I was immune, it might be because of my characteristics.

Dariush always sat next to me, I was knitting ,and he was a sewing tapestry ,which established our friendly relationship. He said his mother was a single parent, and he and his brother sewed tapestries with her to cover their cost of living. His mother believed everyone should have a product and not waste time. He thought a surgeon should have tailoring skills. After we finished the medical reports, we discussed the medical case when Ana and I crocheted and Dariush sewed a tapestry. Behrouz and Bijan had also learned from Dariush; they sometimes sewed tapestry when Dariush were present. People carelessly labeled and mocked others. I wish they would consider their limitations and respect human rights because the emotional wound scare stayed with us forever. Bijan and Behrouz's participation in tapestry sewing had changed some attitudes, and Dariush seemed calmer.

Sometimes a simple movement, even if not a cure for a wound, might recover it. Bijan and Behrouz said that tapestry embroidery increased their precision during surgery. Although Bijan and I are together, we are gradually drifting apart. The outward silence was the chaos inside him that he was trying to hide from me.

Meanwhile, Bijan asked Behrouz for help with my concubine. Behrouz said that he wondered how Neda did not have a boyfriend and knew Ana had hidden something from him and told him what was between Neda and her was our secret, and he did not ask her anything else so that she would not get upset. Behrouz suggested that Bijan search for my dad's advice. They agreed that Behrouz did not say anything to Ana. They told my dad they wanted to be alone and talked about a critical issue, and they met him outside the house.

Two young doctors told my dad about the concubines. My dad was shocked and cried that night and wanted to talk to me, but he encountered Bijan's resistance. When Bijan found out that my dad was unaware of my concubine, he got upset about why he told Behrouz and my dad, and he wanted a day to prepare me for my dad's intervention.

Bijan asked Behrouz to pretend to be unaware and stay in the hospital when my dad came to see me, and Bijan opened the issue. This was a part of their conversation that I heard from Bijan. That night my dad came alone for dinner. It seemed to me that he was sick and older than before. In response to my question, he denied it. After dinner, Bijan went to our room and called me. He was sitting on our bed. He took my hand and asked me to sit next to him. My dad came to our room and asked.

"Why did you come here?"

Bijan held my hand and spoke.

"I am glad you came alone tonight. I have a problem and want to share it with you."

I never thought that he might talk about me. He started explaining about my concubine, and my father listened to Bijan's words with a strange calmness. I was melting and wondered why Bijan was saying these things to my dad.

My dad was looking at me and asked Bijan to leave us alone; Bijan left the room. My dad sat next to me. I squeezed my head between my hands and could not bear my dad's look. My dad spoke.

"What is your decision now?"

I was surprised by his calmness. I remember the night when Madam came to our house for the first time, he was disturbed by Marzieh's words, but now he is calm. I told him the story of how I did this stupidity.

My dad asked quietly. "Are you afraid? Whenever you want, we will leave here for America, even if we must walk and go tonight, I will come with you. I told you that I have lost my loved ones and cannot bear to lose you."

I was about to explode with so much sadness.

"No, I am not afraid, and I told Madam to help me to end this mistake."

"Are you afraid of me that you did not tell me about such an important matter?"

"I do not know why I could not tell you, but I am sure that I love you more than anyone. I felt you would be upset if you knew, and I did not want to upset you."

"You could not hide this vital matter forever. What disaster would it be if something happened to you?"

"Daddy, I never felt danger until Bijan found out and said you did something hazardous. Because he is afraid, now I am worried something will happen to me. I talked to Madam and believed I could solve the problem."

"Sooner. They must have made all the inquiries about you."

"Daddy, you may not believe that they consider me a dumb and stupid girl."

"Do not trust the desert is empty; it might be the tiger ambushing there."

My dad was upset and was there late at night. Ana came from the hospital and said that Behrouz had covered another doctor. They talked about me all night. I was happy that Behrouz was not there!

They decided to give me a chance to finish the matter myself. My dad said that whenever you feel in danger, do not risk your life because nothing is worth risking your life, not even your degree. Bijan was also crying that night. I thought a foolish girl did a stupid job, and the ten men should get together to look for a solution. What was wrong with me, and why did the foolish act?

It was not my business that Zubeida married a man with fake nicknames. I was constantly blaming myself. When I told them I was regretful, my dad said we should spend our energy on solving the problem now and thanked Bijan. Bijan cried and said we should listen to dad and solve the problem sooner. When we were alone, I asked him why you talked to my dad, and he might have been a heart attack. He looked at me in astonishment.

"I needed help to save you; even thinking that something might happen to you was painful. I could not wait and say I wish I did such and such. My only thought was to ask your father for help because my dad was not here to help me."

"Your fear is contagious, and I am scared too."

The strong surgeon seems like a child who needs to be cuddled in those moments. I thought love changed our characters; it turned me from a fearless liar to a coward person, a strong man into an innocent and crushed my dad with sad news. Yes, it was a trauma for my dad to hear about my situation. In the meantime, Ana was patient and calm and comforted me, which was amazingly effective but did not have Madam's power. Later, Ana told me that she was also significantly terrified that Bijan would leave me alone when I was in love with him. And we were not scared because we were not mature enough and did not see the dimensions of the problem, and not being scared is not a sign of courage. Bijan's fear was a sign of maturity, and he was the one who consciously examined the issues and saw the danger. In this way, everyone talked about my concubine except Behrouz.

Iran Joon, Madam, and Monsieur came to Tehran. In my mind Madam was strong enough and could solve the problem. She bombarded me with hopeful words, and I was ready to finish our concubines' relationships. It has been a long time since I spoke that my mother is sick. Finally, I told them that if my mother could bear the bus, I would take her to Mashhad, and if I did not come, you know that I was not in town. The first concubine was like always, but the second concubine, who was miserly, and addicted, seemed to be seeing me for the first time.

That night, she was checking me out, which was scary for me; the effect of Bijan's words that they were dangerous scared me. I was no longer that fearless girl afraid of dying, how much I love to be alive and healthy for Bijan and by Bijan's side. It bothered me to look at him, and I tried to keep myself together and be the same dumb and wasted girl, a role I had been in for years. My heart was pounding so much that I thought this useless older mullah looked like a giant devil coming out from the glass to take my life. I could imagine Madam beside me. I calmed myself down and started analyzing the situation. He was the same former garbage addict, and, most importantly, I am the same dumb girl.

The impact of words is so significant that it weakens the strong person without having a real presence. My brain washing by Madam gave me power without my physical and educational ability were changed. Madam was my ability source. I wished that Bijan would not be afraid or would not transfer it to me.

I loved Bijan so much that I took everything as a sign of his caution and love for me .I was evaluating my destiny and my happiness with my situation before falling in love . However ,I knew I had chosen the wrong and manipulated high rank officials making money. Marzieh had infected my mind with the story of Zubeida at an early age. The marriage temptation led me to look for a powerful husband with the title ,which was a foolish thought .In the real world, I entered the witches' castle that belonged to Zahakis (ancient Iranian mythology); a man with snakes on his shoulder who devoured young men's brains daily. Fortunately ,they were not interested in touching a poor , stupid country girl because the heavy make-up ladies were there to shield me from my misfortune.

My story may be like another concubine who has experienced smiling and dancing in a stage and laughing at brainless men or crying for herself in isolation. In those days ,lies and tricks were my toys; becoming a concubine was a childish game with no love and affection ,and I did not know the meaning of self-sacrifice .

However ,my past mistakes could not be justified with these words .I was only 16 years old .I did not understand the content of being a concubine ,and I had no love or sexual experiences .I reviewed my fate and understood my dad's situation; I admired him for allowing Marzieh to live in with us the same room in our society .When I returned home ,my father and Bijan were waiting for me ,while my death and life did not affect my concubines .

I want to tell you a big secret, my concubines' jobs were Cole pollen sellers at the end of Arab's bottomless pit (fake title) too. I had become an important person like Zubeida and no one saw me! Do you believe me!?

Bijan and I decided to marry without any ceremony. Although Bijan said his father had provided him with financial resources, I did not care about the formalities. Professor Kiani liked Bijan and suggested we get married in the Hospital's amphitheater. I asked my dad, who agreed.

Dariush and Nasrin decided to have a wedding ceremony like ours on the same day: my dad, Sahar, Madam, Monsieur, and Iran Joon joined us. Dariush's brother, Jamshid, with his girlfriend Rose, and Dariush's mother, Pouran Khanum, also came. Professor Kiani had bought two simple rings for Bijan and me, he asked Dariush who claimed his mother and Nasrin had bought their wedding rings. Professor Kiani turned his face to my dad and spoke with high respect.

"Dear country's elite professors, Dr. Soheil, we request that you be the first speaker of the wedding ceremony and please perform the ceremony."

I was happy that everyone respected my dad, but my dad asked him to manage our wedding ceremony.

Then professor Kiani spoke.

"Are you ready to become Bijan's wife?"

My answer was positive, and he asked Bijan the same question. Bijan's answer was yes, and he called us husband and wife from now on, and all the residents would be witnesses. He repeated the same question to Nasrin and Dariush and then asked Ana.

"Although, you were already married Abbas, were you ready to remarry Abbas again?"

Ana happily said yes, yes, and Behrouz laughed loudly. Ana spoke.

"Now it is not the laughing time, say yes, then."

Professor Kiani: "Then he should cry."

The teacher's wife, Dr. Nahid, who was also in our group, said: "What, we should cry; why his wife?"

We gave each other gold rings and became spouses. We decided to register the marriage in the office of Professor Kiani's acquaintances. At this time, Madam saw the gold rings and turned to Bijan with a protesting expression, as usual.

"If you love her, you should invest and buy the best ring for her, and if you don't like her, it's better not to take risks and marry her. A man should not be stingy in this matter. If you don't have money, say that the woman will cooperate with you, and if you have, use the money. You should buy the best ring for Neda, and I will lend you money if you don't have it. At the same time, it is financial support for both of you."

Madam was a symbol of a feminine characteristics, shined like a queen with her unique styles, and spoke fluently. Professor turned to Monsieur and said:

"It's like you suffer a lot."

"No, Gohar and I had nothing when we married, but she motivated me to work better, and we succeeded.

She ordered me some items from the first day and gave me a deadline to prepare. I remember that I did not have the money for the ring; she said, come back here when you have money for the wedding ring, then I will marry you. If I wasn't available, find a better woman. I noticed that I could not tolerate losing her, so I borrowed money from my friends and family and bought her a ring she wanted, which he still has."

Madam raised her hand and said:

"It was the best ring when we married."

Professor: "What if he did not come back?"

"He was in love with me, and I knew he would return, but he wasn't serious about working hard enough. I knew that he had potential and needed a motivation.

At this time, Monsieur said:

"Let me give you some advice. I'm not a doctor, but I grew up with street people. Whenever your wife tells you to go shopping, leave immediately because the dangerous situation."

Everyone laughed and looked at Monsieur in surprise. And Professor asked:

"Shopping?

"Yes, when the moon is in Scorpio (an ancient Iranian mythology phrase for the awkward and inappropriate situation), you don't know anything and ask questions, or it's days before the women's period. Oh, oh, oh, you must do what your wife says, otherwise, you will be in jeopardy. Get out of her sight soon. Gohar sends me to buy black peas. It was much better than fighting. I leave her alone immediately, and when I thought she had cooled down, I called her to evaluate the situation. I say, honey, I did not find it, anything else I shall do. If she said OK, it meant she come down, but if she says, how did not you find it, I know still the moon was in Scorpio, and I must continue to look for black peas. Or whenever the situation was awkward, I went to the shop to clean it. It is better not to be at home for a few hours."

Bijan asked in surprise: "Do we have black peas?"

Everyone laughed and said it was an expression to look for something that did not exist. I remember Madam asked Monsieur to buy a loaf of bread or yogurt while we had enough at home. And Iran Joon said, Gohar, black peas!

"I told Neda that there was enough money, we could buy whatever she likes, and I would do it."

While we were laughing and having fun, the mullah of the Harassment office came. I remembered Imam al-Zaman mullah, who wanted to marry me and wrote the petition for Marzieh, a piece of paper in mud, so her vows could be fulfilled. Mullah spoke.

"Hello, as if you asked me to perform a ceremony for the doctors."

It was clear that he knew everything. The cunning

mullah had a political manner and said you asked me to come. All doctors laughed when the Professor spoke.

"Your honor is obligatory, these young doctors are penniless, and they got married yesterday; we brought some sweets. When your child gets better, you must read a marriage verse at my wedding."

It hinted that I treated your son, don't step in my shoes. He did not give up and said:

"Professor, to your regards, they are not halal according to Sharia law."

It was an implicit hint that I know you don't accept my verses and did not read it, and the marriage is not Shariah. In their way, both were persuading each other, and we were spectators. Our professor had a good policy for managing idiots without arguing; he immediately said:

"Bring sweets for Haji Agha. Haji sits next to me and tells me what you want to do on my wedding night."

Our teacher was funny. His wife, Dr. Nahid, laughed and said: "Haji Agha, I must find a husband for myself, and you should read a verse for me too.

"God forbid Mrs. Doctor. It is a sin and disobedience."

"Oh, it is a sin if I don't answer my husband. Very well, behalf of me ladies answer my husband."

We laughed, he noticed nobody buy his words, and said: "With your permission, I will go."

"It is up to you."

In this way, mullah left us alone. I could see the worriedness in my dad's eyes, although he was calm and the concubine issue was over, and I was with them all the time. Some friends arranged a dance party in the cellar room, and Monsieur arranged catering. We went to that room gradually, and This was our wedding party. After a few days, Bijan asked me we buy a ring. Madam said salesperson raises prices when a young couple purchases a wedding ring. We buy, you pay for it. Bijan and Behrouz accepted. Ana and I with Madam and Iran Joon went to a jewelry store and bought our wedding ring, had lunch outside. Nasrin and Pouran Joon bought a beautiful ring for Nasrin, and they all came to our house in the evening.

My dad and Sahar also purchased a beautiful wedding

ring, which indicated that Madam's words were a good motivation. That night, my dad announced his marriage to Sahar, making us incredibly happy. I did not ask anything, but I understood that my dad was not married to Marzieh. I did not want to know anything, either. Sahar showed her ring. My dad was happy.

I wondered why I hesitated to know his story. Everyone had a particular respect for him, and no one asked my dad or me anything about his life story, while I felt that Dariush, Behrouz, and Bijan were full of questions.

Bijan had a very stylish house and suggested living in his home, and his father let him to buy a home too, but I wanted to live near the hospital and my dad, and he agreed to live with us. At my dad's suggestion who was afraid that something would happen to me ,we sold our home when we bought three-story house next to his house, and Madam paid the rest . Each story had a two-bedroom unit .We planned each occupied one floor and the first floor for Madam and Monsieur and Iran Joon and her husband so they could have their place when they came to Tehran .But Ana did not accept that we had separated ,and we moved to the third floor .Ana and Behrouz were in one bedroom, and we had the second bedroom .Dariush ,Nasreen ,and Pouran Joon moved to the second floor .Dariush's brother , Jamshid ,lived in Dariush's apartment with his girlfriend, Rose ,and sometimes they came to our home for dinner. Jamshid and Rose loved each other and were not committed to marriage. They studied computers and worked in the same field. The first floor became the kitchen for all of us and the bedroom of Madam and Iran Joon.

The grocery near the University was expensive than the free market. My dad and Sahar would do the grocery shopping on their way. Pouran Joon cooked meal, and we gathered on the first floor for dinner and take our lunch. This was how I saw my dad every day. He was happier than weeks ago when he heard about my concubine. Our life together was charming. Ana, Nasrin, and I agreed to get pregnant around the same time that our children grew up together.

One night, before Madame, Monsieur, and Iran leave our city, and we were together and chat, Nasrin, who always had a question for my dad, spoke.

"Having a good father is the best blessing. Your daughter is good because she had a good father like you. I still wish I had a father, even though I have a good husband."

My dad was emotional and spoke.

"My dear, my sister and I were children when I lost my father. My mother loved my father and never married. She might not have a chance to get married because she had to feed her hungry children. Although she did not have a skill but had great courage to raise us by working. She was a great woman, and I am proud of her and wish we had inherited her traits."

Sadness squeezed my dad's face. I got up quietly, sat next to him, kissed him, and put my head on his shoulder.

"You are the best dad in the world. You instilled in me the ability of learning without going to school, never complained about your life hardships, and never boosted how great and noble you are. I have everything from you, and I love you very much. If I become a doctor, I owe it to you."

Madam also started praising my dad. I turned to Madam because I had acquired speech freedom and dared to express my opinion from her.

"Thank you for explaining my dad's greatness, and you teaching me the courage and bravery to express my opinion and teaching me friendship. If only one person believed in us, she made us. Otherwise, we will be crushed between the wheels of childish illusory, society's unfair events, and bitter life realities."

Madam was sitting like a queen and smiling. She ended Nasrin's discussion, took everyone to another room with a particular skill, and changed the subject. My dad's sadness was noticeable, and I shared this with Sahar who contacted his old friend's doctor and said, he would visit him soon. I was happy that Sahar was taking care of my dad. The important thing was that they both worked at the same place, went to the same university every day, and kept my dad active. Madam and Monsieur were good at taking us for fun at every opportunity. After a few days, Madam, Monsieur, and Iran Joon went to their town.

At home, I read Behrouz's love poems notebook to Ana, and Bijan noticed my interest in his note. He also made a notebook and asked everyone for the best love poems. He wrote a phrase in that notebook daily. In those days, he read Fereydoun Moshiri's poem who said:

"The most beautiful poem in the world is I love you.

Ask me to say more, I love you and tell me more you love me."

I liked hearing the romantic poetry. We had a sweet life. The surgical residency was complicated and busy. I had nausea for a few days, and I thought it was food poisoning. Bijan looked at me and told.

"I guessed that you are pregnant."

"No, I have IUD."

"You have signs and symptoms of pregnancy."

He was right, and this happened when we set with Ana and Nasrin to get pregnant together, but it doesn't always happen what we want. My pregnancy made everyone happy, especially Bijan. Ana protested that we were supposed to get pregnant so our children would grow up together. Ana and Nasrin decided not to take birth control pills anymore. Behrouz had become happy, but Dariush worried and said we still did not have a stable situation and could not afford the child's expenses because many graduated doctors were unemployed and jobless. If I did not find a job, it would be difficult for Nasrin to work and cover the cost. First, I must find a job, and then she will get pregnant.

Nasrin said that I work and could have a baby. These arguments did not convince Dariush. Pouran Joon was a very understanding woman and did not interfere in this matter and said that whatever you decide is the best. Sometimes she was on Nasrin's side and told Dariush that the woman should be satisfied. The burden of pregnancy and the pains of childbirth are on a woman's body, and he must obey his wife.

Madam had heard about my pregnancy, said she

come sooner. Bijan happily informed his parents, who were abroad for treatment, and they were supposed to come to Iran. Although Ana no longer takes birth control pills, she did not get pregnant, which caused everyone's concern. However, the obstetrician and gynecologist told her that it is normal, and it takes several months for a woman's ovaries to return to their normal state after a long period using the contraceptive pill, and she should be patient. Ana's condition also caused Nasrin to say, well, it may have taken several months for me to get pregnant, but Dariush was unhappy. This conversation dragged on until finally, Dariush gave up, while Nasrin had not taken her pills for several months. Since the day I got pregnant, Bijan believed I should decrease my worktime in the hospital and crocheting and rested more.

My dad agreed with him. I told them I would take sick leave whenever I could not continue working at the hospital. I should keep crocheting skills, especially since I assumed it was a sport for my hands and did not consider it as a work. It was like looking with my eyes, chewing food with my teeth, or hearing sounds with my ears and I did not consider as a work. None of them understood my mental perception, and they gave up when I resisted. I told Bijan that if there is even nothing for us one day, I would still provide a part of our living expenses in this way!

Bijan was surprised and told me that people don't need a tablecloth but need to see a physician. He was right, but unfortunately, luxuries were more critical for a group than their health. Iran Joon or Madam placed only a tiny tablecloth in our house on the coffee table. Unfortunately, people had gold bangles and black teeth, and dental health was less critical than jewelry.

Pouran Joon still accepted orders for tapestries and lived honorably. Nasrin also sewed tapestry with Pouran Joon and Dariush, her charitable deeds were contagious. At the same time, my knitting and her tapestry were not necessary items for the house. When I heard that Bijan's parents were coming, I was anxious, and I told Bijan and Ana that I do not know why I am worried. I thought it might they don't like me. Bijan kissed me and spoke.

"What do you say. They will love you. They are lovely people and will love you as much as I do."

His words were comforting. I was in the last trimester, and we would make a list of names on the nights we were together. My dad's depression had worsened, and I did not know his life history and wondered why he was depressed. Later, I guessed it might refresh his memory of his lovely wife's pregnancy. I asked him several times to let me be with him to his doctor, but he did not accept.

"I must be alone so that I can talk. You can't bear to hear my words."

He was right because I refused whenever he wanted to speak to me. I was afraid to hear some things that I did not like. I don't know why not knowing the matter was more comfortable. My anxiety had increased, and I did not know it was related to pregnancy, Bijan's parents, or my dad's depression. Ana did not get pregnant despite all her efforts, which was incredibly sad. Behrouz used to say that it doesn't matter if we have children, we love each other and will have a romantic life. Madam was upset that Ana did not conceive. Ana went to different doctors, and they all said that they did not find any health problems, and sometimes it takes a long time to get pregnant for an unknown reason.

Finally, Nasrin was pregnant and pleased, but she had terrible morning sickness and couldn't work. Although Dariush was not happy, he did not say anything. When he was alone with me said that he had a difficult life and wanted everything to be ready for his child. I told him that life was never easy, and we
could not have everything together. I felt that Dariush was very lonely. Our intimacy started when I knitted; he did tapestry, and we ignored the people attitudes. Sometimes I would laugh and say, don't be sad, we will always be good friends, and whenever one of us fall apart, the other will take care of the rest. We will stay together, help each other, and not be alone. And it was my fault that I got pregnant, and this chaos started. He was silent.

Madam was supposed to come to Tehran and prepare the baby set for me, and at the same time, we expected

Bijan's parents to return to Iran. Iran Joon always came with Madam. Whenever Iran Joon was in Tehran, he visited Aria and said that Aria was depressed, and she was back and forth between our house and Aria and said Aria always asked how Neda was. Madam stayed on the first floor, but this time they left it for guests and slept in our living room. However, Bijan's parents had a very luxurious house in Tehran. Bijan went to the airport and took them home. I wanted to go with Bijan, who said to stay home, you are pregnant, you will get tired. He was right, I was getting exhausted recently, and the doctor said it was due to iron deficiency. I slept a lot and took iron tablets. When I got home, I would fall asleep on the sofa on the first floor, and my father would come and sit next to me for several hours until I woke up. They did not wake me up for dinner until I woke up. As usual, Pouran Joon prepared dinner, and Bijan bought flowers. Madam and Iran Joon organized the guest rooms, and everything was ready.

Bijan's mother, Setareh Khanum, was a beautiful woman. She looked at me dumbfounded for a few minutes, and I was surprised, and she said, oh my God, you, I see you, how happy I am. Koresh Khan, her husband, was also stunned, and after a long pause, he patted his wife's back to go ahead. She held me in his arms and kissed me. She held and stroked my hand all night and repeated how happy she was to see me. Koroush Khan was a quiet and polite man and hardly spoke. Bijan was pleased when we were alone and said, "you saw how much they love you."

In the kitchen, Madam told Iran Joon how Setareh Khanum was looking at Neda as if she had never seen such a beautiful girl, and we all laughed. While having dinner, Setareh Khanum spoke. How nice you were together. We were alone in the USA, and loneliness looked like a black hole pulling a person inside, even though there were all facilities. It seems like you have a party every night. If we have these numbers around the table, it means we have a particular event party.

They had jet lag, and different time zones was eleven hours and took time they adjusted their sleeping patterns. As usual ,we all left the house daily except Nasrin ,who was sick and exceptionally stayed home.

Madam ,Monsieur ,and Iran Joon were going out .After a few days ,Madam and Nasrin said that Mrs. Setareh seemed very curious because she carefully looked at your photos around the house and had many questions. I laughed and said so what?

She would kiss me a lot when I was at home ,caress my hand ,and look at me. I told Ana, "No one had ever kissed me so much; I wondered how much she kissed me."

"Well ,it is about Bijan's love for you. If it bothers you , tell her to come and kiss me."

Two or three nights passed ,and whenever I sat down , both husband and wife stared at me .Once ,when I fell asleep on the sofa ,Setareh Khanum kissed me from head to toe. At night ,I told Bijan ,and he also kissed me from head to toe and said it was my fault that I did not kiss you well until now .That night he was better than ever in his love game ,and he was wondering why I was surprised by his mother's expression of affection .A few days later ,his mother asked him to visit their house ,and Bijan would go with them .It was late night when Bijan called and said we would stay there because some work had come up. I thought they could do it later!

The next day ,when Bijan returned home, his eyes were red ,as if he hadn't slept or cried a lot ,and he claimed it related to challenging work ,and we went to the hospital , but I was wondering what had happened .Bijan's behavior changed significantly .He did not kiss me .His attitude continued when I asked him for an explanation. He gave me the excuse of catching a cold and that it was too contagious because I was pregnant. One night, I argued with him badly.

"After the day that you were alone with your parents, your behavior changed, it was related to your parents, and you did not hug and kiss me like before."

"Neda Joon, you are in the last months of pregnancy; it is better hugging you less so that nothing happens to you and baby."

"Prescript it for your patients. I know how to take care of myself. Tell me, what happened between you and your parents?"

"I swear that nothing happened."

It was the first time I fought with him. I had become such a tiger to attack him. Ana, who had heard our noise, came to our room in surprise.

"What happened?"

"This gentleman has changed and thinks I am dumb and do not understand. He does not want to tell me what his parents told him."

Ana asked me in surprise.

"What? How has he changed?"

"He doesn't even kiss me properly. He also tries to keep his distance from me in bed."

"What?"

She aggressively turned to Bijan.

"Bijan, is it right?"

I wished that Bijan said no. Those moments passed as if my heart was stopping, and I was going crazy and thought how much I loved him; I wish Bijan would say that Neda made a mistake. His pause was killing me. Bijan lowered his head and said:

"Ana Joon, Neda is in the last months of her pregnancy; I am worried; I don't want anything happen to her."

"What? It means that he does not know the difference between love and annoyance. Bijan, your words are not acceptable at all. If you kiss her, what will happen to her?"

Bijan's face was covered in tears.

"Neda, what do you think? Is it related to his family? Bijan, why are you crying? Tell us what happened."

"Bijan's behavior is related to them because he changed after being alone with them for one night. You tell me it may not be related to them. Interestingly, he did not tell me what happened. His eyes were red, and he claimed he got a cold, and this person was different from before." Ana growled.

"Well, Bijan, what explanation do you have?"

"I have a cold, and I love Neda very much."

"Okay, you love her is acceptable, and she is wrong about your family, and they did not ruin your relationship. Now you hold her in your arms and kiss her."

Bijan held me in his arms like someone was forced to make an unwanted request. I angrily pushed him back and said: "I don't want to hug me like this."

Ana was surprised and spoke.

"Are you okay? What is wrong with you? How did he hug you?"

"Ana, I know what I'm saying; it's ridiculous."

Bijan was kissing my hand and crying.

"I love you, dear, and I wish you knew."

"You wish I do not know you are not the previous Bijan."

At this time, Bijan turned to Ana.

"Let me to be alone, I am sick, and I won't kiss her."

"Okay, you want me to leave you alone. I'm leaving, but I'll be back in an hour to be sure she's okay."

I had become a predatory tiger and wanted to throw out all the evil curses. How could a person change like this? I was sitting on the edge of the bed in my pajamas. Bijan was sitting on the floor, putting his head on my legs, and crying. I have never seen him so upset. My heart was burning for him, and I was sure my guess was correct, and something must have happened between him and his parents, which he wanted to hide it from me.

"Bijan, tell me the truth and don't hide anything from me. Whatever it is, it concerns me, and I must know. I love you very much, and I could not bear you crying. Raise your head and tell me why you are weeping."

"Please give me time, give me time, please. I love you very much. You're pregnant."

I asked in disbelief.

"Is there a third-party woman?"

"You know me very well. I have never loved anyone except you."

"Do you remember when I told you that I became a concubine? You believed me and said it did not matter. We would solve the problem together. Whatever happens, tell me, and we will solve the problem together. We promised that whatever happens in our lives, we will tell each other immediately and not be afraid of difficulties. tell me."

"You remember when I told your dad about your concubine, you got angry and made me promise to tell you whatever happened, but please let me to talk to your father first. Please."

I recognized that issue must be essential. At the same time, I could not bear Bijan's crying. I caressed and kissed his head.

"Very well, Bijan, do not cry; tell me what made you change."

"I do not feel well, give me time, give me time. Please stop and give me some time. I do not feel good. Let me sleep on the floor, I'll tell you."

"Bijan, if you sleep on the floor, that increases our distance. I wanted something else."

Bijan's shoulders were shaking from sobbing. I was worried about him and remembered his sadness was significantly affected when he talked about his parents' deaths, but he was not so disturbed. It must be serious. My heart was broken, and I was upset with myself because I made him upset. I wondered why he was crying. Why was I aggressive with Bijan? His head was on my knee, and I sat quietly, hoping he would calm down and tell me what had happened. I remembered my dad's words that everything could be solved except death. We could solve the problem together, and he could share it with me. He could not suffer alone. Later, Ana told me that Behrouz did not sleep and waited for her worriedly.

"What happened? Did Bijan and Neda fight?

No way, I could not believe it. It is impossible because Bijan loved Neda.

"I was surprised too, and Neda explained that Bijan had changed after he went with his parents to their house. She could not make a mistake, and Bijan cried and asked me to leave them alone. I wish my mom were here. This was the first time I had seen Neda like this. She was furious. I don't know why I am worried; I should call Uncle Soheil."

"This time of night! It could not be good."

"My father always told me that if I had any problems, even if I got a boyfriend and pregnant, I would say to Uncle Soheil first because of his knowledge."

Behrouz insisted that was not good at this time of night. Finally, Ana convinced him that she should my dad. This was Ana's philosophy when facing problems. Ana told me dad that Neda had a fight with Bijan and said Bijan's behavior had changed.

My dad had the key to our house, came immediately, and after a few minutes, Sahar joined them. They sat quietly in the hall, and they occasionally peeked through half-open door of Neda's room. Unlike a few minutes ago, Neda was calmer, but Bijan was still crying, surprisingly, and we could hear their words. The sound of Bijan's cry was terrifying and a sign of a severe problem.

"Neda Joon, I told you that I grew up in my aunt's house because I had no parents. When I saw you, you were the image of a beautiful, lovely, gorgeous, thoughtful woman who was always in my dreams."

Sobbing and crying take away his time to talk. There was silence and fear. We sat in amazement, and Uncle Soheil was standing next to Neda's door and listening to them.

"Am I now different that you saw in your dream?"

"You are even more beautiful than my dream. You are a natural beauty, but."

"But what? I love you and don't care what happened in your past. Do you remember I told you I became a concubine? You said it doesn't matter, let's solve the problem together, now we have the same promise. Nothing is crucial except you, and I am deeply sorry that you had so many problems. I love you anyway. Listen, I don't care about anything but you."

We could hear Bijan's crying and said:

"The regime of the Islamic Republic killed my parents."

Sobbing and crying.

"Before he was killed, my father threw me from the wall between our house in the neighbor's house, and later they handed me over to my aunt."

Crying had cut off Bijan's chance to tell the story.

"I had a sister who disappeared that night. Neda, are you sure about that?"

"That, what?"

"Your father. Is your father Soheil Khan?"

"What?"

"Someone stole you that night. You look just like my mom."

Neda screamed in panic and spoke angrily.

"What are you saying? My father is my father. What do you want to say? No, no, my father is not a thief."

Uncle Soheil and I went to her room.

"Someone may have stolen you from our home."

She screamed: "No, my dad is not a thief."

Uncle Soheil said in a sad voice:

"I'm not a thief."

"Dad, say that you are my dad."

Neda ran to Uncle Soheil and threw herself into his arms when she cried.

"Dad, say, I am your daughter, say something."

Uncle Soheil hugged her, and his tears covered his face.

Bijan was terrified and said:

"All my mother's photos showed your images."

The sad atmosphere filled the room. I objected to Bijan: "How did you say it to my Uncle Soheil?"

Behrouz: "Bijan, what are you saying? It is possible to be a common similarity."

I heard Uncle Soheil's sad voice:

"I did not abduct a child."

Sahar, who was at the threshold of the door, said:

"Bijan Khan, you don't know the truth; you and your mother are not allowed to give such labels to a man who symbolizes humanity, honor, and morality."

That night I was terrified, left her room, and called my mother to come home. My mother assumed that Neda's labor had started. Iran Joon was at Aria's house. In a panicked environment, we all lost our balance. I returned to the room as if Sahar knew something, stood next to Uncle Soheil, and kissed his arm. Neda and Bijan were crying loudly. Neda sat on the bed next to my uncle. I sat next to her and robbed her neck and shoulders. Behrouz looked at me dumbfounded; he thought that uncle Soheil might steal a child, no, it is not possible. Bijan was sitting on the floor with his head in his hands, and his shoulders were shaking from crying. Behrouz brought water for Bijan and sat next to him.

"Bijan, drink some water. Tell me what happened. Many people are similar!"

He had just realized that the matter was more terrifying than a resemblance. It means that Neda is Bijan's sister. At the same time, my mother entered without knowing what
had happened. I said softly in her ear that my mother exploded and said to Bijan:

"It is a shame that you have accused an honest man of theft. We know the whole story, and we even have the necessary evidence, and why did not your mother tell me about it first? Why did you tell her? She is pregnant. Doctor, do you understand?"

Bijan spoke with crying.

"The last time I told her father about the concubine, Neda was angry with me, and we agreed that I would tell her first whenever something happened. I did not want to say it, but Neda was furious and insisted."

Madam said aggressively:

"This was not a minor issue you could manage in this situation. Your mother mismanaged it too. Neda, I will tell you, do not be upset you are pregnant. Your father is an honorable man."

"My dear, I encountered your rejection whenever I wanted to talk to you, and I did not know what to do and waiting for you to ask me how the story was." Uncle Sohei used to say to Neda who was crying:

"Dad, say that you are my father. No one is my father except you."

Neda was in denial, running away from the bitter truth. It was a terrible night. My parents and Sahar knew everything and supported Uncle Soheil. Bijan is crying hard. No one slept that night.

My mother forced Neda to lie down on her bed. Uncle

Soheil sat next to Neda's bed and held her hand. It was morning when Neda fell asleep. One of my mother's characteristics was that when she got angry with someone, she would fight with him without any consideration. But I was sure that Bijan had no choice except to tell her the truth because he could not be indifferent to her request. Bijan was upset, and my mother argued with him. Why did he use Uncle Soheil's name?

I was shocked to hear that Neda was not Uncle Soheil's daughter. I was angry with my parents for not telling me about such an important matter. I was about to explode, and the only way to through my anger toward my parents. When Neda fell asleep, I argued with my parents and blamed them, then I went to my room and cried in Behrouz's arms. Behrouz wondered how this incident would damage
the Neda and Bijan's life. My mother used to yell at Bijan as if she were yelling at a child. Behrouz did not know how to calm me down. I fell asleep and woke up from the sound of the bed when Behrouz woke up. Behrouz spoke.

"You rest, I will go to the hospital and report that you are sick, and it is better to ask Bijan to stay at home with this state of mind, and of course, Neda too."

"Yes, all three of us were sick."

I remembered that Neda might wake up and jump out of my bed.

"Where?"

"Neda"

"You sleep. I will check and tell you if she wakes up."

"No."

I went to her room, and Neda was asleep. That night, Uncle Soheil and my mother did not sleep and stayed in her room. My father, Bijan, and Sahar were sleeping on the sofa in the hall. I returned to my room quietly. I knew that we had a difficult day ahead. Sahar woke up and called the university that they were not attending and asked other professors to run their classes. Dariush came upstairs because he heard the noises of walking at night and supposed Neda's labor had started. He was shocked when he found out about her story and said, I am not going

to the hospital either. But Behrouz said he should go to the
hospital to cover the work of Ana, Neda, and Bijan.
Dariush had the utmost respect for Uncle Soheil. He always
said how lucky you are to have a good father, and that day
he was dumbfounded; however, it was hardly read his
thoughts from his eyes.

We had appointment with a gynecologist, I asked
Behrouz to cancel it. He wanted to reschedule it, but I
asked him to postpone it. Although, I tried all the ways to
be pregnant, but the Neda issue shadowed my importance
wishes and reduced it to nothing. Uncle Soheil was in the
hall and suggested my mother go down and talk to Mrs.
Setareh, and it was better not to say anything to Neda at
this stage. Pouran Joon came up. Dariush said something in
his mother's ear, and she did not ask any questions. It was
clear that she knew everything. Dariush went down to
have breakfast, returned, and said that Mrs. Setareh had
woken up. My father and mother went downstairs, and
Mrs. Setareh was unaware that Bijan had told her about
such an important matter. In the meantime, Neda woke up
and went to the bathroom, her face full of tears. I sat on the
edge of her bed. Uncle Soheil sat on the other side, and
Sahar sat on the floor. Neda returned to her bed, put her
head on my shoulder, held uncle Soheil's hand, cried
quietly, and said calmly.

"You are my father."

She was crying and continued.

"I wish I had known sooner."

"Neda Joon, nothing is important but your health. No
matter what happens, everything will be fine."

Bijan came to the room and stood in front of us with
tears in his eyes. Sahar left the room so that Bijan could
have privacy. In the meantime, my parents went
downstairs to talk to Mrs. Stareh, and later my father told
us that my mother behaved aggressively with them and
started a riot. They were horrified to learn that Bijan had
told Neda and even said that Uncle Soheil might have
stolen Neda. They were agitated. My mother told them
that innocent Neda captured Soheil Khan, and this man
ruined his life to take care of Neda without any

responsibility. How did you allow yourself to accuse him
of child abduction?

Mrs. Setareh did not think that Bijan would tell Nada,
did not expect my mother's harshly behavior and were
ashamed of the situation. She wanted to go to their house,
but her husband said they would stay until they solved the
problem. It was their mistake to tell Bijan that they should
compensate themselves. My mother had asked them not to
talk to Nada unless she was present and could calm her
down, and they had agreed.

Pouran Joon, who heard my mother's argument with
our guests and came upstairs, pointed to Bijan, dragged
him out of the room, and told him to go downstairs. Bijan
was helpless, and his mother told him.

"We told you not to say anything to Neda for now."

"She noticed from my attitude that something had
happened, and he argued with me. If I did not speak, the
fight would have continued."

"It was my fault; I wish I did not say anything." She
was regrated.

"As a head of a family, you should say it to Soheil
Khan or me first because they are young, brilliant, and
unique in university lessons, but they do not have our
experiences. Bijan could not tolerate this much pain for
himself and Neda. We should think about what will calm
her down. It would be better for Neda if Bijan leave this
city. It may be better to send Neda to America."

"Bijan will become a surgeon soon; if he leaves, he will
lose all these years." Mrs. Setareh spoke.

My mother says aggressively:

"Three or four years is not crucial compared to Neda's
situation. Intellectual Neda without any education, is
dearer to me than the entire world; her ability is worth the
world. What was Neda's name, or do you have a photo or
proof?"

"Her name was Bahareh, and she looked like my sister
when she was pregnant with her. I have his childhood
photos."

"First, you should have brought a photo and proof
you would have raised the issue."

My dad asked them: "It is better to bring the photos for us to see. Where was your sister's home?"

They said the address., while my mother and father looked at each other but did not say anything.

Bijan: "Did you know our address?"

"No, I just wanted to know. What had happened to your sister's house."

"We sold it with difficulty and left the money for Bijan."

They planned to show her photos the same day and they did. This was my mother report and Pouran Joon was wondering about to take care of whom when I was with Neda. Neda sat between Uncle Soheil and me, and she cried when her head was on my shoulder. Bijan entered the room with her mother, and my mother followed them. When they arrived, Neda turned her head on Uncle Soheil's shoulder. We were sad and suffered. My mother sat next to me and said: "Neda Joon, you should rest and take care of your health."

My father brought a breakfast tray for Neda, and when my mother tried to help Neda to eat it, Bijan and his mother stood silently.

"I am tired; I want to sleep." Neda said and refused to eat breakfast.

We got up from her bed. My mother said:

"Nothing happened. It is possible that my mother or my father were friends with someone else, so we did not know Arman was my brother when we married."

Neda pulled the blanket over his head and said:

"I want to sleep."

My mother remained silent, sitting on the edge of the bed. I sat on the floor next to my uncle Soheil and Sahar. Deadly silence reigned in the room. Behrouz had returned from the hospital and signaled to Bijan to go out. My mother and Bijan went out of the room as if my mother had told Bijan that it was better for him not to be in front of Neda and go to the hospital. But Bijan looked sick, went downstairs, and slept there.

That day, Behrouz told our story to Professor Kiani loved Bijan very much and used to say he was his son.

It was noon when Dariush, who was worried, came home. Dariush was close to Neda. He came to her room and stayed by her bed for an hour, but he did not say any words and was silent. It was noticeable his silent meant a lot about humanity, love, kindness, and care. Dariush was undoubtedly in love with Nasreen and was happy with his marriage, but he had unique feelings for Neda, like a loyal friend. Dariush was silent and did not take his gaze from Neda as if he wanted to register even the sound of her breathing in his eyes. Uncle Soheil, quiet, sad, and silent, sometimes looked at Dariush. Sahar did not stay away from Uncle Soheil for a moment.

It was afternoon, Professor Kiani came to our house to see Bijan and Neda without asking any questions. He also looked distraught; although he tried to maintain his appearance, but his face expression was different. He sat on the edge of her bed and said, how is our pretty girl? Neda did not answer. He greeted Uncle Soheil, drowned in the silence as if the magician had sewn silence on everyone's lips. He was there for a few minutes and left the room. I got up to go with him. He pointed out that he would return. He called his psychiatrist friend and asked him to come to our home. The psychiatrist came to her room with the professor, stood for a few minutes, and called Neda by name, but she did not respond, and he left the room. In the hall, he told us that she was in shock it was better not to crowd around her. Bijan had asked him what he should do to make Neda more comfortable so that he could treat her like before or leave the town. The psychiatrist told him to stay here but not go to her room too much so that she could bear this shock and prescribed a medicine that would not harm the baby during at this stage. He suggested not making the issue a big problem. Professor Kiani told Bijan that none of us should worry about the hospital. It was a blessing that he understood our situation. Neda suffered severe depression that dragged uncle Soheil and me with her.

Mrs. Setareh brought her sister and Neda's childhood photos. Uncle Soheil approved her photos, told them about finding Neda and his efforts to find her parents, and referred to the police unsuccessfully. Although, my mother had already told them all the details. Mrs. Setareh said her sister had a black mole on her neck like Neda and showed her mother's photo. The images showed that Neda looked exactly like her mother. Uncle Soheil told them he had kept her dress all these years; Sahar brought it and showed it to them.

On that day, Iran Joon came to pick up her luggage because they were supposed to go to their city at night. Aria and her father were waiting for Iran Joon in his car. Since Neda and Bijan married, Aria moved out of our neighborhood and never came to our home. Iran Joon told them what had happened and asked her husband to postpone their trip. We all knew very well that Iran Joon loves Neda very much. Iran Joon also joined us. Sometimes she came out of her room and talked to my mother. My mother and Iran Joon understood and supported each other very well. We knew that Aria was in love with a married woman.

Only his father, Iran Joon, and my mother knew his story, but Aria had asked them not to say anything to anyone. No matter how much his father insisted, he did not accept dating girls. Aria was upset and cried after learning about Neda. His father said understanding him and what love means. Aria told his father that suffering because of her, and cried for every woman fate in this country and remembered his mother. They went to their homes and waited for Iran Joon's call. His father suggested drinking alcoholic beverages that might calm them down. Aria said nothing calms me down, not pills, not alcohol, not even death. Nima Khan cried and drink, while Aria prepared meal and asked him to eat something before drinking. Both sat sadly and reviewed their past. Iran Joon told us this story by quoting Nima Khan. In those moments, Iran Joon was restless in our house. Bijan asked professor Kiani.

"Is it better to leave the city?"

"It is better to stay, face reality, deal with it, and get help from a psychologist or a psychiatrist."

My condition was not better than Bijan's. Seeing Neda in that situation killed me. I never knew that Neda was the most important person in my life. Her crying was heart breaking. I hate my mother for not telling me about Neda. To be the first student, and pregnant were no longer critical to me compared with Neda's situation. I saw how great sorrows make a person forget all other sorrows or how a greater love makes all loves fail. I used to read a poem that Behrouz always reads.

"My beloved's sadness destroyed my flight wings and feathers."

I sat next to Neda but could not find anything to say despite we always talking. We were crying in silence. That night, I thought that Neda and Bijan's fight was sad, but later I found out what real tragedy is. We were sad and refused to talk. I wished to suffer Neda's pain. Behrouz tried to calm me down.

Uncle Soheil lost weight, and his depression intensified. Aunty Zohreh found out about the issue and suggested Neda leave Tehran to US, and she accepted her child. Zohreh and Uncle Soheil's friend, Arash, asked a lawyer to apply for Nada's visa.

Neda spoke a few sentences in the first day only. She rested on her bed, did not look at anyone, and did not eat and talk. Iran Joon fed her by force. Even my mother and Iran Joon could not help her. Professor Kiani reported that Neda's diagnosis was pregnancy complex.

Those days, Bijan and I read Uncle Soheil's diary, and we cried. Later, Behrouz said that he read his diary with Bijan and Dariush. Even though we were not feeling well, we went back to the hospital because Dariush and Behrouz covered ours. I returned to work on and off. Bijan had lost weight. He often stayed at home and blamed himself. I could understand why my mother was so angry and argued with Bijan. This was something other than what we learned in the books. It took me a long time to understand why my mother had not told me about such an important matter. In that crisis, I did not recognize that I should not blame her. It was beyond my tolerance to bear this pain. And it is better than I did not know. Otherwise, I would be upset like Bijan, and I could not hold myself and not tell Nada about it.

Professor Kiani's friends, psychiatrists, psychologists, regularly visited Neda and tried to have an open communicated. Neda was in the silence stage. They said it takes time for the medication to be effective. Uncle Soheil did not go to university anymore, and the doctor prescribed him anti-depressants. He sat by Neda's bed for hours and talked to her even though she did not respond.

Uncle kept repeating that Neda must take care of herself and that issue was unimportant. All of us who got married might be siblings in a society that did not consider morals and ethics seriously and have a relationship with a third party. It might not discover which child belongs to whom. There may or may not be a similarity between two people from two corners of the world whose parents were never in contact with each other. Uncle Soheil was trying to turn off the fire that burned Neda and covered its most brutal event. Finally, the psychiatrist could communicate with her on one of those days.

Neda told him, now I understand why my dad's matters was above of my bed, and he let Marzieh live with us without any relationship and intimacy; he wasted his life for me. The psychiatrist said no, he improved his life because of you, loves his daughter, did his best, and became your father. Your happiness is his happiness, and not eating hurts him. She did eat that night. She had not taken a bath for almost two weeks. Even though we cleaned her with a wet towel daily, she needed to bathe. That day she bathed with me. We were happy, but her doctor said we should be more careful because self-destruction is higher at this stage.

It was a time to think about the depth of this social problem and the street children's destinations. They are the victim of their parents' negligence and should pay retribution for another's fault. It is more unfortunate that a parent did not make a mistake. From then on, when I saw the wandering street children, I visualized the innocent Neda who mourn in the black hole with a ghostly life and an unknown future. Knowledgeable Uncle Soheil analyzed every problem from different dimensions and explained everything clearly. One of those nights when

Neda was not with us, I asked:

"What do you think and how we could help her in this situation?"

"Siblings marriage was in Sweden and other countries, although it has recently been banned. The secret and illegal intercourse of first-degree relatives and the result of pregnancy are like siblings' marriage. It was painful when students suffering toxic shame and saying my father or brother was my child's father in private. The one who made a mistake should be ashamed, not these innocents who carry the outcomes, and under the pressure of this problem, they lose their future. Concealment is caused the lying in our society. Because the honor and reputation taboos prevent telling the truth, and as a result, many problems still need to be solved, as if everyone sweeps the dust under the carpet and avoids cleaning. All issues should be analyzed and sought solutions. The people created the law to improve human life, not to have a leash around their necks to drag them here and there or to hang with it. The same is a marriage law and having children. It is essential not to add new pain to an issue when it happens without the necessary knowledge. Imagine if Nadav and Bijan were in Sweden or a European country; no one would be so scared, not even Neda. This has happened, and it should be solved with appropriate tactics. She should learn that her and her child's health is essential. If she likes having a child, that is fine, if she does not, I will raise the innocent child. I will be okay with her decision. I always told her that only death has no cure. We should consider the best solutions and solve the problem. Later, we should not blame ourselves for the decision if we will realize that the result was not the best."

My mother approved Uncle Soheil.

"You have an exceptional insight that I asked Ana always to ask you first."

Behrouz: "Monsieur can help too."

"No, no one is better than Soheil Khan. First, tell Soheil Khan, then me and Iran. Her father is a good person, but he is overly optimistic."

Uncle Soheil never blamed Bijan and always looked for

a solution. Then I asked him about the street children.

"The vast dimensions of this social disaster are long-standing. A country needs a plan for population growth, should know the population growth, and plan to anticipate their needs, including nutrition, health, school, education, work, housing, etc. It is the same way one gets pregnant and needs a particular set. Your mother is here to prepare the baby set for the basic needs of a newborn baby.

All aspects of having a baby require a plan. These helpless wander street children have no plans, and they are target of greedy charlatan people. They are society's victims, and this vicious cycle continues. This is one of the thousands of issues these children face."

That night, in the continuation of the conversation, my mother decided to talk to Nada to find out about Nada's decision. Uncle Soheil told Neda that she was wise and could decide and does not worry about anything else. On one of these days, when Neda was with Uncle Soheil and me, she asked her dad about her story. It was the first time that Nada talked about this issue. Despite her reluctance in the past, Neda still trusted her dad and was closest to him. Uncle Soheil explained:

"Zohreh and I had decided to leave the country. I owed a debt and went to my friend Masoud's house to repay it, because I could reach him by phone, and no one was at his home. On my return, I heard a gunshot. I moved to an auxiliary road and hid behind a tree until the shooting stopped. Those days in Tehran, the Islamic regime raided people's houses and killed those who spoke against Khomeini's dictatorship. That night, I knew they would arrest or kill a few more people. I wanted to protect myself. Regime killed my brother-in-aw, Soroush, and my wife. Zohreh was left with two small children. We had planned to leave Iran. I was not in a good state of mind. While I waited in the dark area, suddenly, I felt something moving next to my leg. I was scared at first, then bent down there; there was a little girl who was wet and cold. I hugged her and wrapped my coat around her."

"I was that little girl."

"Yes, my love, that beautiful little girl was you. I did

not know what to do that night; I took you home with me, and the next day I looked for your parents and could not find them. I went with one of my relatives Hossein Agha and my friend to the local grocers and the police station and asked if anyone was looking for a little girl with these characteristics. No matter what we did, we could not find your parents. When we came to Tehran, Monsieur and I searched again for a trace of your family, which was unsuccessful. When Mrs. Setareh gave me the date that this painful tragedy happened to your parents, and comparing your address and seeing your photos, I was sure that you were their dear daughter.

We even visited your previous home address with Mrs. Setareh, Koroush, and Arman. The buildings changed, but they had photos of your home. Your mother or father tried to keep you away from home that night and left you alone accidentally."

Neda listened calmly and I cried. My uncle's voice was sad. I remembered that Uncle Soheil went out with Bijan, his parents, and my father in those days.

"Do you remember the first time Madam, Iran Joon, and Arman came to our home, and we were sitting in the yard? I was very sick, losing weight, and the doctor said I had cancer; I thought I might die, and you do not know what happened. That night, I told them my life story and gave them my handwriting notebook. You will have some support if something happens to me. You were only 14-15 years old and happy to come with Ana to Tehran. I did not want to ruin your happiness. When I came to Tehran, Arman and I went to the police station to see police officers Shahrukh and Payam, who knew your case from the beginning, but they were no longer there. When I wanted to talk to you, you refused."

"Daddy, so you had a wife, and she was killed like my mother because Bijan told me they killed his mother."

She had a strange voice, put her head on my shoulder, and looked at her dad. I thought her pain was so deep that she could not even cry, and my tears fell silently, and I feared she would not know I was crying. Neda asked her dad about Marzieh.

"I saw her in the street one rainy night and told her to come to our home, I did not expect her to stay with us, but I could not kick her out. I thought you were a little girl; it might be better if a woman cared for you at home. I had no opinion of her and forced myself to live because of you. You gave me the motivation to survive. We had a humiliating situation. I could not and wanted to work before you go to school. I used to live with the money left over from selling my house and car and Masoud until Marzieh joined us. Marzieh gave birth to Sohrab, and I got you a birth certificate and sent you to school and work when you were in school.

You did well in school until you got sick and did not want to go to school anymore. I noticed that your learning ability is much better than in those schools, and then you went to Ana's, which was better than staying home." At the same time ,I was thinking ,did Uncle Soheil know what happened at school that day and why she got sick? For the first time ,I learned not to talk .Of course ,after everyone said that Bijan made the mistake of telling Neda ,I thought I should not say everything I knew. I hated my statues. We grow up to understand better and hide more! I did not like those secrets and considerations. Were those considerations constructive or destructive? I hated my parents. I did not understand that the pain caused this anger and irritation. If they told me and I knew Neda is not my uncle s daughter, how would I know she had a brother? I was hurt and shocked by this incident and enduring post-syndrome stress. But Neda's pain was so deep that no one saw my pain and did not consider it, not even me and my mother. I was not feeling well and may be as a witness suffering more pain, like a mother who saw her child fall. After a few minutes, the child is quiet and continues playing, but the mother is still upset. My relationship with Neda was not a mother and child relationship, but she was not just a friend to me. I wondered why I did not recognize it earlier. I should see a psychologist and have anger management. That night Uncle Soheil talked to Neda.

"Bijan has been hurt as much as you. Please talk to him."

"I was mad at him for accusing you of stealing me.

"Is not Bijan fault. You are both victims of the autocratic regime's crimes. Do not be upset and ignore what he said."

Neda crying:

"Thank you, daddy, for what you said about Bijan; I was angry with him and simultaneously worried about him."

I did not know any word to say and comfort her. We always said that I was the one who could express myself easily, but now everything has turned around. Neda asked her dad about talking to Bijan.

"He was hurt. I could speak to him if you want. It is an exceptional unwanted situation and should be managed wisely so you get hurt less and learn to manage it."

Neda wanted to talk to Bijan.

"I will send Bijan up so that you can talk to him."

Uncle Soheil left us and then I left her alone after Bijan came. Uncle Soheil suggested Neda to talk to Bijan, and I admired Neda's courage to accept his offer. Later, Neda explained to me.

"I told him my dad had taught me that whatever happened was just an incident and we should not blame ourselves. My dad is not upset with you and said you were hurt as much as I hurt. I still love you, but this time like a brother, not a husband. We need time to get over this stage. I decided to leave Iran and raise my child alone. I want to be like my dad, he was the best in the world, and I still love him more than anyone. I love my child and promise to do my best for him. My dad helps me; he has right to be tired of all my trouble, because he has wasted his life for me, I will do the best for my child alone."

Bijan cried and spoke.

"I wish I had your courage and will do everything I can for you. I would not know what I want or what should be done. It is tough to believe I lost my love, wife, and child. I am entirely a loser. It is hard for me to be selfish and want you to stay. It is difficult for me to lose my sister as if all my hopes and all things have been destroyed at once; I am left under all the ruins. I do not know how to be,

I am no longer a good doctor longing for everything I had, and it is no longer mine; I do not know what to say."

"I understand you, but what happened cannot be changed; I must go so that you can bear it better; stay in this house; at least Ana, Behrouz, and Dariush are here to take care of you. I miss you all at once. I must go and take care of my child. Again, the burden is on my dad's shoulders. What would have happened if he were not in my life? I want to see our parents' home together, and do I remember something from my childhood?"

"I have gone there twice since my mother told me, but I did not remember anything, even the buildings had changed. At that time, our house was one story; now, it is a multi-story building. The quiet residential area converted to an apartment building, and you were much younger than me, you don't remember it."

"I will go with my dad and want to see you more these days."

Bijan put my hand on his face which was wet from his tears and said we should understand that everything was gone with the wind, and we could not control and bring it back what we lost, and we must accept the impossible. I went to the ground floor; Aria and his father were at our home to pick up Iran Joon. Iran Joon had invited them inside Nima Khan was saying to Uncle Soheil.

"Aria has been in love with Neda since she was a child. When Neda was accepted to the medical school, I told Aria not to say anything until he got his degree and then proposed to Neda. She felt in love with Bijan and married him. At that time, Aria asked us never to say anything about his love. He heard about Neda, and it might leave this country. I came to tell you that Aria still is in love with Neda, we decided to see you."

Uncle Soheil looked at him and wondered what he had heard. Before anyone could say a word, Aria spoke:

"My father worked hard to raise me, and I owe everything I have to my father. I was in love with Neda since seventeen when she was a little girl, and she came to our shop to buy yarn, but I never had a chance to tell her. I followed my father, advice not to say anything, continue my education, and then propose. When I heard that Neda got married, and I never wanted her to know how much I loved her. I accepted everything. Please tell her that I love her and her child."

Uncle Soheil looked at him with surprise and said:

"My dear, Neda passed along a life difficult phase and decided to leave here."

Aria, who had enough skills in negotiation, or because of his love intensity and did not want to lose any opportunity, took control of the conversation, and said:

"I do not want to miss this last chance; I heard that she wants to leave, so I came tonight to beg and tell you that I love Neda. I am ready to go with her anywhere she wants and live with her at any cost. I do not expect help from anyone."

"Now, I could not tell her anything."

"It is better to tell her now that she knows I am with her to the end of the world, and I love her child too. And nothing matters to me. I work and provide everything for her."

He had made up his mind and came to talk with a specific purpose. This conversation happened in the presence of Bijan's family and at the same time when Neda and Bijan were speaking in her room upstairs. At the same time, Neda and Bijan joined us. As soon as Neda sat down, Aria immediately said.

"I came here to say that I have loved you since you were a child, and I still love you. I promise to do everything in my power to make you happy. I wanted to finish my studies and prepared everything for you, but you got married. I want you to know I was, and I am in love with you. I will love your child and come with you wherever you want."

Neda looked tired and watched Aria with astonishment. After a pause, Aria left without waiting for an answer or saying goodbye. We were all shocked when Nima Khan got up and calmly said.

"I praised my son. Yes, he loves you, and I am sure he will be the best husband and father."

My mother invited him to stay for dinner, but he

refused. Iran Joon went with him to the door, returned, and joined Pouran Joon and Nasrin, who was in the kitchen prepared dinner. My mother said.

"Aria is a worthy boy, and I love him very much."

Bijan was lost in thought and did not say anything. My mother broke the silence and said Arman did you buy a video? I was sure that she wanted to change the atmosphere. That night, after several nights, we were all around the dinner table except Behrouz, who was at work. After dinner, Neda kissed Mrs. Setareh and spoke.

"I talked to my dad and leaving here; as always, my burden is on my father's shoulders. I know my parents were killed, but I love my dad very much; I always know him as my father, and everything I have is from him. He tried to talk to me, I walked away from him."

Uncle Soheil was silent, and Sahar said:

"Soheil told me that we would go with Neda, do not worry; I will take care of her and her baby."

"I asked my dad do not leave me alone until I gave birth to my child."

"Neda Joon, you are more important to me than anything else, do not worry. Zohreh is waiting for us."

In those days, they were looking for their passports. Mrs. Setareh did not say anything; I noticed she looked like Neda for the first time.

"I know my name is Bahareh, but I like to keep Neda."

I could not bear no one could see me, not even my mom. I said:

"Uncle Soheil, what will happen to me without Neda?"

My mother had just noticed my pain and spoke.

"Do you want to go with Neda? If Soheil Khan says that studying is unimportant, it means it is not."

"What should I do with Behrouz?

I was restless and had excuses and hated everything. Uncle Soheil said:

"My dear, talk to Behrouz and see what you want to do."

Those days, Uncle Soheil called Nader in Germany and asked for an invitation. However, uncle Soheil thought we should not rush because a long trip for pregnant women

may be dangerous. In addition, they planned my mother
and Iran Joon travel with Neda and uncle Soheil to Turkey
or Germany by car; when the visa to America is ready,
Sahar and my father will go by plane.

My father will return to Tehran in their vehicle. It was
hard for me to lose Neda. Neda said: "I never thought I
would be separated from you. I remembered how sad I
was when you wanted to come to Tehran, and it hurts me
being away from you now, but with my current situation ,I
have no choice."

My mother had noticed our sadness ,but the Neda
issue had happened so quickly that it had affected
everything. After dinner, Neda said.

"I am tired and want to sleep. I talked to Bijan tonight;
I still love him now like a brother."

She kissed my uncle, and as usual, Iran Joon followed
her such a shadow. Professor Kiani sometimes came to our
home and had lunch or dinner with us. He had a particular
respect for Uncle Soheil. He had become much closer to us
than before. Of course, he was worried about Bijan and
referred him and me to a psychologist.

Since the psychologist and psychiatrist had told us that
the rate of suicide is more at this stage, no matter what
Nada said, I trembled that she might commit suicide and
told us her last will. Eighter Iran Joon or all of us do not
leave her alone.

In the absence of Neda, we spoke about Aria. Aria was
a handsome man who had finished engineering. Since our
school years were long and we still needed a job and
income. He had entered the job market early while he was
a student. He worked in consulting engineering companies.

I remember that Iran Joon said Aria came to Tehran
because of Neda, but at that time, we did not take the issue
seriously, and Neda was also incredibly young. Iran Joon
used to say that whenever I tell Aria to get married, she
says no, I am still in love with her, and it is not fair to ruin
another girl's life by lying or pretending to love her.

Whenever I can free myself from the trap of that love, I
think about marriage. After graduation, Aria opened her
own company and was phenomenally successful. My

mother went to his home and told me about his high-end living style. It was the first time I saw him speak like that, while Neda and I always thought Aria was a handsome, shy, and quiet boy. I told my dad I liked Aria who spoke decisively and did not wait for anyone. He knew what he wanted and was ready to take the necessary risk. My father also confirmed that Aria did the right thing, and a man should have the courage to speak out and not miss the opportunity. Dariush was silent as always.

Mrs. Setareh asked everyone.

"What is your relationship with Aria?"

"We are all friends, love each other without having a family relationship. Indeed, it was good that we were intimate and were not worried about relationships or formality. Iran Joon was like my mother, and Uncle Soheil was the closest to me.

Dariush, Pouran Joon, and Nasrin became our family members. Uncle Soheil was the center; my father did not play an active role, but my mother is a controller and undoubtedly played a key role and did not let the reins of work be left out her hands. My father and Iran Joon were my mother's auxiliary forces."

One day we went out with Neda to see her parents' house. Mrs. Setareh gave us their house photos and said that the home entrance was on the street, and the backyard was adjacent to the backyard of several neighbors. On the night of the shooting, her mother's body was found on the street, and her father's body was inside the house who were killed by gunshots. It might be that her mother tried to keep the child out of the guards' reach, left her child on the street, and returned to save her son. At the same time, their father dropped Bijan at the neighbor's house to be safe from the mercenaries and went back inside the building where he was shot. My uncle Soheil knocked on the houses in an alley behind their house. Neda was looking dumbfounded.

There was no trace of the tree where Uncle Soheil had found her. The Islamic regime had also cut down the old trees in that area. Bijan had been there before and was looking at Neda. My parents and uncle Soheil were

standing by Neda. I was amazed by this lousy luck of
Neda's fate, thought that if her parents had not died, she
would have had a good life, she never had come to our
city, and I would never have seen her. Neda's dignity was
hereditary. Neda turned to Uncle Soheil and said:

"The nightmare was I got a cold and grabbed yours.
Was I able to record the memory of that time in my mind?"

She immediately continued:

"I don't want to see this place anymore. It is near Mrs.
Nilofar's house. Let we go there. I have not visited her and
the shop manager for a long time."

We all went to Mrs. Nilofar's house together. She
kindly invited us inside. He had a luxurious home and a
good lifestyle.

"Do you remember one day you offered me knitting on
the bus? We built a workshop with that income for
children."

"Please tell me if you need help."

"No, I came to thank you before I am leaving your city,
but your good memory is always with me."

"Where?"

"I studied and became a doctor, and I am pregnant. I
planned to go to America or a foreign country. I just came
to thank you and say goodbye."

Mrs. Niloufar was appreciative that she remembered
her. We went she say goodbye to the shop manager. His
coworker was cleaning the shop. Neda's eyes stared at the
corner of the shop and spoke. "Where is your boss?"

The young boy with tears in his eyes said.

"He died. He had an automobile accident while
coming from the other side of the street. He was my
brother."

"What? You always said he is my boss."

Meanwhile, Neda went to the corner of the shop and
said:

"The tablecloths are here. You told me you sold them."

"My mother said to buy them from you."

"What, your mother?"

"Yes, my mother."

A picture of Mrs. Niloufar was on the storage shelf.

"You had fewer customers."

"Whenever my mother goes somewhere, she takes one of these as a gift."

Neda sat on a chair, rested her head on her hand, and gazed at him. We just discovered that the lady asked her sons to buy her handcrafts and how a woman's kindness had created hope for someone. We were amazed by so many contradictions in the society, the great virtues of innocent people, and the evils of ignorance, madness, and oppression of the religious regime. We praised pious people's integrity and cursed religious people's ignorance and madness.

We returned home. There was a car at the door. My father said: "It is Aria's car, he asked Soheil Khan to travel with his car, which has three rows of seats, and Neda can rest better, and but he refused. Aria left his car there. Soheil Khan, please accept it, and if it bothers you, I will buy the car, return it, and give it back to him."

Uncle Soheil did not say anything. Aria transferred the car registration under Uncle Soheil's name so they would not have any problems during the trip without saying anything. Neda and Uncle Soheil's passports were issued with new family names with help of my father's family who know someone in the passport office.

Neda's job in her passport was housewife, and my uncle's job was as a worker. Uncle Soheil returned to the university for one day, and all the students' work was with Sahar, who calmly compensated for her husband. Uncle Soheil submitted his resignation, but the dean did not accept it and said here is your home, and we will wait for you to return.

The last nights when Neda was in Iran, I slept in her bed; we talked, reviewed our memories, laughed, and cried. We promised to be together wherever we were, and we read Uncle Soheil's diary, the country's elite professor at Tehran University, and we cried. Now that I got to know Bijan and
Neda better, Uncle Soheil is a holy man, and I understand why everyone respected him sincerely. On the day of the trip, Neda hugged and kissed Mrs. Setareh while crying.

"You are my niece. Count on us if you need anything."
Koresh Khan kissed Neda.

"We are relatives. I love you and Bijan, and we are
interested in seeing you more."

Seeing Bijan hugging Neda and crying was difficult.
When we were outside the house around the car, Aria
came with his father in a stylish sports car and brought Iran
Joon's suitcase. Nima Khan said goodbye to Uncle Soheil
and wished them a good trip. But Aria with a dark
sunglass was standing next to his car. Neda thanked him
for his car and spoke.

"Don't want to say goodbye to me?"

Aria, after a long pause in a manly voice said.

"We never have goodbye; I am with you."

Then he left there before Neda left. Neda left Tehran
with Uncle Soheil, my mother, and Iran Joon. The house
was sad after them. Let us go back to the diary of uncle
Soheil ,one of the country's elite university professors ,and
see what the Islamic regime did with him.

CHAPTER 5, SOHEIL

Zohreh was one year, and I was four years old when we lost our father in a car accident. My mother talked about him with respect and love and said he was a great man. My mother was 24 when she faced the bitter truth that she had to carry the burden of life on her own. There was not any social support for my mother. Even one of his wealthy relatives willingly adopted us if our mother would never see us again. My mother told him that my children are my husband's most precious relic and lost their father, but their mother is still alive. She worked hard and saved our lives from poverty but sacrificed her health. She suffered from joint deformity rheumatism. I started teaching and tutoring math in high schools and private students when I was 15 years old, which helped my mother. Eventually, my sister and I went to the university. We were both distinguished students. At 22, I received my master's degree with the highest rank, and Tehran University hired me as a professor assistant. At the same time, I was student and employee of the same University.

At 24, I got a Ph.D. in physics and math and became a professor at the University of Tehran. In 1979, the Shah of Iran awarded me a gold medal. The University installed my picture with the Shah at my office, and the photographs were published in Iranian magazines. As soon as I have a stable job, I bought a small house on Amirabad Street near the University of Tehran with a bank loan and lived there with my mother and my sister.

Zohreh was a student who met Soroush and loved him. I met Soroush at her request. He was a self-made worthy man and passed his last residency year. The only disadvantage was that he was a political activist before. I shared his political issue as a flaw, and my sister spoke.

"I love Soroush, and I don't want anyone in this world except him. Being a political activist is not his problem, even though it is his excellent trait that does not consider only his interests."

My mother, who was upset by our conversation, said.

"Why do you use disappointing words? Soroush is a good man and loves her. What do we expect?"

"Mother, I'm worried about Zohreh's future."

"What do you worry about? Soroush loves Zohreh, and he is a doctor who can manage his life."

"Whatever you want, I love her and want her to be happy. I love Soroush too, but he has political issues that worry me."

I met Soroush many times, and he talked about his past; he had been arrested for several days and was in Evin Prison with Lajavardi. Soroush was imprisoned because he had told a group of students that White reforms were not the right for all parts of Iran and that agriculture would be destroyed because the peasant did not have the financial backing to manage his agriculture and life. SAVAK had arrested him. SAVAK was the National Security Agency (1957-1979) founded by Mohammad Reza Shah. The prison-in-charge colonel asked the prisoners to repent and signed the forgiveness letter. Lajevardi signed the letter. Soroush refused to sign a repentance letter because he did nothing to regret, and they will find in the future, even though many years later, we have seen farmers abandon the land and come to Tehran as peddlers. We became commodity (wheat) importers instead of exporters.

The university was home to political activities students in those years. Whether I was a student or a teacher at the university, I would never enter a political activist. I would focus on learning science and paying my family's expenses. My mother's pain had blinded my eyes to see other people's pains. I did not recognize it might others to suffer more than us. My mind would rotate in a closed circuit, and I imagined this was the best way of life.

I fell in love with one of my students, Hayedeh, who was in the final year of a master's degree in physics and mathematics. She was firm and capable of systematically presenting mathematical arguments without using any notes. She discussed the relationship between known dimensions and unknowable factors that had been developed and the creation of new formulas. All the professors admired her, and she was openly lecturing about the root of social problems in public when others feared and would not dare to recount them in private. She praised me for knowing my mother's pain and seeking to cure it. She believed that I should strive to eradicate the underlying cause, not cure the symptoms of the disease, and have vision to look at the different dimensions.

Also, we need a proper social system, and then we can hope that mother and nobody should suffer. She said many times do you think I'm crazy and could handle the pain in prison? We will succeed if we are all together, then the high authorities would pay attention to what we request. You were in a closed mind, and don't know the problem's roots. Hayedeh believed in intelligent work instead of hard work, these lessons were an insignificant part of our lives. The real meaning of life is to be effective. Even these wooden pillars of light have a significant role. Are we less effective than these lamp sticks? Effectiveness is the existence sign. The silence and fear of changing is death, and it credits to the oppressor. Ineffective means dead and must pray on our moving corpse. Society structure is like a human body that has several organs, the eye is one organ only, not the whole human body, and one who pays attention to the science of physics is just paying attention to the healthy eyes and forgetting all other organs when the rest of the body doesn't work. Man can survive if all organs work correctly, it is essential for a healthy community. More than your science achievement we needed for a healthy community. I understand the value of studying and living in a healthy environment; although I am your student, you must work on this subject.

At that time, I thought politics had nothing to do with me. unfortunately. Later, I learned that whether we liked it or not, even the bread on every poor or rich table has a direct and indirect connection to politics. Hayedeh ignited the first sparks of this awakening. I loved her, but I did not understand her, and these memories hurt me badly.

In those years, many of my students were intermittently in Evin prison; the student called Evin "the center" when they were not in class. Evin Prison was a

political prison in northern Tehran belonging to former
Prime Minister Tabatabaei. In 1970, it became a place for
political prisoners (mainly students) arrested by SAVAK,
its nickname was Evin University.

After obtaining my Ph.D., Zohreh and Soroush,
Hayedeh, and I married on the same day. Hayedeh was
arrested the day after our marriage and sent to Evin Prison
for three days and was released. She said Shah's sister
should not be CEO, and her friend Dr. Ansari was the head
of the organization. Hayedeh was a human rights activist,
not a communist, believing everyone should be equal in
front of the law and we must have Social Security.

Soroush, the cardiologist, joined our family after their
marriage and had a steady busy life. He loved my sister
and his family and had nothing to endanger his family's
interests. After a few months, we went to Amol, and he
bought a home for his mother, Ava Khanum with his
salary saving. He considered that his mother would live
comfortably. We were all happy that his mother was
delighted. When my sister got pregnant, Soroush rented an
apartment near the hospital where she worked and moved
in. Although we married at the same time, my sister gave
birth to two sons, Kaveh and Kamyar, the difference
between their ages was only eleven months, and we were
waiting for our first child. Soroush started the night shift
on call to take care of their sons because Zohreh was at
university. My mother moved with them to take care of
their babies even though she was sick.

Soroush recounted the prison memories and the harsh
treatment of the guards with himself and his mother,
saying that his feet had become numb from the cold and
had burned as he approached the heater. He made a
mistake in telling his mother the truth. Afterward, she was
constantly worried that he was cold on his feet. His mother
was poor and saved money to buy him a pair of socks and
bring it to prison. The cost was not only the price of socks,
but she also lived in Amol and had to spend for a bus ticket
to Tehran, sleep behind the prison door and wait to visit
him. During one of those visits, while he was waiting in the
other room, hearing her mother crying because correctional

officer had taken the socks. She was crying and said, sir, if you're angry, tell me whatever you want, but let me get the socks to my son. She wouldn't see Soroush in those moments, and he wanted to die but not hear his mother's crying. Soroush said that some memories, such as the exquisite photo frame, were forever on our memory wall. This lousy memory remains in my mind. I asked him what did he think about the situation after the 1979 revolution?

We no longer see correctional officers mistreating prisoners; we witnessed many murders without trial by Khalkhali, it was my comment.

He said, "it is a disaster, but we must wait until the dust settled, then we judge."

My opinion was against his opinion, and I said that a good year appeared by its spring. It is a tragedy that Khomeini came with the promise of freedom, not captivity and killing. Khomeini came with the promise of free homes, water, and electricity, not poverty, but he opened a hundred toman bank accounts and asked for money from the first day. Khomeini spoke clearly about death and killing, even saying that Islam is the religion of the sword, and Imam Ali killed many people, but it was enough, the cultivation of this population must be done. Khomeini has come to murder and kill people. Soroush agreed, surprised and said there must be some opportunists who take advantage. My arguments did not seem necessary because I did not have a political background, I might be wrong, and the truth is otherwise. Soroush expressed his feelings and showed his love for Zohreh; bought flowers, sent a small cards and notes were on the wall around their house for any occasion, even when they had ice cream for the first time. He knew the magnitude of the moment well and was very romantic. There was always a candle on the table and a loving note on its side. I was trying to learn from him and create a better environment for Hayedeh. I asked him to teach me how to treat my love, following him and his expressing love note and affection for Hayedeh, such a parrot.

Soroush did housekeeping and even bathed their children before Zohreh returned home, prepared the pacifiers and bottle of milk, arranged my mother's clothes, and made the house tidy if it was unordered. It was his regular job, even nights that shouldn't have worked. Hayedeh said he was more organized than a woman.

Zohreh told us that I was a guest in this house and had nothing to do except relax and be with my husband, children, and family. We often gathered at their home with his sister, Manijeh and Hossein Agha. Hayedeh said we should be happy that Soroush taught us our duties because Zohreh, Hayedeh, and I still needed to learn to do housekeeping. Soroush laughed and said it was the fault of the devoted mothers. My mother said that the world had been changing, and I always thought it was my job to do everything. Soroush hugged my mother, pointed to us, and said she should sit like a queen and order these bully servants here to do what she wanted. My mother blushed her face out of shame and said, oh my goodness, if I dare. I gradually learned from Soroush to look around as soon as I entered the house and do what it is. There were fun and happy times with Soroush in our company. He always said that we suffered all life hardships and how glad we were to be with our loved ones and beloved. We studied and had a good life; we should not do physical work like our mothers. What else do we want? When your baby is born, your happiness will be completed like him. We all laughed, unaware that everything would be lost.

One night, as usual, when Zohreh arrived home, Soroush went to the hospital. The following day, Soroush's colleague called my sister and said that a few revolutionary guards had taken the doctor from the hospital last night. When he protested that they had had a legal reason and the prosecutor's order to arrest him, they told he would shut up or strangle him, and he was not in custody, just go with them answering a few questions, then they had taken him by force. The doctor's colleague apologized for the bad news, did not have any choice except to because he knew the doctor would take care of his children daily and Zohreh would go to university. My sister called us and cried, and I took his phone number and called him to make sure, and we went to Zohreh's house.

Hayedeh immediately began searching and eventually, through her friends, found that Soroush was in Qasr prison. Qasr Prison was a palace built for Fat Ali Shah in 1790 and was a place for holding political prisoners. After 1979, many high-ranking officers from the country, including Nader Jahanbani and Amir Hossein Rabie, were executed by order of Khomeini; there without trial. Khomeini had come to power, seized Iranian property, and wanted to kill patriots who might rise to defend the country. In court, patriotic officers said they were loyal to the kingdom by oath.

Hayedeh was most terrified to hear that Soroush was in the Qasr prison because she knew more than us what it meant to be in that prison. At the same time, she controlled her emotion and tried to keep Zohreh calm.

From that day on, our job was to visit Qasr prison, requested a meeting time, and asked for his arrested reason. At the same time, we considered finding a lawyer to defend Soroush's rights. The promises of Qasr prison were misleading to us. Soroush and I were like brothers. I was sure he had not committed to any political activities since I knew him. I admired his kind and calm personality with all his moral qualities. We had disagreements about politics, and he was very optimistic. My sister said the only unusual event happened recently Soroush visited his patient, and one patient's visitor was Lajevardi. Soroush asked him about his prisoner period, and he denied it.

"Do you still remember that prison?"

Soroush wondered and spoke.

"Do not you?"

He had shaken his head and changed the subject. Soroush had remained silent. Soroush had said that if Lajevardi were a political activist, he was not an activist like him. He was the same self-sale cunning who repented and signed the forgiveness letter. Hayedeh told me it probably started from that point and did not tell Zohreh. After this incident, Zohreh did not go to university. She cried, and we did not have a better time than her while keeping our calmness to help her dominate the situation—what a fantasy. We took the older child when we went to Qasr prison because my mother suffered severe pain and couldn't take care of both simultaneously and spoke.

"I wished to suffer Zohreh's pain, what could she do with two children?"

Perhaps she imagined Soroush's death and could also remember her destiny and responsibility for two children. During the 20 days that Soroush was in prison, every day, without exception, we went to the jail in the morning and afternoon because that was the only way to hope to see Soroush.

Anyway, we called everyone for help. Several friends had hidden, and a few real friends would do but could not do anything. Sometimes they helped us with buying the baby formula. At that time, infant formula and children's diapers were scarce. During this period, we were only allowed to visit him twice, with a party recommendation. Throughout the visit, they were examined and interrogated us such as a professional villain and criminals' person with extreme care and physical torture that we were not imagining. We endured and were happy to be able to meet Soroush for a few minutes. On the first visit, Soroush told Zohreh.

"I am innocent, and if something happens to me, you must marry. I hope you will be happy and take care of our sons."

"What do you say, did they say something to you?"

"No, but there is a killing party nightly, and they kill people more quickly than drinking a cup of water."

"You're a doctor, and they're counting on how many years must be spent and worked hard to become a doctor, and what you're saying."

"Soheil, they do not have logical thinking. I have a friend, Dr. B, had reached power and wealth in this government because his father, Qum's mullah. You call him and ask for help. I was in jell before, but they are the most irrational people I've ever met. Tell my sister and mother that Soroush is on a mission instead in prison if they call you."

Those meetings were also done after They gave us

many empty promises. In those days, Manijeh and Hossein Agha had returned from Amol and wanted to come to Zohreh's house. But Zohreh said to have a cold and would call them later. She said to call them after Soroush's release; she hoped Soroush would be back soon!

I went to Dr. B.'s office, occupied with many clients waiting for their medical records approval for the currency exchange for abroad medical treatment. They had used the sickness excuse to take advantage of the black-market currency exchange and would sell it at a higher price on the free market. My appointment was at 2 pm, and I met him at ten pm, introduced myself, and told him that I was Dr. Soroush's relative. He thought that I wanted currency exchange, but when sure that I was not looking for the currency, he calmed down, changed his attitude, and talked about his university and how nice Soroush was. He even remembered Zohreh and Soroush's love story. After hearing Soroush's situation, his attitude changed 180 degrees, and he said harshly.

"I should see my patients. I could not do anything. You'll need to contact the court."

"Considering your father is a Qom's mullah and gave you this position, you must have enough influence to help an innocent well-educated doctor. He was your close friend."

"Sir, what could I do?"

He pointed out to his maid to bring the next customer. I was disappointed and returned when they were waiting to receive good news. I decided to lie to Zohreh. I reached home at midnight; I said Dr. B would talk to his father and call me. Hayedeh and Zohreh had gone to Qasr Prison unsuccessfully. When I was alone with Hayedeh, I told her the truth. Hayedeh also confirmed that Zohreh no longer tolerates anything from friends or untrue friends. The third appointment was set for us, and we returned without visitation.

Those false promises were repeated to us, and we had no choice except to accept their lies and hope to see Soroush. The last time we asked for an appointment, the jail officials said he would be released soon. Those days, we stayed at Zohreh's house. One day we went to our house and for grocery shopping. We decided to go to jail and tried to see Soroush on our way. After much delay, Hayedeh told me that she had been in pain.

When she begged the officer that she was in pain, he said that Soroush would soon be discharged, and our efforts to visit Soroush were unsuccessful. Along the way, Hayedeh said that Khalkhali was the devil ruler and bloodthirsty executioner in Qasr Prison. He killed Hoveyda and Nasiri and numerous heads of the army and ministries. Khomeini had appointed this devil as a judge. He issued the killing order for the bus passengers, innocent people, without any trial. In a live interview with Los Angeles Radio 670 AM, he was proud of the killings and said it was done with Khomeini's orders. I told Hayedeh that there was no hope that Soroush would survive, and she remained silent. To end the silence, I spoke.

"Did you know Zohreh's classmate, Abbass, had been arrested because he erased the word "America" and wrote "Khomeini" on the phrase "Death to America "on the university walls."

"The word "death" is a mark of dictatorship. The people's slogan shall be a sign of the consciousness of that society, and it should be a construction message for more motivation. Khomeini and America have their hands in one bowl. We heard Colonel Oliver North's interview broadcasted live on U.S. television. He was in Iran during Reagan's presidency to help Khomeini, the USA sold weapons to Iran and Iraq, who were at war with each other, and Khomeini said death to America, the Great Satan. Khomeini had accepted the allies' conditions in Paris. The U.S. and Russia were two of the ALLIES who supported him in Paris. Their connection, Qotbi, had been killed to cover the secrets, just the story of the Kennedy killer who had to be murdered and the murder of the murderer. Why did ALLIES not support Shah? What did Shah say that was against their interests? Russia created SAVANA to control Khomeini instead of SAVAK, which was the US founder."

"What is your opinion about the Revolution of Iran?"

"It was a disaster started with the Portugal pirates arrived in Bandar Abbas and noticed the warm waters, knowing an underneath energy source. The greedy European countries' attention turned to the south of Iran. Now we see Dubai, Kuwait, and others with foreign capital invested in towers, which is a part of the massive projects. All aspects of Iran's situation, including its natural resources, people, and geographical position, should be analyzed. In the political issue, the western countries and their allies are united to preserve their interests against our interest. The Asian continent has the most resources in the world. China and Indian populations, and the existing oil and other resources such as uranium, copper, silicon, etc., are heavy weight in this part of the world.

First, England and now its allies coveted this part of the world to devour everything together. The theory of divisiveness and the government has been implemented by England in different countries for many years. The allies planned, reviewed, and then executed it; their plans have yet to happen suddenly.

England has no wealth and sucks the people's blood of the world. They were determined to decrease Iran's power and executed their plan step by step. They sold weapons to Iran to withdraw the oil money that had been paid and propaganda that Iran was the regional gendarme, then pulled him down and weakened Iran and other regional countries.

The Allies noticed that religious tool was good enough to destroy a community, such as Russia's last Caesar experience and Rasputin. They knew that a cunning mullah could kill the people of a country and a region. The policy was based on the theory of division and rule. The Allies sent spies under the umbrella of kind pious missionaries to gather data, namely espionage. They had seen that Iranian women were no longer Qajar women. So, controlling half of Iran's population with religion was more effective than the communist sickle. Reza Shah, a hardworking and patriotic man who recognized that the primary source of sedition and corruption were the mullah, said the country did not need a mullah."

"Keep your words here; people said Reza Shah was a dictator."

"Words such as dictatorship, democracy, or territorial reforms should be measured in the dimension of time, place, and social situations and whether the result was helpful or harmful at that time and place. For example, the emergency ward requires the manager to decide immediately and tell them what to do or not to do. The authority must act like a dictator to provide the highest benefit and least harm to the majority. If they say that Reza Shah was a dictator, we should praise him for not being fascinated by the contentless simple words of deception.

At that time, he was an excellent leader eave labeled as a dictator. Imagine a home fire, and there are many children. If you want to save them, you can hug two and get out of the fire. Now, if you put all in one bed sheet and drag them on the floor, you saved all, but their legs and arms will be injured and bloody. One could take a photo at that moment and defames you and will prove his claim with one photo. Those who want to plunder Iran are well acquainted with these type documents and its use. Uninformed Iranians see one photo unfortunately, which is unfair and not wise."

Hayedeh continued.

"Look at the situation of Iran during the reign of Reza Shah and the table of human needs written by Abram Maslow. You will see that the most basic human needs, whether scientists or illiterate, poor, or rich, are physiological needs such as air, water, food, clothing, and shelter. After that, in order of healthy and safe, live without fear, and have financial and social security.

In the next stage, emotional and social needs are love, having a passionate relationship, self-respect, self-confidence, finding the value of oneself and others, respecting oneself and others, and social values. Self-sufficiency and self-fulfillment, accepting facts, accepting responsibility, searching for solutions to problems, creativity, and ethics are human needs. And this happens when human beings have met their minimum needs. In the highest part of the human need is freedom (Nirvana).

An Iranian phrase said that you have not starved to forget your love. The basic needs are so strong that it squeezes human being in their clutches: they must be overcome so that there is an opportunity to reach a higher stage. Although in some societies and some very exceptional people, such as Indian ascetics, these criteria are less clear, and the change can be seen to some extent.

Now we should understand Reza Shah's situation better. He was general when the country faced famine, diseases, insecurity, poverty problems, foreign countries influx into Iran's privacy, and the threat to Iran's national independence. There was not any responsible in charge. Reza Shah was not selfish to save himself instead save Iran and met basic human needs. Still, the Allies worried that someone like Reza Shah would stand up and fight their plundering program. For this reason, they defamed Reza Shah's character, and ignorant friends watered the enemy's plant. Western governments did not want our developed country and invited him to negotiate to take him away from Iran. He had nominated Mohammad Reza Shah as his successor before he left Iran. Mohammad Reza Shah did not know the importance of his father's work in destroying mullahs and spreading superstitions. As a result, it provided an opportunity for the breeding of mullahs.

Mohammad Reza Shah saw the opposition's words against himself, not against the Allies' plan. The Shah was oblivious to those who created distance between him and the people and wanted to exploit the country's wealth. The Shah assumed some university students were hostile to him. The head of allies, the U.S.A, had established SAVAK to take care of their interests and remove anyone who opposed them. While most patriotic students opposed some plans that the exploiters planned to harm the Shah and the country, they had protested and arrested by the SAVAK. If the Shah had paid attention to the dissidents talking, the situation would have been different.

Later, we heard Shah's friend, Army general Rafighdoost, betrayed him. In The last speech, the Shah said the oil cartels having a stake in this conspiracy, designed those protests. Oil cartels meant Allies who created SAVAK and killed the patriots. In short, wealthy Allies invested significant capital in the region's countries, creating internal turmoil to make the most benefits. The Allies wanted executive obedience servant's mullah who distributed the internal superstition for plundering people's property.

They inflated the stupid grave reciter and threw them into the community to keep people busy with Fatwa and hadiths (hijab etc.) and limited their rights and activities. Mullah is a scarecrow in front of the stage. There are different groups, Revolutionary Guards, Hezbollah, Jundullah, Basij, Taliban, ISIS, the Revolutionary Guards, Savana, the martyr's family, Maddahs, etc., stood behind the scarecrow and ready to follow the real boss's order, shoot to scarecrow's heart, then kill the killer because the secrets should be hidden and then they will point an innocent.

The colonists and exploiters do not like the mullahs, they used them and throw mullahs in the garbage bin. I wish illiterate mullahs would learn that they would have a terrible fate like bin Laden. In the best mullahs' interests, join the people before it is late and used a fatwa trick like the prohibited tobacco fatwa. The only people's solution is to unite, be armed, fight for their rights, and neutralize the conspiracies. If people learn this, everyone will be better off. We must be one and fight against the real enemy, Mullahs.

We got home, heard Zohreh crying, and Hayedeh forgot her pain. Zohreh was wailing, and my mother told us about a phone call to Zohreh from Qasr prison.

"Did you know Dr. Soroush, and what was your relationship?"

"I knew him! What did you say? He is my husband."

"He was your husband. Come tomorrow, take his ring, watch, and clothes."

"What."

"He was executed, and his corpus is in Kofrabad."

Zohreh screamed, cried, and said no, it's not possible. My mother knew from Zohreh's crying that she had a bad news and tried to calm her, and the two children crying.

"Zohreh, please call the prison to be sure it was the call from jail, or someone called here by mistake."

It took about 10 to 15 minutes, she noticed that she had dropped the phone on the floor, took the phone to dial the prison, still he was on the line and spoke.

"You screamed enough, you got on your nerves. Listen, you come here tomorrow and get your husband's inheritance".

Around the same time, we were in Qasr prison, asking for an appointment. We said it must be a lie, but unfortunately, it was not. I called Manijeh and Hossein Agha and told Hossein Agha what had happened, and they came immediately. They were not better than us. Hossein Agha and I went to Qasr prison to see if this news was accurate. I cried and did not care that the man should not be crying.

"Maybe it's false news. We must be calm because of your sister and my wife."

In Qasr Prison, as usual, there was a physical interrogation going from room to room. Someone said we did not call. We wanted to hope that the phone was incorrect. They mocked and manipulated us, and after several hours, they said.

"Yes, he confessed his guilt and was executed."

I screamed and said you killed him. He was innocent. He hadn't done anything wrong. Hussein Agha forced me to remain silent, and we were both engulfed in mourning. Hossein Agha asked for Soroush's belongings, which they said should be given to his wife only, a kind of torture for the victim's family. We returned to my sister's house.

Manijeh and Hossein Agha stayed with us. The day after, we went to Qasr prison in two cars while Zohreh and Hayedeh were in Hossein agha's vehicle, and my mother and the children were with me. They told Zohreh that Soroush was a corruption on earth and became a tyrant. Zohreh said that you were a corruption on earth, and he was innocent and helped the people, and it is a pity he saved the stupid people's life like. All the time, Hossein Agha was careful not to let something new happen. After a long wait, they gave Soroush's ring only, not his watch, to

Zohreh. It was painful to see his wedding ring. After that, we went to Kofrabad. My mother was crying silently. The children were restless, and I did not know how help my mother who took care of them!

Kofrabad, 1982

The kofrabad meant a non-Muslim place, it was a dirty landfill in south of Tehran, with many stray dogs eating the garbage. The Islamic regime had chosen that place to bury its murderers. Later, its name changed to Khavaran. Many corpses were dumped in one of the large landfill pits, may be about 30 bodies could be seen at one glance.

Several soldiers were there to prevent the victims' families protests. The young soldiers had come to military service; their appearance and speaking could be guessed from small villages, unaware and brainwashed.

They looked at us as if they had seen their enemies. Hossein Agha was a smart street and knew how to manage them and was familiar with their language. I could say that he used bribe language to ask them for his corpse, and we were able to find him between multiple pits in a ditch. We cried loudly from seeing his bloody body. I hadn't seen a dead person in my whole life and did not know what to do. Hossein Agha advised me yesterday that I had to control myself, and now he cried out loud and said there was no choice except to show him to Zohreh Khanum and Manijeh, even though it was heartbroken, but it was better if Hayedeh did not see his body. Hussein Agha took off his coat, emptied his pockets, and threw it over Soroush's body while crying.

"It's a pity you were killed. What do I say to your mother? No one should see the hole of gunshots on your body."

I couldn't believe what I saw was real. I was horrified by all this vice, injustice, and brutality event.

"Give me a few minutes to see his face. Then I come."

"Okay, I want to see him too. I wished the last visit weren't like this. I told him to take care of Manijeh after my death. I did not believe I had to care of his corpse. You stay here, and I will bring them because they might come here with two innocent kids at any time."

I put my head on his forehead, and I talked to him.

"You were my coach. Tell me how to say farewell. I should kiss your forehead and say, my brother, with a dozen holes in his body, left me here."

It was the worst day of my life. There were several bodies in the pit without shrouds. Even in a movie, you couldn't see such a horrible scene. Hossein Agha, who had noticed that I was in a bad mood, did not go, and he sat next to me and hugged and held me in his arms and spoke.

"You're my son, I feel your pain, but you must control yourself and think about your pregnant woman."

I had never had a warm father's hug in my life. I wanted to put my head on his shoulder and cry out loud.

"My son, we will return here tomorrow and say goodbye to him. Be firm at this moment."

I wanted to scream and cry.

"I must go back now. Be fluent in yourself."

He was right. I did not even have a chance to sigh. He returned with Zohreh and Manijeh, who were also distraught and had their head on his body. Hussein Agha pulled me and put Zohreh in my arms, and Manijeh was in his arms. I had put my head on Zohreh's head, and we were crying. My mother, Hayedeh, and two children were in the car. Hossein Agha believed that Hayedeh was pregnant and better not seeing his corpse. After a few minutes, Hossein Agha grabbed my hand and said:

"Take Manijeh and Zohreh Khanum to your car so that I can arrange a solitary grave."

Zohreh and Manijeh hugged each other and cried. There were no words to reduce their grief. I felt how powerless I was and how unaware of real pain, even unaware of death that might suddenly come.

Hussein Agha talked with the soldiers, and I noticed they put down their guns and dug the ground, and he asked us to go in our car and wait for him. We separated Zohreh and Manijeh from his corpse and took them to another car where my mother did not see them. Hayedeh came to us and could guess from our appearances what had happened, hugged them and cried.

"Now it's my turn."

Whatever I told Hayedeh, it was not good for her to see him. She refused.

"I must say farewell to Soroush for the last time."

She walked with me to see his corpse. She pushed aside the coat from his body, silently shed tears as wide as her face, kissed his forehead, and said goodbye. Hussein Agha
came and told her to get back in the car. While we cried and got to the car.

"How would you deprive me of this pilgrimage?"

"You're pregnant, it was painful for me, and I did not want you to suffer."

"No more chance to see dear Soroush again."

Hayedeh needed my support, but I was weak in the face of this tragedy. She joined them and did not cry anymore. My mother wanted to see Soroush, but Hayedeh said it was not good for her. My mother listened to her. I returned to help Hossein Agha. I thought that one shot was enough to kill those innocents, so why did they pierce their bodies? All were young, and their bodies were torn apart. Soroush was a doctor and should be a savior, and it was clear that these words were useless.

The group grave was a pit in the ground, it was dusk when we put our beloved corpse in the grave and kissed his forehead, something I hadn't done when he was alive. Hussein Agha prayed on his body. I hated God, praying, and his representatives; I wept. Before covering the grave, Hossein agha took the coat to slit its back, wrapped his upper body, fastened it, and spoke.

"My coat should not be the shroud of loved Soroush."

He cried out loudly after a pause said.

"Let's bring Manijeh and Zohreh Khanum for farewell, it is better not to kiss him because its memory will stay with them.

"This is the last kiss before pouring dirt on his corpse."

Zohreh and Manijeh came and kissed his face, and soldiers dropped dirt on his corpse to cover the grave. We returned to the car, and Hossein Agha stayed there until the grave was covered and marked. Hayedeh returned with their car, and I stayed with my mother and the kids. The children were crying and did not have milk. I was changing the baby's diapers for the first time, and I talked to myself that Soroush did not stay to teach me how to care of baby; like a crazy person, I walked around the home and talked to myself about how to do housework. The angry landlord, who noticed our restless condition, asked us to consider the neighbors instead of consoling us. Hussein Agha dragged them down the corridor and talked to them when I heard.

"Shame on you; it's instead of comforting her.

Their neighbor was a poor girl, the landlord's third wife, with several children from the multi-marriage. The landlord was a little considerate, but his wife had no originality that one could expect her kindness. The next day, one officer came to Zohreh's home and said we had no right to cry and go to Kofrabad; otherwise, we would be arrested.

We did not understand how our mourning had reached the officer! We went to Kofrabad several times with Hossein Agha. He told me that he paid them, and they wouldn't report it. Zohreh's landlord did not understand the tragic pain and had begun to be incompatible with Zohreh, and instead sympathy for the bereaved was her regular advice to remain silent! Hayedeh and I asked Zohreh to come to our house, but she said this home was full of his memories and would not go anywhere.

A month later, her landlord asked her to leave. Hayedeh and I insisted on returning to our home, but Manijeh and Hossein Agha asked her to move near them. Hussein Agha rented a house three houses away from theirs due Manijeh could take care of the children, and Zohreh continued her education which was better for the children's future. They lived on Pole Chobi of Shemiran street.

Her neighbors said that Sayed Ali Khamenei lived there and moved out to one of the confiscated houses, Shabanov Farah Pahlavi's uncle in Niavaran. He went to the usurped house. According to Islamic law, God does not accept praying on seized property. Neighbors said Sayed Ali was not financially stable and regularly repaired his old Volkswagen on the street. His situation changed significantly, and he had a private bodyguard and a bulletproof vehicle. The question is, where does wealth come from?

After Soroush's death, I was afraid to lose Hayedeh and asked her to calm down and not involve in the social activity. Even Manijeh asked Hayedeh.

"Compare Shah's era to the Khomeini killing jail and the executioner. You and many students protested and went to prison for a few days, and now the innocent people were killed in jail without trial."

"Now it's a disaster, a thief stole and strayed the people movement, it does not mean the protest was wrong. The situation would have been worse if the fighters did not talk. The mullah will kill and eat our bones if we do not protest. There are always casualties in war that soldiers must accept. In every effort, it must be assumed victory or defeat. Of course, no one is fighting for failure, but it is not humanity to be silent such as a piece of meat in a butcher shop. Everyone has a responsibility in life. We should work to improve the situation. Even unsophisticated farmers had learned to plant, care for, and harvest crops by experience and provide foods.

We are astonished by all the pretentious literate people who have given up and said God will, and God will not. They will do nothing and expect someone to drink water when thirsty and go to the bathroom when urgent. Everyone must play his part. Forough Farrokhzad (poet and cinema director) said.

"I was amazed by many indifferent people with useless hands."

Hayedeh continued "Sattar Khan did not fight against the dictatorship if his thought was improper. At the same time, Iranian were resistant, and their freedom movement was the first in the region. These countries still needed development if Reza Shah and Ataturk were outside Iran and Turkey. If people in Europe had not fought the oppression of churches, they would not have seen this flourish today. They have also been killed. And we have no choice; whenever there is oppression, people must resist regardless of the oppressor, Khomeini or other. We must unite, plan, fight, and aim for victory. We must remember that a fighter needs a plan, and resistance is the key to success."

Zohreh: "What can we do? Soroush were killed and you are."

"Remember that the death of innocent Soroush is not easy, and it does not prevent me from fighting for his blood. They killed Soroush yesterday, if we do not fight, they will kill another person tomorrow. I'm not fighting to get killed.

But between living without dignity and death, I rather die with dignity. Love is not simple. A lover must know that there is a dangerous pathway ahead with many blockages, and he might need to swim in a bloody lake with sharks. Or such as a butterfly to love to visit candles. Writing letters to Khomeini and demanding to consider a trial for killing an innocent Soroush will not kill me, but indifference kill me."

Hayedeh had sent a letter to Khomeini to protest Soroush's death and stated that Soroush was a fighter for human right and Khomeini claimed nobody and Americans living in Iran are not above the law, shall be treated equally, and were not allowed to do anything in our country illegally. You should accept that killing innocent people is shameful.

Soheil: "You shouldn't write the letter. Khomeini is a wolf in a sheep's dress and will commit a crime."

Zohreh: "You see the world through a lady, but they are wild, blinded men fascinated by power."

"Countless Iranian men were fair leaders; looking at it from a gender perspective is not wise."

The Islamic Cultural Revolution & lay off

Khomeini called for the cultural revolution and, indeed, destroyed the culture and the ruin education quality in Iran. Later, Iran became of the quota illiterate degree that issued paper titles for mullah and his relatives in the seminary. Khomeini's cultural revolution resulted in the fall of literacy and education, and the quota university for mullah. Mullah's relatives obtained a Ph.D. and a bachelor's degree within going to school. They became illiterate experts in the corrupt government and an illiterate surgeon with a very high death ratio in the operating room. An illiterate person with elementary education blackjacked the title, and his name was the doctor. After graduation, many top-educated, talented students did not find a job because they knew an illustrated doctors!

Many illiteracies religious mullah's relative was hired to work at the university under the name of the revolutionary guard to spy on professors, SAVANA, and they called each other brother.

On the pretext that shah's photo was in my office, they called me a tyrant and fired me. I was depressed after Soroush's death and was not in a good mood to see anyone, especially this group. I was a tyrant in their minds, but my only fault was hard work and study. An illiterate mullah reached a high position that could not have been imagined and asked all to pray at noon in the university yard. There was nothing except hypocrisy and cunning. They had nothing except to spy on us even though our tea-time should be under their supervision. Everyone said that under the beard of each mullah was a British-made label.

By now I understood Hayedeh idea about a healthy community was not limited to studying. I had been laid off in this situation where my family's income was only my salary. I preferred not telling my family because they suffered hard times, and I would tell them the truth when their wounds healed.

The misfortune was I did not have any other skill except studying, and teaching. Schools and universities were closed, resulting in no jobs and no money. I wished I had learned anything else to make an income covering the cost of living. I even went to the Bazaar one day on the pretext of going to university and watched the hardworking coolie, hoping I could do something. I noticed that it needed a tool that included a hard cushion on back and a rope or string to tie the cargo on the back. And I couldn't afford it. I remembered one of my friend Masoud had his architecture firm, and I went to his office. His company's work could have been more active, and he said he would likely close his office. He asked about my financial situation. I said it's not good, so I'm looking for a job. He did not say anything. When I got home, he called me and said wanted to talk about a project and would come to my home. I wondered why he did not say when I was there.

Masoud came to the door and gave me an envelope, which was money inside, and said whenever you have it, give me back, and I

will let you know if I find a project.

"I did not tell Hayedeh and Zohreh that I lost my job."

"I noticed that I did not come inside."

He came to our home when he was a student because our home was close to the university. Masoud was from a wealthy high-class family and lived on Fereshteh Street. I took the money and told Hayedeh it was about a project.

Those days I was very restless, asked Hayedeh not to talk in public during her pregnancy. My worries did not go anywhere. When I asked her what the result of her challenge, her answer was.

"The result creates from the continuation of the struggle and the process of victory goes forward. Consider the media are in opposite hands and would not let the people's victory be revealed and people to recognize the value of the progressive struggle. An excellent combatant soldier knows that resistance determine the final word, and it's just a few steps away from victory and does not leave the trench. They would swallow us by now if it weren't for our struggle.

Even our pieces of literature help us to send our messages. Even though our hands are empty of weapons, our messages are clear, the pen has been well-spent. Even the jokes and sarcastically speech are people's voice and will be etched on the history. People use the poem to say what they want in a less harmful way, and the poem carries the picture of people's heartache. Remember, if our home is on fire, we could you use our maximum ability to stop more damages including but not limited to an extinguisher.

Remember, if our home will be on fire, we use our maximum ability to stop more damages including but not limited to an extinguisher and try to save our children. Our home is on fire now, is it wise to use everything to save them, and you only talk about my safety. It is not wise to be cowardly silence. I must try to save myself and others, even though no one could understand me. I know there are some casualties in our way, but those who stay will live better. There is no benefit when one healthy organ is in our body, and others are not. It is like our sick society, and I am looking for treatment. Dictators and oppressors do not survive and will disappear; people must protest and resist."

"Hayedeh, what do I do if you will be killed?"

"Everything is possible. We could find any excuse to deviate from the primary goal if we want, but we must be determined. I may be killed, but I prefer death to live with humiliation."

I was begging and saying: "You're pregnant if you're not thinking about yourself. At least think about the baby."

"You are afraid I have Soroush's fate. If anything happens to me, take me for a cesarean section immediately and pick up the baby to survive. Soroush told me that the chances of the fetus surviving are high after six months. Remember, the fear is captivity and death for me, and I die every day."

Hayedeh told Zohreh:

"The great men wish not to die in bed. There is a specific value in fighting and dying for freedom. Soroush was a great man and knew the value of selflessness, and the philosophy of effectiveness. We die in some way, such as through diseases, starvation, accident, etc. I love to live with freedom and don't think about the quantity of life. As Forough Farrokhzad's poem.

The most stretched flame of candle and its last flame openly express and testify the secret of its selflessness."

Hayedeh

Hayedeh was arrested in 1981. Our house heater
worked with oil rationed by the government. We were
deprived while we were the oil exporters. The corrupt
government auctioned the oil and imported the air-
polluting gasoline, which is carcinogenic, and then
switched it to a worse type of gasoline that pollutes the soil
and is as carcinogenic as the previous one. People observed
a tsunami of cancer in Iran. We saved and took oil to my
sister's house, which caused the Revolutionary Guards'
anger. They controlled us even though we weren't
important people. One day I took oil to my sister's house.
When I returned, the shopkeeper at the alley told me that
the revolutionary guard had taken Hayedeh away. We
were a client of Diani local grocery store. He was a good
guy and had seen patrols ambush, stopped Hayedeh, put
her in their car, and run away. It looked like Hayedeh was
their target.

That night, I called Hossein Agha, who came, and we
went from one police station to another until we found out
that Hayedeh was in Evin prison. We decided not to tell
my mother and Zohreh, but we said Manijeh could cover
up when we were not there. For the next three days, we
were able to make an appointment. I received a phone call
from Evin prison to take the baby on the morning of the
appointment.

I called Hossein Agha and Manijeh, and we concluded
that Manijeh should tell Zohreh and my mother because
we must take the baby there. Manijeh had sent some baby
clothes with Hossein Agha. I had a weird feeling, was
anxious and worried for Hayedeh, who endured the pain
of childbirth alone in prison. I was happy that I was a
father, concerned about how to take care of our baby until
Hayedeh returned, and I was sad that my first visit should
be in jail. We went to Evin Prison with Hossein Agha. After
a long wait, let us go to the morgue and see the dead
newborns. I was Crazy and cried loudly. Hossein Agha
kept saying.

"Remember Hayedeh Khanum."

He hinted at Hayedeh's captivity; therefore, I must not

speak. The morgue was a damp, ruined room at the end of the same building. They did not let us to see Hayedeh. There were some dead babies wrapped in dirty cloth. The officer showed them to us. It was painful, and it was my meeting with my baby.

I couldn't figure out which criminal mind could behave like this with an innocent baby. I thought to whom I should complain. Complain about my fate or thugs? I hated everything and remembered Hayedeh, who said, Reza Shah was right to say that our country did not need mullahs and that everyone must work. If the shah had listened to his father's advice, we would not be in this situation today. I had never seen a dead baby before, and I couldn't tell which of these babies was my baby. I was crying. A young boy was there, talking angrily.

"It is embarrassing, and a man doesn't cry. You have seen your baby go out." Hossein Agha comforted me.

"Doctor, when Hayedeh comes out, another child next year. Hayedeh is a healthy woman, and you have it again." He invited me to remain silent. We are unaware of Hayedeh's life and death. We went to my sister's house and told them what had happened. We were grieving for the baby and praying that Hayedeh survived those thugs. The next day we left the children with my mother, and we went to prison. They told us that we should pay for bullets. At first, we did not understand what bullet money meant.

They had killed Hayedeh and asked us for bullet money to hand over her corpse, so my love life had ended. Hossein Agha paid them, and they referred us to Kofrabad. We went to Kofrabad, and they claimed her corpse was buried, and we did not even see if Hayedeh was there. Hayedeh's name was on the list that was tagged on the wall. I was sick for several days. My mother cried a lot, and Hossein Agha did not let me return to my house. I lost everything and wanted to die.

Every day, my situation degraded, and I could not do anything. I assumed my mother's resistance to this event was reasonable compared with us, whereas my mother had no opportunity to complain about the pain because of us.

After a few days, I decided to go to my home with

Hossein Agha. We entered my house, which had been damaged, and someone had robbed the place. We had a TV and a rug that wasn't there. There were no valuable items in our house. Several scientific books and notebooks were taken, which was not on the level of thieves to study. We could have guessed that it was the Revolutionary Guards. I later learned that my telephone book was also taken away.

When Hossein Agha asked me if I had left any money at home, I recalled that Masoud had given me money. Hossein Agha was worried that was stolen, we found money in my coat pocket, which was left in Hossein Agha's car, and I had forgotten it. I looked at the house where my love Hayedeh was living with me. She was no longer there, and I missed her and those memorable moments. I wanted to register all her memories in my head forever.

After her, I suffered from severe depression. My condition deteriorated daily, and I was unaware, like the metamorphosis people. Zohreh's grief and my situation robbed our mother snatched the opportunity to care for her problem. She increased her medication dosage, her joint deformities increased, and she tried to draw our attention to two innocent children. I did not even know how to help myself. The older child was restless and took his father's excuse. I was lying, and my mother put the younger one beside me and asked me to feed him with his milk bottle. Kaveh had a teddy bear that he would hold and said, my dad, which was painful.

I tried to play with the older kid, but I stared at a spot. My mother sent me to buy a loaf of bread as if I had been a kid again. It was my work after all those educations. Zohreh followed me with her baby carriage. My mother also dragged herself into the alley. Because there was no safety. Manijeh would come to Zohreh's house after Hossein Agha went to work and stayed until Hossein Agha returned, dined together, and then went to their house. It was their daily routine. In the meantime, Manijeh and Hossein Agha burdened us, financed our debt, and other life problems.

When I look back, I see that my mother was very sick in those days. As a family man, I had to care for her when I was in the worst situation. One day, Soroush's friend, Dr. Omidi, came to our home at my sister's request, and prescribed medication for me. Zohreh took care of my medicine. I was sleeping most of the time. One day, Hossein Agha spoke.

"You come with me to the shop tomorrow. Staying in the house is not suitable for you."

It was several days since I did not go out of the house.

"I will go to work tomorrow."

Which job? There was nothing to be done. I did not know that everyone knew that I had lost my job and that the honorable man was watching over my sister's life all the time.

"We would talk about it."

In the meantime, Hossein Agha called Ava Khanum occasionally and imitated Soroush's voice; she thought it was his son. Ave Khanum told Hossein Agha that she had cataracts and could not see well, and her doctor couldn't do surgery due to her heart problem.

Hussein Agha suggested we visit her, as her eyes would not see correctly. Zohreh called Soroush's friend, Dr. Jamshidi, who lived there and talked about Soroush and asked him to take care of ava Khanum. We finally visited Ava Khanum for one day. Zohreh and Manijeh were supposed to kiss her first to make sure she could not recognize the face, then Hussein Agha imitated Soroush.

Ava Khanum said. "Soroush your aroma is different."

"I changed the washing powder."

"No, your body aroma."

Manijeh changed the subject. I wondered how long he could play this role. We returned the day after, early morning before the weather lit up, and she could see better in the light and recognize that the person she was kissing was not her son and did not smell like her son. Ava Khanum protested why did we leave soon. Zohreh said Soroush should go to work. My mother had stayed home, and we did not tell her the plan. I hated myself and my life. There were frustrations, so I did see my mother go away.

My mother was on medications that required blood tests to determine the dosage. Soroush always checked her blood tests. Zohreh's house was one bedroom where she slept with two children and closed the door so that when her children woke up, not disturb us in the middle of the night. My mother slept next to the heater on the floor, and I slept on the sofa in the hall. One day when we woke up, we found my mother dead quiet and hassle-free. I saw that she was relieved of the suffering to endure for us. She went, and we were lonelier than ever. She was about fifty years old, she was my father too, and now we had lost our parents at once. Zohreh called Manijeh, and she came.

I always wished I had a father like the other children. The situation was worse, and how I did not see that this delicate statue was my father, mother, and everything to me? She was a breadwinner and a refugee for us. I wish I'd put my head on her feet and cry. I couldn't even cry and she left us alone with two children. Manijeh and Hussein Agha came forward to help us without any expectations. Manijeh took Zohreh with children to her home and Hossein Agha stayed with me.

My mother's death was another shock to me. I wanted to stay alone with my mother and kiss her, something I hadn't done in her lifetime, and put my head on her feet, And Hossein Agha asked me to go with him and bring the doctor to write the death certificate. I told him that I needed to be alone with her. He agreed but regretted it before leaving and speaking.

"I don't want to leave you alone. Remember, Zohreh Khanum and children need you and me more than ever."

I assured him that I would not do anything harmful. He went to call the doctor from his home and returned sooner because he was afraid to leave me alone. When I was alone with my mother, I kissed her hands and blame myself for not kissing her when she was alive and did not take care of her. I regretted why I did not hug her before she died. I did not learn to show my affection and express my feelings, and it was too late. Manijeh had asked one of her neighbors to take care of the children and returned home with Zohreh. My sister has also blamed herself for not taking care of our mother. We had nothing to say except remorse. The doctor issued a burial permit.

Hossein Agha arranged my mother's funeral in Behesht- Zahra commentary. A black car stopped in front of the house, and the neighbors came and put my mother's body in a wooden box of coffins. They would carry the wooden box in the raised hand; they said we all go back to God and put it in the black car. I hated this God for sending my mother to him. We should drive behind the black car to the cemetery.

In Behesht- Zahra, the coffin was sent to the mortuary to be washed, shrouded, and buried. Hussein Agha went to the office and paid the bill with a tip, especially for the corpse washing 200 Tomans. A woman who washed my mother's corpse came where we were waiting and complained that it was very difficult, and she had washed her corpse well because of us. Hussain Agha gave her a tip again and spoke.

"I gave your tip in the office."

It was less than 20 minutes that we were in Behesht-Zahra. My salary was 15,000 tomans monthly for eight to 10 hours a day when I was teaching. I received 500 tomans daily, and a mortuary worker tip for 20 minutes is 200 tomans. I remembered Shamloo's poem.

"I never feared dying, although his hands were more fragile than vulgarity. I feared dying in a land where the wages of the badger were more than human freedom."

I was always afraid of death and thought that if my father had not died, I would not have been an orphan, and my mother would not have suffered so much. It was the first time I wasn't afraid of death. Here in my land, human life was worthless. The wages of the commentary worker were higher than human freedom, and the tip was more significant than the salary of a university professor.

When we waited there, a beggar with a child in her arms came to us, and Manijeh gave her money, and she left. Manijeh noticed that she went and came back with another chador and another child, and this was repeated several times. Manijeh made sure that the woman regularly changed her appearance, and she told the police that the beggar was a charlatan and changed her clothes and her child. Surprisingly, the police told Manijeh that it was not her business. Hossein Agha quickly walked towards Manijeh and told the police to forgive us and took Manijeh's hand and pulled her aside. He said I wish you'd told me first. They are the charlatans and thugs Ganges all over in the market, and they're all together, and the police are partners of that group. They carried these unknown kids for business.

For a moment, the world turned around my head, shooting all my spine and wondering if one of these kids might be my child. I was staring at him. Hossein Agha noticed my mood changed, the issue of the baby was targeting my wound, and he changed the subject and was upset.

"One of these kids might be..."

I couldn't say anything else.

Manijeh: "No, Doctor, they are the gypsy children who change with each other." Her word was not effective to relief my pain.

Zohreh cried along the way and spoke.

"After this, I must take care of you. My mother worried about you and said that my son had just learned to study, and someone should take care of him."

I was older in terms of age, and could support my sister, but I couldn't even manage myself. Manijeh's neighbors took care of Kaveh and Kamyar, tied up Zohreh's house, took out the mattress from home, and prepared lunch. We returned home, and the mother's vacancy was clutching to our hearts, and her loving shadow was no longer over there. On Manijeh's advice, we have not cried in the presence of children. During this time, the doctor increased my antidepressants, which bothered me, but I should take it for three months. I had not been out of the house for weeks. Hussein Agha and Manijeh's help in our painful situation was a great blessing, and thanks were not enough for them. After my mother's 40-day ceremony, Zohreh and I decided to sell my house and car and leave Iran for another country and we expected Nader, Hossein Agha's son, would send us the invitation from West Germany. Then we would have a passport, an invitation and apply for a visa.

I had brought in much debt after losing my job,
Hossein Agha had paid my loan, and I spent the money I
had from Masoud. I bought my tiny old house in Amirabad
St. for 555,000 Tomans, added one bedroom, and repaired
it. I sold it for 1,400,000.00 tomans and paid off my bank
loan of 440,000.00 Tomans and Hossein Agha debt. I kept
Masood's loan and 150,000.00 tomans for tickets and visa
fees, and I gave the rest to Hossein Agha to exchange for
foreign currency. He converted the funds into DM Deutch
Mark and US dollars. We planned to go to West Germany
and apply for a U.S. visa because we were familiar with
English language.

When Shah was in Iran, the dollar was always equal to
seven Tomans, and it did not change. The price of Deutch
Mark changed around 2-3Tomans. On average, one US
dollar equaled three Deutch Mark or a little more. When
we wanted to exchange Deutch Mark was 22 and the US
dollar was 71 tomans, almost ten times more than the
former price, and there was no hope to decrease. Hussein
Agha, who worked in the bazaar, told us to convert our
money sooner because the situation was unstable. He
exchanged 500,000 tomans for foreign currency. It was time
to apply for passports. I had never traveled abroad and
needed to learn how to obtain a passport and visa. I left
home at 7am to be the first in the passport office, and when
it was our turn to call Zohreh to come.

Passport and home for sale

Getting the passport was difficult because the airport
was closed to public after the Iraq attack to Mehrabad
airports, and the exit was banned from the country.
Binational people, parents whose children are abroad, and
patients for treatment if treatment is not possible in Iran are
allowed to leave Iran. It was almost one-two months to
Nowruz when the passport office was opened to the
public. A passenger should get a foreign county visa with a
valid passport, then buy a flight ticket and leave the
country.

The passport office was located on Shahrara Street. I
reached there early but it was crowded. I could recognize

the depth of disaster when all were disappointed, wanted to run away and pointed mullah and government with ugly title. The passport office was separated from the street by tall, heavy-iron fences, like a prison. Due to the overcrowding, I could not get even close to the gate. Polices were standing at the entrance, clearly indicating that it is a bribe party. Because some people touched the police's hand, they passed the gate and pretended should see their boss, and people said loudly he paid, the money miracle. Around noon, the police announced that the officers would not see more clients. They should deal with the cases from this hour onwards and asked the customers to go home and come back tomorrow. I returned home with empty hands. And I heard people say they would come very early tomorrow morning.

That night, in the news, Rafsanjani said that he saw people crowding in front of the passport office and wanted the authorities to create a system to prevent wasting time. Recently, I did not wake up early morning, became lazy, decreased my abilities but I left the house at 3 a.m. I was always getting up early in the morning, and now it was painful to wake up early.

The streets city was quiet, but it was in a long queue in front of the passport office at 3:30 a.m. Even though I was wearing warm clothes, shivering, and drowning in my thought. It was close to eight o'clock when I heard someone called my name and touched my shoulder. He was university professor Arash.

"I did not recognize you at first. I crossed you twice. It looked like you emerged in deep thought. How is your work?"

"I am fired."

"Good news, I have cleared up, too. Who wants to work with these bastards? You seem so grieving. With your literacy and knowledge, you will be hired quickly. How is Hayedeh?"

My tears collapsed incontinently and stayed silent.

"Bad news, tell me what happened. No, no, don't say she, Hayedeh."

I shook my head.

"Tell me what happened."

"They killed her."

He put his head down and wept. A few people who heard our conversation were saddened and swearing at the mullahs.

"You do an excellent job leaving, and the best universities would hire you."

He started to console me. Arash graduated from a US university, was hired at our university, he did not have any experience in Iran and was very annoyed. At that time, he would come to my office, consult with me, and favored me. There was a man behind me who spoke.

"I knew we would wait a long time and put a big flask of tea in my car. Here's the hot tea, please."

He now knew I was a university's professor. He treated me with compassion, and his name was David. The man in front of me expressed his sadness too.

Arash said someone had filled his spot instead him.

He told Arash:

"The door opens at 8:30 am, and they call me, stand here, or wherever you want, then you come with me."

His name was Shahryar.

"How do they call you?"

He said something under Arash's ear.

"The rest will be with me when we are inside."

They shook hands. Now he knew that Arash was a university professor. Arash said under my ear.

"He paid a bribe to the front door police and promised him more. Also, my classmate is a colonel who worked here. Last night I tried to contact him, but I couldn't. I came to see him. Now, we wait and see what will happen."

During this period, everyone was walking to keep their body warm, swearing at mullahs and saying they were black reactionaries and ruined our country. Arash spoke.

"It is a pity these important people leave Iran, but what could they do? I was labeled and fired as a tyrant."

"Why are you a tyrant? Did you have a picture with Shah?"

"I don't know where these labels came from, but it was an excuse not to let us work here."

At 8:30, the police posed as a king who talked to his servants, came forward, had a file, looked at the crowd, and read three names; one of them was Shahriar. David who was after me asked Shahriar to come with us, and Shahriar agreed. We went forward. The police looked at Shahriar in anger. Shahriar put his hand in his pockets with money, pointed to the money nonverbally, and said "I left all my passport in your kiosk."

The policeman was familiar with his hint and pretended all documents were there. After going up and down a few times, the police went to his kiosk, and Shahriar followed him. Shahriar returned and stood next to us calmly. After a few minutes, the police came and spoke. "The Colonel waits for you."

We passed through the gate. Arash laughed and said: "You know their tricks very well."

The man who accompanied us was a doctor and said: "I have a friend I couldn't get him on the phone. You stand in line when I am looking for him."

Arash: "Let me to find my friend too. Follow me."

We went to Colonel Kamran's office. We arrived in his chief of staff room. His room was not comparable to our simple university office. He did not take us seriously. Arash noticed his cold shoulder and the officer's attitude. He frowned and said with authority.

"Go now and tell Colonel Kamran that Dr. Arash is here and cannot wait."

The chief of staff stood up and said, yes, sir. He might think we were important, so he immediately went to the colonel's room. The Colonel came out with the officer. It meant that we were important to him to greet Arash and us respectfully. In short, we were in the colonel's office. The Colonel ordered tea. He was very cordial. Arash said:

"Kami, Soheil has priority over all of us. Remember when I came from America and told you it was hard for me to work at the university? This is Soheil."

Kamran interrupted his remarks and said:

"Soheil, the distinguished university student and elite professor, it is a pity you will leave."

Arash got up and leaned over his desk and said

something in his ear that I thought told him about
Hayedeh. His face showed his sadness, and he spoke.

"Give me the docs."

"I couldn't get the form yesterday."

Except me, other had their passports that needed to be
extended and stamped. They were also required to fill out a
form they did not have. The colonel pointed to me and
asked:

"How many are you?"

"Four, my sister, two kids, and me."

"How about your brother-in-law? If he isn't coming
with you. Your sister and her kids need his permission to
get out of Iran."

"He was killed."

"What? Arash, did you say his wife or her brother-in-
law?"

Arash returned to me:

"What did you say? Are you telling doctor? Soroush?
No!"

"Yes, the government killed Soroush."

I closed my eyes so I could keep myself calm. Arash
knew Soroush. They often saw each other at our weddings
and family and friends' parties. The Colonel spoke in low
voice. "Don't say anything for a moment. He called his
office manager.

"Bring a passport application form and renewal form."

He came back with a bunch of forms. We filled out the
forms. I did not have the headshot photo. And we decided
to return tomorrow, and I will bring the photos. There, we
found that David is Gynecologist. He said there is no place
to stay in a country treating doctors like this. I graduated
from Sorbonne University in France. Those who know the
Sorbonne University know its scientific value, and for those
who don't know, I don't need to explain it, and my time is
worth more to spend on medicine and scientific research
instead to explain for the mullah. He decided to return to
France.

Shahriar studied in Germany for a few years and then
gave up his study and started importing heavy machinery
from Germany. He knew how to bribe the police. He sold

his business and intended to return to Germany. He explained that in the market, mullahs asked for ransoms; they were thieves, and their robes had large pockets that never would be filled, and I could not tolerate these grave reciters anymore. Shahriar quoted his father as saying that before Reza Shah, thieves would stand on the road outside the city and attack cars and trucks at night. Based on Khan's order would steal people's belongings and kill them. My father once drove between Shiraz and Yazd, and his vehicle was full of stuff that was attacked by thieves. He would fearfully hide between two truck wheels for his life. Even though it was cold, he took off his white underwear because they might see his white lingerie in the moonlight between the two wheels. Thieves were customary to shoot and kill the owner of the goods after they stole items. My father went to Khan in the morning and spoke.

"Khan, your thieves stole my truck last night. Tell them to return it with my stuff."

My father knew Khan well because Khan asked him to marry his daughter. Khan seemed to be surprised! A few hours later, he returned the truck with his stuff to him. My father said we would have been killed 100 times if Reza Shah was not in Iran. That time thieves were stealing in the dark, and now they're all over daylight. Every day they send one to beg that Haj Agha asked for Khoums and Zakat, whereas they took khoums and Zakat for one year a month before. It means that every hardworking must pay mullahs one-fifth of the gross income for Khoums and one-tenth of the gross income for Zakat without any question. And again and again, they asked for money to build a mosque. Their demands never ended and continued. My father advised me to leave here.

When they spoke, I thought that all of them were in one of the foreign countries except me. They knew the country and its language. I just stayed wondering what to do. They asked me where you were going, and I said I had no place, so I decided to go to Germany and apply for a U.S. visa.

Our file was completed after four days. Colonel

Kamran explained the process of issuing the passport; the files must be sent to a newly established department named the Protection Agency, which is the same as the previous SAVAK. This paperwork takes two weeks. It was a time killer. I went home; I considered selling cars because I had better do things in order.

We agreed with Zohreh to sell the household items to Manijeh's neighbors, who paid the fee and decided to have the items when we left the country. People were good and trusted each other, but no one trusted the regime. I thought I did not need a car anymore, and I went by taxi or bus.

Hossein Agha's friend bought my vehicle. We had already dated to see Arash, Shahriar, and David in front of the passport office after two weeks. That morning, Hossein Agha gave me a ride to the passport office. Arash and Shahriar were there. David was a little late and said he did a cesarean section. We thought that this time there was no need to give a ransom. However, Shahriar knew the way of going to the passport office because he was dealing with these groups, and we were such a pearl inside a shell in our limited circle. In our little world, everything was simple, whereas, in the outside world, the confusing clutches of simplicity was evoked. And we offered to pay our share to Shahriar, he refused, as if he were in an excellent financial situation and needlessly. Also, Shahriar wanted to buy the man and said that my family should also come here, and I must give a ransom to this doorman who is the gatekeeper, to facilitate the rest of the work. As usual, the police went to the kiosk on the pretext of seeing the passports. Then we went to the colonel's office, where he took us with respect and pleasure. Arash and Shahriar's passports were ready, and he gave me my sister's passport and told us.

"Yours and Doctor David's passports were not issued. For the doctor, the easiest way to get his passport is an invitation to participate in a medical conference. But you are on the country elites list who should be allowed by the Ministry of Science."

His words were such a hammer on my head, how I would tolerate being banned from leaving. What about Zohreh and her kid? I was happy that at least Zohreh could go. We were all upset. Arash was sure Kamran would have done it if it had been under his control. We came out of there, and they wanted to have lunch. I did not feel well and wanted to attend the Ministry of Science, and they came with me. Shahriar bought sandwiches for all and drove to the Ministry of Science. On the way, they talked and asked me what I did.

"I sold my house and car and prepared to travel with my sister and her kids. I should try to get permission to leave."

"Do you know anyone there." After he hear that we had no acquaintance in the Ministry of Science, he told.

"When we got there, I would separate from you to get some clues to solve this problem."

At that time, I thought about how to give thanks for these strangers' kindness. I remember my mother always saying thank people at the same time when they do something for you. Don't wait for good words. And I did not thank her when she was alive and kissed her when she died, and how much I regretted it. I told them my thought and how grateful I was for their kindness. The sad atmosphere filled the space broken by Shahriar's voice.

"We must break this spell anyway. The pay is with me. Like other government agencies, they are good at ransoms."

"I will pay with the money I have."

Shahriar interrupted me:

"We will talk about it later. Now we will find the spell breaker."

He kept talking; maybe he wanted to decrease my sadness. He defined that he has returned to Iran 12 years ago, started doing business with his father, and then became independent. When he referred to any office with numerous blockages, as soon as they saw the money, the country's law would be drafted, and problems would be solved. He compared Iran to Germany, where the German people enforced the law, and if they took money from clients, they would be expelled.

David said from France that he was always in the medical field, had nothing to do with the business, and

never saw a Frenchman to blackmail. But whenever he had
a problem in Iran, his family and friends said, come on,
we'll fix it. It's a formality.

Arash talked about the United States. Everyone must
work their lawful jobs. In the meantime, I did not know
anything about business, and was in the books since I was
a kid, and I did not have any experience abroad to tell. Like
the captive bird of the cage, who saw nothing but six walls
of the cell, I had deposited the day to night and the
unknown tomorrow in my lonely cocoon. I was thinking
the depth of Hayedeh's vision and conversations, a man
with a healthy eye and all the disabled
organs left on his owner's hand. Arash asked.

"Soheil, why are you quiet?"

"I was thinking about Hayedeh, was heartbroken when
she tried to wake me up, and I thought it was just enough
to study. I was educated and did not understand what was
happening to our country. Even in some cases, the people
were screaming lest the country falls into the hands of
mullahs because they were in the community and knew
these England parasites.

We, educated people, like a robot, had a longstanding
habit of reading books and thoughts about the book we
read. They should have shared with us about the country's
work and decision-making. One person ordered, and a few
people understood and protested. The fear prevented a
healthy and constructive dialogue that should be clear
about who was saying what. We were unaware and fearful
of SAVAK and arrest. Anyone who said different things
were ridiculed. In such an atmosphere, we lost the point
that the fight was not only about Mullah's Marsudin's quilt
but also about his shorts. And now, we must see that we
are penniless in our community, and we burn from the
inside because the illiterate trickster mullah became the
people's blood-sucking.

"I am reviewing Hayedeh's memories and her
leadership and her decisively speech. At any gathering, the
professors talked and praised her courage, and said she
was right, but no one dare enough to speak publicly."

I listened to Arash and reviewed Forough 's poem.

"The innocent pigeons are full of hidden spites, looking at the crowd from the height spot of the white tower look at you.

Come to the meadow, to the grand meadow.
Call me in public behind the voice of silky flowers,
Such a deer calling his soulmate."

I talked to myself, yes, dear, we were not a good role model for innocent pigeons and children. If we were united and came to the grand meadow with you, and those groups whose voices were submissive to the wind joined and followed you. In the big square together, we announced our demands, and we did not leave you alone, and then this tragedy wouldn't happen. If there is no complaint from others, it would be from me who needed to understand and help you on time. This pain will always be with me. We reached the Ministry of Science. The corridors were crowded with educated people, and in talking to them, we found that the majority were those who were banned from leaving Iran. Shahriar left us, and I saw him enter a room. There were three rooms in raw, and one was for the academic records assessment of foreign graduates, full of the graduates who watched the commutes. Their expression was spectacular. They talked loudly that all this chaos due to mismanagement and it had a solution. They were unfamiliar with domestic affairs.

The other group knew the awful situation, frowned, and spoke.

"Sir, you did not see the situation of mismanagement. Wait to dry up your sweat and discover what a chaotic desert is here."

One was in front of me and had just talked to three young, manicured men with neat appearances who had just came from abroad.

"Listen to me; if you have two feet, borrow two more and run away from here, you go back. Remember my words and leave here sooner."

The young men looked at him dumbfounded and did not understand him. Shahriar finally found someone who took care of my case and gave him 2,000. Tomans. Shahriar

refused money from me. David and Arash insisted on
sharing the cost, but he declined and urged us to forget the
expenses. The man found my file quickly and told Shahriar
to follow him to the administrator's office. We went to his
office; the administrator was an inexperienced young boy
who looked at the file and spoke.

"Sir, you are an elite who could not leave the country
without the supreme leader's permission. Anyone with a
high education degree should stay and work here.

David pointed to me and spoke.

"He is sick and should go abroad for treatment."

I remembered Soroush and the doctor of currency in
charge for the patients, and I thought about what the hell I
did when I studied, became an honor student and teacher. I
wanted to be stupid and wasn't here with these killers.
Shahriar spoke.

"You are the boss and should sign the documents."

"I'm not the boss."

"Who's the boss?"

"Go upstairs."

"You come with me, and I'll give you a car if you take
care of this case. What else do you want?"

The young man looked at him and said:

"Look at the list. Not eighter we have it, but also the
passport office and the airport police have it. In this way,
they control each other and report."

"Who made this list?"

"The Department of Protection."

"Do you know anyone at that office?"

"No, but it's possible if you have a familiar mullah."

"What does mullah want?"

"You don't know what mullahs want? Mullahs want
money and money."

"I know, you find the mullah."

"I do not know any mullah in that department. Please
give me time so that I find one to change the list. Could I
count on your promise?"

"Yes, come to the door and see my car. I will give it to
you."

"I accept you."

I was disappointed and returned home after wasting my day inconclusive. Manijeh was with my sister. Hossein Agha came home and said that Nader was sent the invitation by someone and gave it to me. It was the German language. Hussein Agha's friend paid 180,000 tomans for the car, and he exchanged it for dollars. I trusted he would make the best decision. I told used car price is higher in Iran, such as the antique, because the original price was half five years ago. There was a high inflation rate. It looked like everything was famine. For example, Soroush bought a video record for 60,000 tomans, and it was sold to a neighbor for 90,000 tomans. It was not a good economic sign and was perilous for the market.

I should pay Masoud's loan. I could not contact him because my phone book was stolen from my home; I went to his office twice, which was closed. I decided to go to his home at night. Zohreh said the city was unsafe at night, and you go there during the day. I postpone it to the day after, placed the money envelope inside my shirt so nobody could rob, put a coat over it, and went to pay back my debt.

Masoud's House

Masoud's house was a mansion in the highest economic area of Tehran. The houses on that street were large and far apart from each other. It was a green area with old trees, and the excellent weather was colder than in other parts of the city. The soft moonlit lights made the quiet street poetic, giving it a unique quality, and it was famous as a lovers' street. I walked with Hayedeh in Fereshteh streets after sunset. The girls and boys stood under the moonlight next to the old trees, whispering for hours. When Masoud invited us, Hayedeh said we go early and walk there before his party.

When I got there around sunset and Masoud's house lights were off. Although it was not easy to ask the neighbors about Masood, I knocked on the neighbors' door to find out about Masood's family. They did not know or did not answer the door. The people's behavior in different parts of Tehran were distinguished. People of the south of

Tehran knew each other and shared all information about their neighbors. North of Tehran, people were in a high economic situation and did not share any information about each other and pretended they did not know anything, the questioning about him was useless.

The weather was going cold and gradually darkened, and a gentle breeze blew. The street had a dime light, no more girls and boys were there, and the road was quiet. I walked from Fereshteh to Pahlavi Street to take a taxi home.

I was reminiscing about those good and memorable days in nostalgia when the sound of successive shots nailed me in place. And I sought refuge behind a tree so no one could see me. I had no choice but to stand there until the shooting stopped. My whole body was shaking, and I did not know if it was cold, fear, or both. The sound of shooting was terrifying. Hard minutes passed, and there was no choice but to wait until the street was safe.

Suddenly, I felt something moving next to my leg. I was scared and stuck in my place for a few moments, bent down to see what it was. In the dark, I could see with difficulty, looked carefully, and surprised to see a child with his tiny hands wrapped around my leg. My hand touched his cold face. I hugged him and realized she was a little girl who had wet herself and was shivering from the cold. I wanted to put her on the ground and take off my coat to wrap her in; she was tightly clinging to my neck and wouldn't let me go. With difficulty, I took off my coat with one hand and wrapped it around her. I asked for her name quietly, and she started crying. Out of fear that the killers with guns could hear us, I gently pressed her face to my shoulder and caressed her. Her head was on my shoulder, and she fell asleep, although her feet were still cold.

I had to wait until there was no danger threatening us. In those days, Khomeini's special guards would attack people's houses and kill people in the name of "war against Allah" or conspiracy and plotting against the regime or other words such as the Tudeh's party or leftist groups.

They would tell on news with aplomb, so they were

terrified people. The NEWS bolded it to terrorize the
people. A few days ago, it was in the NEWS that they had
attacked a house in the north of Tehran killed a team and
did not let the toddler children stay with their
grandparents. They took the toddlers with them. It was
about Masoud Rajavi's group had worked with Khomeini
to achieve power. When Khomeini came to power, he tried
to eliminate his companions.

Pity for me that I lost Hayedeh, my child, and my
It was cold, and I could hear the steps of someone
running. I remembered the days when Masoud had the
party, and he would invite my family, especially my
mother. He always told everyone that my mother prepared
his desired meals, and he had good lunch at my home
every day. Whenever my mother did not want to come, he
said he would come to our home, but he would not eat
lunch. He did the same even though my mother insisted
him, but he did not eat. Then my mother would be with
us. Masoud's mother would take my mother to her
bedroom to rest when she was tired until the table was
ready, and she would invite my mother to the table first.

Pity for me that I lost Hayedeh, my child, and my
mother. Good memories with Hayedeh in that alley filled
my mind, and I wished this was my child. Zohreh said that
the streets were not safe. The money envelope was inside
my shirt, a child in my arms, and what could I do with this
child? I had the dilemma couldn't leave her alone in a dark
street, should take her, but if I would be arrest, it might be
accused of stealing money and kidnapping the baby. If I
would search for her parents, no one would open the door
especially after the gun shooting because they hesitated to
respond me previously. No one would open the door after
the shooting. I was there for several hours to ensure no one
was around and the shooting was over. The baby warmed
up and slept. My clothes were wet with baby clothes, and I
was frozen, and there was no choice but to take the baby
with me and come back and look for her parent day after.
It was late, and I knew that Zohreh and Manijeh were
worried, I checked the alley, walked down like a thief, and
trembling to get to the street when no one was nearby.

On Pahlavi Street, I got the first taxi. At least it was

warm, and I wasn't trembling from the cold. Taxis went straight and picked up more than one passenger. I was looking at the baby and trying to keep my appearance calm. The taxi driver in the front mirror checked the passengers one by one and asked me the child's name. For a moment, I thought about the baby's name and said Hayedeh.

After checking the passengers, the driver spoke.

"Do you want to listen to Hayedeh's song?"

Everyone happily said yes and cursed Khomeini. I was talking with myself and going through my misfortunes. Hayedeh's song was.

"Good King, I complain from the sadness of separation.

My life is over, and it is time you come back."

I was incontinently in tears and thought, Hayedeh never returned. I wished to die, was restless and checked the baby's appearance and what to do if they accused me of kidnapping. The baby's hair was clean and tidy, and it could be guessed that the child belonged to a prosperous family, and I wished this child was Hayedeh and me. The taxi driver rightly recognized my discomfort and pain when he asked me a few times.

"Mr., what is wrong with you? where is her mother?"

"She died."

The driver was convinced I should not be happy and tried to comfort me. At the end of the trip, he did not want to accept the ride fee, but I paid it. I went to Masood's house to pay my loan and returned with a baby. After those painful incidents, Manijeh always stayed at Zohreh's house until I returned home. Both are surprised to see a beautiful little girl in my arms. I explained what happened and wanted to put the baby on the sofa when she woke up and started crying. Zohreh wanted to change her clothes, but she resisted and held my neck. My sister changed her clothes with her son's blouse. The baby did not talk and fell asleep in my arms. I sat on sofa with fearing that the baby would wake up and cry and wake up my nephews all night and thinking about my life's event that I never expected, now a child. I would be glad to find her parents, and they will be happy to have their baby. I wondered if my child was dead or if they lied to me. I thought I would leave Iran anyway. It would be my fate to take care of my sister and her kids, and I looked for a light that was not in my life's dark tunnel. The next day, Hossein Agha came to Zohreh's house with Manijeh. It was evident that Manijeh told her the whole story.

"I will go to the shop, return soon and we will search for her family together." Hussein Agha spoke. The baby had woken up and looked around with a surprised look. I fed her with a milk bottle, and she relaxed in my arms.

Zohreh could get her attention by playing with her kids. She joined them playing and, a few minutes later, came back into my arms. Manijeh said this little girl is brilliant. Even after one night, she prefers to stay with you. Kaveh and Kamyar were sixteen and five months old. Manijeh said the girls talk sooner than boys. This little girl is either late, or her family is all tall and probably 8-9 months old because she walks and has front teeth but doesn't talk. Zohreh suggested I keep my distance from the baby so that she would not suffer when I leave home. The kids get to know each other sooner and play together.

Hossein Agha returned with two sets of girls' clothes purchased at Manijeh's request, which were large for her. Hossein Agha and I went to find the child's family. On the way, he said that his friend gave him the exchanged currency, and we agreed that he would keep it. He always talked to me with love and respect and said that it was better I marry again. And he always wished to study, but it was never possible to achieve his dream. He worked and had many gains and losses until he could stand up, and Manijeh never complained and stayed with him. He loved Manijeh and her family, and it was a pity that Soroush was not alive. He loved Soroush like his son, and his death broke his heart. And about Ava Khanum, when his eyes would treat what we could tell her about her son.

We parked the car near Masood's house. We went to the same sub alley on Fereshteh Street and cautiously knocked on the door by the door. Some did not open the door, and a few people talked to us. We asked about a missing baby and wondered if they did not see a little kid, and when people trusted us, we said we found a little girl, and we gave them Hossein Agha's phone number. We went to Masoud's house, where no one was there. We could guess that Masoud's family had traveled.

Hussein Agha told me to search for a local grocer and give him the telephone number. There were only two local stores. Hossein Agha told them his friend had found a child here last night and that if anyone missed a baby, call him. On the second day of searching for her parents, Hossein Agha said it was better to send Manijeh as people trust women more. People might be scared when they see two men behind the door and assume they are thieves. It was supposed I would care for the kids, and Manijeh and Zohreh followed the case. The baby was a little comfortable with her kids, but like someone who lost something, she came out of the room, looked after someone everywhere, and suddenly started crying. From the sound of her crying, my sister's kids also wept, and their voices occupied the whole space. I was surprised to care of which one first and noticed how difficult it was to have kids, remembered my mother, and how she had suffered. The next day, Hossein Agha came, but Zohreh did not feel well. Manijeh and Hossein Agha left for searching her family.

I was at home when Arash and Shahriar called me, and I told them I was busy, but I did not say what it was happened and promised to call them. All problems came to me at the same time. A few days ago, my travel was banned, now a baby, depression, sold my house and must apply for her visa.

I decided to go to the German Embassy and apply for Zohreh's visa. Then I followed my case in the ministry of science, hoping they would issue a permit to leave this country. Hossein Agha, who passed by the German Embassy daily, saw a long queue. I had passport office experience, and I knew I should go morning and wear a warm dress.

Zohreh did not feel well and said she would leave when I could leave Iran. I tried to keep her calm and said don't worry about me. Let's see what happens. She was

worried about words such as Mam and daddy. We all
agreed to select a name for her. Hossein Agha suggested a
name that Hayedeh liked. We called the child Neda.

Hossein Agha Asked me to go in his car to the
embassy, which I refused. I woke up early and took the taxi
to the front of the German Embassy on Ferdowsi Street. As
expected, there was a queue. People had been sleeping
there the night before, but they said the embassy was open
at eight in the morning, and the line was going fast. I was
unfamiliar with the processes.

I was educated and expected to know the basic things,
but others knew better than me. Inevitably, I asked them
what to do, where is the form and how to fill it out.
Someone in line told me that there was a man who sold the
form, I bought it, but I did not know Germany, and how to
fill it out. Someone told me the embassy would give you
the form and help to complete it which was a wasted
money and a form.

They started on time, and my turn was at about 11:00
AM. A person at the embassy knew German and Farsi
would fill out the form from her birth certificates and
passports and said your sister should come here and sign
the document herself, and I could not
sign for her. I tried to set an appointment, but she said no,
she should be in line. It would be better come back with
Zohreh tomorrow.

When I returned home, my sister said Shahriar called
and would come here with Arash and David tonight. They
were so kind and met me a few weeks ago, and I did not
expect them to be so gentlemanly. Manijeh and Zohreh
prepared dinner, and I took care of the babies. Neda had
distinguished behavior that showed that someone had paid
particular attention to her. She picked up the toy and
 kissed and patted it in her arms. My nephews had boys'
toys and Teddy bears. Neda played with a bear that was
brighter than the others. Manijeh said she only took this toy
since morning. My heart was broken because I thought my
sister and I were the most miserable children in the world
who did not have a father, my sister's siblings also suffered
our destiny, and now I saw this child's misery. More

miserable than this child is her parents.

All afternoon I was reviewing misfortunes like a round of rosaries. These thoughts approached me like a stone wall from everywhere and pushed me into a corner. I stayed in the room and stared at a point all day long. I was 26 years old. Manijeh and Zohreh noticed my depression. I thought my duty was heavier than before and I would live for Zohreh, nephews, and Neda, but I couldn't move forward.

At dusk, Hossein Agha came from work. I saw how valuable was for a man to go to work for days and return with full hands, which was impressive and satisfied the men's feelings of pride. And I was lying like a carcass in the corner of the house, which I would never have thought of. I started working when I was in high school, and always active. Now I was like a useless tire that would not repair and was not pleasant. That night Arash and Shahriar and then David came.

Arash knew Zohreh, Manijeh, and Hossein Agha. They had seen each other frequently at parties. Arash talked about Soroush, and I put my head on the dining table and cried loudly. Zohreh told them about my depression.

"Why you and Manijeh wore black dresses? I had studied in the US about Iran history for many years, and I know that Iranians were not dressed in black for the dead. The color itself is not happy. You must take off the black dress because of Soroush."

I noticed that they have been wearing black since Soroush was executed. Then their conversation with Hossein Agha heated up, and I went to the kitchen to help Manijeh. When we had dinner, Hossein Agha said it was time to visit Ava Khanum. I found out that they decided to go to Amol on the weekend with the long SUV belonging to Shahriar.

Shahriar: "We will go in one car."

"I am busy and do not come."

"I know the visa still needs to be completed. Why did not you tell me? We will do it tomorrow. I will take care of it."

"There is a long queue."

"I know I'll send one to stay in line, and then we'll go to the embassy. In Germany, I will do my best if you want to live in Germany. And if you don't wish, I will help you with the U.S. visa. I know Nader lives in Cologne, I know Germany and it is easy to travel by train."

Shahriar picked us up from our home at 10am. We all went to the German Embassy in Shahriar's car, and after a few minutes, we went in. Shahriar spoke German, and Zohreh signed the forms. The passports would be ready in three days, Monday, because the embassy was closed on Saturday and Sunday. Shahriar said we would go to Amol with peace of mind. From there, we went to have lunch based on Shahriar's suggestion. He did not let me to pay for lunch and spoke. "By the way, we will come to your home tonight. Because Arash's mom wanted to see you, we invited ourselves, and David might come."

Manijeh and Zohreh wanted to go home and prepare dinner.

"We think about it at night." Shahriar spoke.

I noticed how comfortable about lunch and dinner who lived abroad, while we had to stay home when we had a guest. Shahriar talked about Neda during lunch time.

"I have a friend at Saltanatabad police Station; You might talk to him and find a solution."

I did not know why none of us thought we should go to the police station. We went home after lunch. Shahriar was very intimate. He called David from my sister's house, and David said you are my guests tonight.

Zohreh: "No, it isn't easy with three kids, and we would have dinner at home."

"All right, I'll call David and Arash."

Shahriar talked to Arash and said his mother would come and bring dinner for us. We knew Arash had cooks and servants. Then he called David. Whatever Manijeh and Zohreh insisted on making dinner, he did not accept.

"No, I promised them on your behalf, let's go to see my sheriff's officer friend."

He was a gentleman and asked Zohreh and Manijeh if they needed anything to buy, which was a negative answer. We went to the police station and met Shahrokh who spoke.

"Tajrish and Sultanabad police stations are two separate branches. I'll send you to see my friend."

Shahriar asked about the legal process for finding the child.

"When a child is found, we will keep him at the police station for almost a day because a parent looking for their child may come to the police station to report a missing child and claim him. We will ask for the child's details, check their identification, and give them the child if their claims are valid. During this period, although it is not the police duty, they care for the child kindly and are very accompanying. If no one claims the child, we will send the child to the court or the orphanage with a police officer based on the court order. Then it will be the prosecutor's responsibility to appoint a guardian for the child, assign the orphan house, and consider the child's life and safety."

I explained her story.

He was very sad and said:

"Can you keep the child? Otherwise, this child will be crushed and will be our future prisoner. I have seen many cases where these innocent kids are future criminals."

He seemed very upset and said:

"Wait for me to contact my friend, Payam, at Tajrish Police Station and find out what happened there."

He phoned his friend and asked him to wait for us. We went with him to the Tajrish police station. He asked him to come out.

"I don't want to tell her story in the police station lest anyone hear it."

His friend was a very gentleman. Shahriar introduced me as a university professor and told him the story.

"There were clashes a few days ago, but it wasn't my working hour, and I heard that some had been killed and several people were arrested that night.

Payam, like Shahrokh, believed that the child would indeed be hurt during the legal process. I am right to give the child to the police station if I cannot or will not want the baby. But when the child goes to the orphanage is so crushed that these children can never have a regular life.

I was supposed to keep the baby, and they checked all cases so that they might find her parents. But he knew no one had reported the missing child to the police station.

"The issue of missing children always has high priority, and when the shift changes, it is reported to ensure that the child is found or still missing. No one has reported the missing child to the police station in a few days."

"We will go to Amol tomorrow and return after three days."

"I'm worried that I would accuse me of kidnapping."

They both promised to support me if there was a legal problem. Shahriar and I returned home. I was grateful to him for helping me in such a difficult situation, and I thought what a blessing it would be to have a good social relationship and friend.

Shahriar: "I am happy to be able to do something for you."

Zohreh and Manijeh made Mirza Qassemi, and Zohreh remembered that Arash liked it. It was the night: Hossein Agha, David, and Arash cam, and Shokoh Khanum brought dinner, two sets of pinkish dresses for Zohreh and Manijeh, toys and clothes for the children. She apologized for not knowing the bad news about Soroush and Hayedeh and wondered how much Zohreh and Manijeh lost weight, they were thinner than before.

Before the dinner, Shokoh Khanum asked Zohreh and Manijeh to change their black clothes. Hossein Agha explained that it is one of the Iranian traditions that take off the mourners' black clothes and serve dinner.

"I wasn't even wearing black."

"You were hit enough from all sides and did not need to wear black, and I did not wear black because of you."

After a long time, I looked at my beautiful sister, her sad face was moonlight color, and her clothes were loose. Manijeh was thinner and had a sad face like Zohreh.

"We would go to Amol, and my dad might come with us too. It has enough seats." Shahriar said.

"I will come too." Shokoh Khanum responded.

We went to Amol, Shokoh Khanum was caring Neda

kindly all the time and playing with her. Shahpoor Khan, Shahriar's father, did not come because his wife was ill. Manijeh was worried that her mother recognized that Hossein Agha was not Soroush. Hossein Agha would ensure her that he played his role well. Hossein Agha brought and wear Soroush shirts that had his body's aroma.

Arash had a flight ticket to the US for a week after. He tried to assure me that the university would hire me, even though I did not know the language, but I was good in mathematics and science. Arash and Shahriar would keep in contact via Manijeh, and Shokoh Khanum, who were in Tehran. Everyone said that Zohreh stayed in Germany because the U.S. visa was more complicated. Zohreh said that she does not know Germany and should work to cover her kids' expenses, and if she could not work, she preferred to stay in Iran and work.

Arash did not know about immigration laws, so he went to the U.S. on a student visa, which was not difficult. Then he got permanent residency as a student, even though he never thought it would use it. He said people give their work to experts, and the best thing is to hire an immigrant lawyer in the US. He was married and divorced in the US before he came to Iran; after he was fired, he contacted his university friends, and they made some promises to him. When he gets a job, he hires a lawyer.

Hossein Agha and I told him not to wait for his career and that we would pay for her lawyer. We were two days in Amol. Men tried not to be before Ava Khanum during daylight when she might see clearly. In fact, according to Zohreh and Manijeh, her vision diminished, and she did not see correctly. She was happy that everyone was there. Hossein Agha was sometimes himself and sometimes Soroush. He asked Ava Khanum to come to Tehran to live with them.

"I love Amol, and I wouldn't go anywhere."

David spoke little but regularly compared the north of Iran to France, and he regretted that Iran needed a capable manager to use these natural resources well. After Ava Khanum's examination, he contacted Dr. Jamshidi and recommended some tests to be carried out. We returned to Tehran, Zohreh's passport was stamped with a German visa, and we should buy flight tickets.

Purchasing a ticket was difficult. We thought if buying a flight ticket had so tricky, it was better to go in a car. At that time, the flight between Tehran and West Germany (Frankfurt) by plane was about six hours and driving in car was about six days. Finally, Shahriar's helped us to get two tickets and a child under two could sit on her mother's lap.

Zohreh did not want to go without me. I was banned from leaving and Neda is with me, and she should go, we should deliver the rented house. I can escape over the border. Shahriar and Zohreh were supposed to leave Mehrabad airport on the same day and meet Nader at Frankfurt airport.

Shahriar had contacted the Police Officers, Shahrokh and Payam, who told them several people had been killed and arrested on Fereshteh Street that night. The Revolutionary Guards did not report the names of those killed or arrested to the police station and they were not residents of that neighborhood. The police officers were very angry because the revolutionary guards interfered in their work. They could say nothing because they knew the situation was awful. We went again with Shahriar to the Ministry of Science, the gay was not there, and we did not know a mullah. I told Shahriar that I would find a way and did not worry, my sister situation was important, and we should save them. Shahriar told his father about the car and his promise to give it to him. And I could have it because his father does not use or does not sell anything. And I did not accept to have his car.

It was my fault that I was an honor student, an elite professor and well-educated in an Islamic regime with an elementary graduation president. I felt guilty of not understanding Hayedeh who talked about a healthy community, should pay the price, which is my life, and I have a child currently. I thought to flee from Iran and give Neda to the police station, or I would stay in Iran to take care of Neda till to find her family. According to the law, it was not my responsibility to take care of the child; it

is better to give her to the police station and take care of
myself. The world is full of oppression that started in the
name of God, and its branches are in the hands of the
Islamic Republic regime.

The imposed deaths and premature deaths revealed
the effects of injustice everywhere, while the government
yelled behind a microphone of justice words, divine justice,
Justice Ali, etc. Neda's fate would happen like thousands of
other children who grew up without a father. I should not
blame myself for finding her, should join my sister and her
kids, and her fate is not my business, especially when I
don't know her.

The closer I got to my sister's departure from Iran, the
more intense these thoughts became, and I was more
nervous and restless than ever before. I increased the
depression medication dosage so that I could control
myself. At the same time, Shahriar suggested we see his
friends at the police stations again. Our experience and
social consequences lead us to plant a positive or negative
image of someone or a particular occupational group and
extend it to that group, equating the individuals with that
trait. The police imagination in my mind was that they
were harsh. I was always afraid of their guns and their
uniforms. Now I saw that my perception was incorrect, and
false inferences to put everyone in the same image. We
should praise the knowledge of the police officers. When
talking to the two officers, I did not tell them that my sister
and I are more important than the world. Payam was
young and handsome and read my mind. He spoke with
kindness and sincerity.

"You're young and right to think about your own life.
You're in a crisis where it's hard to decide. In this situation,
you feel about yourself, which is nothing wrong with it.
Our social system is unfair. Let me tell you that everyone
who knows me admires me because of my appearance and
behavior. Please don't make this a sign of my selfishness; I
told you this to be a ground for the rest of my speech.
Although my close friend Shahrokh does not know I was in
the orphanage and had bad behavior, I am not shy to say it.
The noble man- Sanatie Kermani institutionalized and

curated all his goodness in me. I learned how to behave well from him, which is admired by everyone today. I am the manifestation of that man, and people have praised him. I owe him all the good that he planted in me, which is my religion, and I must practice every moment of my life. He was a great man, an artist, and a painter, and I learned his art. He told me that being an artist meant starving. You must have a carrier, and the artistic job would be your hobby.

I loved the clean chick suits of the police officers, and several of my orphanage brothers went to different universities. I decided to go to the police academic college. I am pleased about my decision because I am among my community and know people's pain and sorrow. You are right if you don't want the baby. Please give me a chance.

My wife is going through the last month of pregnancy after giving birth and taking care of the baby, we adopt her, or I find someone."

I knew he had read my thoughts correctly; I was so ashamed of myself and my feelings that I stayed silent. I had been in this conflict for a while, and when I looked at Neda's face, I hated my selfish person. It was the end of my killing inner conflict.

My selfish part had failed, and I was separated from the purgatory inside. The last time I was with Shahriar, who wanted to leave the car for me as the employee's gift, I told him that if they issued my passport without bribes, I would take my final decision. But we knew I would not make it without a liaison and bribe. Shahriar was familiar with people's social behavior and told me that you fell in love with this child and that the Payam talking was effective. I looked into Neda's eyes and thought that to leave and abandon this innocent child spooked and made me crazy, I would start my life with Neda and see what would be next.

1984, Mehrabad Airport

Flights to Germany were at 10:00 A.M. We had to be at Mehrabad Airport at 4 A.M. Mehrabad Airport was in the west of Tehran for domestic and foreign flights, a large hall on the first floor, which was a place for gathering of domestic and foreign arrival and departure, companions, and attendees. A half-story-like balcony was a restaurant. We could sit there, have some fast food, and watch the first floor, a theater for himself. A curtain separated one section of the first floor from the checkpoint where the officers controlled the luggage, and we could see the inspector's area well. Several people came for each passenger to welcome or say goodbye.

The entrance was a happy area, kissing and cheering with families about their special visit. The departure, it looked like they are separated forever, and these journeys had a particular predicate. The phrases, forgive us, do not forget us, and if we could see each other again would be heard repeatedly. It looked like the mourning and wedding parties were mixed up. I was amazed because never I saw such a show, and I wondered why they did not separate the two sections.

Behind partitions were the spectacular inspectors. The inspector must ask the passenger what he had and collected his data, but he asked him to open the suitcase and rolled his hands in the briefcase when he held his head up and looked in the left and right directions. I wondered about the inspector's skill that he could evaluate with his hand and did not need to use his eyes! I was not like others who were relaxed. A man sat at our table, noticed my gaze, and spoke.

"You're so surprised. Is it your first trip?"

"I'm not going, the traveler is my sister, and I'm surprised that the inspector's hand was inside the suitcase, he turned his head left and right and did not look inside the bag."

"He worried that the intruder could avoid, getting inside the suitcase and looked for coins and gold."

"Why gold?"

"Easier exchange for money."

Shahriar returned to the table and entered the discussion.

"It's better to put the money in the passport because they are not interchangeable."

"This gentleman traveled a lot and knows the lawless laws."

"Yes, this is the special unfair rule. In Germany, giving money to an officer is a crime. The officer reports it immediately and a large sum fine is issued, so the guilty person remembers never to bribe to any officer."

We had breakfast, and Shahpoor Khan was a quiet man.

Kaveh, Kamyar, and Neda were running around the hall.

Manijeh was crying. Hossein Agha tried to calm her.

"When Zohreh rents an apartment, you travel and stay there for a few months. I could not take you anywhere. Now we have money, and you can travel."

Zohreh was worried for me, I tried to distract my attention, watched the airport theater, and talked to Shahriar.

"Why did they not organize and separate the two parts?"

"Do you think they read any management book and understood the value of an organization, labor, and energy consumption."

Shahpoor Khan turned to Shahriar and said in a sad voice: "Speak with a low voice consider your safely."

"The experienced man shook his head when his eyes were tearful and watched his only son sadly. Every passenger came with his family members except Shahriar was with his father only, and later I knew his mother was disabled.

Shahriar told me to care for his father if I was in Iran, although he always does his job.

"Father, I told Soheil to be in touch with you if you need anything."

The departure time got closer, Shahryar pointed to me and spoke.

"Let's go, pass the luggage, and return."

We went together and took the suitcases to the other side of the curtain. Each passenger could take two suitcases weighing 20 kilos each. Iranian bags packed with food items, such as saffron, pistachios, berry, dried vegetables, and fried vegetables, that Manijeh prepared for Nader and

Zohreh. It was as if there was an Iranian food famine in
Europe. While we placed the suitcases on the table,
Shahriar gave the passports to the inspector. We opened
the luggage, and the officer who got the money recognized
briefly that there was nothing in the suitcase, closed and
locked it. A man placed the bags on the trolleys to carry to
the plane. We went back to the balcony with the passport.
Time passed quickly, and I remember Sohrab's poem.

"The waiting person could recognize the time volume
value."

Yes, the time volume declined and would inevitably
separate the only person I had, Hayedeh, my baby, my
mother, my brother-in-law, and Zohreh. I would miss her
too. We cried and I said we would see each other soon, and
I don't know why I did not tell her how much I loved her.
My weakness was that I could not express my feeling.
Shahriar understood that I was tied up in Iran, watched me
sadly, and said goodbye. It was time to leave and Zohreh
cried. Her kids wanted to stay with Neda, and Neda pulled
Kaveh's hand. Neda was crying and wanted to go behind
the screen. They passed across the screen.
We stood up and watched Zohreh with two children and
Shahriar. I talked to myself about a good chance we could
meet Shahriar. Shahriar held Kaveh in his arms, Zohreh's
bag with his bag on his shoulder, and Zohreh had Kamyar
in her hands. They looked like a couple traveling with two
children. It was heartbreaking, and at the same time,
Manijeh had the same feeling, and we wished Soroush was
next to Zohreh. Little by little, they became out of our sight.
Shahpoor Khan asked us to have tea, and Hussein Agha
immediately agreed and pointed out that his father did not
feel well. Manijeh was hugging Neda and walking around.
From that balcony, we saw them waving at us. We stayed
at the airport, until their flight departure was announced,
we said goodbye to Shahpoor Khan, who asked me to call
him when I needed help.

On our way home, Hossein Agha insisted that we stay
and live with them, which is better for Neda, and I refused.
He said he and Manijeh would care for Neda if I found a
job or left Iran. Neda was restless in the car and could not

express her discomfort except through crying. I imagined the volume of her sadness and suffering separation anxiety is more than ours. Manijeh tried to keep the baby quiet, and Hossein Agha stood in front of a toy store. In the store, Neda started playing with a doll. I bought it and hoped to keep her quiet. We returned to the car, and after a few minutes, Neda was crying again.

We went to Manijeh's house and from there to Zohreh's house. After a few hours, Manijeh came with her red eyes indicated that she cried a lot, worried about Neda who is an intelligent child to endure the family separation at this age. She called the neighbors, and they came and took their pre-purchase items, the only remaining was heavy equipment such as beds, refrigerators, and kitchen equipment, which we would deliver it to them on the day of the evacuation of the house. Neda was in my arms, cuddling her so she wouldn't cry and walk around the house. I couldn't even go to the bathroom and thought about how the housewife would do everything, including babysitting. Neda carefully checked the house. I thought how much this child hurt and how I could withhold myself from her. I increased my medication again and told Manijeh that if anything happened to me, someone would know what to do with this kid. Manijeh played with Neda, who was entirely in a different mood. She was in my arms, and my hands hurt. Neda recently talked with her childish tone to say, "o for me, o for e." Zohreh told them. "One for you and one for him", not to fight for toys. I thought where I'd get "him," and she should learn to say one for me, one of you. That night she slept on my chest, and I was on the sofa. Being alone was good; I could cry, although you can't solve a problem, but I should weep quietly not loudly, lest Neda wakes up. It was in the middle of the night that Neda had wet herself and me. I just remembered that I forgot to change her diaper; every housewife has ten eyes and hands instead of two. I changed her and my clothes. The baby slept in my sister's bed, so I slept beside her.

In the morning, I heard Manijeh and Hossein Agha talking who were in the kitchen. I got up, and Neda was still asleep. Hussein Agha spoke.

"We came here to have breakfast; it is better you come to live with us. Last night Nader called, and we talked to him and Zohreh Khanum. They arrived on time, and Shahriar Khan waited for Nader. Zohreh Khanum called you unsuccessfully. We came here and saw you were asleep on the sofa. You would call them today. Manijeh was in pain last night, and I stayed to take her to the doctor. If you want to go to the Ministry of Science, we will take care of child."

"I am not in the mood today. I will go there later."

We had breakfast, and I called Nader and talked to Zohreh who was crying. She said the weather was cold, Nader lived in a dorm, and Nader arranged us to see one apartment. Its rent is expensive, 2,000 DM. I told her that no matter how much, you would rent it, and I would consider its expenses later. Manijeh left with Hossein Agha. I was glad the baby slept quietly. She woke up near noon when Manijeh returned and said the doctor had given her medication and tests and emphasized that she should do the tests soon. She played with Neda and went to her home to make dinner and latter brought it for us when Hossein Agha came. Day after, Hossein Agha said that Shokoh Khanum called and said they would come tomorrow night to have the post- passenger's Aash, and she brought dinner. Manijeh made Aash only. Shahpoor Khan and David would come too.

Post Passenger Party (Aash)

The Iranian tradition is to arrange a party and cook Aash three days post-passenger departure. The post-passenger departure creates the vacancy of a loved one, and the companionship of friends and acquaintances decrease their loneliness. Manijeh made Aash, and they came at night. Shokoh Khanum brought dinner and nice girls 'clothes and toys for Neda. As soon as she saw

Manijeh said:

"You have lost weight since last week."

"I went to the doctor, he ordered the test, and I'm going to see another doctor tomorrow."

"We did not want Soheil Khan to know it; I was worried for her, and we would go to Soroush's friend office tomorrow." Hossein Agha said.

"Come to my hospital tomorrow, all the tests will be done, Soheil, you come too. I received the invitation to the medical conference. We will go to the Ministry of Science after visiting my patients."

"I must take care of Neda."

"Come with Neda."

Hossein Agha said Manijeh needs to have fun, and we will visit Ava Khanum this weekend.

Shokoh Khanum said I will come with you.

"I came here to leave your car based on Shahriar's order." Shahpoor Khan spoke.

"No, I am on the medication that makes me drowsy. I don't want to drive."

Hussain Agha agreed to have his big car for the weekend.

"I'm not coming with you because I don't want to leave my wife alone."

The next day, we went to Dr. David's private hospital. He examined Manijeh and ordered the necessary tests. Then we went to give the invitation to the Ministry of Science, and his permit letter is issued then we went to the passport office.

"We must use the Shahriar's method." David said.

The same policeman was there.

"Officer, I must give the passport to the Colonel."

"Yes, Doctor, give it to me to call the Colonel."

David gave him the passport with the money inside. He went to the kiosk and came back.

"Doctor, the Colonel is waiting for you."

While the colonel did not know we were there! We went to the colonel's office; his manager knew us, and we did not need to brag. He kindly accepted us and told me about my daughter and how pretty she was. I had a good feeling that he thought I was her father.

After a few minutes, we went to the colonel's room, and he happily accepted us and thought she was my nice.

"Shahriar told me they were leaving the country with your sister and two children."

"Yes, they left."

David told him what had happened. He was looking at me in amazement.

"What a beautiful girl. It might be the best thing to happen."

David gave him the passport and he said it would be ready next week. I repeated that it might be the best thing to happen. It might be the best thing to happen.

"Soheil, when was the last time you see your doctor and
he controlled your medication dose?"

"I don't know."

"Do you have your doctor's telephone number?"

"No."

"What is your doctor's name?"

"Dr. Omidi"

We returned to the hospital. Manijeh was in mammograms. David asked Hossein Agha for Dr. Omidi's number, but he did not know. David told us to go to the cafeteria, and he would come there. We went to the restaurant, ordered food, and Neda fell asleep on my shoulder. After half an hour, David came, and he talked to Dr. Omidi. I needed to have a blood test that he ordered it.

"Why?"

"Your medication has some side effects, and you need to have blood test."

"Did I show any symptoms?"

"do your blood test now, then Dr. Omidi will see you."

"You saw something that concerned you, let me know the truth, to determine the child's situation, I'm worried for her."

I remembered my mother needed blood test and Soroush always took care of her.

"Do you remember talking to yourself at the passport office and repeating the words."

He was right. I've been talking to myself a lot recently and repeating everything. I did not think it was unusual. We went to the lab with Neda and Hossein Agha. Neda refused to go to Hossein Agha's for a minute when I was giving a blood test. When Manijeh's mammogram was finished, some of blood test result were ready.

David said the blood test and the mammogram result would be ready within two or three days, and I should see Dr. Omidi. We left the hospital to leave Neda and Manijeh at home and go to the doctor with Hossein Agha, but Dr. Omidi called me to say he would visit me at my house. He came at night and wondered why I increased the drug dosage and did not tell him. He changed the medicines and reminded me not to increase or decrease them without his consultation. He gave me medication for only three days.

"I bring medicine every three days."

He was afraid I will take it more. That weekend, we went in Shahpoor Khan's car to Amol. As usual, Hossein Agha was sometimes Soroush. Ava Khanum had pneumonia and kidney problem with severe edema. She said aging has a thousand flaws,
and it is time to say bye. Although vision is an excellent blessing to appreciate, sometimes it comes up that not having it is better. Like a mother who has lost her son and no longer recognizes that the one who kissed is not her son. Or someone who has Alzheimer's and does not remember losing a loved one. Ava Khanum couldn't see that the talking person was not her son. How painful it would be if she knew he was killed and couldn't do anything, but she was alert and asked.

"Who is Neda"

"Hayedeh Khanum's baby." Shokoh Khanum said.

"Hayedeh was pregnant."

"This kid is from her first marriage."

Manijeh changed the subject. On this trip, Shokoh Khanum took care of Neda and said she was in touch with Arash. Whatever Manijeh insisted on bringing her mother to Tehran, she refused, and Manijeh should return due to her health problem. We returned to Tehran, and Hossein Agha promised Manijeh they would return to Amol after the doctor determined her situation.

David called our house and said that the test results were ready. We went to the hospital; her diagnosis was

breast cancer. and needed surgery We were upset about
her diagnosis, and David got his flight ticket and would
leave Iran within two weeks. She could do her operation if
Manijeh were ready. Hossein Agha reported it to Nader.
They even thought that Manijeh would go to Germany and
have her surgery there, but we believed we met an
excellent surgeon accidentally and David to do her surgery.

Manijeh did not tell Zohreh about her diagnosis. I
thought that Zohreh is her close friend and needed to
know. Then I concluded that I hid the possibility of staying
in Iran from Zohreh, and Zohreh did not tell Manijeh about
Soroush's imprisonment. We are all captives of secrecy.
I was ashamed that I did not tell my sister the truth. We
learn what is good after post experience. It was Zohreh's
right to know and to decide it. However, Manijeh believed
she had just rented a house with two children and would
be unhappy when she knew and could not come. She will
tell her later. She talked to Nader and decided to have
surgery in Iran. Manijeh underwent surgery, mastectomy,
she was hospitalized for five days. Shokoh Khanum visited
her every day, came to our house, brought us food, played
with Neda, and helped me with the housework. She was
down to earth even though she had a maid and a cook.

The telephone call was also expensive. We agreed with
Zohreh to call me once a week. Manijeh returned home,
and worried about her mother. Nader stated that he would
go to Zohreh's house for dinner on nights when he had no
class and take her for shopping when it is not rainy.
Shahriar was often called Zohreh. David went to Paris and
left Manijeh's treatment with his colleague. It was planned
for chemotherapy after six weeks. David will follow up on
her treatment via phone.

Hussein Agha asked Manijeh to have a trip to
Germany, change her mood, and see Nader and Zohreh. At
the meantime, Hossein Agha went to Amol in the morning,
returned at night, and said that her mother's situation was
the same as before. And when Manijeh gets better, they
will go to Amol. Ava Khanum's neighbor called them
when I picked the phone and said that she was very sick
and hospitalized. I called Hossein Agha, who came, and we

went to Amol. Ava Khanum was so ill but recognized Manijeh and Soroush's voices. Her diagnosis was kidney failure, and she died in the hospital day after. His burial was more straightforward than my mother's funeral in Behesht Zahra, simple folks without tricks.

After two days, we returned to Tehran. Manijeh did not feel good, and Hossein Agha insisted on sending her to Germany before chemotherapy began. She wanted to stay for her mother's 40th-day ceremony.

It was the end of the month, and I had to deliver the purchased items and the house. I was feeling better after the medication was adjusted. Dr. Omidi did not need to control me every three days. He could trust that I could manage my prescription correctly. But he visited Manijeh and me regularly.

Manijeh and I handed over the belongings of the house we had sold to the people and evicted the house. I was convinced that it would be better for Neda to move to Hossein Agha's home. In this way, we settled into their home. Hussein Agha said that Manijeh worked very hard, and we never had any fun. With all the pain that Manijeh has suffered, it is better to have a vacation.

Hossein Agha was even afraid of the word cancer and said the damn disease. Manijeh convinced to travel to Germany before Chemotherapy and left Mehrabad Airport, and some memories gripped and depressed me. This was another blow for Neda, who became sick and had a fever. I hugged her, and her head wetting my shirt and shoulder. Dr. Omidi visited her, gave her medication, and asked me to go to his home that night. I looked at myself; that was not clean and neat, and I told him I hated my shape recently.

"It is due to depression, Zohreh lost weight significantly.
I am glad she left and separated from these sad memories."

"But I gained weight."

"Some depressed patients gain weight. You were very active, and the excessive grief of losing Soroush, Hayedeh, and your mother caused you to be overweight. Do not worry, and you will lose weight when depression would be under control."

"Staying at home as an idle person bothers me. I will go to work with Hossein Agha and take Neda with me."

"Do not drive when using medications, which is dangerous."

"I am up and down, going around a cycle.

"It is post-trauma syndrome. That takes an average of about six months to a year to recover. I never wanted to tell you how painful it was to lose Soroush. We were like two brothers, and I took medication too. Everyone thinks that we're the doctor and we do not get sick. Our body structures are the same. If I don't complain, I did not cry and talk; it's all forced out of necessity. How could I say I'm in pain when people bring me their pain and look for a solution? They expected a cure for their pain. If I say I can't heal my pain, how do I tolerate their frustration?"

I noticed he like Zohreh and me lost Soroush, and we never asked him how he was.

"Soheil, you have three times the burden of grief, and remember that the standards scale cannot measure any sorrow. Sometimes you convince yourself by the logic scale that you must endure pain and that it's not rational to complain. Moments later, you're so distressed that you cannot tolerate the pain, and the logic scale and logical thinking could not manage pain. You could see yourself in a quiet and stormy sea at the same time. Calm on the logic scale that dictated I should be tolerated because there was no choice, and on the storm, emotional scale, I could not be taken any more pain. You switched between two strongly positive and negative poles and were more disturbed. This restlessness is neither rejected nor acceptable. It's like you stay in a vacuum space and away from the air when there is air. You grabbed a straw hoping to be released from the trap of this storm, and a moment later, refuged to a logic scale that could not convince you and cover your need entirely. Give yourself time and bear this difficult time for this baby."

We went to Dr. Omidi's house that night, he talked, and we cried. The day after, he gave me a ride. Neda had a fever for a few days, and Shokoh Khanum brought us food daily. She was a very kind woman and thought I, clumsy men, couldn't cook. She wanted to change Neda's clothes; all her dirty clothes were gathered in the corner of the room. She suggested washing the clothes, which I refused.

That night, when Neda slept, I got up to clean the house and wash her clothes, and by midnight I had just cleaned and organized a room, there was still a kitchen. I told myself all these jokes about women saying they're doing makeup from morning to night, so who's doing all these chores? I spent time with Neda and clean the house at night. Manijeh and Zohreh kept calling and asking for Neda, and Shahriar called too. Arash called and said he started working in a private company and applied for university.

David called from France, and I gave him Zohreh's number. Manijeh was supposed to go to France and see him. As they said, they could travel by train across Europe. Zohreh and Manijeh were good, and here Hossein Agha was restless. It was the first time he was away from Manijeh, and he had noticeably lost weight in the last few days.

1984: TEHRAN BAZAAR

After Neda's health improved, I went with Hossein Agha to the bazaar for working. In bazaar, nobody came to work with a child, and Neda was good in the first hours. Hussein Agha told me to sit in the back of the store and do bookkeeping and accounting because after the Soroush tragedy, he did not take the receipts home for Manijeh, and he is behind. It was an excellent opportunity to compare the bazaar environment with the university. It was much better for me to come out of home even if I did not make money. It would make me happy to help Hossein Agha because our plights did not leave him an opportunity to do his own thing. Comparing bazaar with universities, the level of contact within the initial group was more than the university. In Bazaar, the businessman deal with street people daily, which is about selling, profiting, and paying.

One party's profit means a negating effect on the profits of the other party. Marketers have their language, tricks, and political policy, talking about money, the payment plan, late payments, and a return check were stressful. The liaison at the university is limited to teachers, lecturers, scientific discussions, teaching, and student. There is specific course subject and respect or strictness. There are teaching methods skills in the scientific circuit and stress of learning and exam for the pupils in university. Working in the bazaar was challenging, it is necessary to adjust the expectations of highly educated men for Working in the bazaar. There was bad language and a thousand times cursing of their sister and mother which was tough and incompatible with my mood. Although the cusses were not related to me, the environment was full of violence words. I was not exposed to this swearing, the bazaar's words.

As soon we entered the shop, Hossein Agha involved with sale, order, customer, and who paid or didn't. I did not hear him cuss or use foul language. But the shopkeepers
talking to each other; their words and their reliance on their words were swearing, which was ordinary for them. I bought a box of crayons and a painting notebook, and I kept Neda entertained to pay less attention to the surroundings. "Do you notice how many cusses were said in this market. You could bring the receipts, and I do bookkeep from home and do not hear to cusses."

"These are their common words and get worse when there is a fight. I've been in the market since I was a kid, but I know it is difficult for you because you are a doctor."

He spoke about his wife when we returned from the bazar.

"I am worried about Manijeh and missed her. We had a very challenging life, and I must take care of her before to be late. I did not do anything for her. I must think about the shop. Do you want to work in the bazaar?"

"Working in the market is not compatible with my situation."

"I understand, it was difficult for me, but I am used to it. I did not know anything else. You have studied, become a doctor, and you can find another job."

I did not realize that Hossein Agha did not know or not say that the mullah regime did not need an educated person. We witnessed four educated leave our country last week. The education death happened with the mullah's arrival. They want illiterate people who would work in the murder field, and they get paper doctoral titles, assassins like Khalkhali or Lajvardi who don't know "A" from B. This tribe did not even read the Quran, they just learned to kill Imam Hussein and sell God for money, brainwash naive people, and capture their minds. Mullah does not create anything except pain. They have written death for all. It is easy to see the mullah's blood-impregnated hands. Khomeini said that Islam speaks with swords, and even at the beginning of Islam, the Prophet Muhammad could not kill people and adequately implement Islam. Imam Ali killed 72 people in one day! Yes, they say all these traits with pride. A variety of assassinations, such as throwing buses (writers and poets) into canyon, shredding women, and her husbands at home (Forouhars), executions in various names (smuggling or waging war against God), beheading (Bakhtiyar), shooting at airplane, shooting innocents, and simply saying that they were guilty, wanting money for bullets, acid spraying on women's face, etc. This is their primary work.

After a few weeks, Manijeh returned to Iran. She seemed satisfied with her first trip abroad, and her mood improved. She brought Neda many souvenirs. They visited David with Shahriar in France. David was confident with the outcome of the surgery, and she did not need radiation therapy, only required to take one pill daily for five years and an examination occasionally, no matter whether Iran or Europe. Manijeh said that if Zohreh settles, she would like to live in Germany and care for her nephews so that Zohreh continue her education. Nader said he would not return to Iran after Soroush's death. Hussein Agha also promised her to retire. Manijeh talked about Zohreh and her good decision to live there.

Also, Shahriar had spoken to his lawyer to apply for a US visa for Zohreh. The lawyer has offered to apply for a visa to Germany too. Zohreh agreed to pay for it. Now her lawyer had all documents, and she should not worry about staying in Germany and learn German. Shahriar quoted her lawyer that Germany would pay for her living cost until she cares of her children and learns a skill due to the declining German population. It provided good conditions for Zohreh.

I was happy to hear about her because it was a nightmare for me when the money ran out, and I did not have a job, what to do with my sister's situation in the foreign country. During this time, I did Hossein Agha's paperwork, and he wanted to pay me, but I refused. I thought it was time to be independent.

Neda situation, my recovery and finding Neda's parents were essential to stay in Tehran, but the cost of living in Tehran was expensive, and we could live in a small city. I told the police officers Payam and Shahrokh that we were going to the small city and inform them about my address so that if they found her parents, I would need their support. I told Hossein Agha about my decision. He suggested I live in their house because he found someone to buy his shop and wanted to travel with Manijeh. In Manijeh's absence, he said that he was afraid of the name of cancer and did not want to come the day when he regretted why he did not take care of Manijeh.

High Interest= Financial Suicide

1983: Hossein Agha sold his business quickly, put his money in a savings account with more than 20% interest per year and told me that toiling produced less than 20% net income. I talked to him about the real meaning of 20% fixed interest rate!

"You know this type of saving meant financial suicide, the country's economic damage, decreased currency value, and increased poverty and misery."

"What do you mean?"

"It means people's misleading, seducing, and financial suicide. You said to make more money if you do not work. Knowledgeable and wise administrators run the developed countries, and the governments pay a living cost so that people learn skills, build their future, and be a producer, not a consumer. They create work for people so that high production and over production are exported, and money flows and currency to their country. As a result, the financial capacity of the people and the government will increase the people's well-being. The high saving account is fooling people by alluring them and destroying production, disabling people's financial situation and the inadequacies of the country's economy.

The corrupt government of the Islamic regime is a traitor, creating conditions to destroy the country's production, increase unemployment, and flow the country's wealth into the pockets of foreigners. Reduce the financial power of the people, the country, and the country's currency value. It would increase imports, item prices, unemployed, and the economic crisis. Soon, the cost of dollars from 71 Tomans will reach 710 Tomans, and DM will go from 25 Tomans to 250 Tomans.

This is another example of England's political behavior that subtly destroyed construction with distributed opium for free in the south of Iran, Kerman, and Baluchistan many years ago. They allured people to smoke and sell the burned opium (opium residual after consumption) to addict people and destroy construction. Now, the same policy is used differently to cripple the people of our country. To kill people's entrepreneurship with this trick. To eliminate the country's products and to increase imports. They even imported Chinese prayer stamps. People published the mullah photo in front of England embassy, and they knew they were the England servants and made England labels under their beards. England became allies and united to plunder the wealth of other countries."

Hussein Agha was astonished at what I was saying and asked, "What can I do now?"

"We can only teach others not to be fooled by trickers. If you put money in the bank, remember the currency value decreases, take advantage of it, but keep your profession, because idle paralyzes you and causes economic disaster."

"What does monopoly mean?"

"Monopoly meant one person controls one product without any competition. Mullahs divided the control of the necessary items between themselves and took advantage of basic human needs. They monopolized from bread on the table (wheat) to vehicles and their share. Indeed, they stole the people's basic. Result, one grave reciter mullah did not have any medical knowledge, became the hospital head and distributed gold coins at his son's wedding! When he must decide on a vital situation, he rotates a rosary that if it comes good, it will be done! The same mullah wished to have five tomans, praying and kissing the shah and queen's hand, to wrap a meal in a newspaper to take home. Now he has stolen money from the people and sent his children abroad to have a lux lifestyle."

Hossein Agha and Manijeh traveled to Germany, and I got a bus ticket for myself and Neda and left Tehran.

1983, Dorud

We arrived in Dorud at night and went to the inn near the bus station. I found a rental room for 400 Tomans monthly, which was proportional to my financial situation. Elderly couple lived in one room in the corner of the house. I tried to cover out cost with some money and recover from my emotional trauma. I was with one child compared to my helpless mother, with two without funds and support. I had studied and gained skills, but I was weaker than my mother and crying out for my destiny.

Childcare might be more comfortable if this child was a boy. But this beautiful, clever girl has become the love of my life. I must spend all my energy on her happiness and finding her parents. I sent a letter to the police officers.

Zohreh's residency in West Germany was processed. I had gained some control over my depression. I called officer Payam from time to time to see if there were any clues from her parents, and his answer was negative.

I've been playing with Neda all day. I bought daily newspapers, and she quickly learned the alphabet on the newspaper, drew a circle around it, and showed it to me. I used to make toys with torn newspaper for her. She

talked to me all day long and had many questions.
Thinking about her school bothered me because I did not
have her birth certification. I had never thought that not
having a sheet of paper called a birth certificate could make
someone so miserable and so effective in one's life. If my
sister were here, she could take care of Neda, and I would
look for a birth certificate and her parents. I thought to her
parents that losing such a beautiful child was severely
bothering me.

On the other hand, how to create a birth certificate for
this child has become a big problem. If I go to the city
record office with this child, they think I have stolen the
child and will take her from me. Sometimes I felt I had so
many friends, but there was no one to help me in this
situation. We looked like beads of a ripped string thrown to
an infinite space without any address of each other. I have
walked patiently in the dark alley screws and kept hope
alive until dawn. So many problems, one after each other,
had slammed me into the rocks of life that I had lost control
of everything.

I always thought about what the phonebook would do
when there is the city's information center. My phone book
was stolen with our books, and I did not know I would
have days when all doors closed. With the mullah's arrival,
disaster had come, and everything was messy. When I
called the information center, there were no numbers, or
they had been moved, the numbers had changed, or
something might have happened to them. I could not reach
them and could not change our situation. I should manage
our live with the limited fund and stayed in this shelter for
a while. My education was halved. Philosophies were not
even a crutch to support my sick soul and could not help
me financially. I saw all the doors closed. I did not dare go
on a trip after we came to a small town. I wished to stay in
Tehran and have more financial means. And the only profit
was that I endured fewer financial concerns.

We went out with Neda to buy groceries daily. The
town was small, and the shops were constrained. We were
in this humble courtyard alone. The elderly couple was
always in their room, and sometimes the man went

shopping.

Two years passed, one day when we went for grocery shopping, I saw a beggar with a child sitting in the alley. I remember my mother's death, Behest Zahra, and a beggar woman who changed her clothes and the child. My mother's face was embodied, and thought why begging, she can work like my mother. This must be like that beggar's woman in the cemetery. Might the child not be hers? After weeks, I asked her why she did not work. She put down her chador and showed me that she was pregnant.

"How can I work with pregnancy and baby? I remembered Hayedeh saying we needed an organization to support the poor people to prevent them from begging. He was arrested for this reason. One rainy day, I asked her.

"Where do you sleep at night?"

She pointed to the barrels at the end of the alley.

"Behind those barrels."

I was sorry about it.

"My home door is open if you want to sleep there at night."

"I don't want it because men want to rape me."

I trembled and thought how hard it is to be homeless and cold and encounter the villain and bugger masculine who did not consider their limitations. I thought about her fate and what men did to her that she accused and judged me without knowing what was in my mind. Never I thought I would rape a woman.

"I have a daughter and don't rape anyone."

"From the day I sat here, I would see you with your daughter, and I wish my husband were alive, and my child's hand was in her father's hands."

Her words hatted my head with such a hammer, remembered my childhood and my frustrations.

"If you want to sleep at my house at the bottom of this alley, I only have one room with my daughter."

I gave her some money and went grocery shopping. I imagined my mother with Zohreh and me in a cold area. I bought a loaf of bread for ourselves and one for her too.

When we returned home, I noticed she was checking

me out. I gave her the bread, and she was silent, whereas she usually said.

"God bless you" when I gave her something. She spoke when we continued walking home.

"Can we sleep behind the door and no one kicking us? I'm not an evil woman."

"I wanted to help you. You can sleep even in my room and be assured that I will not do anything to you. I will leave the door open."

We went home, and I thought about my destiny, my mother, and the students' protesting that I never understood their pain. And it may also affect the fate of thousands of desperate and helpless women with their children who don't have shelter or social security. Neda was asleep, and I was reading books when I heard sound. I waited a few minutes, but the sound was interrupted, and I thought I was wrong. I was sorry for this dear child's fate away from her family. Again, I heard a sound, and wanted to check what it was. There was no one in the yard, so I looked at the door and saw the woman lying behind the door in the hallway. She jumped out of her place when she saw me, and I spoke.

"I won't touch you. If you want, you can come to my room." I pointed to our room. She hugged her baby and came after me. I gave her my blanket and mattress, she put her baby on, lay next to her baby, and I slept on the floor over Neda's head. The next day, she told me her name was Marzieh, she slept comfortably last night after a long-time, and God blessed me. I got upset and paid her some money to bathe and wash her clothes. I went with Neda and bought two mattresses and two blankets.

From then on, she has been living with us. She sleeps with her children, and I sleep as usual over Neda's head, where I sit. I did not expect her to stay with us, but I could not ignore her poor situation either. I wondered where the pregnant woman with her baby could find shelter if she did not come to my house. I couldn't support her socially and financially, although it might be better for Neda to be a woman at my home. I did not want to marry or have a relationship with her and any woman.

1985: Marzieh had labor pains, and I took her to the
hospital. In the taxi, I was in the thought that I should have
taken my beloved Hayedeh to the maternity hospital. How
hard for a person to be full of sorrow dense clouds and
nowhere to weep, and in his lonely bed. I wished that
Hayedeh had called me so that I might have eternal peace.
The driver guessed my sadness and tried to calm me down.

"Sir, I drove to the maternity ward four times for my
wife and 100 times at night for people. Do not worry. God
will give you a son, and your children will have a brother."
He was recognized my hidden pain but did not know the
reason. We arrived at the delivery room with two little
girls. A woman who was at the receptionist spoke angerly.

"How many children? What was going on with you?"

"God-given." Marzieh replied:

"God! How did not God give it to me?"

Everyone laughed. I remained silent and did not know
what to say. I couldn't leave her alone in that situation and
did not regret why I helped her, but I was worried that I
had to take a heavy responsibility for taking care of two
children in this situation. She was an ordinary woman and
preferred cold alleys to work. I was immersed in my pain
and worried my financial situation would end and we sat
in waiting room that was receptionist too. She asked
Marzieh some question and she gave birth to her son and
was discharged from the hospital after a few hours. After
weeks, Marzieh wanted to go to the record office for the
child's birth certificate, and she was afraid to go alone and
asked me to go with her. Without asking any questions, I
went with her. I wanted to know how the situation would
be and if I could get a birth certificate for Neda. As soon as
we arrived an employee was behind desk asked us.

"Father's birth certificate." I did not expect it at all.

"My birth certificate was lost."

"Give the children's birth certificates and 10,000
tomans to issue the certificate.

"All lost together."

He looked at Marzieh's birth certificate, which Marzieh
handed him.

"Your name is not in. How many years have you been

married?

"Nine years." Marzieh responded.

"So, how old are you?"

"Thirty years."

"Hey, unfairly, this miserable girl was not half your age when you married her. Damn, son of a beach, f... you."

He cursed me. I put my head down and was upset about his swearing. I thought he might be a conscientious man.

"You are right. I made a mistake."

"Now you know! Spit to the cowardly."

Marzieh was trying to support me.

"Sir, I swear it was not his fault. I loved him, and I wanted to marry him."

"You were a little girl. You had to play with your doll."

I was standing quiet, listening to cussing. He made himself entitled to cuss me. He might have learned from a bitter experience that child marriage is wrong, and he considered morality. I took Neda out of the office, so she did not hear his swearing, and I stood in the hallway. He yelled.

"Well, come to pay for the certificate."

I told Neda to stay in the hallway and went to his office.

"How much do you have, and what's your work?"

"I am unemployed and have 25,000 tomans only. How much should I pay?"

"25,000 tomans."

"No, I'm responsible for their dinner and could not pay it to you."

"What? You did not feel responsible when you married this innocent little girl under half your age. When she got pregnant, you were not responsible for what you did. All right, give 15,000 tomans for birth certificates and 1,000 for stamps."

I paid him 16,000 tomans and returned home with Neda. After a few minutes, Marzieh came home and gave me the certifications, and I was shocked to see them. Neda Varparideh's birth certificate was eight years old. At that time, Neda was 4 or 5 years old. I was the father of three children and a wife, and my name was Murad Varparideh.

My wife was Marzieh Dehkenar, and three children Neda, Roya, and Sohrab. Marzieh was 21 years old at that time. I thought the man had the right to curse me! I told Marzieh what was on the birth certificate was just the paper appearance. We will not have any relationship, and she should find a place and move out.

Later, it was revealed that when Marzieh was in the delivery room, she was asked about her husband's name and she said Varparideh, then the maternity department assumed and issued the baby's birth certificate under Varparideh last name.

The record office employee assumed everyone's family name was the same except Marzieh, and he asked Marzieh the children's names and ages and her husband's name. Marzieh said Neda was eight years old, and her husband's name was Murad. In those moments, I did not care if I heard a curse or what my name was, but I paid 16,000 tomans in that bad financial situation. At the nearest school enrolled Neda and claimed she knew the first and second grades. They took an exam and put her in third grade. I found a job in a print shop where the owner agreed that I would be at work only on the hour my daughter was in school. I told Marzieh that if Neda came home sooner than me, she should take care of her. Marzieh cried and said, I saved her life. When she was homeless, feared men, and slept behind the barrels while dogs gathered around her. All night, she was afraid the dogs would tear up her little girl. The dogs were howling and hungry. The place was full of rats and flies. She claimed I did not know what it meant to be a homeless woman with a child, sleeping on the street, and hearing cursing from people who thought she rented the baby. It was all her brother's fault. Murad and she were in love. She thanked me and me her story.

In this part of his diary Ana and I were crying, and I spoke.

"How hard was for my dad to endure Marzieh in a toxic environment to protect me from the rotten community mislabels? He always asked me to write my memories."

"Since my parents and aunt had come to your house and knew Uncle Soheil, they had a particular respect for him."

There was his relatives and friends' information list and a letter for me and his letter.

My dear Neda, I love you and am sorry it was not in my ability to provide you with the lifestyle you deserve. I wrote you a part of my life story. You can trust the names I wrote here if anything happens to me.

You can call them and live with them. They pay for everything you need. On the bottom of the wooden box is an envelope included your earning and the small amount I could save for you, and the clothes you wore on the first day. You're brilliant, and you will have a perfect future. Take care love of my life.

CHAPTER 6, IMMIGRATION

Ana talked about Neda's immigration. Neda, Uncle Soheil, my mother, and Iran Joon left the house to apply for a US visa in Turkey, and if the U.S. embassy were strict, they would drive to Germany. Uncle Soheil had obtained an International Driver's License. Our house was no longer as warm as before. Behrouz and Pouran Joan looked after me and did not leave me alone, but I missed Neda. Our hope was for my mother's call every night, telling us where and what they were doing. When they arrived in Turkey, my mother called, and I talked to Neda. My mother reported. We stopped at a few places along the way. Iran's border with Turkey, the police carefully controlled them inside the car, and when Uncle Soheil gave them money, their accuracy dropped sharply, allowing them to continue their trip. Soheil Khan had learned the loosening law with money trick from Arman to loosen his pocket so that the rules would be gone, and the police would be the most flexible.

Based on other passengers, we were the lucky strangers less hurt. When we were getting away from home, Neda looked back and said I never believed that one day I would leave Ana and Bijan. She immediately claimed that she was tired and wanted to sleep. Soheil Khan was driving carefully so that Neda would not be hurt and asked her where he would stop. They stayed in a newly built hotel opposite the U.S. Embassy. The hotel is very stylish and uses the best marble stones. Still, there is no elegant touch, and no standard welfare equipment protects their building, so not even a shower curtain is installed around the bathtub that prevents water from pouring on the bathroom floor.

Soheil Khan and I went shopping around the hotel when Neda was sleeping, and Iran stayed with her. There were two police cars there, and we heard pleasant music.

The police officers were standing at the intersection.
We thought they were there because of the US Embassy,
and we went further and saw that several cabarets and
dancing were there. An Iranian was there and asked us if
we had just come, and why we got a hotel so expensive, we
could sleep there at night, which is cheaper. Soheil Khan
thanked him and said we were here temporarily. I was
interested to see his hotel. The man showed us the
economical hotel and said you could sleep here at night.
Girls go dancing at night and sleep here during the
daytime when you're not here, and their clothes stay here!
Soheil Khan pointed to me to go back to the hotel. On the
way, we saw a group of villain men standing in the hall.
We left there immediately, and when we returned to the
hotel to see the officers smiling, they were relieved that
strangers had returned safely!

They went to the U.S. embassy early morning and
should stay in line. Therefore, Neda and Iran Joon returned
to the hotel till they called them when the time came.
Another Iranian man was there and told if they wanted a
room for rent. My mother said she was interested in seeing
that room and asked Soheil Khan, but he said it might be
like my last night, go with someone. My mother asked the
man to call the hotel in the afternoon, and they might
interest to see the house. My mother said it was like
everyone trying to deal with newly arrived Iranians and
use their needs.

They provided all necessary documents to the US
Embassy. Neda said it's better to say that she is in the
second semester of pregnancy to let her fly. Sahil Khan
refused due they would find at the medical examination.
The Embassy set an appointment three days later and
explained the process, including reviewing the file, an
interview, and a medical examination. After receiving the
medical reports, review the case, and the visa will be issued
if approved.

In the afternoon, the Iranian man came to the hotel,
and we went to see the room for rent. There were five beds
in one dirty room for $200.00/ per person/ one week;
when he noticed our reluctance and said he had a better

place for us. In short, everyone is profiting from Iranians.
Istanbul weather smelled the coal-burning fireplace. There
were many mosques, a group of women wearing hijabs,
and another group with the latest fashion open clothes.
They are poor and did not respect others, there were flies
all over the place. The next day, my mother said: Neda was
depressed and wanted to sleep. We went to a better hotel
near the embassy and got a unit with two rooms and three
beds. I got the hotel phone number. No one asked about
our relationship, although, I was ready to say that Soheil
Khan is Iran's husband. Soheil Khan watched Neda all the
time. We watched Turkish TV advertisements combined
with a sexy woman. There was good food, but the flies
were on the food, and I was afraid Neda would get sick.
We prepared the meal for her, but she did not have an
appetite, and Soheil Khan was worried.

During this time, Zohreh and Arash had sent the
necessary documents and a letter from a senator, Arash's
friend. The recommendation letters affected the processing
time. Also, Professor Kiani wrote a recommendation letter
for Neda and introduced her as the most talented student
in medical school. The US embassy gave her case priority
due to her pregnancy. They should have a medical exam at
a hospital approved by the embassy.

Immigrant health is essential for the US. The same day,
the embassy set Sahar's interview date, and Soheil Khan
asked for a letter for her medical examination, which was
rejected, and told them that Sahar should be there. Their
nine-day medical examination and Sahar interview dates
were set two weeks later. At the same time, my father
arranged for Sahar's visa and flight ticket so she could be in
Turkey before the interview. My mother was glad to have
an opportunity to visit Istanbul like a tourist.

Bijan's parents moved to their house after Neda left,
and Bijan would come to our house in the evenings and
stay with us until he heard about Neda. He then left or
slept on the sofa instead of going to his room. This was the
first night we had no news of Neda, and Bijan was
extremely worried, continuously trying to call her hotel. He
even called his parents to let them know he would be

staying at our house because Neda hadn't contacted Ana.
His parents also came over. Behrouz and Dariush were in
the hospital, and Nasrin's health was improving, but she
was getting tired earlier and going to bed. Pouran Joan was
with us, providing much-needed support.

On the other side, Nima Khan called Iran Joon every
night, so Aria found out about Neda's situation when she
noticed there was no answer on the phone. They came over
to our house to see if we had any news about Iran Joon and
Neda, showing the unity and support among us.

"Nobody answered in her room." Aria spoke and his
concern was palpable.

"Maybe they went for a walk or dinner." My father's
words did not calm us down and he fell asleep on the
couch.

"Might her labor start and go to a hospital? I wish she
had stayed here until the baby is born." Bijan spoke.

"I had heard from my mother that Zohreh had gone
from America to Germany, and she said she couldn't wait
any longer to see her brother. She planned to go to Turkey
with Manijeh. They might have gone to pick up Zohreh
from the airport."

I talked to Neda the night before, and she spoke about
herself, and everyone wanted to know what she had said to
me, so I explained a little bit. Neda talked about her feeling
when she left the house, she felt she had buried herself in
this house and escaped from herself like a ghost. She cried
for her fate and her parents, whom I had never met. She
thought about Uncle Soheil, who cared for her without any
expectations and still supported her. She talked about Bijan
and was restless to see him at any moment and be with
him, and she was overwhelmed with pleasure and joy. She
expected a bright future, and her child would be the
happiest to have the best father in the world; she would
never let poverty bother her child, and suddenly, all went
with the wind.

She talked about me as a friend, that we grew up
together, and that I was a sun without shadows for her. She
lost everything but a child. She must consider all the
criteria for her child's happiness, burn with all pains, and

despair and make a better life for her baby. The
Immigration situation is disappointing, and it did not
matter whether it was mandatory or an option. In my
nightmares, the image of a little girl who suffered from the
cold weather was carved, and now I must add my
frustrations. Neda cried for what was painful and cruel,
then excused her fatigue and wanted to sleep so she would
scream silently. She said she could not tolerate so much
pain and wanted to cover her face with a bed sheet because
she felt everyone was reading her mind.

I reviewed her memory; sometimes, she felt happier
than street children. At least she knew her parents and
brother; her dad was loving and caring. Madam and Iran
Joon were always there for her. She was grateful that I was
for her and supported her from our elementary school. She
had regretted leaving her home, and this doubt bothered
her. She had looked behind and wanted to return to her
house, but she was on an unreturned way. The doubt had
killed her and sank into depression.

In the meantime, Neda had thought about her baby,
the only relic of her love, and must care for her baby, the
fruit of her love and passion with Bijan. She cursed herself
for forcing Bijan to talk and causing his charmingly
cheerful man to have a sad look and weeping eyes. She
blamed herself for creating the problem. She did not dare
enough to return due to her love for him because she
feared people's judgment if they knew she loved her
brother. Bijan was saddened, and it was painful to see him
grieve. Bijan always said to support her, but this tragedy
ruined his strength. However, these tragedies could be
expected in a dictator regime saturated with power, crazy,
and ignorant.

Also, she wished that she was not pregnant and killed
herself or her child, then Bijan and her dad would be
relieved, and Bijan would not feel guilty and would not
have a sister that could not look into her eyes. She was a
captive of society's taboos, and her dad described that
Swedish siblings were married before; she wished she was
Swedish, had been born several years ago, and was no
longer forced to swim against the river trend. All thoughts

about elementary school, home, Tehran, concubines, love, marriage, pregnancy, and undesirability were marched in my mind. Even she talked about Dariush, whose absolute joy was to speak with her when they were alone; although it was not secret words; he was alienated from all except Neda. She looked for ambiguous points that should be rooted in his childhood. Neda was upset about his loneliness, and now her situation was like his, and she could not talk to anyone about her secret and was inside her lonely cocoon; she drew her execution plan because she could not suffer this expensive burden. She wanted to be comfortable and sleep forever and ignored her dad's grief.

Neda explained that my mom rubbed her legs and knew she was not sleeping; she should eat something, but she did not answer. On the road, her dad stopped in the rest area, which had a dirty restroom she couldn't use as a toilet. She told her dad she couldn't bear all this burden anymore and wanted to kill herself.

Her dad said life is about managing unwanted situations, and it has sunny days, scorching times, and cold nights. You speak about the intolerable situation; if you mean the baby, I will raise him enthusiastically, and all of us will accept him. I know it's a hard time. If it's an emotional burden, emotional issues are like a wild rogue horse, which becomes more rebellious if you want to rope them around. So let the energy stored in the tunnel of his mind erupts and empties so there is no explosion. What is the solution? The life was not made based on our order. That is what it is. We must use wisely whatever it is. My dad's words were logical, but my storm inside did not calm down; Neda was talkative, and I listened as if she had compensated for her silence period. I remembered Neda's words. In our home, the waiting hours passed slowly, especially when Neda was far away, and we could guess something had happened that my mother did not call. Finally, the phone rang with my mother who said.

Neda was depressed, did not eat, and wanted to sleep; her situation was worse than before, although I kept giving her antidepressants. Soheil Khan looked for a doctor to visit her and asked the hotel manager to provide us with a phone and the address of a nearby hospital. Soheil Khan talked to Neda to see a doctor or let a doctor visit her.

"I could not eat due to my nausea."

"During these months, you should not have nausea. You are a doctor and know it is not normal."

"Wait till tomorrow if I do not get better. We see a doctor."

"Why do we wait till tomorrow?"

"Now I am falling asleep."

"All right, I'm asking the doctor to come here."

In the meantime, Neda vomited and agreed to go to a medical office.

"Something must have happened."

"Like, what happened?'

Nada paused after a few minutes said.

"Vomiting is a sign of toxemia, and I feel the baby's movements decline."

Iran changed Neda's clothes, and Soheil Khan asked for a taxi and said that we did not know anywhere in this city, and it was better to go to the hospital where we should have a medical examination.

After a long wait in the hospital, a doctor examined Neda and asked her about the baby's movements because he could not hear the baby's heartbeat. Neda asked him for his stethoscope and said, I am a physician too. The doctor got upset, showed his sympathy, and did a sonograph to make sure and said there were no heartbeats, her child had died, and she should have induced labor or a cesarian section. Neda got upset and asked to be discharged, so we returned to the hotel. Her mood is not good.

Bijan took the phone and talked to them. His parents looked at him. My father woke up from our talking. Aria was pale and restless and stared at me and spoke.

"Is it life-threatening? Tell me what we could do. You are a doctor. Could you tell me what it means? I will go to Turkey."

"What about a passport and Visa?"

"I have both."

Koroush Khan: "We are US citizens and did not require a visa. However, we will research, and if there is no need for a visa, we will go to Turkey with Aria."

"Over sea flights start at 5 a.m. daily, and passengers are at the airport at 4 a.m. If there are any flights to Turkey, I will buy a passenger's ticket under any circumstances and go on the first flight. I will go in the car if it is not a flight to Turkey."

Aria asked Koroush Khan to call him at 4 a.m. He had a mobile phone when we thought it was unnecessary to have it! Aria was a very mature and mighty man, even though he is young. His father always accompanied him. We were concerned about Neda. We did not have a passport, and only Aria had taken his passport when Neda decided to leave here. It might be that he knew he should go after his lover. Aria and his father left us; he went to scream his sadness in privacy.

I was so upset and did not know what to do. Bijan and I decided to go to Turkey, I informed Dariush and Behrouz. Dariush said he would come with us. We were skeptical about the diagnosis and the possibility of misdiagnosis. But Dariush said the chances of misdiagnosis were rare in this case. My father said we apply for our passports tomorrow. We expect the passport process and Visa will take at least one week. I asked Bijan to tell Professor Kiani I would not go to the hospital, even though I was sure that Bijan would talk to him. Dariush informed the head of the department that his sister was sick and would not be at the hospital and asked one resident to cover his shift because he wanted to apply for a passport. The head of the department could have been better with Dariush because he had told Dariush in front of many doctors that tapestry art is a feminine job. Dariush had told him, I'm proud to do feminine work and not be a brainless doctor, which was unpleasant for him; he always gave a hard time to Dariush. Dariush has ignored his inappropriate behavior and talked to Neda, his only friend. I told Dariush that this might cost him badly. Dariush said, "Don't worry. I have a high tolerance."

Sahar had a flight ticket and a Turkey visa, but her work needed to be completed. She was supposed to talk to the dean of the university, who was my father's friend, and if her work were done sooner, she would come with us. It was a tough night. Bijan was so sad and profoundly unable to know what to do. I had thought about Neda's words that these men had muscular bodies, but their emotional capacities were less than that of women. I noticed I was weak; men and women are no different; our situations change our abilities to overcome problems, and emotional pain is fatal. Bijan was in bad condition and did not know for which pain he should cry.

Passport office

We prepared the necessary documents and went to the passport office early in the morning to apply for the passport. We took the headshot photo before we entered the passport office. Dariush said Ana come with me to find out who the boss and start from there.

My father spoke. "We should stay in line to deliver the documents."

"You stand in line. We will come back soon."

I went with Dariush to the boss office. Dariush spoke.

"I am a surgeon, and my sister is in the hospital. Please issue my passport today as tomorrow is late, and the day you need me will surely compensate."

"Who is this lady?

"This lady is also a surgeon, and I will take another surgeon with me to perform the surgery if necessary."

After a long pause, he asked several questions:

"Is she your wife?"

"No, my wife is pregnant, and she stays here."

"What commitment do you give to return?"

"Accept my words, manly. If it is unacceptable, please tell me what I should do, whatever you say."

"The boss should order to do it out of turn."

"All right, who is the boss? I know you're the boss. However, if anyone is higher than you, I will beg him."

The colonel seemed impressed.

"Go to Haj Agha's room there."

"Please come with me, he accepts your words better than us."

"Where's the other doctor?"

"They are in queue. The doctor will ask them to come here."

I immediately went to my father and Bijan, and they
came with me to the boss's office.

"Who is this gentleman?" He pointed to my father.

"He is my father because my husband stays in the
hospital, and my father comes with me."

"Is your father a doctor?"

"No, my husband is a surgeon."

Then we went to Haj Agha's office. A mullah was there
with dirty clothes, a dirty neckline, and a rosary in his
hand.

"Haj Agha, these gentlemen wanted to see you."
Dariush spoke.

"My sister needs surgery in a foreign country, and
these doctors will do her surgery. We need to have our
passports today. Let us go, and we will return after the
surgery. I will
be with you the day you need me and compensate for your
kindness."

"Are You a surgeon, and where is your office?"

"My office is in the hospital."

"What is your specialist?"

"I am a gynecologist.

Haj Agha laughed when shown his dirty teeth:

"We don't need a gynecologist."

He still needed to finish his words.

"But your wife and your daughters should need my
skill."

"Astaghfarullah, they go to the female doctor," then he
turned to me and said:

"How about you?

"I'm a surgeon.

"And you?

"I'm a surgeon, too."

"What a commitment you give to return."

My father: "What commitment do you want? They are
surgeons; you are an understanding man who could
recognize their honesty."

"Are you a surgeon, too?"

"I am her father. Her husband cannot go because he
has had surgery and wanted me to accompany her."

"We need to ask the Ministry of Science for an inquiry."

"What do you need? I'll bring it to you. I'll go on a motorcycle due to the city traffic, which will be faster."

"Do you not have a car?"

"I have a car, but I use a motorcycle through the city traffic easier; you can call the head of the surgery department and ask for their positions, and I will bring you any papers you need."

I thought about what my father words who did not have a motorcycle. Haj Agha, who prides himself that we needed
him, said with arrogance:

"So, let's see what I can do."

Bijan Wept and said: "Please."

"Is that your sister?"

"No, his sister is my wife, and I must go."

"What is your name?"

"Bijan"

"What's your wife's name?"

"Neda. My wife is his sister."

He asked Dariush and me my name and shook his head and said:

"So, you're from a minority.

"Yes, and my father is Monsieur Arman.

"Why don't you convert to Islam?

"Haj Agha, if you were born into a Jewish or Christian family, you would be Jewish or Christian. I love my religion, and we have the book."

Haji did not expect me to talk because I was silent like a dead rat. He was rolling his rosary in his hands and talked under his lips.

"When I obtain your documents from the Ministry of Science, I will look at your files to see if you can leave."

My father: "Okay, you stay here. I'm going to get the paper."

"No, they must go."

"Haj Agha enjoys talking with three young doctors. I will bring you the document. I'm doing it faster because my children always studied, I did their work. Tell me, what do you drink? I will bring it for you. Which one, Wine or whiskey?"

My father read his hand of the bastard Haji Agha well. "Istaghfarullah."

"Haj agha, enjoy this world; nobody came from the post-death world. Please tell me what you drink to bring it for you. How about you, Mr. Colonel? What do you drink? I used to sell alcoholic beverages."

I was scared to death by what my father said that ruined our chances. You could not believe it was the opposite, and Haji started talking friendly with us. My father pointed to Mr. Colonel and said:

"I can move my car while you write what forms Haj Agha wants from the Ministry of Science."

My father left the room and returned after 10 minutes with a plastic bag in his hand. He stood next to Haji and said something under his ear. He put the plastic bag next to his feet. Later, I learned it was two Johnnie Walkers and promised them more.

"Haji Agha, what form should I bring from the Ministry."

Haji Agha softened and pointed to us.

"You stay here. Monsieur come with me to the colonel's office to see what forms are required."

We stayed there based on his order! My father went with Haj Agha, and we were looking at each other.

Dariush: "Your father did his job well."

Bijan said in disbelief: "Means?"

Dariush: "Yes!"

We were waiting to see if they would give us passports.

My father returned with Haji to the room. He spoke.

"Bring the forms in the afternoon after the praying."

"Yes, Sir, for sure."

My father pointed us to leave.

"What is your decision, Haj Agha?" Dariush asked.

Haji, with a proud look, spoke.

"Monsieur knew what are required. I will give you a passport if you are not corrupt on earth."

"Is it a particular form?" Dariush asked.

"Monsieur knows what is needed."

"Come, we will be late for the Ministry." When we reached outside, my dad pointed to us to be silent. In the car, he told us that he bribed them, and we would get our passports.

"That is, it?"

"Yes, my daughter, they are the ransom machine only, nothing else."

While we were at the passport office, Aria and Bijan's parents were on their way to Turkey. Aria and his father had gone to the airport early in the morning, found out no flight to Turkey that day, the US citizen did not need a Turkish visa, picked up Koroush Khan, dropped his father at home, and driven to Turkey.

At night when Aria arrived at the Neda Hotel in Istanbul, we informed them we got our passports, apply for the visa, would be there if her doctor would postpone her treatment. My mother said the doctor insisted on giving birth as soon as possible, but Neda refused to go to the hospital. Uncle Soheil told us I should watch her closely because she once talked about suicide. Elsewhere, she had said this was the only relic of her love and wanted to keep it. My mother continued that Aria and Setareh Khanum arrived in her room, and Setareh kissed Neda, who disregarded them. Aria greeted her, stood up and watched her without her response, then talked to Soheil Khan while keeping an eye on her, and the presence of others did not interfere with his behavior. Neda closed her eyes.

"I'm going to buy dinner. What do you like, and what does Neda like?" Aria spoke.

"The restaurants and stores are closed at this time of night."

"Except for hotels, their restaurants must be open."

"We cooked dinner because we fear contamination. It is better if you have dinner here." Iran Joon said.

"Okay, I'll be back soon." Aria left the room.

Setareh Khanum explained that except on the Turkish border, we just stood at a few spots to use the toilet. Despite my husband's insistence on Aria taking a little break, he said driving helped him to endure the time. Aria returned and pointed to Setareh Khanum.

"Your room is ready on the same floor.

The services man brought a bouquet and put it in Neda's room. When Aria started talking to Neda, Soheil Khan noticed that Neda had paid attention to his words and left her room with Koroush Khan. Uncle Soheil told my mother that he wanted to shower and please watch Neda even though Aria was there.

My mother stood at the door to see what Aria was talking about but did not hear anything except Aria say you should be yourself and tell Bijan what you felt and forget everything you heard. Then my mother entered the room on the pretext and saw Neda's red eyes. She did not say anything and left them alone.

Aunt Zohreh had called me from the US several times since Neda was in Turkey, even though she had talked to me before. She called me from Germany to learn about Neda's health situation and decided to go to Turkey with Manijeh. I gave her the hotel's number, and she will have a flight from Germany to Turkey that takes about four hours.

Turkish Trip

Getting a Turkish visa with bribes took one day. We should owe this fast-receiving visa and passport to my father's skill, who got along with them to get bribery. I was so happy to see Neda. We left Tehran for Turkish early morning. Sahar came with us regardless of her ticket. It was the first time I had a long trip abroad with so much stress. My father agreed with Dariush and Bijan to drive a few hours each and could get to Turkey faster. I had my head on Sahar's shoulder, and I was scared something would happen regarding their driving. Although my father was sitting in front, he was careful and talked to them constantly. The Turkish border was too hardening to get us all messed up.

My father was calm and told us not to say anything and not lose our patience; otherwise, it would get worse. We were my father's students! After the search, even though my father bribed them, we continued our trip and reached the hotel. We were restless to see Neda sooner.

"You go, I will park the car." My father said.

Sahar stayed with my father to take our stuff and come with my father. We saw Aria in front of the hotel. I wondered if it was a coincidence or Aria was waiting for us there. We greeted him, and he took Bijan's hand. Dariush and I continued to the hotel, assuming he would need privacy and did not want us to know. Suddenly, Dariush returned and said:

"Look at Aria, son of a beach, who has fought with Bijan, keep my bag, and I will be back."

Dariush was right that Aria had taken and waved Bijan's shoulders, and Bijan was trying to put his hands away. Dariush yelled, "Son of a beach," and went to them. I was apprehensive about what would happen and wished my father was here. How bad were we fighting as soon as we arrived? I was nailed in my place for a moment and looked at them. Aria had not yet given up Bijan's shoulders, and I took Dariush's bag and walked up to them. I heard Dariush.

"Aria is right."

I thought, what happened? He went to assist Bijan or Aria!

"Do not touch me." Bijan spoke loudly.

Dariush said. "Yes, listen to Aria. Aria is right."

Aria stated firmly "You should do what I said."

I wondered what are they talking about?

Bijan said "All right."

"Listen to Aria and go to her room first." Dariush spoke.

He grabbed Bijan's hand and came toward the hotel. With his lip-biting, Dariush invited me, not asking while I wanted to know what had happened. When we arrived at the hotel, I returned and saw Aria leaning on the same light pole. I wanted to know what they talked about. We walked into my mother's room, and Dariush talked under Bijan's ear, "remembering Aria's words." Bijan confirmed with his head. The room was packed. The door of Neda's room was half open, and Dariush pointed to Uncle Soheil, who was there, grabbed my arm, and said, "Bijan first."

Bijan entered Neda's room, and Dariush closed the

door. My mother held me in her arms. We had yet to have
the opportunity to greet Uncle Soheil. I saw Zohreh and
Manijeh for the first time. Mr. Koresh and Setareh Khanum
sat there. I wished to see Neda and couldn't wait anymore.
I asked Dariush.

"What happened?"

He pointed me to be silent. Sahar and my father
entered the room. Sahar and Uncle Soheil hugged and
kissed each other intimately. In the meantime, my father
has kissed and hugged my mother romantically.

Uncle Soheil introduced Sahar, Darius, and me to
Zohreh and Manijeh. I went to Darius's side and asked him
again. Dariush whispered slowly in my ear.

"Aria said Neda needs Bijan and his love more than
ever to overcome this shock and requested him for
different behavior."

"What does the difference mean?

He did not explain to me what the meaning is of
different. I wanted to see Neda and went to the door to see
her, and I saw Bijan hugging Neda in her bed; I looked at
the surprise, turned to Dariush, and said under his ear.

"What did Aria say to Bijan?"

"She needs Bijan's love more than ever."

"What? But. But…"

He cut my sentence.

"But! No, but. I know what you want to say. Aria is
right."

I saw Aria standing next to the light pole from the
window. Uncle Soheil was staring at us, but he did not ask
anything. Iran Joon also noticed I was looking at Aria.

Dariush, whose eyes were teary, said:

"Aria is a great human. Each of us has a portion of
love, a life-maker love, or a life-burner love."

He was the person who cursed Aria a few minutes ago,
and he went to be with Aria now. I had no choice but to
stay there until Bijan came out. I was impatient and
restless. Sahar sat at Uncle Soheil's sides, both in his arms.
Aunt Zohreh was a simple, beautiful woman whose hair
was on her shoulder, and Manijeh was too. Setareh
Khanum was sitting next to her husband. In the meantime,

my mother was sitting on my father's knee, and he whispered under her ear and caressed her hair, which was my father's habit. I looked out the window again, but no one was there. Where were Aria, Dariush, and Iran Joon?

We were concerned about Neda without any blood interfaces with difference religion. I got up and watched Neda and Bijan from the small gap in the half-open door. Bijan and Neda were in bed in each other's arms, and Neda was crying. I went to her room and kissed Neda while Bijan and Neda hugged each other lovingly. How much I missed her and after a few minutes, I came out and saw Uncle Soheil standing behind the door and looked surprised. He walked away and spoke.

"How Neda was."

"She is fine."

"Where is Dariush?"

"He might be with Aria. Aria advised Bijan to behave differently in this exceptional case to pull Neda out of this shock, such as an antidote for poison."

Uncle Soheil shook his head several times and remained silent. I thought Aria, his love and sacrifice for Neda, and his effective action at the right time taught Bijan the best lesson on time. It couldn't have been better, especially when Neda suffered from severe depression. It might be the best shock at this point.

I had just come to know Zohreh and Manijeh. It did not take long for Bijan to go to the toilet. I went to Neda's room, laid down next to her, and she spoke.

"I felt the baby's movement was slowing down, did not believe it was severe, and the doctor said that the baby had died. I was guilty and had caused the child's death, and this pain has killed me. I wished I had eaten enough and did care. I want one thing to happen: the doctor made a mistake. I cried a lot. My dad put his mattress on the floor beside me and talked to me. I asked him to wait because it might be diagnosed wrongly, and I don't want to lose my baby. My dad understood me and my pain because he was in this situation before and wished his child would be alive.

My dad had lost his newborn baby and had not told anyone about his pain for years. Madam and Iran Joon were always there for me, and they talked to me. My dad insisted I see the doctor, and should I decide sooner if his diagnosis is accurate? I hated my dad for asking me to end my child's life. I don't want to go back to the hospital, and if this is going to be the only relic of my love, let me die with him."

Neda had become talkative, and I listened to her and thought Aria perfect recognition of saving Neda.

"The doctor did the sonogram and said that the baby was dead and that I should have a cesarean section, but I did not want to lose my baby. This is the fruit of my love, even if the child is not alive. Ana, I know it's stupid. It's tough to understand what it means to be pregnant and the child's death. I remember one night when I was in the hospital, a woman gave birth to her baby, and her baby died after a few minutes, and the woman cried badly. I told her could have a baby year after. Her baby might have had a fundamental problem that she couldn't survive, but she was crying. I have her face ahead of me, and I'm that miserable one that my heart ripped apart. I want to die."

"Are you happy to see Bijan? We were worried about you."

"I'm so glad that he still loves me. I love him. Aria talked to me to see other aspects of love. He is a thoughtful, wise man who told me I loved Bijan. Before, I thought I loved him like a brother, but Aria brought to my attention that I love Bijan and should not suffer. He said there is no sin. These are man-made rules that were imposed out of ignorance, and sometimes, they thought it was the public interest in these hypotheses. Still, in exceptional cases, a different decision should be made and not be afraid. He spoke so determinedly that he gained my trust incontinently, and when Bijan came and kissed me and said he loved me, I was pleased. What do you think? Is it bad I am in love with my brother?"

I wondered what to say, I learned not to be myself and to answer expediently. Aria is right that it should be an exceptional decision in a unique situation. I said some words when I couldn't understand its depth correctly.

I just knew that Aria had prepared Neda and Bijan for

this shock!

"I don't know why I told Aria about my love for Bijan. Aria said you have the right to love someone unconditionally. All laws and regulations tried to improve people's living situation, but some hanged us unfairly. I told him, but now I know him to be my brother. He said when you fell in love, you did not know. Your evaluation criteria are now different. It would be better to free yourself from the bondage of the constraints and love yourself.
I love you, but I do not beg for your love, and I would have begged for everything if you loved me. So, you can see that begging and not begging are two sides of one coin, not far from each other, and they are not the main issue. The important thing is a decision based on a particular situation.
Don't worry that you love him; love is everyone's wish. Be yourself. When you measure the criteria, it is not love. The accounted thinks about profits and losses and is trapped in the marketplace of phony credits. It is a fair condition if you love yourself and be honest with yourself. Otherwise, you get away from yourself and are not genuine. Let's eliminate everything you've heard. All people are profit thinkers.

I asked Aria what your profits are. Aria said I've been in love with you since I met you. I captured in your love circuit. When you came to our shop, I was slow to keep you longer because I thought your job was compulsory. I was concerned about you being free from work for a few more minutes, and it was not about me seeing you more and you wanted me to work faster. I was happy to keep you waiting and spent time in the back of our shop. You are my life dream; I am with you wherever you are. You want to know where I stand. I'm comfortable saying that I love you so much that, most importantly for me, it's your comfort and happiness, not my happiness. That's why I'm telling you to be yourself and my favorite profit is your happiness. I'm also a profit thinker. I had a particular respect for him. He is wise and unique, like my dad. But Bijan's love confused me and was tainted by guilt. Aria's conversations helped me to think of other aspects. Even though I knew he loved me, I did not understand why I told him about Bijan's love, and maybe I wanted to tell him that I loved another man. Perhaps he spoke so powerfully and gained my trust. Aria did not take his look away from me when I remembered that I couldn't look at Bijan when I fell in love with him.

There was a world of differences in his behavior and his self-confidence that manifested in his actions. I commend him for his courage in his speech. I wished that Bijan would tell me how he was feeling. I was pleased tonight when Bijan came."

Neda was talking, and I was drawn into my thoughts and saw that I am now a prisoner of my beliefs that have been planted in my mind for a lifetime, which are the product of the harvest of past generations. I wanted to know what Arya told Neda and Bijan that both had changed. From

Tehran to Turkey, we sat like statues and didn't think or plan to solve her problem like Aria. Dariush came to see Neda, and I also went to see Aria.

In the other room, everyone was gathered, and of course, they were worried for Neda; we knew that each of us needed to be alone with her and had thousands of unspoken words. I searched for Aria and asked Iran Joon in the corridor about Aria; she had seen him in the restaurant. I went to the hotel restaurant, Aria was not there, so I returned to our room. I fell asleep on the sofa. I woke up after an hour and went to see Aria when he was in the hallway, wanted to talk to me, and we went to his room. I was full of questions, but he started without delay.

"Ana, you must prepare Neda for surgery. I asked everyone about the city's best doctor and hospital, and I called him, who will probably come to visit Neda here tomorrow. Her surgery or delivery should be done as soon as possible."

We disturbed that we did not talk about this critical issue.

"Okay, but Uncle Soheil was taken Neda to the hospital, where they were supposed to have a medical exam."

"You're right, but maybe the best surgeon in this city

has the best equipment because of his name. The best-known surgeon in the city should do her delivery; even if you want to do surgery on her, you need a hospital, equipment, and a surgery room. It is better to have the best-known doctor by your side, or you'll be by his side."

He was right; we are not allowed to have surgery in this country and cannot do the surgery in the hotel. He had selected a well-known hospital and doctor.

"Ana, please go back and talk to Neda before falling asleep. To make sure the operation is done tomorrow. In addition, I asked a girl who knows Persian and Turkey well to be with you all the time to facilitate your communication. I asked her to be here early morning. If Neda has any problem tonight, we will go to the hospital and inform the doctor."

Then Aria gave me a piece of paper with the hospital address, the doctor's name, and the telephone numbers.

"All right, I have a question: What did you say to Bijan that he changed?"
"Was Neda happy?"
I looked at him in surprise.
"Answer me, I asked you."
"How was Neda's reaction?"
I looked into his eyes.
"Tell me, what did you say?"
From his steady look in my eyes, I could understand that I had only one choice: to answer him first.
"Yes."

His shoulders were pulled down, and he was relaxed. The previous nervous pressure on his face disappeared. He turned around to the window and looked far. I traced his staring. He was thinking about his love and pain. Aria's suffering hurt me badly, and it was difficult to see him in pain, whereas I loved Bijan very much. I stood beside him, grabbed his arm and put my head on his shoulder. He put his hand on my hand and remained silent. We should be quiet because I could not find any words that could have soothed the heart of the lover man or what he could complain about. I whispered.

"Aria, you're a great man."

He was quiet, crying in silence, and did not want anyone to know about his suffering. His grief was so heavy that I forgot why I came there. Moments passed in silence, and he calmly said.

"Ana, go get Neda ready."

When I left him, I saw Iran Joon standing in his room corner; I grabbed her hand and pulled her out. She had come barefoot, and we did not hear her footsteps.

"Aunt Iran, he might want to be alone and cry."

"I stood quietly there if he needed me."

Iran Joon raised Neda and me for many years in our house with love and affection, and now she has given her passion to Aria. I never saw that she wanted anything. With love and affection, my mother challenged her about what she should buy, wear, and eat. My mother said Iran was my real sister. I would go back to the room to see my real sister. I hoped to ask Dariush what Aria told Bijan, joined Uncle Soheil and Dariush, who stood in a corner and could guess Bijan was in Neda's room, and my mother joined us. They talked about Neda.

"Aria had asked me to prepare her for the labor or surgery and that a doctor would come to visit her tomorrow, and if she were in pain tonight, we would call the doctor or go to this hospital. Aria researched, and this is the best doctor and the most equipped hospital in the city.

Dariush: "When I walked down the corridor, a Persian lady asked me how my wife was, and I was lucky that this doctor accepted my wife. This doctor is very famous and does not accept patients easily. I was surprised; I guessed it was Aria. I explained he was my brother. She said that your brother loves his wife very much, he cried and gave them a bunch of money.

I asked if she was there. She answered no, her friend who is a translator told her."

We just discovered that Aria found the doctor, went to his house, and paid his fee.

"Aria did not tell me, he just asked me to talk to Neda."

"Aria is right. We selected hospital without any research. And it might not be the best in the city. We don't know this city, and I will speak to Aria and pay his money."

"Uncle Soheil, as I know, Aria will not say anything, and he did not even tell me what he said to Bijan to change."

"You're right."

Madam: "Our children listened to ours before, but the situation changed, and they decided whatever they wanted. Neda was stubborn recently and did not listen to me."

"Mom, she is not stubborn. Have you ever lost your baby?"

"No."

"So, you could not understand her."

"So, what happened, another kid?"

Uncle Soheil had tears in his eyes.

"Neda said this to another woman one day, she clearly did not understand her feelings, and your judgment on this case needs to be corrected."

"You are out of our control when you grow up."

There was a big gap between our mentalities. I wished to think like my mother and have the false peace and calm down."

Setareh, Koroush, Zohreh Manijeh, and Sahar sat in one corner and were not curious like us. They waited until we told them what was going on. Sometimes, they seemed to be indifferent, but they weren't. I went to Neda's room. Bijan was sleeping next to Neda in his suit. I kissed Neda's hair and asked how she was.

"Fine." I started gently.

"I must go to bed early and have a busy day tomorrow, so we should go to the hospital."

Neda had shaken and said:

"But I do not want."

I ignored her words because I learned these tricks from my mother and Iran Joon. Whenever I was stubborn, they ignored me and politically followed their goal. I noticed it is better to copy and follow the same approach, although I was always not too fun of those manners and thought a man should say his words comfortably and clearly. I saw how we changed. Yes, I was also in a position where I would ignore and become a monkey, not see, not hear, or understand what Neda said. After a long pause, I laughed and talked to Bijan.

"It is excellent; you slept all the time. We are tired, too."

Bijan stared at me and might understand my plan but did not dare enough to help me. Minutes later, I heard Neda.

"What did you say?"

"We must go to the hospital tomorrow."

"What do you mean?"

I was silent again. Neda said.

"I don't want to go to the hospital.

I remembered Aria, who did not give anyone any respite and did his project.

"So, if the labor pain starts, we're going tonight. We don't know anyone here, and it's better to find the best doctor and hospital in town to let us be with you."

At that time, my mother came to her room and then took my words and said:

"Neda Joon understand better than all of us and should end this problem tomorrow."

My mother always used the phrase Neda knew the most. Neda knew me well that I did not change my words; my mother was my accomplice. Neda remained silent and said nothing, and Bijan looked at us astonished. Again, this one-sided lecture was continued by my mother and me.

Uncle Soheil joined us, then Dariush, Stareh, and Iran Joon. Bijan, who was in her bed like a motionless statue and looked at us, got up and sat in bed.

"Neda Joon, I'll sleep next to you tonight."

"Good enough, giant bear, why are you going to sleep here?"

I said with a laugh:

"Mom, I became a doctor, who a giant bear is."

"Take your doctor title for your patients, not me."

Everyone laughed except Neda, and Bijan. One by one, they left Neda and Bijan alone. I went to the next room to sleep. Aria was there and said the doctor would visit her early in the morning.

Dariush went with Aria to sleep in his room. Aria had taken rooms for Bijan, me, and my parents on the same floor, a little distance away. I preferred to sleep next to Iran Joon. Uncle Soheil and Sahar stayed in our room to be available just in case. Behrouz called me, it was the first time I had been far from him, my first trip to a foreign country and missed him so much. Dariush talked to Nasrin. I woke up early, showered, and went to Neda's room. Neda and Bijan were sleeping next to each other. I returned and had breakfast with Iran Joon. Uncle Soheil showered, and Sahar woke up when Dariush and Aria came to our room. Aria dressed in an elegant suit with a tie and spoke.

"The doctor will be here in half an hour. Don't worry if she does not let the doctor visit her. Nothing will happen."

"I prepared her to some extent last night but did not say the doctor would come here. I will tell her now."

I went to her room, turned around her bed, and kissed her hair, and she was awake.

"The doctor should see you today."

"Do you understand me, I don't want to go to the hospital." Neda was angry with me.

"Well, I arranged it."

I did not say anymore. Bijan went to the bathroom, and I lay down on his spot next to Neda, and I said:

"Look, you should not hurt yourself and us."

I did not give her time to talk. When Bijan came back, I said:

"Now it's my turn. You get out."

Bijan sat in the corner of the bed, and I spoke.

"Go to eat breakfast; you did not eat anything last night."

I hit him with my foot and pointed him at the room door with my eyes. Bijan walked out of the room, and my mother, Iran Joon, came and kissed Neda. Uncle Soheil came after them. None of them talked as if they had been a team. Setareh Khanum did not come to Neda's room because Neda gave them a cold shoulder.

Zohreh and Manijeh treated her differently with

different manners. They believed they should respect Neda's choice and not force her. We thought it did not matter what she wanted in this situation, and her health had priority over her decision. We talked in the same language and were from the same land but had two different manners, indicating two different ways of thinking formed in other times and places.

We looked forward to solving her problem. It was not clear based on which criteria we had established it. There was no opportunity to analyze our behavior in those critical days. I was sleeping next to Neda when someone knocked on the door. Uncle Soheil welcomed someone coming in, followed by a woman. I guessed he was a doctor, and he laughed and said in English:

"I must see two pregnant women." I laughed and said in broken English.

"You must help me to be pregnant.

He laughed and said:

"I am not usually the one that handles it. Someone other than me should take it!" His accompanying woman translated very formally. Dr. checked Neda. Her depression was noticeable. The doctor told her cautiously.

"I'm sorry, but you are a doctor and know we should decide sooner. We will start to induce in the hospital; a cesarean section is the only option if it doesn't work."

Neda noticed to surround from all sides. The doctor held hands and continued:

"Stand up. Let's go to the hospital; doctors are responsible for the patient's life in this country."

It was a kind, polite and threatening proposal without any terrifying words. I was happy that her health would not be compromised. Neda pulled her hand back.

The doctor said kindly but firmly:

"I visited a beautiful girl, and you will come with me."

"I want to take a shower."

"In the hospital which is better equipped than this hotel."

He kept Neda's hand.

"I am not ready.

"I can't wait for your health to be compromised. Come

with me."

The Iranian woman translated it, my mother said:

"All right, we're coming."

I saw my mother as the woman whom everyone feared her. On the way to the hospital, Neda said:

"If I die, take my suitcase with you, and keep the Bijan poetry notebook. I will deliver my baby and my corpse here. My share of love will be completed to be in a foreign country's grave."

I was horrified by her words. Dr. Yilmaz started intravenous induction, which may begin labor. Neda was silent, ignored her surrounding area and did not speak. The medication dosage via serum was regularly increased, but there was no labor pain, and the decision was made to have a cesarean section. Koroush Khan and Setareh Khanum kissed Neda and said they loved her. Dariush did not talk, grabbed Neda's hand, and looked at her. Aria stood before Neda, smiled at her, and said you are perfect, and be yourself. Bijan said goodbye to her and wanted to kiss her, but she did not kiss him and put her cheek on his face. I did not understand if she was still in love with Bijan or had abandoned his passion. I asked her when I held her in my arms.

"Why did not you kiss Bijan when he wanted to kiss you?"

"I wanted to feel his warm breath on my cheek. I don't love him anymore. It looked like my wish's chandelier had collapsed; each lamp was broken into a thousand pieces, and each piece was a needle that tore my heart apart. My love memories hurt me, and the rope of love around my neck kills me. I never believed the day I would reach the end of the dead-end alley from every side and be left in the depths of a dark well."

I did not understand if she was still captive in Bijan's love. My courage to ask was dead in me. The fear that my question would be annoying limited me, and it was the silence between us. I regretted our childhood, how easily we said everything in our minds recklessly, and now there were a thousand stones in our connection way in the name of expediency. Yes, the expedient brick walls between us hoisted up and killed me behind the regret walls. I wanted to know how she felt and thought.

Neda was taken to the operating room. Bijan, Dariush, and I went to the operating room. Dr. Yilmaz performed a cesarean section. While Dariush was his assistant. I stayed next to the anesthesiologist, and Bijan's face was pale, the surgeon who was a university idol. The operation was over; Dariush said Dr. Yilmaz did a great job. The baby's condition showed that the death had occurred several days ago. When we left the operating room, I saw Bijan crying when his head was on his mother's shoulder.

There are moments in our life when we need at any age and position to have a shoulder for crying: a handsome, a tall handsome gentleman like Bijan or a weak woman like me. Aria was not around, but I was sure he was in the hospital, although I had seen him behind the operating and recovery rooms. They asked us about which way the baby should be buried, Bijan did not have any opinion, so we left it to the hospital. Neda refused to see the baby after waking up. Neda's depression peaked a day after surgery, and the doctor prescribed her medication.

Translator Roya told me about the night they visited Dr. Yilmaz's house. The doctor refused to accept the patient first, and Aria sat there and asked them for water. He told Roya to go to the toilet and wait there because he wanted to be alone with them. Roya left them and stayed in the corridor, not to be seen, but she saw Aria was sitting and they were standing. They spoke English, and she did not understand. Then, they sat at the table quietly. Aria put a bunch of bills on the table. Dr. Yilmaz's wife told her husband that we did not tell him how much. The doctor responded that this person needed us, and we should accept his patient and his fund, no matter how much we would return his money. The doctor took the money.

They told him something in English, and I saw Aria put his face between his hands. The doctor got up and put his hand on his shoulder. When Aria Agha got up, she returned and pretended that she did not see them. Before they left, the doctor said he would come to the hotel tomorrow morning and get the hotel's addresses, but he

did not tell him how much the fee was. She translated to
Farsi. Aria said, tell them how much, and he will pay
tonight. They said it was enough and talked about it later.

When we were in the hospital, Dr. Yilmaz had not
asked about Aria; that was clear intentionally. My uncle
Soheil wanted to pay the hospital bill, which showed a zero
balance. We learned that the private hospital was Dr.
Yilmaz and had done the treatment for free in Aria's
respect.

Neda was discharged from the hospital to the hotel.
Every night, Behrouz called me, and we talked for a few
minutes. During this time, Professor Kiani contacted Bijan
and us. He had a father figure who worried about Bijan.

Nima Khan called Iran Joon every night. I wondered
why he did not talk to Aria. Iran Joon said that Nima called
Aria's mobile about workers several times daily. Nasrin
called Dariush and when I asked Dariush how Nasrin was,
he said, you should ask how Ana and Dariush are and
stared into my eyes momentarily. He was right, we should
separate from our dear friend, and there may be no more
chance to see her again! I should consider our emotional
situation.

Uncle Soheil made appointments for the medical exam
for Neda and himself and Sahar's interview with the US
embassy. Manijeh and Zohreh returned to Germany.
Manijeh asked Uncle Soheil, Sahar, and Neda would stay
in Germany and then go to the US. Bijan's parents stayed
with Neda in Turkey.

On our first trip abroad to Turkey, we saw two streets
along a river, the road between the hospital and the hotel,
and a heavy traffic jam with people in dirty clothes and the
latest fashion clothes. Our hotel was in Taksim Square and
had a city view. Taksim, in the Persian language, was
divided too. Aria decided to stay in Turkey until Neda was
there. Dariush was trying to spend time with Aria, and he
said we should keep an eye on Aria. As two men, we sat
quietly beside each other and were not talking much. You
could sit with Aria and encourage him to express his
feelings and release the emotional pain because he saw
Aria drank alcoholic beverages every night. I went

down to the hotel bar restaurant when it was crowded around Neda. Aria had sat, played with a glass of beer, and stared at it for hours. He did not talk, and his grief was observable.

It was the first time for me to be in an alcohol bar and did not know I had to order anything. I thought I couldn't go and sit there because it's a business place. My father taught me to order something even if I did not drink and pay the tip. Any business had a specific rule. When I told Aria, he made me sure it did not matter. I guessed he would pay them a good tip because they were constantly hanging out around Aria. My father was there a few times and saw that everyone had a particular respect for Aria.

Dr. Yilmaz visited Neda one night, and then we went to the hotel restaurant where his wife had dinner with Aria. I joined them and asked why they did not charge us for the hospital bill, and they said you are doctors, and in honor of Aria. That night, Dariush and Uncle Soheil joined us. Aria had a particular respect for Uncle Soheil. Neda's behavior had changed, and she ignored Bijan significantly and even told him she no longer loved him. The psychiatrist could understand all these changes. She had not even talked to me and was imprisoned in her shell. The Neda silence before our separation was too heavy for me.

Dariush, Bijan, and I returned to Iran in my father's car after a week. My father and Aria had planned to return to Iran in two of Aria's cars that were there. My father said.

"I pawned the property deed at the passport office. It is important your passports would be stamped on arrival."

"Why did you not tell us?"

"Your mother asked me not to tell you."

My mother: "You wished to be with Neda. If they take up the house, we work together again and buy another one. We must appreciate the moments."

"Where do we get back the property deed?"

"Nowhere. Just be careful that the passport is stamped then I can get the deed of home back."

Bijan apologized to Uncle Soheil for the child abduction accusation. Bijan and Aria were hugging each other at the time of separation, and both were sad, had a

common concern such as two sides of a coin and had been
so far and close to each other. Bijan thanked and told Aria,
"I will leave Neda to you" and cried. Aria had a particular
manner and specific skills that even Bijan needed to learn. I
assumed Neda loved Bijan, but she was noticeably away
from him, which might relate to her depression or her love
chapter ending.

I loved Neda and did not want to bother her with my
questions about Bijan. Unfortunately, our last togetherness
moment was not good, and passed in silence.
When I wished we could review all our memories together
and talk for hours without interruption as we used to
without hesitation, but her depression had hijacked our
opportunity.

Return to Iran

On our return to Iran, we were sad. Along the way, I
thought about Behrouz, and if this problem happens and
we separate, I will kill myself and understand Bijan's
situation. Bijan occasionally sighed loudly from the bottom
of his chest. I was glad that Bijan had good parents and a
professor who loved him sincerely; unfortunately, they
could do nothing in this situation. There are moments
when all roads are dead ends, and we wander between the
sorrows and think about what to do. Dariush was as
quiet as usual, and all his conversation was for Neda only.
Iran Joon had said about Aria and his fate that the Islamic
Regime had stoned his mother before his eyes.

I was so upset to hear his story that I did not want to
listen. The imagination of anyone stoned skewered my
body, and I thought Aria had many challenges inside. But
he still sacrificed and helped Neda and Bijan to make Neda
happy. Who is he, and how can we describe all this
sacrifice? None of us did what he did. Aria was right to be
silent! From which pain could he talk that we could put a
salve on his wounds? I was resting in the back of the car
and thinking about the fate of my loved ones. I was happier
than them. The most considerable sadness I endured was
when I fell in love with Behrouz and he pretended to
ignore me; I thought it was enormous sadness in the world.

Later, I felt immense regret for not getting pregnant, and now I see that my pain was nothing compared to Neda's problem. I had not thought about my brother, Varouge, for a long time and what pain it would be if I did not know him and fell in love and married him. I saw how easily the period of unknowingly passed and the problematic experiences had come, and I did not believe I would have this hardship in person. The people's sorrow was painful; now, I could see other people's problems. I was too young to understand its depth and remembered the Sohrab Sepehry's poem.

"Love, only love.

Only love motivates humans to see the extent of people's sorrow.

Love inspires humans to have a vision to go far beyond the barrier and search for solutions, like a bird's motivation for flying.

Sorrow could motivate the creation of antitoxin, an elixir that could treat human sadness."

The depth of this sorrow draws me to the extent of the street children's pains in our society. Does anyone come to make a life-giving elixir for those innocent people bravely? According to lousy Islamic regime government statistics, which is far less than reality, the Iranian street children are more than a million.

One can be Neda, who is unknowingly getting married to her sibling. It is a painful memory for someone like Aria, who witnessed his mother stoning. One might be Varouge and me, and the thought of Varouge and Behrouz in one position as a husband and brother was far-fetched for me, and I trembled. Does anyone come to solve and prevent these harmful incidents? Does Switzerland have street children, and a mother is stoned to death in front of her child? We were approaching the Iran border when Dariush made me wear a scarf. When we got to Turkey, I forgot I did not need to wear a headscarf. I saw what religion is Islam that would be ruined with my hair exposition, but what could I say, especially when I was a Christian? Suddenly, I remembered that if they arrested us, we were not wife and husband and were not confidants. What could we do?

"I wish your mom had come with us." Bijan spoke.

"It made no difference. My mother would be accused of being your girlfriend, and I am Darius's girlfriend; then, we would be arrested and stoned."

I thought about how they could justify this wrong social behavior. In Turkey, I was alone with Aria in a room, and there was no problem. And I was sure that I should not explain to Behrouz because we trust each other. We could never have the idea that Behrouz being alone with Nasrin is a problem. We must be crazy to think stupidly about this kind of turban Muslim regime behavior. More interesting, mullah told me why you did not convert to Islam!

This is Islam, we should not want it for our enemies. We reached the border, and we did not have my father's skills to encounter the fools, so we panicked. As we guessed, our problems began when the officer asked.

"What is your relationship?"

"We are surgeons and come back from a medical conference."

"Sit in that room."

Their order had its special meaning that you were in trouble. They searched our car. We hadn't considered it before because we were obsessed with Neda's situation and forgot the rest. We used a public phone to call Professor's home based on Dariush suggestion and he talked briefly.

"As you know, we and Dr. Ana returned from the medical conference, and we have a problem at the border."

He delivered his message to the Professor. Then Bijan spoke with him.

"Did you say you are the best surgeon and should attend the next conference?" Professor asked.

"Yes, but they did not believe us."

"Could you give me their office number?"

I went to the other room and asked for the phone number. There was a cheeky woman with a black chador who was reluctant to give me the number even though I said it was for Ayatollah. Bijan gave the number to the professor.

"I ask the Ayatollah to call them personally."

It was a trick. We stayed there for two hours and assumed someone had called them. The cheeky woman told me my husband would not send me alone with two men if he had zeal and honor! I was silent because the answer to a fool was useless when her measurement tool was in the middle of the lady's legs, and they did not know the honor meaning and assumed savagery was the zeal meaning. They believed the men's brutality against women was a sign of manhood and bravery. They did not know those wild, muscular men were not men, and their manhood died. We studied at the university but did not learn how to encounter these wolves, and I remembered the Forough Farokhzad poem.

"In such a cold and dark world
Some people kiss you while, in their mind, knitting a hanging rope for your neck."

This was the objective embodiment of the Revolutionary Guards who had to maintain security! After several questions and wasting time, they allowed us to enter our homeland. It was late at night, and we were exhausted. We decided to stay in Tabriz for one night and continue our trip the day after because we were afraid that we would be held captive by these idiots in the middle of the road at night. Dariush said that if desert roads are left to young single truck drivers at night, it is safer for the naked, single-alone woman than the Revolutionary Guard. One of them in a province is enough to create an unsafe crime area. We have heard many stories of the manhood of truck drivers. It is better not to be on the road at night and not encounter fools like the border guards.

Hotel

In Tabriz, we did not find any vacancy in the hotel. We were surprised that the business was so good! The same story repeated from one hotel to another. Finally, Dariush asked a taxi driver what was happening in your city and that all the hotels were full. The taxi driver surprisedly said.

"There was nothing and all the hotels were empty. Who says no vacancy?"

"Wherever we went, they claimed they had no room."

"No, it's impossible. Are you together?"

"Yes."

"Is your marriage document with you?"

"We are not wife and husband and wanted separate rooms."

"Now I understand it. Hotels are not allowed to give women a room."

I was crazy and spoke. "In the Islamic city, the woman must sleep in the street to be available for mullah's raping."

"You recognized correctly; everything is possible of these bastards."

You should go to the registration station and ask for a hotel. Then, a mullah assigns a hotel for you."

"What and where is it?"

"The registration representative is at the police station."

We followed him to the police station. Dariush said:

"A hotelier said that; I thought it was the hotel's name."

I was so angry that I cursed everything the fornicated mullah. In the police station, Dariush and Bijan told me to sit in the car till they got a hotel. Then they returned to take me and asked me to make the headscarf tightly.

"It was as if my headscarf was the seatbelt of Islam. There are no lice on my hair. Otherwise, I would have tightened the headscarf to preserve Islam!"

Dariush: "To be calm. They are worse than schizophrenia mental sickness and have deceitful delusions."

We entered the police station, and a mullah with a dirty collar and dirty teeth was there, named Haji Agha, who asked.

"Where is your Haji Agha?"

"Who's Haji Agha?"

In a nasty and ridiculous tone, he said:

"Haji Agha.

"I do not understand what you mean, and who is he?'

"So, you don't have Haji agha?"

"Who's Haj Agha?"

There was a woman there to say he meant your husband.

"My husband is a surgeon not a Haji."

A similar process had been repeated that we had at the border as if we were trapped in the psychiatric hospital. I remember my father saying the fools get worse if you say anything. If our time was not wasted time at the border, we would have been near Tehran and would not need to get a hotel. They were time killers and did not understand the time value. When we were there a lady who was a tourist arrived. Later, I learned that she had been taken by taxi from this hotel to that hotel. The taxi driver took advantage of an unfamiliar customer and turned her around the city to make more money. Eventually, she should refer to the police station to get a hotel room. Mullah asked her.

"Where is Haji Agha?"

Like me, she did not know the meaning of Haji Agha. After a few repetitions, I thought the bearded dirty mullah had sadism and deliberately tested people. He knew we did not know the meaning of Haj Agha; he wanted to gain something from his flirt in this way. The woman responded that she is tourists, and her husband is in the US.

"Where's your daughter?"

"She fell asleep in the car."

"She should be here."

The woman left and returned with her daughter, who was about 12 or 13 years old. She was holding her sleepy daughter's headscarf, and to the extent that I understood the girl was cursing in English about why they came there and wanted to return to the US. Her mother tried to keep her calm. Finally, the mullah, who thought he had a significant position, said:

"Don't be upset, my sister. I take these measures to preserve your honor and take all precautions so that you are not in agony in the Islamic country, and now I will write you a good hotel."

I said under my lip. What agony was worse than to see a fool like you who insecure the places. After she took the paper, she said that she was very sorry for mullah to allow himself to accuse women if a few did not behave appropriately. He shouldn't insult and disrespect most women in a few cases. She left without caring about the mullah's response, and I thought she was right. Mullah allowed himself to insult women, whereas they were the primary source of sedition and corruption, and worse than them, we sit quiet and tolerate them. I got up and said:

"Why are we waiting so long, whether there is an available room? It is unlogic we stay here."

Dariush and Bijan were worried about me. Dariush stood up and said:

"She is sick and shall have to speak at conference."

It was clear that Dariush and Bijan tried to show that I was an important doctor, and I had a delirious fever.

"We are careful that no one upsets you."

"Who wants to upset me at the hotel, for example? You made these rules to upset people, and if one is a prostitute, one can do everything in this room behind your desk."

The mullah tried to keep me quiet.

"Mrs. doctor like you should not talk loudly. You should learn from Fatima that non-mahram did not hear her voice."

"Were you there and saw Fatima?"

I said it in a low voice. We noticed that Mullah's job was to take advantage of female passengers under the name of the hotel guest registration every night, while other mullah with his secretary were the titer of foreign media. The English Major Journals article was about the turban and non-turban Islamic governments' corruption. Velayati, the Minister of Intelligence, was caught with his secretary in a New York hotel. World journalists and photographers are admired in civilized countries and rewarded for good news on time rather than punishments. In Iran, photographers and reporters are guilty if they report the mullah's corruption, embezzlement, and crimes, because it should be hidden! The photo of the sleeping parliamentarian mullahs during the government meeting in their seats. It was hard to believe, but it was true that the photographer had been arrested for taking pictures. What happened to the photographer after arrest was unknown. In civilized countries, journalists promote the growth of society and the advancement of constructive goals of the country, not destruction. The police are responsible for maintaining security, not disrupting the people's peace. While the Revolutionary Guard is paid to disturb the order of society.

Dariush explained that "The guards' members were a young boy hunted by hyenas to convert those confused lambs to wolves and kill people. It is an ultimate victory for an illiterate rejected boy to see people waiting for his decision and it compensates for his inferiority. They did not recognize that they were the victims, and the foundation was wrong."

On our trip way, we saw ourselves in the mullah's fire while we did not have this feeling in Turkey. It was tough to believe that we were foreigners in our own country. I was willing to move away from this land, and how regrettable can it be to express this bitterness? I remembered Zohreh and Manijeh's peaceful behaviors; might they have thought about our stressful behavior unwillingly? The lack of friendly behavior was due to an insecure environment that made us vulnerable. We were uncalm people who jumped into the air with every spark.

Where did we stand, and who stole those best gems from ours, good thinking, good talk, and good practice? We, educated people, were less than foreign illiterate people because we needed a proper politician. I was afraid all the way and was careful not to take me as a prostitute person. Our trip problems inside our country were awful, which forbidden hand sprinkled the bitter insecurity seeds in our land, and it had grown all over.

I cried a lot, Bijan was very upset and told them I would leave at the earliest opportunity if my crime was to be a woman, and I should not be humiliated and insulted; I would not belong to an insulted area. I studied to experience a better life, not hurt more. Dariush believed there were some problems in childhood and at a young age, but we could not analyze them deeply. When we know the root of the issues, we can see all the heartbroken dimensions that have made people vulnerable recently.

I called Behrouz from the hotel's public phone, and I

looked like a child who complained to her teacher about the ridiculous people who hurt us for nothing. Dariush talked to Nasrin and Pouran Joon. We also called the professor. He was worried about us and told us to call him tomorrow before leaving. His support was magnificent during our hard times.

We informed my mother that we would stay in Tabriz that night and she reported the Neda situation the same as before. Aria was with them but did not go to Neda's room. My father told them he wanted to have fun and see the city like a tourist. I knew my father to look for pleasure and wanted to see everywhere. I went to one room, and Bijan and Dariush went to another. We left early in the morning Tabriz and arrived in Tehran.

Our home after Neda

I was worried about Dariush and asked him to be cool in the hospital. He said I would no longer tolerate those stupid behaviors, preferring to be a peddler and not tolerate anyone. My mother and Soheil Khan had raised their children by working; I can work as a worker and cover the cost of our living. I will not tolerate anything I kiss everything and put it aside. I was worried what would happen in the hospital. People created difficulty for each other unfairly. It looked like mullahs and guards who were stupid could not understand that autocratic and unhealthy behavior ruined the people's civilization and peace. We were sorrier when the educated man gave Dariush a hard time for no reason. I knew Dariush had reached the border of rebellion. He was a person who talked rarely, and he verbalized it when he was very serious. He reached the level that he would ruin whatever he had built hard.

We returned to the hospital, and I was apprehensive. Also, Bijan talked to Dariush the night before, and he said I could no longer tolerate anything. When Dariush passed the hallway, he saw the department head, who came forward and asked Dariush about his sister's situation; then he apologized for the past.

Dariush did not expect such an encounter, staying quietly, staring at him. He said you are surprised; I waited for you to come and apologize and tell you how unfair my behavior was. I hope that you will forget it. Dariush told him I also thought the world was not worth it; I tolerated the hardships and decided to leave the hospital with no excuse. He invited Dariush to his office to drink tea together. Bijan guessed that the Professor talked to him because Bijan spoke about his behavior.

At night, my mother called and stated that they visited the city. Uncle Soheil is not going anywhere because he is worried for Neda. My father requested that they go with him to see an island, Princess Island. He forced Soheil Khan to come with us. Uncle Soheil also asked Aria to be with us. I love Aria like Neda. We went to Princess Island and on a big boat full of tourists. The island was a hill full of tall trees, two police cars, and one fire truck. The tourist s walked around. There were also some horse carriages for those who did not want to walk. We stayed in line for a carriage to visit the island. Neda said.

"We could imagine that once a princess has been deported to this island by the prince or the ruler of the city, its name is Princess Island, and there is always a reason for naming."

Each carriage or a horse ride was for three people. Koroush Khan, Soheil Khan, Sahar, and Arman walked around. Setareh Khanum, Iran, and I were in one carriage, and Neda and Aria in another. Then we returned to the same boat, and sometimes Neda stared at one point and thought deeply. This makes Soheil Khan worried. We were on the boat when I noticed Neda and Aria were absent. I looked around and saw Aria grab Neda's arms tightly on the boat's deck and shake her.

At first, I thought they were joking, but I remembered you told me that Aria had tightly grabbed Bijan's arms once. I approached them, stood there so that Neda and Aria could not see me and listened to them. Aria talked firmly, and Uncle Soheil noticed and joined me. We heard Aria say that life was never easy, and no one sent us an invitation and did not ask us what we wanted. According to Buddha, there is always some pain from birth to death. We should learn to handle it. Dying is easy, eventually, we are gone and should leave. No one lasts forever, you should be dared enough to stay for others. You are here to play your best role. We don't belong to ourselves to make decisions just for our convenience. We're a piece of a collection, and if we go, the group collapses. Did you think about your father's situation, Ana, Bijan, Dariush, Iran Joon, and so on? We must live, learn, change, grow, and tell others what we know. Think of your father and we should learn from him.

Aria was in an aggressive state, like an orator, not leaving Neda and holding her arms tightly. He may have seen something. Later, I asked Aria if she wanted to commit suicide. Aria quoted her that if one fell into the seawater, fish would eat it, and it would be relieved. This way of speaking is dangerous for someone in a depressive phase or whose depression has diminished, and I did not want to miss an opportunity. My mother said that Aria's words frightened her.

We talked about Aria when I said what had happened on their boat. Bijan confirmed Aria and talked about that night we got to Turkey; he had taken his arms tightly.

"I was so angry with his arrogant attitude and how he had allowed himself to grab my arms that I hit his hand, but after a moment, I saw that he was right. I should listen and accept what he said. If this is the only way to get Neda released from depression, I am very selfish to resist.

Neda was shocked by the misadventure, and Aria was right. Another shock may be the antidote to that incident. He must have seen Neda at a stage where he commanded me so strongly as a commander who spoke to a soldier. We did not learn in school that we must act differently in exceptional cases. Perhaps Aria had numerous special occasions. Like an attacker and an orator, he must have effective speech and think about a solution. Going to school and learning is good, but it is not enough. We learn to deal with problems, especially emotional issues, not escaping from problems, and daring in any actions are something beyond the schoolbooks and should be learned in the furnace of life." I did not want to tell Bijan that Aria had prepared Neda, then him.

Dariush: "That night, I thought he had attacked you, and I had come to help you, which I saw was different."

"I also thought that Dariush came to help you and attacked you, what we wanted, and what we got!"

Bijan is right: sometimes misery can be a good teacher and teach us valuable lessons if it doesn't crush us. When you face adversity and defend yourself, you learn practically, and you could not learn from books. These practices are more effective than just reading about them. Just like how hardships can turn iron into steel, making it strong and resistant to rust, Aria also has a solid and unwavering presence.

After Neda, we were sad. I spent time with Nasrin, a curious girl. I didn't mind her curiosity as I had nothing to hide. Though I wasn't as close to her as I was to Neda, whenever we were at home, she would come to my room and talk. Nasrin was happy that her baby was growing but worried that the baby might face the same fate as Neda's baby. She became sensitive to the baby's movements and sometimes expressed concerns that Dariush seemed more worried about Neda than about her and loved Neda more.

I was surprised and explained to Nasrin that her doubts about Dariush's love resulted from her lack of self-confidence. Nasrin said that all our conversations were about Neda when she wanted to discuss their baby. I compared her situation to imagining Behrouz saying I don't love Ana because she talked more about Neda. I emphasized that just because I love Neda doesn't mean I don't love Behrouz. I reassured Nasrin that Behrouz wouldn't be upset with me if I talked to Dariush or someone else and that her lack of self-confidence was the basis of her doubts. Unwillingly, Nasrin was upset.

After a few days, when I ignored her, she kissed me and said I was right. She observed that Behrouz had no attitude when I talked to Dariush and Bijan. She was sad that she had hurt Dariush and promised to work on her problem. I was happy they would have a better relationship. I wasn't in the mood to see a gynecologist anymore. Having a baby was not a matter for me anymore.

Dariush was silent as usual, no longer did tapestry,

and said he was not in its mood. It is evident that When Dariush was alone and wanted to talk to me. Perhaps he found a successor to Neda and filled her vacancy. We both made a desperate, unsuccessful effort. One day, he told me that talking with Neda was like breathing for me when there was no air. I loved her without being able to define any specific interface. Talking to her was a cure for me not to see myself alone in this world, and her absence was a heavy blow. We talked about Bijan and how hard it is for him. Bijan had lost everything at once, and now, by separating from us, his friends.

That night, we talked to Behrouz, and we thought it would be better if Behrouz asked Bijan to come back and live with us because he went home after we returned from Turkey. He came every night to hear about Neda, slept on the couch in the hall, and did not go to his room. He lost weight, told Behrouz his stomach hurt, and was taking medication. Behrouz asked Bijan to come home and be in the same room till he passed this stage, and he agreed without pause. My mother called us and reported In the US embassy, they should have blood tests, chest X-rays, and physical exams, and they could change their names. Later, I talked to Neda, who said she had asked Aria's opinion about the name change, and Aria said.

"Did you hear the Phoenix story, which re-establishes itself from its ashes? This means that whatever is uncomfortable, you must burn and build a good one. It did not mean a physical burning but also a change of mentality and annoying things. As a human, I have been made of the existing mindset and the cultures in the environment.

We should be daring enough to make a better "I" for a better future and discard the previous grief. It would be best to create a new life, even with a new name. You imagine the past story was a movie, good or bad. You could not change even its small scene. Forget what it was, move on, and there is no live space behind you. Start today with the name you like."

"My father selected my name, Neda."

"It was the right thing to choose a name for you at that time, and we know it wasn't your father's chosen name. If

you change your name; it does not mean you did
something against him. If you like to change it, do it, and it
is acceptable for your father."

"The name my aunt said is the name of a season; is it a
good name?"

"Each name is based on the selector's taste means; it
doesn't mean good or bad. Take it easy."

"I will tell Ana about my choice and later to others."

Aria had told Uncle Soheil that he was happy to hear
this because it was a sign of hope and emotional
attachment.

Nima Khan went to Turkey to talk to Uncle Soheil
about Neda again and told Neda to answer him whenever
she would be ready. After Neda left, Aria's family, Bijan's
parents, and my parents returned to Iran in Aria's vehicles.
My mother had brought back the Neda's baby set. I
suggested keeping it for Nasrin's baby, which my mother
refused, and she with Pouran Joon and Iran Joon, bought a
new baby set for Nasrin and Dariush. My mother paid for
it. Pouran Joon was upset that she did not have the
financial means, and my mother told her we were together
and shared whatever we had in our house. Dariush gave
Neda's baby set to a mother with a newborn without
clothes in the maternity ward.

Neda in Germany

In telephone call from Germany, Neda said Aria was
sad in the airport and stared at me, and I was heartbroken
for him and unable to compensate for his love and
kindness. At the last minute, he took my hand, and I said
goodbye, but he said "there is no goodbye, I am always
with me and loved you, and no goodbye. Just take care of
yourself." He spoke firmly with his sorrowful voice. I just
looked at him. Iran Joon watched us with her tearful eyes. I
believed her motherly sense of love for myself and Aria.
When Madam held me in her arms, I remembered the day
of the vice president's proposal and Madame told me that
whatever I wanted to do, she would be with me. I wanted
to ask her to come with me. Even though I grew up and
could stand on my feet, I still needed her love.

I looked at them behind the airplane window, thought about Aria and Bijan, and thought about my fate. Sahar kindly caressed me like Iran Joon, and my dad watched me. Eventually, the plane landed in Frankfort, which was very clean and sorted, with no air pollution like in Turkey and Tehran, without the smell of gasoline or exhaust pipe smoke.

We waited at the airport because we had to fill out a form. The police requested the Iranian passenger fill it out and guided us on where to take the subway to the central train station and which train to take to the city where Manijeh lives. We wanted to get a taxi. Their taxis were Mercedes-Benz, but the Iranians told us that the subway was cheaper and faster. We changed three trains to the city where Manijeh lived. The train officers guided us to figure out which train to pick. The train officers dressed in police uniforms would help us quickly get our luggage to the next train. We have yet to see this kind of cooperation among our people.

Manijeh lived in a charming city with pleasant rainy weather. Compared to us, people walked in the street in raincoats, carried umbrellas, and not running away from the road on rainy days. I'm in a better situation; maybe antidepressants are effective, and maybe my father and Aria's logical words have helped me accept the terrible reality of the world.

In Cologne, all stores are closed at 6:30 p.m., like an office. No one else is in the street except late at night when people go to the pub, which means bar. All stores are closed on Sunday, and people walk and watch the glass shops to come and buy during the weekdays. Their lives are regularly clockwise. The streets are washed up, and the store is clean and busy.

Pedestrians waited behind the line to turn the traffic light green. No one walks in the street and cross the street at a red light. If someone wants to cross the street between cars, they must think he is crazy and need a psychiatric evaluation. Their social behavior is different; we look at and copy them and ask Aunt Manijeh what to do. Nader and his wife Brigitte visited us at Manijeh's house and left after a few minutes. Manijeh said they couldn't stay longer because Brigitte was paid to care for her granddaughter tonight and should be there on time. We were surprised that she must get a fee for her grandchild's care.

In another phone conversation, Neda told me that my dad's friend Shahriar visited and invited us to his house, where we went with Manijeh and Hossein Agha. They live in another city. Hossein Agha was driving fast without any speed limitation. We noticed that people could drive at any speed on some freeway. Driver must keep the left lane open for another car. They use light instead of horning, and the car pulls into the right lane. No one is beeping, so the city is quiet and peaceful. I see how even the beeps can disrupt the environment's peace. Here, people used car and driving rules properly, keeping social peace, and not disturbing each other.

Shahriar had a young girl who came to the room and, without paying attention to us, turned on the TV and put her foot in sneakers on the coffee table in front of the sofa. If it was in Iran, we thought, what an impolite girl, but it seemed very normal here. When Shahriar came and told her something, then she left the room. Later, Manijeh told us that Shahriar said put your feet down. She did not answer, left the room, came back only once, and gave Shahriar a phone that her Moti (mother) wanted to talk to him.

Abroad phone call fee was three DM- Deutsch Mark per minute which was expensive. Aria asked me to call Neda from Tehran because it is cheaper and cost to his company. He wouldn't say how much, and company belonged to him. After every phone conversation with Neda, everyone expected me to explain all the details.

I returned to the hospital and did not like school and hospital as usual, although my life was spent studying, and I did not know anything else. Aria called me every night or visited our home with Iran Joon, who lived in Tehran, to find out about Neda.

Whenever Aria came to our house, Bijan sat on Aria's side, and none of them wanted to look at the other. The heavy silence such a stone wall between them was noticeable, and both diligently preserved it. Aria rented Uncle Soheil's house for his parents and gave the monthly rent to my father to send to Uncle Soheil.

One of those nights, before my parents returned, my mother talked about Aria's house and asked him to have a party at his house. Aria invited us to his house. Bijan refused. At the time of his leaving, Aria asked Bijan to go out with him to talk. They left together. When Bijan returned, he told me he would come with us to his home. We discovered that Aria had told Bijan that he had loved Neda all his life and that she fell in love with Bijan and married him. He was happy that at least her choice was right and married to a good person, and if he were not good, Aria would have prevented her marriage under any circumstances. Aria does not have any grudge against him or hate him. It wasn't Neda and his fault if They fell in love with each other. Now that everything has changed, does he mind seeing Aria?

Bijan told him it seemed we had run away from each other and tried to keep our distance. Aria replies that whatever it is, it should be solved sooner. Don't fool ourselves. We love her and want her to be happy. He accepted Madam's suggestion, and it is better that Bijan joined our party, and he accepted.

Aria House was a modern two-story building that did not match our simple lifestyle. Upstairs were seven bedrooms, and each room had a bathroom. There were two offices, one bedroom, and one maid room on the first floor.

"It was a good decision that you study engineering and build your life. We did not finish our education yet."

"These are all from my father's efforts, who trusted me, sold his only property, shop, and he believed my theoretical plan. Sometimes, I was afraid that if I failed, we would lose my father's funds, and at the same time, I worked in two consulting engineers' companies. Then, I bought land and built a home for sale. And that was our primary investment project. I opened my firm, which my father helped me with, and I worked in three places. I bought this land and started building it, and I planned to propose when the house was finished."

"Why did you build a seven-bedroom house?"

"I always thought about having four children, a babysitter, and a room for my father."

"Is there a bedroom downstairs?"

"Yes, my father suffered back pain, and if he could not come upstairs, to have his bedroom. The house remained empty, my dreams were gone with the wind, and my love did not stay here."

We reviewed engineering vs. physician programs with Aria. "You should study for a shorter time, establish your work, and set your life."

"Remember that all people dream of having a doctoral title when they get a Ph.D. in engineering; they are fascinated by a doctoral designation."

"How about you? I know you got your master's degree."

"No, I left the master's degree unfinished."

He sighed and continued. "You know why. Sometimes, we reach a point where nothing is important. You think for what, for whom, and all these efforts are fruitless! I felt I could work with my degree if I wanted to work. If I wished for a title, I had a motivation that I lost. For what? To make more money or show off? If I wanted to learn more, I could study at home. And I look at myself; nothing has any attraction to me anymore."

"Aren't you depressed?"

"Ana Joon, you are the doctor and know better than us that Iranians suffer depression caused by our environment. Even there is a crying sound in his drunken laughter, and in the dance songs that people dance with, is the mourning sound."

He was right, and what a bitter truth. Before my parent returned to their city, my father went to the passport office with documents to remove the bail they had placed on the title deed. Mullah was not willing to remove the bail! My father said mullah is the most cunning on earth. Finally, my father got the deed after many efforts and the ransom. Iran Joon and Nima Khan stayed in Tehran at Uncle Soheil's home.

Uncle Soheil and Neda gave power of attorney to my father to sell their properties. Neda said her share of our house is for Bijan; if Bijan does not want it, it is for Ana. Bijan parents bought him everything, and he was financially needless.

Bijan returned to his room, who lived before, and reviewed his memories. I had become a boxing bag for Bijan and Dariush's emotional pain and suffering. Only Behrouz said we should be happy that Neda is a better place, and she will make everything much better than before. Behrouz worried about me, and I missed Neda. I reported to Neda whatever happened.

Bijan's parents invited us to their house, had a luxurious life, and welcomed us very well. They were worried about Bijan and wanted to go back to America. This togetherness helped us tolerated better Neda's empty place.

Neda's letter

The telephone call was expensive, Neda and I decided to send a letter to each other. In one of the letters, Neda attached a letter for Niloufar Khanum and asked me to give it to her; here is part of her letter.

Dear Niloufar Khanum, I went to the shop to say goodbye to the store managers, know the shopkeepers were your sons, and learned that your son died in a car accident. My condolences to you for this great sadness. In their shop, I found the demands for my handcrafts were an illusion: You helped a girl in financial need with dignity without damaging her self-esteem. I saw all the tablecloths left in your sons' shop. The sojourn days have provided time for thinking about what has happened in my life. Your lovely image sits in my memories, and I don't know if I'm happy or sad about discovering this truth. I have a double feeling that is accompanied by your goodness.

During my academic year, how indescribable joy I felt that I could pay for the cost-of-living, which was not real, and I was immersed in my hallucinations. I don't know if I should laugh at the fake past joys or weep. But I know with certainty that your magnanimity played an influential role in the structure of my self- confidence, so I must thank you for your helping hand, which spread kindness seeds throughout others' lives.

I wrote this letter to show my appreciation. I left Iran and will never return to where my parents were killed. Hearing about the murder of my parents by the Islamic regime was painful and distressing, which drove the fate of my life and my brother so that we fell in love without knowing our relationship. We did not think we were siblings. Finally, I decided to escape from that environment, although there was no escape from the game of destiny. I don't know where or what to do, but I know I will go far. I want to get away from myself and escape my fate, but I will take myself everywhere. In all these hardships, a man was my father and my mother and tolerated me and still. He is still with me. I admired his humanity, and he suffered my restlessness. I was happy that he had accepted me and taken care of me. I have survived because of him. I learned many lessons from people's kindness, including my father, my friend, and friend family, and you. I have a wounded body from life hardship. I present this Rumi poem to you.

"Our existence could give life to others.

Our wounded experience could be created treatment for others' wounds.

"If the existence of the heart was scrutinized

Then, we could say each soul is a savior."

My wounds fruit must be a treatment for others, and I will try to do so. I owe all of you. I will pay one day, where I don't know, but I will remember your kindness, and I always sow the seeds of hope in every way under your names. I hope to hear from you. Neda had signed the letter.

Behrouz and I gave the letter to Niloufar Khanum, who was happy, read it and cried. She asked me about Neda. There was a table next to her with a tablecloth made by Neda, and her medication was on. It was the only decoration in her room. I knew the medications.

"We are doctors. Please tell us if you need anything."

She shook her head and spoke.

"It was a small world, sure."

When we left her house, I cried, and Behrouz took me to Tajrish, a restaurant where I had been with Neda before. I did not feel good. I did not want to eat, and I was nauseous. Despite Behrouz's insistence, I could not eat, staring at the spot. I reviewed the memories about how much laughing we had for nothing, and now nothing made me happy.

The nausea continued, and Behrouz noticed I was pregnant. I was sick of the smell of food. I asked Behrouz not to tell Bijan and Neda because they could be upset. Behrouz said it was not right for you to hide it. By hiding, you tell them that your pain is enormous, and you should be upset with everyone who gets pregnant. This behavior exacerbates their pain. It is better to say both as soon as possible. I noticed my stupid argument and that secrecy would worsen it. My nausea, compared to Nasrin's sickness, was not bad. I got pregnant without treatment when I did not expect it, and I had long dreamed, but it did not matter to me now. Behrouz was happy, and I was indifferent. I told Neda that I was pregnant in a letter. It usually took a month to two months to receive a letter from each other. I gathered her letter, and her letter's content was interesting.

One of Neda's letters from Germany to me was about the family relationship: Dear Ana, I feel the people's relationships in Germany are cold like their weather, whereas humans need a warm relationship. One day, Hossein Agha told my dad. "I was wrong. I left Iran because of my son's Nader, and he did not care that we were here because of him. Here, our children find themselves solely responsible for their lives and have nothing to do with their parents, while we think and do differently."

My dad tried to decrease his emotional pain by talking. I thought it might be that my dad would say the same thing in another way years later. When Hossein Agha was not with us, I asked my dad if he thought the same, and I would leave him alone. He said that he never was in that position and does not expect me to stay with him or will do something for him. My heart is broken for my dad, who never expects anything from anyone. Remember how badly missed him when I came to Tehran, told him it is acceptable parents request to see their children. I noticed Nader's official behavior, such as a stranger.

In another letter, she wrote. My dear Ana, I changed my name to Bahareh, and Aria helped me get to know myself better. This time, spring will be the scene of my life; in my mind, I will visualize my dance like blossoms dancing in the spring breeze. Will these blossoms bear fruit, or an unknown storm will destroy them from nowhere. Or will my destiny suffer another game? Do you think our existence and destination are our options, or our fate will unconsciously drop us like straw abandoned on a shore or hit our head to the rocks? If life is optional, which option was with us, with which feet can we escape the harrowing events, and find a salve for our deep wounds?

Sometimes I'm very depressed. Where is a rain of mercy to refurbish my heart wrenching? I have lost everything. I am glad to have a good dad and friend like you. Let me visualize a spring season in my vision. I should rebuild my life; call me Bahareh from now on. Maybe if my mother were alive, she would be happy to give me to my dad. I hope Bijan will rebuild his life. I want to be full of spring freshness, and you will be my twin, and maybe spring will be able to flourish my life. Let Bijan read my letter as well, and I hope he tries to rebuild himself for my and his good parent's sake. We must build ours again from our ashes. I have learned this thinking from Aria. I read her letter and felt I loved her by any name and gave Bijan her letter.

Nasrin was happy that her baby would be born soon. I knew very well that I was no longer the previous Ana. Behrouz was concerned about my health. I slept more, was quieter than before and thought everyone was sad in the hospital. My pleasure was Neda's letters. The air overflowing with nostalgia had affected my sweet marital life. Nasrin's beautiful boy was born by natural delivery, looked like Dariush and named Dara. My mother came to Tehran for Nasrin delivery and preparing the baby set for my baby. Pouran Joon kindly cared for the baby, and Nasrin returned to work.

Behrouz asked me to prepare a baby's name list, and I wasn't even in the mood to think about it. Sometimes, I was terrified that my baby would die in the womb, and these nightmares hurt me. Professor Kiani kindly suggested that I travel to change and return to a normal life situation.

Bijan finished the surgical residency, was sadder and lost weight than in the past. Bijan's clinic was formed by Professor Kiani in his office. The handsome and successful young surgeon made a name among the surgeons. He was alone, sad and his companions were us, and news from Neda, who loved her passionately. In his private life, he would not accept any women. Behrouz said that Bijan needed time to heal his wounds and regain himself. He had broken from the inside while he seemed a powerful and successful surgeon. As we expected, Neda passed the U.S. Medical Board exam, we all believed in her success.

My son was born naturally. He looked like Behrouz. At the time of my delivery, my mother informed Zohreh that I was in pain and went to the maternity hospital. Bahareh called the hospital room, and Aria picked up the phone. Aria talked to her while everyone and Bijan were in my room. And then he gave me the phone. The baby's coming had changed my mood a lot. I happily started talking without thinking she might be upset and saying, I wish her baby had been born too. Everybody stared at me as to what I said. Then I spoke to Uncle Soheil and Zohreh. At the end talking to Bahareh who asked me to give the phone to Aria again, which surprised me. I could hear her thanking Aria for his advice. Aria's face was blushing. I could hear her voice, are you still on the line, Aria responded with a long pause. I heard Bahareh saying, I'll call you tonight, and Aria said he had Zohreh Khanum's phone number. Bijan stared at the corner of my bed motionless. Dariush and my mother said nothing, and Iran Joon was happy. Later, I spoke to Aria, who said he knew Bahareh would call me and did not want to lose the opportunity.

I watched the unforgettable moments when my baby was in my mother's arms, Behrouz bent over and kissed him, and Dariush was taking pictures. Aria had quietly left the room after Bahareh's call. I still did not have a name for our baby, and it was my fault that I couldn't focus and choose a name for him.

Holding my baby in my arms, I stared at his breathing and thought he wasn't breathing. Behrouz was laughing. Motherhood taught me although education and literacy are good, but emotional issues influence the logical pathway when you want to take care of your own baby. It was good that my mother, Iran Joon, and Pouran Joon were with us.

But about Bahareh, I wonder why I was looking for Neda yet! I know Neda was gone and took her old name with her! Here is one part of her letter about her immigration.

My dear Ana, I never knew and experienced freedom in Iran, so I could interpret the difference between prisoner's pain and freedom. But now, in this land, where there is no terror of the Islamic regime, brothers and sisters' guards, etc., I can see the differences between the earth and the moon. Nobody bothers anyone, even if you sit by the street by night; no one asks where you came from and what you do. Even if they want to help, not harass, they consider their limitation. People commute with free wings in the street without fear of sudden attack or touch. In contrast, we expected sudden attacks even at university and borrowed four eyes to check our periphery so that the regime-made monsters would not attack us. This was while we were good students and did not do anything wrong. The social behavior of guards and greedy men was pathetic in Iran. They talk about the promiscuity of foreigners which it is not true. They don't steal anything to hide it. The Muslim religious men's greedy eyes, the light talk of the married brainless holy men at the university, and how cheeky they were and talked were toxins. I am embarrassed about their rudeness when I remember them. I have never seen such a look at myself from any man here. I do not know if I was ugly for them or so beautiful in the greedy Iranian men's eyes that they greedily attacked us. Their behavior created a complex socialization.

I wish they would review and evaluate their behavior.

Do they know that their action makes the Iranian woman disregard them and not consider them? And these simple issues cause their inferiority complex. Has anyone ever told them their behavior is not manhood, consider dignity, and do not touch the women? Here, I feel the meaning of freedom, even though I haven't been able to adapt myself fully; for example, I'm still considering how to dress. Here, the people wear a T-shirt and a pant or shorts. They have their food in the best and high-class restaurants or fast food, and they have the hands of the one they love in their hands. And they do not care that we look at them or what we think of their clothes. But I'm still considering what to wear and the color harmonies. I still like the color harmonies that my dad taught me.

CHAPTER 7, USA

The immigrant life based on Bahareh's diary and our chat. My dad talked to me. "You should forget everything that happened and not let depression captivate you. The loss of Hayedeh, my child, Soroush, and my mother was hard for me, and the depression robbed my strength. You are wise and can overcome this sorrow; your grief is my pain." I promised him to try to overcome my grief. Changing my residency was the right thing. I missed Ana and Bijan and wished Ana was here and we talked to each other. While traveling to the United States, an Iranian traveler helped us fill out an entry form. At the border, they control the money quantity to prevent money laundering by smugglers, plants and fruit control to prevent damage to the agriculture and farming business. More than ten thousand dollars per passenger should be reported at the entrance.

Zohreh and Uncle Arash welcomed us at the airport and were happy to see my dad and said they missed him badly. Aunt Zohreh said that her children were working and living separately. Along the way to their home, Arash told my dad that they bought this new car for my dad, which had three seat rows. Their house is two stories and has four bedrooms on the second floor, where they have arranged a room for my dad and Sahar and one for me. We had jet lag due to the time zone change. The streets and shops are clean. We are waiting for Zohreh to tell us what we do at the store.

One day, when we passed a clinic, I asked my uncle to stop in front of the clinic so I could get some medical journals.

"Do you know English?"

"No, my dad taught me to read and write from a newspaper before school. I can learn English through the English Medical Journal and be familiar with the medical exam questions, which are common topics."

"Soheil, how old was Bahareh when you taught her to read newspapers?"

"Bahareh was very smart, about two years old.

"Okay, we'll go to my friend John's office and get medical magazines."

We went to his office, and his secretary gave us some magazines. In the car, I said.

"I go to my room, find the English topic from the magazine, tear them up, and stick them on the wall, and my dad cleans after me before we sleep and he never complained about how much I hurt him, and still."

"My intellectual daughter."

Sahar: You play, and I clean up.

Once, my dad asked Arash about rental apartments.

"Soheil, after a long time, we see you, you should relax, Zohreh explains about the house.

"Soheil John, when you sold your house and car, you gave me all the money. I had no choice but to accept it for our living cost. I've told you to send you money several times, but you told me you worked and had money. I later learned you had a hard time, and I was sorry. I bought a house with your money, and its mortgage was equal to the rent. Then, I was hired and had a steady job, and I bought a house for myself. If you want to live alone by Sahar, we will go to my house."

"Soheil, I came to this city because of Zohreh. I bought a big house and asked Zohreh to marry me. When she did not accept, it was rented out and I came here. If you want to live with us, that house has more space, and we can live here or there. Zohreh told me and wrote in her will that this house belongs to Soheil, and our children also know."

My dad just listened and did not say anything.

"Soheil, what do you think?"

"My concern was Zohreh's comfort."

"Zohreh and I had no vacation and waited for you to have fun together. Refrain from talking about work; you have plenty of job opportunities."

"Uncle Arash, what do you think of my work?"

"We must have fun and think about it later. I hear

you're brilliant. Congratulations to Soheil for raising such a good girl. Also, Professor Sahar has plenty opportunities."

"I must write to the medical board to let me participate in the board exam. I don't know English, but I know the medical topic."

"Don't worry, I'll teach you English." Zohreh said

The weather was perfect, so we went shopping. Zohreh told me to buy whatever I wanted. I remember she sent us clothes, and I shared them with Ana. I said I had to buy two of each, for myself and one for Ana. Once, Uncle Arash turned the pages of a scientific journal and talked about a few job ads. He mentioned a firm that would hire a scientist with an annual salary of $150,000.00-200,000.00. My dad and Arash spoke about it, and I feared losing my dad again.

"I will come with you if Sahar lets me," I said.

Uncle Arash laughed and said, "What would you do if Sahar disagrees?"

"I'll be sad. I would return to the little town where I lived with my dad." Tears covered my face.

"It's impossible, Soheil, and I came here because of you. We will never leave you alone," Sahar assured me.

My dad hugged me and said, "I'm not applying for that job."

Uncle Arash apologized, "Sorry, I was joking."

After a long pause, I asked:

"Uncle Arash, I am interested to know about that job."

"I don't want it; forget that ad." My dad protested.

"Dad, I would like to know what that job is."

" Uncle Arash, your expertise in this area is invaluable. Could you shed some light on this project?"

"That project is about developing mathematical models to create software with the desired application."

"Do you teach these things at university?"

Their answer was positive.

"I suggest you call them and ask how many will work on this project and the term period. Then send them a proposal you want to do with less time and less price. For example, write the term one year instead of three years and a million instead of two million. You do not lose anything.

Have you written a math model before?"

They looked at me with amazement and spoke.

"Yes."

"Daddy, you work from home for three months instead of three years, and your income will be more or equal.

Uncle Arash: "If we can't."

"Nothing happens, you pay their money back."

Sahar: "Great, what a good idea."

Uncle Arash looked at me and said "Soheil the outcome of your work is excellent, an intelligent girl."

"Gohar Khanum said Bahareh is an exception, and she found a customer for herself on the first trip. Bahareh, we are not going anywhere. I asked Arman to sell my house, and we would have enough money to wait for a job."

Aunt Zohreh was silent until that moment.

"Bahareh's offer is excellent. Why do you miss this opportunity? Arash can take three months off from the university, and we have a house if they pay in advance that we don't spend their money, and if you can't get the project done and you spend their money, then we sell one house and refund their money. How do you reject good offer?"

"Bahareh Joon, my daughter, I never made computer software."

"Dariush's brother, Jamshid, and his girlfriend, Rose, can do this. I will contact them."

Uncle Arash said: "If they refuse."

"Arash, please listen to Bahareh. You will only miss time and learn something new. I'm following Bahareh. Kaveh and Kamyar worked on software a few years ago, and they can give us a clue."

When we were alone, my dad asked Sahar and me where we wanted to live. Sahar said:

"Wherever Bahareh wants."

"Daddy, it would be better for us to stay with Aunt Zohreh till we learn English and you find a job."

Sahar agreed. Later, I talked to Zohreh about my dad's temperament and that he doesn't like living where someone pays the cost. Zohreh said your father gave me his money when I was one year old. We agreed that I would talk to Madam when she told my dad that he had

bought my dad's house and would send its money to
Zohreh account. Zohreh paid my dad monthly, and we did
not tell anyone about it.
I talked to Madam that night. A few days later, Monsieur
called my dad, when I heard my das said a fair market
price, and then Madam talked to me and knew what to do.
I contacted Ana, Behrouz, Bijan, and Dariush and got
Jamshid's number. I called Jamshid who lose his job and
possibility of a project and building a software, he assured
me that he could make it.

After a week, we visited some interesting points when
we adjusted to the time zone. Zohreh and Arash had
already planned our trip and booked the hotel. There were
many rest areas, restaurants, and public telephones on the
roads between cities. Zohreh bought me a calling card so I
could talk to Ana. Zohreh said phone companies have
different plans for family members that end cheaper, and
she had ordered it. My dad and Sahar said they did not
need a mobile phone or a vehicle.

Zohreh disagreed and said you need to have your
phone. Most of the time, Arash drove, sometimes Zohreh
and my dad. Zohreh said that she bought this car with
Soheil's money. My dad was quiet. Disneyland was a
beautiful place; we were there for two days. There were
also beautiful parks in nearby towns. I brought the medical
journals, and my dad had the scientists' journal. Zohreh
told:

"When we returned from the holidays, I would become
the professor's secretary and call about those projects."

Arash laughed and spoke.

"It's good that your family came. I am more honor and
have a secretary, so be careful I do not reduce your salary."

"I will be Professor Soheil's and Professor Sahar's
secretary; my aunt Zohreh is my boss."

I saw the grant word in medical journals and asked.

"What is grant?" Arash explained:

"The meaning of the grant in this journal is a fund for a
medical institution or physician to research a particular
project paid for by rich people or companies. Often, the
grants are not refundable for helping to improve scientific

jobs. Suppose one article is accepted by a scientific institute or medical university and published in a scientific journal. In that case, it brings unique credibility to that individual or group, and the immigration office considers this an important position."

"I translate an article and send it to Ana with the original article. She publishes it in Iranian journals, which helps me learn English, will be helpful in the medical field, and is suitable positions for Ana, Behrouz, Bijan, and Dariush. When they come, we will apply for Grant. Maybe passing the medical board exam is the most important thing I must achieve."

Once, we went to the shore and played on the beach. All our clothes and shoes were full of sand. I looked like a kid again. Dad watched us enthusiastically, and I told him we were children, and he laughed and said, I'm also a teenager, and then we both got German baths, and you're wondering what the German bath is? When we were in Germany, Shahriar's daughter went to the bathroom and said I got a bath, and I asked Manijeh how she took a bath so fast, and her hair was not wet. Manijeh said the German people are accustomed to washing and cleaning themselves with a damp towel and soap because of the cold weather and the high price of water. I thought my dad had been taking a German bath in Iran for years, and his body did not smell.

It's an excellent way to use others' experiences, save time and water. In addition, the Germans fill a bathtub once a week, wash their hair and body in the same bathtub, and then dry themselves. It is called the full German bath, so they pour less water than we do. I asked if they would not shower after the tub! Manijeh said no. Even their dishes are placed in the kitchen sink filled with warm water and liquid dish soap, pulled out plates and utensils, and dried with towels. This was also dishwashing! I asked if we ate meals on those plates. She said no, it might be that they used the dishwasher.

I wrote to Ana that I thought I knew English. Now I see I must learn English. You must be surprised. People speak in the streets differs from the language we learned to understand scientific subjects. Now, we listen more to the radio to learn about regular conversations. In the store, we are busy converting dollars to rials and figuring out how much it was there and how much it is here. In stores, we could find everything, and no one watched us. The doors were open, the hidden cameras worked, and everyone was busy with their jobs. Unlike everywhere else in the world, the measurement units are not metric. The weight measure is in pounds, which is a little less than half a kilogram. In the first few days, we made the wrong calculation; we thought the price of the goods was in kilograms and assumed it was very cheap!

The length unit is an inch (2.5 cm), feet (30 centimeters), and yards (90 cm). The speed is in miles, which is less than two kilometers. The date format is month, day, and year, unlike everywhere else, where it is as day, month, and year.

Upon our return, Aunt Zohreh's plan was put into action. Three big-screen computers and three mobiles were delivered to our home, a fantastic surprise. Zohreh's idea was for each of us to learn English on our computers to track our progress. We committed to spending two hours daily reading English and watching an English movie. Zohreh taught us common daily words used in ordinary conversation, while Uncle Arash took on the task of teaching Sahar, my dad, and me the scientific words with the correct pronunciation.

Zohreh took us to the bank to help us open an account. I was prepared for the usual chaos of an Iranian bank, but to my surprise, the hall was spotless, and there were only a few people. Zohreh insisted it was crowded, but I compared it to the long queues that often extend outside Iranian banks. In the bank, each customer is tended to by one teller at a time, ensuring privacy for each customer.

One weekend, Kaveh and Kamyar came to visit us. They were tall, handsome gentlemen who spoke Persian with us. My dad said how much they resembled their father. They were close with Uncle Arash, even engaging in wrestling together. Arash and Zohreh left to work daily, and we were learning English. I received a digital romantic text message on my cell at 8 a.m. daily and assumed it was to everyone. Zohreh, with Uncle Arash's approval, called several institutes seeking to hire a scientist. They requested an in-person meeting with the professor. Zohreh said the first step is for the professor to know your project. After he accepts your case, then an in-person meeting will be set. During the phone call, Sahar listened to their conversation, wrote the appropriate scientific answers and questions, and gave them to Zohreh to tell them.

I asked Aunt Zohreh to write a letter to the medical board. My dad asked her to indicate that Bahareh entered the university without attending school. Of 1,250,000 applicants, only 153,000 were admitted to the university that year, and she was among the first 20 top applicants' while deliberately not writing some answers. My dad had the precise statistics data that Zohreh wrote. I asked her to add that although English is my second language, I can pass the exam successfully if they let me take it. Zohreh contacted the board after sending the letter, and they asked for the documents. I called Ana to send me my medical certification. I translated some medical articles, and Zohreh or Uncle Arash corrected them before I sent them to Ana to publish under their names, and I hoped it would be effective for a US visa in the future.

Shokoh Khanum came to the US because she had a green card, and her traveling from Iran to the US was unhindered. She talked about my childhood memories. Kaveh and Kamyar called her by name, Shokoh Joon, loved her, and kissed her a lot. Also, I called her Shokoh Joon too. Zohreh said that Shokoh Joon has always looked after Kaveh and Kamyar like a mother.

Uncle Arash's house had more room and was three stories; we moved there. It had more bedrooms. Manijeh and Hossein Agha also came from Germany. I moved to the library on the street level and then to the basement to have more room and prepare for the medical board exam. I hang interesting medical articles all over the basement walls.

Uncle Arash reached an agreement with a scientific institute and signed a contract after he asked his lawyer to read the contract and add some phrases to protect his rights. The institute paid one-third of the fee in advance; the remaining payment was made when the project was delivered. Their first project was finished successfully in collaboration with Jamshid and Rose. Arash opened a limited liability company with equal shares between partners, including my dad, Sahar, Zohreh Arash, and me. I rejected his offer because I did nothing, but Arash said he would have to pay a significant tax if he did not share the income with us. Also, My dad received an offer to work at the university where Uncle Arash worked, with a salary of $120,000 a year, while my dad made it three times more in less than three months.

One day, I asked my dad if I would call Aria, and my dad agreed. Nasrin and Dariush have a son. I passed the medical board exam, and Ana's son, Behzad, was born.

After Behzad's birth, I started talking to Aria nightly. Our nighttime was his daytime working hours, and he said I should not be worried because he did his job on my sleeping time. Als, our talking time was the best time of his life. His words were pleasant, and he had my number when I wanted to give it to him! The phone call was cheaper from the US, and he agreed that I call him from US and pay less. I had told him everything, including my dad's successes, and put my name as a shareholder. In one of our conversations, Aria suggested I call Bijan, who should return to his normal life situation. I was surprised. Then I talked to my dad about Aria's suggestion. My dad liked his suggestion and said Bijan was hurt and needed support. From then on, I call Bijan, like the phone call to Ana and Dariush.

Aunt Setareh and Koroush Khan came to the US and our house. She brought her medical records and said you were my doctor from now on. I regretted why my behavior was terrible. They are very kind and modest and invited us to their house for a long weekend and stressed that Shokoh Khanum and Manijeh with Hossein Agha should come with us. We went there in my dad's car, which was spacious, and we met their children, Pegah and Pedram, and Koroush Khan's sister, Kimia, her husband Farhad, and their children, Farid and Farideh. Pedram and Pegah spoke Persian, but Farid and Farid said Persian with an accent and inconsistent pronunciation, which was a cause for laughing. They were excellent and tried that we have a good time. I also spoke to Ana and Aria from their house.

Their house, a grand palace with eleven bedrooms on the second floor, a swimming pool, a jacuzzi, a sauna, and all amenities, stood in stark contrast to our humble abode. They even had a detached guest home. They graciously prepared a bedroom for each of us in their building. I wanted to stay with Shokoh Joon and two queen beds, but Setareh Khanum gently set me in another room. They treated us with utmost respect, a special reverence reserved for my dad. Kaveh and Kamyar were very stylish and dressed in fashionable clothes. They worked for a wealthy company that paid for their first-class travel expenses. They visited us on weekends and came to my aunt Setareh's house. One day, I asked Kaveh about his job.

"Kamyar and I work for a big oil company and travel to different places to check out small, financially troubled companies. We buy them for our company if they have a future."

"Why don't you do it yourself and have your own company?"

"It requires a significant amount of capital."

"Tell me what vast capital means."

"We must have millions of dollars for this type of deal.

"That company will make how much profits."

"Billion dollars."

"You must do it for yourself. You can start negotiating and set the necessary conditions for the transaction. For example, say
I would buy that company for 100 million. If I couldn't purchase it on time, I would pay a penalty of 10% of the purchase price. If it's worth a billion, you sell it for 700 million. You lost 10 million or gained 600 million."

"The main problem is the initial ten million that we do not have."

"Imagine you have that amount. Could you?"

They both looked at me, and Kaveh said.

"We did not have the amount."

"Imagine I have 10 million. Do you have enough knowledge and enthusiasm to do this independently?"

"Yes, over the past few years, Kamyar and I traveled independently, made deals for the company, and added billions of dollars to their capital."

Zohreh: "Listen very carefully to Bahareh's words. She believed me and confirmed me like Madam.

"I talk to my dad, and if he agrees, I talk to Uncle Koroush about the initial fee."

Kaveh and Kamyar looked at me and Kaveh spoke.

"We should talk to my father" and he looked at Uncle Arash. Uncle Arash shook his head to the confirmation. After I talked to my dad, he agreed I talk to Uncle Koroush.

My dad's friends, Shahriar with his wife and two daughters for a month and Dr. David with his French wife, his daughter, and son for two weeks came to our house. I was interested in meeting Dr. David and discovering what was happening in France's medical sciences. We drove in a few cars together to the city's landmarks, which was much fun. Aunt Setareh and Uncle Koroush visited us, and Shahriar and David discussed my childhood memories. It was as if they were testifying to my dad's innocence, although it was unnecessary, and I prefer him to everyone. This great man taught me humanity, patience, and creativity from nothing in the poor, empty room when it was not his duty. He had lost his life's best years, his well-being, and even his health for me. I remember he bought everything for me, not for himself. In the presence of everyone, I asked Uncle Koroush about my parents' life and death.

My dad looked at my face surprisingly and said:

"My dear, you've suffered enough. It bothers you to open this up."

"I need to know what happened."

Uncle Koroush, when his eyes filled with tears, spoke: Your father's name was Cyrus, and your mother was Soraya. Your father was my cousin and my best friend. We married two sisters, and almost all our plans were together. The night the tragedy happened, Setareh talked to Soraya about the weekend plan. There was nothing unusual. You had a big home, gardeners, baba Rahim, and housekeeper Fatima. Your father built a two-room unit in front of the building with a small window facing the street and a large window facing the yard for Baba Rahim, the gardener and security guard. The doorbell was also connected to Baba Rahim's room when someone rang the doorbell, and Baba Rahim could see who was through the window. The housekeeper Fatima had a little child and went to her house at night. Sometimes, Soraya came to our house and gave our phone to Fatima to call if she had any questions.

The day after the tragedy, Fatema called our house and gave the phone to Baba Rahim, who had asked Setareh to go to your house and said that Mr. and Mrs. did not feel well. Setareh called me. At that time, we remodeled our home and lived temporarily in a rented apartment on Takht Jamshid Street above my office. We put our children with my office staff and went to your house, the disaster scene.

Baba Rahim told me that the night before, as usual, your father's office manager was there for an hour and left. The doorbell rang. It was Siavash Khan, your father's brother, with some people, Cyrus Khan said to open the door, and they went inside the building. Then your father called Baba Rahim and told him to turn off the lights in his unit, pretend nobody was at home, and not open the door for anyone. According to Baba Rahim, I guessed that someone was chasing Siavash. He was near your home and had no choice but to seek refuge in your house. He went there with his friends so he would not get caught.

Some people came to your home, rang the bell, and knocked on the door. Baba Rahim did not open the door and saw them jump the house wall into your home and rush to the building. There were too many of them, and they were there to kill. It seemed your father dropped Soraya and you from the back yard wall to the neighbor's house because it was tall, and Soraya could not climb that wall. And then your father dropped Bijan in the neighbor's yard, maybe at the same time your mother put you on the street and returned to save Bijan.

Bijan knocked on the neighbor's window. They took him inside and tried to figure out where this kid came from. They noticed their yard door open, so they assumed that Bijan had come to their house from the courtyard door. When they attacked your house, Baba Rahim hid behind his building so he could not be seen, but he heard the gunshot and Soraya screaming from the street in front of the house. After that group ran away, Baba Rahim went into your building and saw your father, Siavash, and three others were killed, then went on the street and brought your mother's body into the building. He did not have our phone number, the next day, when Fatima came, he called us. When we entered your house, the scene was very harrowing. I sent Setareh and Fatima home. I asked them not to tell anyone till I found the children. Baba Rahim said he did not see them carrying our child. Your neighbor asked Bijan how he came into his house. Bijan said my dad threw me from the wall into your house. The neighbor looked at its height and thought he was a kid who did not know what he was saying.

He put on a ladder, and he went up with Bijan. Bijan said this is our home, and he called Baba Rahim loudly. I was in your house, told the neighbor to keep the child, and would take him because I did not want Bijan to see that heartbreaking sight. I called Setareh to pick up Bijan from the neighbor's house. I asked your gardener and housekeeper not to tell anyone and wash the blood from the street's pavement.

I called one of my friends, a doctor, and asked him to write a burial certification, which he said the coroner should write after the autopsy because they were shot. We sat down and thought that if the coroner found out about the issue, legal issues would arise, custody of Bijan, and your property would be gone. I said burying them personally without a burial permit would be better. He told me that he heard that in Behesht-Zahra, a group would take the money and bury corpses. I decided to bury their bodies in a cemetery near Shemiran, which was very painful. I called his office manager and asked him to wait for me after work hours. Your father was a good boss, and

the employees loved him. I had an accounting firm, and my responsibility was all the financial issues in your father's office. His office manager brought all bills, receipts, and checks to my office every other day, and I had your father's checkbook, and I managed his accounts. His office manager had the safety keys also. I went there, told him the tragic story, and asked him not to say anything so we could prevent more problems. He opened the safe box and made a list of them. With his help, I transferred your house to Setareh in an escrow to sell it without going through the probation process and claimed the Bijan custody. I sent a message to the merchants who had repeatedly offered your father to buy his business, said I
owned the company and sold it on the condition that he would keep all the employees.

Setareh was sick for months, and I asked Fatima to care for our children. Fatima was the honest woman and knew the place of your mother's gold and jewelry and cash, collected and gave them to Setareh, and cleaned the house before selling. She and the gardener were mourning for a long time, but I told them not to wear black so that no one knew anything, and they agreed. I sold your father's house and business, and your father's office manager helped me get the customer's debts. I bought him a home because if he did not help, I couldn't keep your wealth. Baba Rahim and Fatemeh were good people, and they never disturbed us, and I bought a small garden for Baba Rahim in his village and a house for Fatima in Naziabad. I exchanged all your wealth into dollars and deposited it in Kimia's US account.

But that's not where it ended. You have a step-aunt who wasn't good to any family member, especially your father. When she discovered that your parents had died in a car accident, she claimed I had stolen your wealth and sued me. I claimed the house and business belonged to me; your father was my employee. She went to that merchant and dragged me to court for an extended period; your father's relationship with me was cordial, and the office manager helped me proved it. As I said, I compensated for his affection by buying him a house with your father's money, and he still worked there.

Your aunt failed to prove anything in court and defamed me with the family that I was stealing your estates. I showed Soheil Khan all the documents and bills. I also wrote down the address of your father's office manager. Fatema still worked for us; before leaving Iran, I told her you become a doctor, and she was pleased.

"Uncle Koroush, did you complain, and Bijan knew our history?"

"Complaining about what to whom? The complaints in the Islamic regime looked like complaining about thieves to the thieves' boss. No, darling, I did not complain. If I complained, we encountered other problems, and they might have given Bijan custody to your aunt. But in Bijan's case, I did not tell him anything your parents were cautious because he was a sensitive child. Bijan passed the university entrance exams well, but Pegah and Pedram did not. Bijan liked to study, and I waited for him to finish his education come out of Iran and tell him not to cause any problems. We stayed in Iran hoping to find you. Baba Rahim called us every month, asked about you, and said, "Sir, don't worry, don't cry; I dreamed that Bahareh Khanum is a good place."

Before we traveled, we went to his village and told him that you had become a doctor. He cried and said, I am relieved and showed us your picture with your father in your house and said I would sit in front of this photo every night and pray for Bahareh Khanum."

I remembered that Bijan had said that maybe my dad had kidnapped me, and Uncle Koroush was also accused of stealing.

"Unfortunately, whoever did the right thing was mislabeled."

My dad knew what I meant. My parents' murder story saddens everyone. For the first time, I saw even Uncle Arash crying. That night, when Aria called, I said I was not in a good mood to talk because I listened to my parents' murder story. Aria, as always, he does not abandon the command platform, said, you must talk and get the poison out of your body tonight. He was talking to me until morning when I fell asleep. Near noon, my dad, who was worried about me, woke me up. I put my head on his shoulder and cried, and we talked about my fate.

"All these bad things happened in my life, if Bijan had known, he would have died of grief because he was shocked when he found out about my concubine."

"That was horrible, and I was dying too. You don't know the mullahs are mafia."

"They are no one and worthless, no value, but people made a giant monster of them."

"Precisely, they are useless idiots who can do terrible things no human can. Even the Mongols have not committed as many crimes as the mullahs have done over the years. These are the rootless people who have come to power with the help of foreigners. They even killed their son (such as Gilani and Mohsen Rezaei), their brother, and their friends and announced in newspapers and media to create terror. Never trust any mullahs."

We went upstairs to have breakfast. Aunt Setareh and Shokoh Joon said we should go shopping today, which I refused. My dad said you should go and distract your mind. If you want, we all go to have ice cream. I laughed and looked at my phone. Aria, Ana, and Madam had called several times. At the same time, Madam called that I did not have clothes to buy me two blouses. I was surprised and said you never wanted anything!

"I'm jealous, Ana's clothes are beautiful!"

We went shopping. I was in contact with Iran regularly, including Bijan. In one call, I asked Bijan what his idea was about my marriage to Aria. Bijan was happy and said I'm glad you can manage your life well. I told him that he should make us happy too. Ana told him the same thing. In Iran, a man can divorce his wife in her absence without any notice, and I asked Bijan to divorce me because it psychologically helped Bijan close our marriage file. After that phone conversation, Bijan went to Aria's house without telling me and told him that Bahareh wanted to marry you. Aria did not know and was delighted to hear it. Bijan also told Aria that my dad had invested in our inheritance that belonged to Bahareh. Tell her to use it. Aria refused and said you should tell Bahareh or Soheil Khan. That night, Aria asked me if I wanted to see him and that he would come to America.

"Yes, I'd like to see you."

"I'd like my dad and Iran Joon to come with me, what do you think?"

"I'd love to see them, too."

"We are going to Turkey and applying for a US visa, and if I can send them, I will come anyway."

Aria did not say she saw Bijan. Later, Bijan said that he went to Aria's home, and he was happy that you would marry him, so I understood why Aria asked me "do I like to see him!"

I told my dad that Aria said he wanted to come to the US with her father and Iran Joon and if I could give them the money to help them get a visa. My dad said that if it weren't for you, I wouldn't have enough guts to accept that project, and the money is yours, and you could spend whatever you want. Then I told Aria that I had $250,000.00 and that he could have it if necessary. He did not say anything and arranged to travel to Turkey. Madam and Monsieur were also in Tehran and cared for Behzad at that time. They decided to travel with Aria, and if they got a visa, come to the US, or return to Iran in Aria's car.

Aria told me that after my trip from Turkey, he sent a flower basket to thank Dr. Yilmaz. Then he went there to thank them personally and asked them what they would like to have from Iran. They looked at him, and his wife said a light-colored Iranian rug.

Aria asked them for the address for sending by mail. The doctor had said no, wait, my acquaintance would come to Iran and take it from you. Aria gave them his office address. After a few weeks, he called Dr. Yilmaz that no one came, and he said, "We did not and do not expect any present." However, Aria sent gifts and was in touch with them. Aria called them before leaving Iran for Turkey and asked them if anything was needed from Iran. The doctor said they didn't need anything, and when did he come? Aria gave them the information about the travel date by car. Dr. Yilmaz asked Aria to call him before getting to the border and have an acquaintance on the Turkish border.

When Aria was at the Turkish border, he called Dr. Yilmaz, who asked him about the color and model of his car and asked him to wait for officer Yousef. Yousef, a young officer, came to his car, took their passports, stamped and asked them to follow his car. Monsieur said I should buy a good present for Yousef. He would take them straight to Dr. Yilmaz's house. Yousef was Dr. Yilmaz's cousin who worked on the Turkish-Iranian border. Aria had given them a pair of Persian rugs and wanted to go to the hotel. Dr. Yilmaz and his wife, Özer, asked him the reason for his trip and where he wanted to go. Aria explained that they intended to get a U.S. visa. The doctor said to stay here at his house. Then he called someone and told Aria to go to the U.S. Embassy tomorrow morning and see Mr. J.

Aria called me happily, saying they do not waste time; they come on the first flight if they get the visa. I talked to my dad if we might reserve a hotel for Aria and his parents. When my dad spoke to Zohreh and Arash about hotel reservations for our guests, they said we were delighted they came to our home; we had not had such a warm family gathering for many years. Zohreh said it might be difficult for them to go upstairs, prepare two rooms at the street level, and take some items and books downstairs. Aunt Zohreh ordered two queen beds with mattresses delivered to her house the same morning they came. We also took several books downstairs. Downstairs, he had two rooms where I was always there to talk to Aria more easily.

"Well, Aria, in your room." Uncle Arash said in my ear.

"No, in your room."

"Wow, Zohreh will kick me out of her room."

Bahareh and Aria Marriage

When Aria came to the US, my dad, Sahar, and Uncle Arash worked on their third project. Zohreh was still teaching at school. I was waiting to get a surgical residency at a university hospital, and I was the professor's secretary and answered the phone when Zohreh was not at home.

My dad, Sahar, and I went to the airport. I was happy to see Iran Joon, Madam, and Aria. Aria kissed me in front of everyone while circling me in his arms and gave me a brilliant necklace with the word "Love." My dad welcomed them. Aria said they were at Dr. Yilmaz's house and left his car there.

"Soheil Khan, I love you very much and will come after you wherever you go." Monsieur spoke.

Iran Joon was crying when Aria kissed me. Nima Khan was fascinated and looked at Aria enthusiastically.

"Where did you buy this beautiful jewelry so I can buy it for my love?"

Madam was full of energy as ever and spoke.

"Arman, don't worry, I'll find a jewelry store here. You, Soheil Khan, and Nima Khan can buy it for us."

Aria held and caressed my hand all the time. Zohreh, Arash, Shokoh Joon, Manijeh, and Hossein Agha welcomed them. The same night, Nima Khan told my dad that we came here to propose to your daughter, and we would like to hear your answer. My dad, as always, said in a gentle way that I should talk to Aria. Madam and Iran Joon chose the street-level rooms, and we were there when Nima Khan asked for Aria. After my dad talked to him, came to the room and grabbed my hand, and we went to my room downstairs. My dad and I sat on the edge of the bed.

"Nima Khan told me about your marriage; Aria is a good man. What do you think?"

I started crying because I feared separation.

"Aria always said that we would have four children and that my baby died before birth. Think about what will happen if my baby dies again."

My dad hugged me.

"You're a doctor; your words don't make sense. Even if you don't have children, it doesn't matter; you're important."

Madam came to my room and said:

"What's going on?"

"Bahareh is worried about having a baby."

"It doesn't matter if you will have kids or not. He came here for you, not for the kid."

"I know he loves children and has often said that we will have four children, but I have always refused to pursue this."

"It doesn't matter. I talk to him now and give him a clear picture. I spoke to him, and he promised me he'd always keep you happy."

"Daddy, I will talk to him."

Madam asked for Aria. Then they left us alone while Madam roared, Aria, do not kiss her too much. Aria wondered.

"Why are you crying?"

"My child died before…

He broke my voice, held me in his arms tightly and said: "Only you are important to me. I came here because of you and promised your father that I would always keep you happy. Let's go upstairs and marry me."

Madam came into the room and said:

"Did you leave any space for our kissing? Is a problem?"

"We don't have a problem." Aria said.

"Come up soon. I want Arman to propose to me. He will be miserable if he doesn't. Arman, are you ready to ask me for marriage?" When she climbed the stairs.

"My Love, I will die for you." And his kisses could be heard. As always, he did not hesitate to kiss Madam romantically in the presence of others. At the dinner table, Madam spoke.

"Who wanted to ask for marriage?"

Aria grabbed my hand and pulled me out of the chair, kneeling before me.

"My Love Bahareh, do you marry me? As I promised your father, I will make you happy."

He took the wedding ring out of his pocket.

"Yes."

He put the ring on me and kissed my lips. Uncle Arash also kneeled in front of Aunt Zohreh.

"I've always promised you I'll keep you happy. I love you. Do you marry me?"

Hussain Agha said Zohreh Khanum said yes. Manijeh stood behind Zohreh and said yes. Then Zohreh said yes.

"I am sleepy now. Later, I will ask my love, Gohar, do you marry me after many years." Monsieur went to their room and slept. Aunt Zohreh and I got married on the same day. Uncle Arash came next to me and said in my ear.

"I told whom that room belonged to."

"Your room."

We laughed; Uncle Arash told my dad:

"You do not ask Sahar Khanum to marry you."

My dad laughed and kissed Sahar. Iran Joon gave me a bracelet that matched my necklace; it had the word, Love. Shokoh Joon went upstairs and brought Zohreh a diamond ring and a chain necklace for me.

Uncle Arash: "What about my gift? What else do you want? Here is your favorite daughter-in-law."

"Your gift, the best wife in the world, what else do you want?"

"We will buy my ring tomorrow." Aria spoke.

Madam responded, "We will buy it, when a young man goes to shop for a wedding ring is more expensive."

"Here, stores label the price of the goods." Zohreh said.

"People don't bargain here." Arash spoke.

"People bargain here, too, under the name of the sale. It means the shop owner unsuccessfully tried to sell the goods at a high price. Then, it was labeled as a sale. It's the same Iranian bargaining in the opposite direction. I hear they sometimes give up to 50% discount."

"We've lived here for years and have not compared the sale with bargaining yet."

The time zone was changed, and their eyes were sleepy, and they went to their bedrooms. Aria came downstairs with me. The day after, Sahar and my dad told me they would buy us a house as a wedding gift. In response, Aria thanked and said he would sell his properties and business in Iran and build a good home. My dad said calling Setareh Khanum about you would be better, and I agreed. When my dad called them, they congratulated us, and then Uncle Koroush talked to Aria and had many questions about what car was good. Aria wondered and said it depended on the person's budget and what was available on the market. They would like to use it in the city or desert, and the higher models with more features, more amenities, and bigger cars are more expensive and consume more gasoline. And he wasn't in the US to give a good suggestion. But he heard that electric cars would be coming to market.

Aria told why they asked me. I need to familiarize myself with the US market. My uncle Arash and my dad continued the issue of which car was best!

Aunt Setareh emailed Uncle Arash our wedding gift, a Hawaii honeymoon trip for a week, including airfare, car, meals, drinks, etc. That night, my dad took us to the airport. And we went to Hawaii. They threw us a flower lei at the airport, our room was decorated with rose petals, and all services were prepaid. Our room faced the ocean, and the light of the gas-burning torches in the waters was spectacular and dreamy. Rose petals were scattered on the bed. Hawaii was a pleasant and peaceful environment.

I thought about my dad being there to alleviate his suffering somewhat. We talked the whole time, although we used to speak to each other two to three hours a day, and I told Aria, except you, the only person I talked to this much was Ana. We reviewed our memories together. Aria said that in those days when you came to the shop, I thought you were at Ana's age, and you are petit and wanted you to stay longer and watch you. I'd tell my dad you'd take this girl for me. He asked me you shall study and have a job when you want to propose to her. I was surprised when I learned you were in medical school because I knew you did not attend school. My dad said her father was a wise man and taught her at home and told me that when you love her, you must study then we propose. Because they ask about the groom's job. I told my father to say the groom is an engineer! He said, okay, you must study and be an engineer, but don't talk till you get your degree. Later, he felt guilty about why he did not propose sooner. We had a great time. I told Aria to be careful. I got pregnant with an IUD. He would laugh and say, "So we shouldn't do anything. Might I be sterile?"

Aria was handsome, strong, kind, very disciplined, and romantic. He had a beautifully skilled limb and a strong arm, giving me a good feeling. I fell in love with him while I always thought it was impossible to love anyone except Bijan. He told me that we should provide ourselves with conditions like this hotel. Look, it costs a little. Two or three pretty bed sheets, a bouquet, and a series of beautiful towels can change the room's atmosphere. Hawaii was a small island that could be visited within a day. Aria did not think he could come to the U.S. quickly, had left his job half-finished and managed it on the phone and said that when Bijan told me that you marry me, nothing was significant because you are the most important to me. I will accomplish the half-finished work anyway. I have enough money to spend in a few months, and you always buy the best for yourself. I work harder and make it. The day after we returned, a stylish car was in front of the house with red ribbons and our names. It was Setareh's and Koroush's gift.

Then we understood why they asked Aria about the car. After we left, they consulted Nima Khan and my dad about what car to buy as a gift. The dealer had agreed to cancel the deal if we did not like it. Uncle Koroush said that if the marriage still needed to be registered, it would be better to consult a lawyer, which we did.

They planned to celebrate a three-day wedding party at Uncle Arash's house. Kimia Khanum and her family, Pegah and Pedram, also attended our wedding party. We became 25 people in total. Aunt Zohreh said I would order everything from the outside.

"Zohreh is glad I married her and wants to buy everything ready."

Zohreh was silent and smiled. Our home was warmer than before. Shokoh Joon responded to Uncle Arash's sense of humor.

"I am on Zohreh's side; think twice about what you want to say."

"Arash, you and I sleep in the work room and set the upstairs bedrooms for Setareh Khanum and Kimia Khanum. The boys and girls sleep downstairs on the sofas. Kaveh and Kamyar can use their sleeping bags."

"I sleep like Kaveh and Kamyar."

Madam: "You're grown up."

My dad and I laughed.

"Why are you laughing?"

"I remembered a memory when I was a kid playing and getting tired; I complained of my leg hurt. Daddy held me in his arms and carried me home. Once, a lady said, why do you hold this big bear in your arms? I frowned, cried, and said no, I'm not a big bear. My dad tried to calm me down and said she meant you were growing up. My respond was crying and saying I don't want to grow up. Fine, don't grow up. When I heard the sentence growing up, I remember it, and after that day, I stopped spoiling myself. Now, I am Kaveh and Kamyar age."

Aria was laughing and shaking his head.

Uncle Arash said, "I'll tell them."

"No."

Madam, Zohreh, Sahar, and Iran had bought the ring for Aria, Arash, and Zohreh. Uncle Arash said.

"The bride should pay for the wedding expenses in America, but a man pays in Iran. Zohreh and Bahareh must pay for the cost."

"We are Iranian, you should pay for the wedding cost."

Shokoh Joon: "You have good wives and no room for argument."

Uncle Arash said with the villain accents.

"We are yours sincerely. We are your menial, your servant, Haji Khanum.

"Arash, you must buy a black velvet hat to complete your role."

"We are your menial, Soheil Khan. We are yours sincerely. We buy it. We will be your servant."

The cleaning lady, Olga, came once weekly; Zohreh asked her and her sisters to come that weekend; later, she requested Olga to come every day except the weekend to sort out the house. When they attended, Aria and I thanked them for their presents. Setareh and Uncle Koroush also gave me a set of diamond jewelry. We wore a bridal gown and a tuxedo that was prepared for us, music and danced for two nights until near the morning, while Madam and Monsieur were with us all night long. Aria changed the wedding songs of his choice, put my name in the lyrics, and sang in his pleasant voice. Monsieur and Madam slept with us in the basement. At first, Koroush Khan and Kimia Khanum insisted on staying at a hotel, but in the end, they were happy to be at home with us. The home environment was warmer and heartier. I missed Ana. Aria would wake up early, run around the house, and then return to bed. The next party was arranged at Setareh's home.

We went to Aunt Setareh's house, at an appropriate time, I told Uncle Koroush that I preferred everyone to have a green card and that I would pay for everyone, and about my dad's moral qualities, who doesn't expect and accept anything from anyone and never complains about anyone or anything.

"I recognized that your father was a great nobleman. You were a lucky person with such a father. As you said, they need to get a green card. Send me copies of their passports. Your father and Sahar are scientists and won't have a problem."

"What about the rest, Bijan, Aria, Ana, Behrouz, and Dariush? Aria is restless about finding a job and likes to be creative."

"Aria is a good man, and we all love creativity. He must learn to invest. It has more benefits and less trouble if he can maintain the original capital. In this way, I was able to make your money fruitful. Bijan is my son and has no problem with a green card. It would be best if you spent your energy on the research. Every doctor can see the patient, but every doctor cannot be a researcher and analyze the heart of the particles. Everyone believes that you're brilliant, so use your talent. Your father was an intelligent man, too. You and Bijan inherited from him."

I talked about Kaveh and Kamyar, and Uncle Koroush promised to speak to them.

Pegah, Farideh, Kaveh, Kamyar, Pedram, Farid, and their American girlfriends had formed a group, gathered in one corner, and their loud laughs filled the space. Kimia also invited us to her house. When we were all together, Uncle Koroush said.

"I wish you would come here and be together."

After a pause, Aria suddenly said:

"Your house is lovely and beautiful for you. My children should live where they neither feel superiority nor inferiority. I make a good home for Bahareh, my children, and my family."

His voice was loud and firm. Everyone was watching him quietly. I did not feel good about his reaction and how he talked because my uncle did not say anything to Aria. After a long silence, Uncle Koroush said:

"You're my son now, we talk like family members, not strangers. I agree with you. I did not mean this building or that building. I talked about our friendly family relationships."

Uncle Koroush walked to Aria and told him to get up, then hugged and kissed him. My dad asked Aria to sing. He sang Hayedeh's song with his pleasant voice, and Kaveh's group also joined us. We returned in two cars. Kaveh and Kamyar flew separately to their workplaces. I missed Ana all the time, although I kept talking to her. After we returned, I talked to Iran Joon and Madam about the green card and passport copies. As always, Madam was my assistant, and she had all the documents because she was afraid that one of us would lose the passport; she took a copy of each and asked Ana to send it. Ana said Pouran Joon had cared for babies Dara and Behzad, so when would she return? Madam would tell me to look, my daughter, where you pulled us.

"I missed Ana so much. It's time Ana come here."

"Ana missed you and got your excuse, and Behrouz is willing to emigrate because of Ana. Now, we all have a reliable base."

"Remember the first room we rented in Tehran? Your brother was a major general or a brigadier general. I was scared, and Ana said to stay here; my mom told us not to go anywhere. I would say no, I should call his brother."

Madam told the story, and we laughed.

Aria was in contact with Dr. Yilmaz and sent them a thank-you card. Dr. Yilmaz wanted the last surgical textbook that we posted to him. Once alone with my dad, I talked about Aria's behavior, who spoke like a commander to the soldier or the king with his soldiers. I wish I knew who Aria's parents were.

My dad had tears in his eyes. I put my head on his arm.

"Maybe years ago, you had the same question."

"I guess you're from a good family. When we went to the small town, I dared not go anywhere because I was scared to lose you, and I let Marzieh live with us. An Islamic regime is a terrible place."

"There is no more of the previous horrors in your eyes."

"You were brilliant, and it scared me that you were attracted to the opposition. I read from your eyes that your mind is preoccupied, but I did not know where it was."

"I hurt you so much and never thanked you for losing all your opportunities because of me. Please forgive me."

He hugged and kissed me. Like my dad, Aria was restless about renting a house and said we should have a home. I don't want to be at anyone's table. I told him there was no one at another table. We are one family. One day, I told him.

"I love to live with these members, now in this house or another. Will you be sad if my dad and Sahar live with us? Would you be sad if Zohreh and Arash lived with us?"

"No"

"It is the same situation, except the deed title is not in your name. If you want us to live alone, Aunt Zohreh has a house when her tenant goes; we go to live there. If you want to build a suitable building, wait until you buy and build it." He agreed to wait until he can build a house. Aria was the centerpiece of Nima Khan's attention, who spun around him like a butterfly. Of course, he paid particular attention to Iran Joon, never made excuses to rent a house, and he was a fired university professor, a quiet man who spent his time on his book writing. I was waiting for a residency program and reading research on medical materials. There were many Grants with different titles, and I was willing to research vital medical issues and did not have a rash.

One of the exciting events is Pegah with Kaveh and Farideh with Kamyar getting closer, and they have been together everywhere. Once, they had come to our house when their girlfriends were not in the room; Uncle Arash told them.

"Be careful. They are family."

Kamyar: "You had many girlfriends before my mother."

"Your mother was different."

"They're different, too."

Kaveh went and said something under Uncle Arash's ear and kissed his head, and they whispered quietly Kaveh answered no.

"We will wrestle, if I can't knock you down, you'll knock me down. Kamyar, what is your plan?"

"Like Kaveh."

Uncle was quiet and then took them to the corner of the room and talked to both. Kaveh and Kamyar were happy. The relationship between father and sons was warm and cordial. I guided Aria, Madam, and Iran Joon during this time. One day, we went to the DMV with Aria to get the driving manual so he could get ready for a driving test because the international license was validated for a short time. Aria asked to have the test. I said you don't know the language. He spoke. "Okay, I'll try."

I suspected that he knew English because I remembered that he had talked to the restaurant owner in Hawaii. He said everyone knew a few words. He passed the driving test, took English courses in Iran, regularly practiced English, and wanted to surprise me. Since Aria came, my phone text messages have stopped. It was his text message; he had my phone number from day one.

At the same time, Uncle Koroush taught Aria about investment and guided him on how to invest. Aria became eager and started working with a computer from the corner of our bedroom. Uncle Koroush talked to my dad about Kaveh and Kamyar. He established the limited company that all expenses and income would come from one account, and Kaveh and Kamyar would be the shareholders.

Kaveh said that according to the labor law, we have a contract with the company, and we must resign, and I have ideas that will make a good income. They left and embarked on their first project. Interestingly, the two brothers worked in special coordination, and Kaveh responded spontaneously when Kamyar looked at him. Uncle Koroush promised them that he would support them financially and move forward with confidence.

Uncle Koroush had a lot of contact with large institutions due to his business relationships, through which large projects were sent to my dad. Through scientific projects, my dad, Sahar, and Uncle Arash made millions of dollars independently.

Although Zohreh and Arash were financially stable, they said to owe their financial success to my dad and Sahar. Uncle Koroush taught them how to pay less in taxes legally. Everyone agreed to buy land to build the house. Aria said it would be better to buy a big lot where he could make several units, offices, playgrounds, and classrooms.

Madam said with a laugh. "Wait till the baby comes and then think about school."

"Ana and Dariush had children, and then our turn."

They bought a large lot near Uncle Koroush's house. Aria asked the whole project should be under his supervision to gain experience in construction. Uncle Koroush agreed and suggested that give each part of the job to one and supervise them because he is good in investment.

Aria responded: "Well, it was the same in Iran. I gave each part of the job to someone who had a good resume and knowledge, or I had experience with, so that the work would go faster properly."

Aria Bought an engineering map design desk and drawing software and carried out the building design from the corner of our bedroom. At the same time, I studied the medical research there seriously. Uncle Koroush suggested the units could be easily converted into small units because the small units would be sold sooner. On the plan, Aria had six-bedroom units that would be converted into three-bedroom units and could be quickly returned to six-bedroom. He kept asking me what I liked, and which design was best. The project had a four-story building with all amenities and 20 residential units, office, classes, parking, elevator, a sports field, a swimming pool, and all safety measures. He studied and considered all the city's building codes.

Aria was happy and occasionally stared at me with a smile, but he did not say anything. I thought he was thinking about his future children. Uncle Koroush and Uncle Arash opened a limited liability company and bank account for the building project, and each of us had an equal share.

My dad and Sahar deposited all their money into this account, and then Uncle Arash and Uncle Koroush deposited the equivalent. Uncle Koroush said that if it is short on cash, we get a construction loan, or he feeds the account. One day, Monsieur told my dad.

"I will sell my property in Iran and pay our shares."

"You gave me your share in Tehran."

My dad was a world of goodness.

"You do not ask what happened to your house in Iran?"

"I trust you."

Madam struck him (to be silent) and said:

"What do you say we bought his house; we paid some."

Aria: "I sell my properties and business in Iran and pay for our shares."

Uncle Koroush: "Don't rush. There's enough money for now. I will sell it when I go to Iran. You keep all the invoices and receipts that are used when taxing."

"Iran has the same laws that are not enforced, and bribery is common."

Aria would no longer take the excuse to rent a house. My dad, Sahar, and Arash moved his office to the library on the street-level floor. Madam and Monsieur changed their bedroom to the upstairs. Aunt Zohreh ordered a large screen TV for the street floor, and the basement was entirely set for Aria and me, and no one would come there.

The immigration lawyer suggested that Madam and Arman and Iran Joon and Nima Khan would be the best way to invest $1 million directly to get a Green Card.

Madam was kidding and told me that if she knew I

was rich, she would turn around me a thousand times daily. Iran Joon said it is enough time to do it. Madam and Monsieur went to Turkey to return to Iran in Aria's car. We sent medical journals and souvenirs to Dr. Yilmaz and his family, Ana, Dariush, Nasrin, and Pouran Jun. My dad and Sahar sent scientific books and periodicals to their university. When they left, Iran Joon would have spent her time with me if Aria was not around. She told me her story.

"My ex-husband was not honest and had lousy language. He beat me under any pretext that if my mother-in-law mediated, he would beat her, too. My mother-in-law was a kind woman living with us, and once he beat me, I had a broken paralyzed arm. I did not file for divorce because, in Iranian law, the child's custody is with the father, and if I had divorced, I would have been deprived of even seeing my child. I was not allowed to leave the house without his permission. My baby was sick one day, and I begged him to visit a doctor, but he disagreed. I decided to take my baby to the doctor's office. My husband followed and beat me in the alley about why you left the house. A neighbor who was Madam's student saw the scene, and the next day, Madam heard it.

Madam came to my house with Monsieur and threatened my ex-husband to cut his head off if he beat me again. They took me and my baby to a doctor who said it was too late, and the toxin entered the baby's blood. That night, Gohar was at my side while my baby died, and then she took me to her home. I filed for divorce; he rumored everywhere that I was an evil woman, Monsieur was my boyfriend and divorced me. His nonsense words did not matter to me because his mother was always with me and knew he was lying." Iran Joon spoke, and we cried.

One morning, I was nauseous. I slept and did not have breakfast. Iran Joon brought me breakfast. I said I wanted to sleep. Aria returned home and saw I had nausea and might be pregnant. Aria was happy, while I was worried. Occasionally, I called Bijan, who asked about Aria; he had completed my divorce request but did not use the divorce word. He took a painting class on the advice of Professor

Kiani's daughter, Parnian, to overcome his depression. Ana said she was a beautiful girl and a skilled painter, and they gradually became closer friends. I was glad that Bijan returned to life because I was worried for him.

Aunt Setareh and Uncle Koroush decided to go to Iran. Ana, Behrouz, and Dariush were waiting for their surgical residency period to be over. Aria wanted to sell his properties in Iran. He gradually acquired skills in the investment, so Uncle Koroush was satisfied and said he would be very successful because he would move cautiously.

Aria said that he studied stocks and shared the results with Pegah and Pedram to be sure he understood correctly. Aria was a world of passion, love, and hard work; I greatly loved him. When I cried that if the children died before the birth, he held me in his arms and spoke.

"Look at my eyes; we'll have many children. I dreamed that the kids were twins and healthy. You must have good nutrition, relax, and take care of yourself."

I wanted to ask if there were twins in his family, but I did not say anything. I learned that common questions like this are sometimes uncomfortable for someone with our background. "One is too much for my body."

He hugged me like a kid and walk around the room. Aria was strong, and his muscular, solid arm was a resting place for me, such as a relaxation pillow.

"Aria, I don't know why I'm so restless and nervous like a spoiled child."

"I love my spoiled child."

After that day, he wouldn't leave me alone. When he wasn't home, Iran Joon was with me. He had reduced his work hours, worked nights when I was asleep, and took me out for a daily walk. Once, I was alone with my dad, and I spoke.

"I never imagined I would love anyone more than Bijan, and now I would love Aria if that love was not real. How is your passion for Hayedeh and Sahar?"

"I love Sahar, although I remembered Hayedeh. Weep is useless for what cannot be replaced. Life flows like a river and cannot return to the river's source. Although I loved Hayedeh, we must accept the tragedy. There is no choice."

"Yours and Zohreh's situations were different from mine. You had no choice and must accept the incurable conditions, but I gave up Bijan and separated from him. If I was not in your life, you married and had many children."

My dad hugged me.

"I have the best daughter in the world. You imagine you drove in the opposite direction of a one-way street and should return. I'm glad you're intellectual and helped Bijan dominate the situation."

He held me in his arms, and I cried.

"Dad, you, highly educated, had hard work unfairly and a hard life because of me and here you could work safely."

"The product of the knowledge tree should belong to the country that planted and watered the tree. In our country, illiterate politicians did not learn the country's capital value. Illiterate and ignorant thieves who are satisfied with a colored balloon in the air instead of gold mines are the Ally servants. The Ally knows how to manage the stupid and steal the foreign country's capital.

Manijeh and Hossein Agha had tickets and returned to Germany. The construction work was going well. Aria would leave early in the morning and return at about 11:00 a.m. He took a shower and then brought me breakfast. He had discipline, and his work was followed in a specific order. At night, when I was asleep, he did the investment work. I told him to work less and not need to work hard. He said this amount of work is nothing compared to his working hours in Iran.

Aunt Setareh and her husband went to Iran to attend Bijan and Parnian engagement party. Before they left, Aria gave Uncle Koroush a power of attorney to sell his house, office, and cars. I sent gifts to everyone, including Bijan and Parnian.

In 2008, I was relaxing at home due to pregnancy, studying research, and Dr. John, Uncle Arash's friend, gave me medical journals. When I read the research articles, I noticed each research pointed to a methodology which is a

key to research. I studied the methodology, and thought it
needed to go further. It might become with a different
result. I saw that some research had flaws that related to
the research method, human error, and ignoring reporting
some details at the time of the investigation or not
reporting the complete facts altogether. Every research
result should be thoroughly evaluated. I talked to my dad
about reviewing the research result, its neglected points,
and their errors. Surprised, my dad said, "Great, start this
field." I was looking forward to accepting a surgical
residency, and there was enough time to study the subject
in depth. My dad said.

"Forget the surgical field. Your health is most
important currently. The course of surgical residency does
not fit your current situation."

It might Aria talked to my dad because he said.

"You needed to sleep well and rest. The surgical
resident must be ready to manage a medical emergency; it
is unfit for your situation."

I started exploring medical research methods. It was
nearing the end of the surgical residency of Ana, Behrouz,
and Dariush. I registered their names and Bijan to attend
the medical symposium and sent their invitations. They
went to Turkey and came to America with the help of Dr.
Yilmaz, and I was pleased to see Ana after almost three
years. The residential building was still under construction.

We thought it would be better for them to use Aunt
Zohreh's house, which we used to live in. Zohreh asked her
tenant to evacuate. After a week, we noticed traveling
between the two places was challenging. They moved into
our home; Ana and Behrouz slept in the adjacent room
downstairs to me, and Behzad, Monsieur, and Madam in
the basement hall.

Nasrin and Dariush moved to a bedroom upstairs, and
Pouran Joan and Dara to the bedroom on the ground level.
Iran Joon laughed and said, "We are in Ghamar Khanum's
home." It was the name of an Iranian TV serial with many
tenants in a small home. Each family had one room only
and had to use the common area, including one bathroom!

Bijan and Parnian lived at Uncle Koroush's house. I

was excited that Ana came and told Aria that Ana and I would sleep together and talk.

"Okay, after you fall asleep. I'll bring you back and put you in our bed."

Behzad looked like Behrouz, and he was amusing and had his stunts, telling me that Taleh (instead of khaleh (aunt in Persian), was attracting everyone's attention pushing her face forward and lying on our lips to kiss him, saying I kissed you. Lovely Dara was always with Pouran Joan, and she would put whatever he ate in our mouths. Nasrin was happy to leave Iran and said we were free from hell. Aria and her father's suits were very stylish and unique. He told me that he met a tailor in a wheelchair who said that he was ready to sew a suit for him if he liked it to pay. Aria had said.

"Why? I give you your fee first, and then you sew my suit."

"I don't have a shop, my house is poor, but I know my job."

"You make a few sets for my dad and me."

He left the color and purchase of fabrics to the tailor. After that, he sewed Aria and his father's dresses and was sad when he heard Aria leaving. Aria promised him to send more customers, told me to order a suit for my dad, and asked Koroush Khan to pay him the fee in advance. We ordered some clothes. The tailor sent them with Ana, and his work was unparalleled. Then, Kaveh and Kamyar ordered their clothes. Ana, Behrouz, Dariush, and Nasrin were Zohreh's English class students. They had computers and iPhones and repeated words to learn the folk conversations. Behrouz was an honor student, studying the medical journal at every opportunity.

My dad, Sahar, and Uncle Arash were working on their projects, and I was the professor's secretary if I was not tired. Aria was in the construction job or trading on computers. Gradually, Bijan and Parnian visited us more often.

My doctor told me that I was pregnant with twins. Aria was so happy sitting down and combing my hair, caressed and kissed me, and said that your kisses would give me

life. I said Aria had a dream and told me they were twins.
Uncle Arash asked Aria, "what else did you dream of? You
are precise and throw the ball inside the target!" Aria was
laughing, Nima Khan was pleased, and my dad smiled
gently and put his head down. My dad's behavior was like
Zohreh's behavior, which was identical to their mother's,
based on my dad's words.

Dariush's restlessness resembled that of my dad and
Aria, who wanted to find a job and look for a rental
property sooner. I told him he had to be patient and focus
on the medical board exam. I talked to Ana, Behrouz,
Dariush, and Bijan regarding the process of being a
surgeon in the US. At least one year for passing a medical
board exam plus five years of residency term in general
surgery. It would be better to create a new field when they
wait for the board exam and review the medical research.
It's not profitable for a physician to concentrate on that
subject, and if we can create this field, it will be very
effective for human life compared to visiting some patients.

And I read some medical research and that the research
method was fundamental. If we succeed in this field, no
one can ignore us, which may be effective in accepting us
in a surgical residency. Also, my dad, Uncle Arash, and
Uncle Koroush confirmed my idea. We agreed to educate
ourselves, read methodological books for scientific
research, and focus only on one subject initially.

Uncle Koroush said they could legally pay us some
funds for the Medical Research instead of paying taxes,
which would not affect the taxpayer's total net income. He
then opened a medical research limited liability company,
and we became shareholders. A portion of the payment my
dad, Sahar, Arash, and others had to pay as taxes was
poured into our account.

I got tired early during pregnancy and feared losing
my baby again. We were working on the project when I
wasn't tired. Dariush provided surgical equipment with
Dr. John's help, checked up, and made a medical record for
each family member, who would have the basic medical
information. I knew that he worried about me and wanted
everything be available. The babies were getting bigger,

and I was more tired. Aria was with me day and night
except when Ana was awake and with me. Aria took me
for a walk daily, and when I complained of tiredness, he
wanted to take and carry me in his arms to our home. I
often sit down with Ana, Nasrin, and Parnian, joking and
laughing. I told them about Aria's comment when he
kissed me and said my kiss gave him life.

We laughed when Madam said, "What are you
laughing at it." After hearing our joke, she laughed and
said, "What a great thing to tell Monsieur to tell me that my
kiss gave him life." We laughed so much that they all
understood what Aria was saying, and Uncle Arash was
kidding with him and spoke.

"Now our work has come to the point where I have to
imitate you, or Zohreh will divorce me."

It was time to choose names for the kids. I told Aria
what name I liked, and he was delighted and said, "Great."
I asked him not to tell anyone, but I told Ana, and he
agreed and said, "But don't say all of our words, such as
your kiss gave me life. I laughed and said, but I did. Aria
said, "Honey, I love you, and you can do whatever you
want." I was approaching the last few months and was
more
afraid of what would happen if the children died.
Aria tried calming me down so the children would be safe.

In my eighth month of pregnancy, my back was sore. I
woke up at midnight, and I assumed I urinated. Aria
jumped out of bed and said, "What happened, baby."

I was embarrassed and said:

"I am wet."

"It doesn't matter, I will change your clothes and
sheets."

I got up, that he changed the sheets when I noticed the
water bag was torn, and my delivery started.

"No, I did not urinate, put the sheet back, I should lay
on the bed and wake Ana immediately."

He hurriedly turned on the light to wear his clothes.
Madam woke up from our voices and spoke.

"What's going on?

"Wake Ana up; Bahareh's labor was started."

Madam and Ana came to our room.

"The children's movement is good, don't worry. Mom, please go to wake Dariush."

"My dad, too."

Dariush examined me and said that the delivery had started, and we would go to the hospital immediately and call the gynecologist. Aria hugged me, put me in the car, and we went to the hospital. They prepared me for the surgery. I said the children must be underweight and need to be in incubators, but I don't want to be in the hospital for a long time, and I take care of them at home. Before I was transferred to the operating room, the children were born, and Dariush gave birth to them.

I kept asking questions; they were alive, breathing, and crying. Aria hugged me, kissed me, said I love you, put his face on my face, and his tears wet my face. At the same time, he was holding the babies on my chest with his hand. My dad was happy I did not need surgery. At the hospital, everyone was surprised that I had so many companionships and asked about our relationship. I said, "Ana is my sister, mother, and dad, and her parents. They laughed: two sisters, how many parents, three surgeons, and a natural childbirth. When I kissed my dad, I cried.

"Must you have remembered Hayedeh?"

His eyes were filled with tears.

"I'm glad you're okay."

I was sweaty, and I smelled. Ana spoke.

"Get up to take a shower."

"No, she gave birth now; I clean her." Aria spoke firmly.

Ana laughed and said: "Don't worry, I'm a doctor!"

The children were six pounds each, identical, and looked like Aria. Dariush asked me to stay in the hospital for a few hours to ensure no internal bleeding. We did not have baby car seats! We put the children in two hospital infants' baskets and the basket in the Dara and Behzad seats and drove home. Two little baskets were placed on the side of our bed. Aria told me I would do everything; you only rest and feed the babies. Iran Joon, Sahar, Shokoh Joon, Zohreh, and Madam came to our room while Pouran Joon cared for Dara and Behzad. I told my dad that we were two and had one room and now four people in one room.

"Bahareh Joon, you and Aria go to our room, Sahar and I care of the kids."

Love and humanity were parts of my dad's nature. The kids were three days old when we had a party to announce our chosen name. We put the selected names in the basket, and Ana had no right to participate in the game. Only Iran Joon had guessed right. We asked Nima Khan to choose the name of the first child from the basket; my dad read the second child's name left on the basket. The first one was named Soheil, and the second was named Nima. The children's age difference was three minutes. The first one had a slightly rounder face. Both looked like hairless Aria and the size of Aria's hand that I feared would fall out of his hand. Aria would be gazing at them with enthusiasm. Their sleep was good at first; later, they were restless and hungry. They grew up rapidly, and their clothes were shrinking.

I was happy and looking forward to the new house when Ana, Behrouz, Dariush, and Bijan waited for the medical board test. Ana said.

"You have two kids; we decided to have the second one."

Nasrin did not tell Dariush for fear that he would be upset. Parnian was pregnant. Bijan, Aunt Setareh, and Uncle Koroush were happy. Parian was an artistic painter, and after she saw the building, suggested the mural corridors and ceilings should have a style that embodied an old palace. She hired two painters and oversaw their work. The corridor walls were painted with the picture of ancient palace pillars, and the ceiling with an image of a sunny sky with scattered clouds. The end of the hallway has painted an image of a palace door. All the ceiling lights moved to the sides and covered with molding. As we walked down the corridor, it was the embodiment of walking down sunny day on the aisle to a palace. We were enthusiastic to go to the new building earlier.

Aria was eager to keep my tastes in every case, asking

which color and design was best and what I liked most.
The red carpet had a flowery fringe for the entrance and
corridors, and the rest of the building was a hard wooden
floor. He asked each of us to choose our favorite curtain for
our unit. In the front yard of the building was a round pool
with a circle of red flowers and a fountain and waterfall
dancing with classical music. The front yard floor was
made of red bricks, which were space for guest parking,
and our parking was under the building. The building had
a beautiful design of iron fences and a gate.

Since Zohreh and Setareh knew how to order things
online, Aria asked them to order decorative items for each
room, especially towels, bedding sets, and flowers, like
Hawaii hotels. Aria believed our living styles should be
compatible to create a healthier environment for our
children. We should use our energy and time in our
profession, spend the remaining time with our children,
and enjoy life.

Aria spoke to my dad, Arash, and Koroush and asked
them to tell everyone to consider their health and being
with the children, leave the housekeeping and cooking to
Olga and her colleagues, and not worry about the kitchen
and cooking. Also, Aria talked to Zohreh and Setareh to set
a plan for each family member to have a regular exercise
daily, healthy diet, and check-up with Dariush. Ana
laughed and said:

"Aria was made to command God, bless Bahareh."

The new building was beautiful, and we occupied
eleven units of it. Kimia Khanum, Farhad khan, Farid, and
Pedram did not come to the new house and stayed in the
own home. Aunt Setareh laughed and said Pedram and
Farid were single and needed privacy, and it was better to
be away. I compared my life to the past in an old room
with no facilities with hungry children. While my dad had
the same education, and how much he suffered because of
me, and if it wasn't for me, he wouldn't have to stay there.
Aria hugged me and spoke.

"I would never let you suffer. Also, you remember that
children are always hungry because they are at a growing
age. We also lived in the same shop with no facilities. My

dad would send me to buy bread; I ate half the bread on my way and was nothing. My dad ate a small plate from the pot of food, and I had two large plates. A few minutes later, I was hungry again. My dad suffered a lot because of me, and he risked selling the shop and giving the money to me, which became my initial asset. Do you remember you fought me one day?"

"What did I do?"

"I told my dad she was an intelligent girl. The next I will give her less or more change and see her reaction. My dad said, give her more money and see what she's doing. If you give her less, we will be named as cheater people. When you received the change, you counted the money and told me where you were and why you gave me more. My dad said Excuse me. It was my mistake. You said no, your son made a mistake. Later, my dad and I would laugh that his son made a mistake. We had many memories of our childhood.

One side of the first floor was the kid's classroom, the middle part was the exercise room, and the other side was the office. The receptionist section was next to the stylish meeting room, separated from the professor's office. Each group had its own office. Aria and Zohreh had chosen the room names and group titles like the scientists' office.

Dariush chose a health clinic room, and Uncle Arash was kidding and said that our wealthy situation required an in-house surgeon. When professors and investment groups had meetings, we sat behind desks in the receptionist section. We did our jobs, which was an excellent décor, especially for young Kaveh and Kamyar, which means we are a large company.

Iran, Parnian, Pouran, Zohreh, Shokoh, Gohar, Manijeh, and Nasrin manage the classes. Each of them oversaw a work, such as a painting class with Parnian. Zohreh loved teaching and spending time with children and said I would run Soheil teaching methods. She had two students, Dara and Behzad, and Madam and Pouran Joon were teacher assistants. Iran, Shokoh, and Manijeh Joon cared for our children. Occasionally, one of them went to the kitchen for a new recipe. They knew very well that they

had to leave the job to the chef. Uncle Arash and Shokoh
Joon had a cook in Iran but were very modest and never
talked about it.

Based on my dad's reports, Shokoh Joon cared for me
when I was a child and now cared of my children.
Sometimes they went shopping and bought more
children's clothes. The children were growing up fast. I told
Aria,

"Look how they grow up; at birth, they were the size of
your hand."

He laughed; "They would be taller than me because
their nutrition was good. You do the breastfeeding."

At the same time, Kaveh and Kamyar did their first
deal successfully. Ana was pregnant, and Behrouz was
happy. Uncle Koroush was a good accountant and showed
us that it's better to build a private hospital with our capital
instead of paying taxes. My dad and Aria said we offer free
treatment for poor people.

We bought land to build a hospital, and Aria said I
needed to gain hospital construction experience. I had to
carefully study the required hospital codes and find the
most well-known builder. He met several contractors and
received their offer to study. He consulted Uncle Koroush's
lawyer to read and approve the contract to get the job done
under Aria's supervision within a specific time.

Nasrin was pregnant, and Dariush did not protest. I
told Aria that we should consider the preventive method.

"All right, wait, now that you are breastfeeding the
children."

Our children were five months old, and I was pregnant
again. I was very nervous and fought with Aria, which is
your fault. I abort the baby.

"No, you don't risk your health."

I had a bad attitude, he tolerated it and looked at me
and spoke. "Do not be angry. It is not healthy."

I thought that he talked to my dad. Because my dad
came to our room and pretended not to know I was
pregnant while I had told Ana it was Aria's fault.

"Of course, it's his fault. No, then you wanted to say it
was Ana's fault!"

My dad was smiling and shaking his head.

"What happened?" Why are you angry with Aria?"

"I'm pregnant again."

"The excellent news."

"What if it's twins?"

"Fantastic, then You will have four children."

"Uncle Soheil, I am lucky she said it was Aria's fault; otherwise, it was Ana's fault."

Aria was in our room and pretended to study the hospital codes, but I knew he was watching us.

"We shall listen to Dad. Whatever he says."

"Daddy, I became a chicken incubator machine."

Later, it was joking. Everyone was laughing and saying it was Aria's fault. Uncle Arash said that "Aria knew well how to aim. Aria is a rooster if you are a chicken incubator machine."

Aria had stayed and worked from home and looked after the children and me, although Iran Joon was with me full-time. Ana and Nasrin were not angry with their husband like me! I was ashamed of my behavior. I apologized to Aria later.

Dr. Yilmaz's family came to the US for two weeks, and we had a good time together. While Ana's group was preparing for the medical board test, we started our work with published research on cancer reports in a well-known hospital. We wrote an article and asked Uncle Arash to read it, then he suggested we mention that we are an independent group and not affiliated with any group or institute because most universities depend on parties and groups and are prejudiced. And a lawyer should review your article to prevent a future legal problem. Remember that research authors and hospitals are legally and financially strong and have all the legal tools to suppress or push you back. They are gangs, and most of the time, they are selfish. If they make a mistake, they are unwilling to accept it easily. It would be best if you protect yourself legally.

"The lawyer has no medical knowledge."

"He has the legal knowledge and does not change the medical information, but by adding clauses, replacing the keywords, protecting, and blocking the other party's routes to a legal claim, complaints, and convictions against his client."

As expected, Ana, Behrouz, Dariush, and Bijan passed the medical board exam successfully, and we were ready to send our first article. Uncle Arash suggested that we write the names of women first. I said it is also a form of discrimination; it is better to be based on alphabetical order. My name was last names of my dad and Aria. I added the title of the surgeon from Iran after their names. I was the only one who was not a surgeon. We sent the article to the top three medical journals with the hope that it would be read.

Surprisingly, our report was published. A university invited us to lecture, which we accepted. Behrouz and Dariush were pleased and said it was time-consuming, no income, study a lot, but it's worth it and will be an essential service to the medical field. One of the social media offered us grants without our request. Kimia Khanum, Farhad Khan, Farid, and Pedram were often with us and later joined us. Kaveh and Kamyar were engaged to Pegah and Farideh. Monsieur had calculated how much we spent to provide and serve meals to forty to fifty people in our house, and he could give all groceries to the kitchen. He opened a small supermarket. Hossein Agha and Nima Khan helped him in the shop and said working was fun.

Uncle Koroush told Monsieur that the shop would be under Hossein Agha and Manijeh's names because they did not have green cards, and he agreed. Uncle Koroush's lawyer had previously applied for Madam and Monsieur's green card. Nima Khan published her book, and Aria was delighted. Children go to daycare and kindergarten every morning and learn to paint, read, write, and find alphabet letters from magazines, counting who found more letters. Zohreh, the school principal, Nasrin, Parnian teachers, and the other ladies are the teacher assistants. Iran Joon was the babysitter of Soheil and Nima. One day, I talked to my dad about our life situation, destiny, and where we were.

"The US was in Afghanistan for 20 years at the cost of three trillion US dollars, withdrew its troops, and left all army weapons for Taliban! Even someone who doesn't know about politics can see that at least five US presidents from two parties had enough time and funds to make changes. Ultimately, they encouraged Afghans to leave by plane and deliver the country to the Taliban, who had meetings with US authorities before. The US gave the Taliban the country with army equipment and took the patriots away.

This is the story of our country, Iran, where Jimmy Carter agreed with Khomeini in Iraq and Paris to hand over Iran to Khomeini. On the other hand, the people in this land never thought about the immigrant conditions. Recently, we had 25 people living in one house, and we worked all day; even Arman, Nima Khan, and Hossein Agha went to the shop early in the morning. Aria, Pegah, and Pedram worked from midnight to morning. Ladies worked in daycare and kindergarten all day.

None of us sit idly by, performing more than one full-time employee. You and Aria were in the same room with two kids, and Aria was simultaneously producing and managing two firms 24 hours a day, and you worked. Even an illiterate who comes to this country does some work that the US people are unwilling to do." I was listening and my dad.

"We have finished our education in Iran and owe and shall return the fruit of the education to that land. Unfortunately, mullahs caused turmoil in our country and forced people to leave their homeland. We must have a wise plan to remove the toxic mullah from our country. We are all wounded by the Islamic regime and must move forward with proper planning for our country's freedom. No one feels sorry for us. We must think about ourselves and our country, and we should not just go to the fight without equipment and a wise plan because the enemy is ambushed to kill the fighter, which will reduce our forces." We were crying.

Parnian due date was approached, Professor Kiani and his wife, Nahid, came to the United States for her delivery. Our full house was joyful. Professor Kiani, Arash, and Monsieur had warmed us up with humor. Dariush's office was a busy free clinic for pregnant women, and we laughed at Uncle Arash's words, saying that we were all incubation machines.

Parnian had a natural delivery of a beautiful girl named Paria, who looked like Parnian. Ana and Behrouz's second child, Bahram, and Nasrin and Dariush's daughter, Delaram, were born. I was pregnant with twins again. The children were born seven months with a natural delivery and were named Ariana and Irana. Aria is so happy that we have a kindergarten at home and always had one child in his arms. Soheil and Nima started talking. In addition to the hospital project, Aria began to build another residential complex and kept asking me what was wrong with this property to improve the other one. Aria is an excellent husband and father. I love him passionately.

Now I have reached Nima Khan's word, "my daughter, be patient; everything will be fine, and you'll be happy." At that time, I was stupid and did not understand the meaning of these words, and my thought was about Zubeida's suitors and her husband's title!

We chose to live in the US, where the law governs the country, not a dictator who has ruled the people. Mullahs or reciters at the grave are losers who kill people with evil, sexual vices, and steal people's estates. The rulers were afraid and hated people, carried a gun, and killed patriotic people and doctors, therefore, they needed treatment in a foreign country. At the time of illness, they go to other countries for treatment with a fake passport. One of them went to a German hospital for treatment and fled at midnight from the hospital and left Germany because he feared the patriotic Iranian protesters. Bulletproof machines are not a badge of dignity but a badge of people haters of the mullah's tribe. Sitting up the top of the wall, such as the weeds stick, is a sign of the humiliation of thorns, not the thorn's dignity.

The mullah is obsessed with stealing the people's wealth, hoping to cover his inferiority. The quota schools that issued the fake certifications and degrees indicate illiteracy. The grave reciter calumny mullahs with the stigma of the home-sell label on their foreheads will last mullahs' shame history.

Hope, this brief can help the reader not get caught up in the black religious swamp of ignorance of the religious theocracy.

I asked Kaveh and Kamyar, who are permanently on social media based on their jobs, to find my dad's friend Masoud to make him happy, and you will read its story in the next book.

Other Author Published books
1. I love you very much.
2. I do not know if there is a God or is not.
3. Loot Desert.
4. Neda, Ian - America online / Persian
5. Neda, Iran- America paperback / Persian
6. Neda online / English version
7. Neda, paperback / English version

www.ingramcontent.com/pod-product-compliance
Lightning Source LLC
Chambersburg PA
CBHW062358090426
42740CB00010B/1318